Ritual

RITUAL

What It Is, How It Works, and Why

Robbie Davis-Floyd and Charles D. Laughlin

berghahn
NEW YORK · OXFORD
www.berghahnbooks.com

First published in 2022 by
Berghahn Books
www.berghahnbooks.com

Library of Congress Cataloging-in-Publication Data

Names: Davis-Floyd, Robbie, author. | Laughlin, Charles D., 1938- author.
Title: Ritual : what it is, how it works, and why / Robbie Davis-Floyd and
    Charles D. Laughlin.
Description: [New York, New York] : Berghahn Books, 2022. | Includes
    bibliographical references and index.
Identifiers: LCCN 2022019386 (print) | LCCN 2022019387 (ebook) | ISBN
    9781800735286 (hardback) | ISBN 9781800735309 (paperback) | ISBN
    9781800735293 (ebook)
Subjects: LCSH: Rites and ceremonies. | Ritual--Psychological aspects. |
    Cognition and culture.
Classification: LCC GN473 .D38 2022 (print) | LCC GN473 (ebook) | DDC
    306.4--dc23/eng/20220705
LC record available at https://lccn.loc.gov/2022019386
LC ebook record available at https://lccn.loc.gov/2022019387

British Library Cataloguing in Publication Data
A catalogue record for this book is available from the British Library

ISBN 978-1-80073-528-6 hardback
ISBN 978-1-80073-530-9 paperback
ISBN 978-1-80073-529-3 ebook

https://doi.org/10.3167/9781800735286

From Robbie:
I dedicate this book to my co-author Charlie, whose early work on
ritual taught me how it works on the human brain and body and
inspired me to study it more deeply.

From Charlie:
I dedicate this book to my lovely daughter Kate and her magnificent
Tim—may they live long and prosper!

CONTENTS

ILLUSTRATIONS

Figures

Tables

FOREWORD

Betty Sue Flowers

As series consultant for Bill Moyers's PBS program, *Joseph Campbell and the Power of Myth,* I was often asked what accounted for Campbell's amazing popularity. "It wasn't just his knowledge of mythology," I would answer, "but his great storytelling abilities, his capacity to personalize the study of myth so that he presented himself as a student, just like us, and his inclination, always, to relate myths to the concerns of everyday life."

In *Ritual: What It Is, How It Works, and Why* and its predecessor, *The Power of Ritual,* Robbie Davis-Floyd and Charles D. Laughlin have done for ritual what Campbell did for myth—tell stories, personalize the study of ritual, and relate ritual to the concerns of everyday life.

In many ways, the power of ritual is greater than the power of myth in that ritual lasts longer. Christians, for example, decorate Easter eggs and Christmas trees every year—the origins of these rituals in pagan myth having been obscured for centuries. And early Christian missionaries, like the Romans before them, found that if they kept the *rituals* of the local gods they were replacing, the local *myths* would gradually morph into versions of the new story that was being imported. Perhaps, at some level, it is easier to change a belief than a habit, especially if that habit is designed to procure favor and protection.

As we know from the way children often insist on a particular bedtime ritual before releasing themselves into sleep, it is the repetition, not the content, of the ritual that creates its power. For a brief moment, our vulnerability to the unknown is set aside because we know what will happen next. As with the principle of "three times" so often encountered in folk tales, we experience the first time something happens as an event; the second time establishes a pattern; but the third time is a qualitatively different experience because we anticipate it. Rather than fate happening to us, we dance with it by knowing the steps in advance.

Repetition itself is a human compulsion, as Freud so famously pointed out, and when members of a group perform a repetitive act together, the individual becomes part of a larger, synchronized whole, at least for that moment. The evolutionary advantage of a group that can synchronize its members to act together is powerful.

All these aspects of ritual and more are explored by two authors whose anthropological insights range from brain function to birth practices and from Brazilian doctors to Buddhist lamas. In *Ritual,* they offer readers a personal journey through a universal landscape.

Betty Sue Flowers, PhD, is a Professor Emerita (UT-Austin) and the former Director of the Johnson Presidential Library. She is an international business foresight and strategy consultant, and currently serves as Chairman of the Board of Public Agenda. Her publications range from poetry therapy to human rights, including two books of poetry and four PBS tie-in books. Flowers was the creator of Joseph Campbell's *The Power of Myth*, which she constructed from his previous writings, and the series consultant for Bill Moyers' *Joseph Campbell and the Power of Myth*. She has served as a moderator for executive seminars at the Aspen Institute; as a consultant for NASA, the CIA, and the Secretary of the Navy; Public Director of the American Institute of Architects; and editor of futures scenarios for organizations including Shell Global, the OAS, the World Energy Council, the CDC, OECD, Malaysia, Eskom (South Africa), Oman, Slovenia, the Five Eyes, and the World Business Council for Sustainable Development (Geneva). Her publications include "The American Dream and the Economic Myth" and "The Primacy of People in a World of Nations" in *The Partnership Principle: New Forms of Governance in the 21ˢᵗ Century*; and the co-edited *Realistic Hope: Facing Global Challenges.*

ABOUT THE AUTHORS AND THEIR PERSONAL AND ACADEMIC ENGAGEMENTS WITH RITUAL

This book is a greatly abridged, revised, and updated version of *The Power of Ritual* (2016), published by Daily Grail Press, Brisbane, Australia, and written by the same two authors, both anthropologists—Robbie Elizabeth Davis-Floyd and Charles Dennis Laughlin—with different histories of engagement with the study and practice of ritual. In keeping with the informal tone we wish to maintain, throughout the book we will refer to ourselves as "Robbie" and "Charlie" rather than "Davis-Floyd" and "Laughlin." Most of the time we will speak with a unified voice, but in this Preface, we will speak individually to give our readers a feeling for why each of us is so interested in ritual and why it is important to us to communicate what we have found out.

Robbie Davis-Floyd

This book grows out of my 30 years of research on ritual in childbirth in the United States and Mexico, and in particular, out of a workshop I have often presented on "The Power of Ritual" to diverse groups around the country. Audiences for this workshop have included groups of priests, psychotherapists, physicists, women professionals, social scientists, health care practitioners (nurses, midwives, physicians, childbirth educators), men's movement participants and workshop leaders, business managers, New

Agers, university students, drug and alcohol addicts, members (or former members) of cults, and aerospace engineers.

During the course of these workshops, I have often noted a high level of confusion among people who are designing and performing rituals on a regular basis as a part of, for example, religious or spiritual retreats, psychotherapy intensives, and self-help seminars. They tell me that they "intuit" what ritual is all about, but their sense of it is vague, unformed. They come to my workshops to find out what they themselves are actually up to! I am always delighted when such people show up in my audiences; one of the major reasons I started teaching these workshops was my concern about the uncritical use of ritual that has characterized the explosion of interest in the "new" spirituality, alternative healing, and self-help movements, to name only a few. Ritual is an extraordinarily powerful socializing tool that can be just as easily manipulated for ill as used for good. The naiveté of many contemporary ritual practitioners has worried me for a long time, and these workshops—and this book—serve as my way of combating that naiveté. This information enables participants to be more conscious and more responsible about the way they use the rituals they create.

My interest in ritual first developed from personal experience. My childhood in Casper, Wyoming, was punctuated with ritual events, many of which focused around the local rodeos put on during the summers, and the seasonal celebrations of Easter, Thanksgiving, and Christmas. But my deepest ritual imprinting came from growing up in the Presbyterian Church. Although I moved away from that religion in later years, the hymns we sang in church every Sunday, the vivid memory of the light streaming through the stained-glass window showing Jesus' ascension, the feeling of peace and completion that would descend over me as the minister raised his arms to give the final blessing—all these still resonate in my being and provide me with a sense of stability. In particular, the words of the Doxology, which I must have sung at least 500 times during my childhood churchgoing years, still give me the goose bumps I used to get as I rose as one with the whole congregation to sing joyously:

Glory be to the Father, and to the Son, and to the Holy Ghost

As it was in the beginning, it is now and ever shall be

World without end, Amen, Amen

As I typed those words just now, singing as my fingers moved over the computer keys, that same uplifting feeling surged inside of me, goose bumps popped out on my arms once again, and I was right back in memory inside that beautiful church staring at the light shining through that stained glass window. Such is the power of ritual to affect our emotions, even decades after the fact.

But now as I reread the words of the Doxology, my critical faculties come into play: that song, which purports to be so timeless and so universal, does not encompass certain facts that I accept as reality. Things are not as they were in the beginning—in fact, change is the one constant of both human and universal experience. Our world is not "without end"—one day, billions of years from now, the Earth will be swallowed up in flames when its sun turns into a red giant. And there are no females and no "female principle" in that song, only a father, a son, and an androgynous spirit, which is the closest the Presbyterianism of my youth—and Christianity in general—could get to acknowledging that males are not the only gender. So I can't even find *myself* in its words—they do not charter my existence as a good myth should. As an experiment, I sing the song once more and note that in spite of my intellectual objections, the goosebumps and uplifting sensation return. As we shall see throughout this book, *rituals primarily affect our emotions*—by triggering a powerful emotional response, ritual can get people to believe or at least resonate deeply with ideologies that they might intellectually reject (see Whitehouse 2005).

In my early years as an anthropology student in the 1970s, I studied shamanism and ritual healing in Mexico and worked for years with two Mexican shamans, one traditional and one thoroughly cosmopolitan. Those experiences, which involved both anthropological observation and personal participation in rituals of various sorts, taught me a great deal about ritual's flexibility as I saw it stretch to encompass the contrasting realities of the pre- and postmodern worlds. I watched with amazement as the people participating in the rituals that the traditional shaman, Don Lucio (now deceased), had been performing for decades suddenly began to include New Agers seeking connection with the Earth—*La Tierra Madre*—and with traditional cultures—in Don Lucio, I guess these seekers found at least a facsimile of Carlos Castañeda's Don Juan. And I was equally fascinated by the postmodern shaman, Edgardo Vasquez Gomez (also deceased). A highly charismatic, wealthy, upper-class Mexican gentleman, he had studied traditional shamanic techniques all over Mexico and was eclectically combining them with a European esoteric spiritual system based on the works of G. I Gurdjieff. Called "the Work," this system invites individuals to "wake up" to a greater awareness of everyday life—to seek to be conscious in every moment. Edgardo's use of ritual to stimulate this kind of awareness in his followers was masterful; watching him manipulate people's states of consciousness was a lesson to me in the intentional use of ritual to achieve instrumental (practical) ends. Sometimes, when I was particularly awake and aware, I could even see the lines of energy that emanated from his hands; he used these lines of energy like reins to pull individuals seeking to practice the Work into greater awareness in the moment.

My next deep engagement with ritual came during my participation in later years with a New Age healing group that evolved over time into a cult. I got involved in part because I wanted to do an anthropological study of that group. I watched and participated and took notes as their at-first tenuous belief system crystallized into an intensely tight and cohesive worldview. For the first two years, I didn't believe a word of it—it was just a story, albeit a fascinating one, and my anthropological detachment remained intact. But the ritual process, as we will demonstrate in this book, can be overwhelming. Embarrassing as it is to admit, against my will I eventually got fully converted to that worldview. The moment of conversion was a devastating experience (described in Chapter 7). I knew it had happened and I was furious about it, but I could not change the fact that in an instant I had gone from not believing to fully believing their story about the nature of the world and the purpose of life.

It took me six months to unconvert myself. Succeeding in that endeavor was a matter of personal self-esteem—I could not respect myself as long as I remained a true believer in a fantastical system that promised the power of Jesus-like ascension to anyone willing to work hard enough to "clear their issues" completely so that they could expand, in the flesh, into "full oneness with the universe"—and save humanity in the process!

Although I suffered greatly during that de-conversion period, I also learned a tremendous amount, firsthand, about the power of ritual to engender belief and influence experience, and about the human capacity for free will and individual choice. We can be heavily influenced by ritual, but we can also make individual decisions about how we will respond to that influence. Since that time, my participation in spiritual ritual has been limited to expansive, humanistic rituals that enact a belief system I consciously choose to hold. Yet I still feel the seductive pull of that other path, one in which the meaning of every event could be forced to fit into a cohesive and intelligible cosmology, and my place and importance in the cosmological scheme were assured. Life seemed so much easier when all my questions were answered by Father André, a spiritual entity ("channeled" by the group leader Karen), who for a time served as my guide through life's bewildering maze. Father André's counsel seemed to remove the bewilderment and offer in its place the comfort of understanding—an understanding confirmed daily by the ritual experiences his followers constructed.

My personal experience of ritual took a new turn following the sudden death of my 20-year-old daughter Peyton in a car accident on September 12, 2000. The Memorial Service (see Chapter 10 for a full description) that her father, her brother, and I designed for her in Austin, Texas, our hometown—followed one week later by a second service designed by her many friends in New York, where she had been living—carried us through the initial, near-immobilizing shock. Over time we have designed and performed many other rituals to help us grieve her death and celebrate her life. None of those many rituals we performed in her honor healed the pain that I thought would never end. Yet each one deepened my experience and understanding of the power of ritual to channel chaos and suffering into paths that lead to meaning and coherence, and thus to increase one's chances of surviving—and perhaps even integrating—the most devastating kinds of loss. Then finally, miracle of miracles, the last one we performed did just that!

Five of Peyton's closest friends accompanied me to my ancestral home in northern Louisiana with the explicit purpose of burying her ashes on the tenth anniversary of her death, in Peyton's and my ancestral cemetery—such a beautiful place, in the midst of the woods—many of our ancestors on my mother's side had been buried there from the early 1800s on. We spent the weekend reminiscing about her and celebrating her life. Then on September 12, 2010, precisely ten years after she died, we collectively buried her ashes at the foot of my parents' graves, right in front of her gravestone.

Our spontaneous ritual celebration on that sunny day in the Keachi cemetery was a ritual that worked—a perfect rite of passage and celebration. I set the lovely Japanese urn containing Peyton's ashes, some locks of her hair, and her baby teeth (all of her remaining DNA, which I knew I had to let go of so that I could stop fantasizing about cloning her) into the hole in the ground that my dear friend Travis Whitfield had lovingly dug, and I let go of it all in that single act. Her cherished friend Brian Hudson perched himself on her gravestone with his guitar, and commenced our spontaneous ceremony by singing "Oh, What a Beautiful Morning"—and indeed it was! And Brian also sang "Sweet Dreams"—a lovely lullaby he had written for Peyton before she died. Then her friend and mentor Jamison grabbed the guitar and sang (to the tune of "Me and Bobby McGee") "Me and Peyton Floyd"—the lyrics were all about the long car trips he and Peyton had enjoyed together and their adventures along the way. Then each and every one present—Brian, Jamison, Corrie, Oliver, Adam, Travis, Mary, and I took turns speaking about what Peyton had meant and continues to mean in our lives. No planned order— we simply followed the flow, together creating in the moment a ritual of both celebration and completion. As a final touch, Adam laid a bouquet of flowers on her gravestone, and we walked away replete with love, awe, and a profound and lasting sense of shared caring—after which, I can say in all honesty, my pain over my daughter's death metamorphosed into a deep sense of acceptance and closure, bringing me, finally, peace. Such is the power of the rituals that we seek to celebrate, and to intellectually and critically analyze in the following pages.

In addition to these deeply personal experiences with ritual, I have explored ritual academically in various ways. For my first book, *Birth as an American Rite of Passage* ([1992] 2003a), I interviewed 100 women about their pregnancy and birth experiences. As I listened to woman after woman recount her birth story, I was increasingly struck by the standardized ways in which this highly individual process was treated in the hospital—which is replete with unnecessary, non-evidenced-based technological interventions such as IVs, Pitocin augmentation, electronic fetal monitoring, and many more.

At first I was unable to explain how a medical specialty like obstetrics, which purports to be science-based, could routinely employ so many procedures that are unsupported by science. Eventually I realized that the "routine" was the key: these procedures were in fact rituals! Every human culture employs ritual to help its members face danger and uncertainty and to make transitions from one social state to another, so every culture ritualizes major life passages like birth and death. US hospital culture could be no exception to this universal human fact; thus it should not have been surprising to me that hospital birth is so heavily ritualized. But in most cultures, rituals are recognized as such, whereas in the hospital, rituals are disguised as "standard obstetric procedures"—as will be described later on in this book.

One day early on in my research for that first book, I wandered through the book displays at the annual convention of the American Anthropological Association looking for books that might help me understand the rituals I was seeing everywhere in US hospitals. At the Columbia University Press booth, my eye fell on a black volume with a gold and very promising title, *The Spectrum of Ritual*. I picked it up and was immediately entranced. Most anthropological works on ritual up to that point had concentrated on the effects of ritual in the social world, but *I wanted to know what ritual did to the human body and brain.* I knew that ritual's effects on human neurophysiology must be the primary source of its extraordinary power to shift human perception—to make someone who is afraid feel safe, for example, or someone who is in doubt to feel certain, but I didn't understand neurophysiology at all. *The Spectrum of Ritual* contained many of the answers I had been seeking. A few years later, at another convention, I was fortunate enough to meet one of its authors, Charles Laughlin, a neuroanthropologist and world authority on ritual. Our rich conversations and mutual passion for understanding ritual eventually led to our co-authorship of this book and its much lengthier predecessor, *The Power of Ritual* (2016).

Charles D. Laughlin

Most of my anthropological work has revolved around a single question: While I intuit with absolute certainty that everything in the universe, me included, is part of a unified, organic whole (the *Thusness*), I routinely experience myself as separate from—and when I was younger, alienated from—the world. When I first became conscious (sometime in the early 1960s) of this dissonance in my being, I had no language to express that insight, nor even the ability to talk about my dilemma with others. Then I discovered the writings of Alfred North Whitehead, particularly his magnum opus *Process and Reality* (1978). This book allowed my rational mind to begin to catch up to that insight. *Process and Reality* became my bible. For some years I had no language of my own with which to describe my comprehension apart from that of Whitehead. He gave me the words to talk about the Thusness and my existence as a part of it, but couldn't explain to my satisfaction why I continued to experience myself as alienated from it. Whitehead had little to say about the brain structures that might underlie my experience. That came later.

Then, with the aid of judicious doses of LSD-25 (about five or six "trips" between 1966 and 1969, all but one well-planned à la Tim Leary's pithy instructions), I came to realize that one could experience harmony with the Thusness through a unitive intuition that generated perception and feeling. I learned that I was capable of numerous states of mind and that my usual state of mind had a lot to do with my inability to experience connection with the world. I gradually learned that I am actually never separate from the Thusness and that the world is continuously feeding me and I am feeding it. The boundaries of "me" are very permeable, and where "I" begin and leave off is a matter of taste and convention.

Then one day a poet friend of mine gave me Colin Turnbull's wonderful book *The Forest People* (1962). That book changed my life. A popular and well-written account of the author's sojourn among the Mbuti Pygmies of the (formerly) Belgian Congo, it was for me proof positive that there are human beings on the planet who routinely experience unitive states of mind. Here were genuinely non-alienated human beings! When they felt things were falling apart, they interpreted this as a sign that "the forest had fallen asleep," and held a *molimo* ceremony "to wake the forest up." That was that! I immediately changed my major from philosophy to anthropology and completed my BA in anthropology (1966).

At some point around 1969, I figured out that my mind states were how my brain experiences itself and its environment. I also became aware that people are walking around unaware that they are bodies capable of consciousness by grace of their nervous systems, which include their brains.

They somehow experience their "minds" as distinct from (apart from, separate from—yes, *alienated from*) their bodies.

I sensed early on that somehow or other there was a mind-body schism at work. Eureka! (This phenomenon is well understood by now, but was not in the 1970s.) I began to understand how I had come to experience myself as alienated from the Thusness. The problem of alienation shifted for me from a philosophical to a neurological one, and moreover a problem that seems to begin with early conditioning—an easy matter to accomplish given our (Euroamerican cultural) obstetric and parenting patterns.

Before I could start my anticipated research with the Mbuti, I had to do my PhD courses (at the University of Oregon, 1972), and by the time I was ready to go into the field, the political climate in the Congo (then called Zaire) was such that doing work with the Pygmies was out of the question. Colin Turnbull (with whom I had corresponded since reading his book) suggested a number of possibilities, and I chose to do ethnographic fieldwork among the So of Northeastern Uganda. Nothing much was known about the So, so I ended up doing fundamental ethnographic research when I got there. One of the first experiences I had with the So was participating in one of their health-related exorcism rituals—which will be described in Chapter 1.

A crucial juncture in my work occurred when I met the late Eugene G. d'Aquili at a conference in 1972. Gene was a neurologically trained psychiatrist and anthropologist; we immediately realized that we had a common interest in the relationship between brain and culture. We collaborated on writing our first book, *Biogenetic Structuralism* (1974), which takes the view that the structures producing universal patterns in cognitions, beliefs, behaviors, techniques, images, thoughts, feelings, perceptions, experiences, and so on, are in fact the brain structures that are common to people everywhere.

At that point, I realized that I needed to seek some training in the neurosciences, so I applied for a postdoc with the National Science Foundation. I was awarded the position, and so became a Fellow of the Institute of Neurological Sciences at the University of Pennsylvania. It was in Philadelphia (Gene d'Aquili's hometown) that I met John McManus. John, trained as a social psychologist at Syracuse University in New York, was an expert on the work of Jean Piaget. John's critique of biogenetic structuralism quickly forced Gene and me to become more developmental in our view of how the brain works.

We decided we needed to do a major study of a single "universal" cultural institution as a practical example of how our approach could be applied. In 1975, the year after the publication of our first book, Gene and I teamed up with John and several other specialists in various fields to produce a book-length application of the theory of biogenetic structuralism to an account of ceremonial ritual, which eventually became the book *The Spectrum of Ritual* (1979)—the one that Robbie discovered by chance (or by fate) and found so illuminating.

As it turned out, the application of biogenetic structuralism to ritual led us to better understand science itself and its profound limitations relative to the study of consciousness and culture. As a consequence, our approach became steadily more experiential, especially relative to the study of ritual and religion. In the process of understanding human rituals, such as ceremonial rituals like the Catholic Mass and the Pygmies' *molimo* ceremony, we came to appreciate how important *symbolism* is to the work of ritual. This understanding led eventually to our most ambitious project together—the book *Brain, Symbol, and Experience* (1990). In this work, John, Gene, and I examined the relations between the brain, the brain's inherent symbolic function, and the phenomenology of experience in the study of consciousness. We argued for combining anthropology, the neurosciences, and inner contemplation as the most productive way to explore and explain consciousness.

Going back in time, in the late 1970s I became convinced that the most direct access to consciousness we have is the study of our own minds. After all, my consciousness is the only consciousness I can know from direct experience. Consequently, I got involved in various systems of meditation, including the esoteric Tarot, Christian prayer, Husserlian phenomenology, Hindu yoga, and Buddhist meditation. I got especially interested in the type of Buddhist meditation practiced by Tibetan Tantric Buddhists, because of their heavy reliance on techniques that involve intense concentration on complex symbols. So in good anthropological fashion, I became a monk (or *lama*) for seven years and spent a great deal of time in Tibetan and other Buddhist monasteries in Nepal, India, Southeast Asia, and elsewhere (never, alas, in Tibet), learning to calm my mind and concentrate on the mental properties that produce consciousness.

As anyone who has done this work knows, the course of meditative practice and the resulting series of intuitive realizations is hard to describe to others. It is literally ineffable—a process so internal, one that transforms one's view of self and world in such profound and subtle ways—that to describe the process in detail is practically impossible. These experiences fed into my understanding of biogenetic structuralism. For instance, at some point along the contemplative path, one comes to fully realize that there is no permanent substance to anything one can put one's mind to, including the self. The illusory conception of a permanent ego utterly fails in the face of direct experience to the contrary and falls away. One consequence of this letting go of ego is that one no longer expends energy looking for the little mental "me," the homunculus in the brain, the "ghost in the machine."

My meditative work was carried out during lengthy retreats in my home or in retreat centers or monasteries in such places as Lumbini, Nepal, Samye Ling in Scotland, the Benedictine priory in Montreal (under the late Dom John Main), a cabin on the banks of a lake near Whitehorse, Yukon, and the like. As a consequence of all this self-study, I came to realize many lessons that have "fed" my writings, including what the full-on experience of loving kindness is like; what Jesus meant by the koan "before Abraham was, I am"[1]; what "bardo" experiences are like; that all sensory experience is constituted by granules (particles, or "dots"); that time consciousness is a cognitive binding together of epochs of sensory experience; that archetypes (universal forms) are alive in the being and tend to become active and to perfect and simplify themselves in visions, fantasies, and projections when the ego-will is not functioning; and so on. In due course, I came to experience and understand what Buddhists call *Nirvana*, or *sunyata*—a transcendent state in which there is no suffering, desire, nor sense of self. All of these experiences and more were suggested and evoked by ritual activities that I was taught along the way or constructed for myself. My appreciation for the great power of ritual to evoke often profound spiritual experiences grew immeasurably over this period.

I later became interested in the Navajo concept of *hozho* or "beauty" (the Navajo are a nation of Indigenous people living in the US Southwest). It seemed to me from reading the literature that ritual is used by the Navajo to return someone to a state of "beauty" and "harmony" only when someone loses that state of mind. Having spent the previous decade learning all sorts of ritual practices geared toward producing a unified mind state, I found it curious that the Navajo seemed to do it "backwards," and I could not imagine why. So, of course, I went to live with the Navajo to find out more about ritual and *hozho*. As a consequence, I shifted my ethnographic interest from Tibetan Buddhism and monastic culture to the philosophy and religion of the Navajo people. In a roundabout way, it was ritual that led to my interest in getting at the *experiences* behind the concept of *hozho*. What were people experiencing that they called *hozho*, and how did they know when they were losing this state? And how did ritual assure a return to that state once it was lost? (For some of the answers to these questions that I garnered over time, see Laughlin 2004a, 2004b).

At some point in the late 1970s, I discovered that there were other anthropologists who were interested in both ritual and alternative states of consciousness. We came together under the banner of "transpersonal anthropology," held meetings, and published a journal. Through a long and eventful history, these early pioneers of transpersonal anthropology formed what is today called the Society for the Anthropology of Consciousness (SAC), a section of the American Anthropological Association.

In a way, this book marks for me a full circle return to the roots of bio-genetic structural thinking. As I have grown older and (hopefully) wiser, my respect for the power of ritual has grown, along with the extraordinary experiences I have encountered exploring the rituals of my own and other cultures. For all the reasons that Robbie listed at the beginning of this Preface in reference to the multiple workshops she has given on "The Power of Ritual" and to the confusions about ritual these workshop participants have often expressed—and considering the fact that everyone sooner or later participates in rituals—a book that addresses what rituals are, how they work, and why, is more than appropriate and informative; it is downright necessary.

Note

1. For me, this statement simply refers to the timeless and spaceless nature of Christ consciousness, meaning that God and being are inextricably connected throughout time and space.

ACKNOWLEDGMENTS

We wholeheartedly thank our reviewers for the first, unabridged edition of this book: Megan Biesele, Claire (Ginger) Farrer, Betty Sue Flowers, Henci Goer, Brigitte Jordan, Robin Ridington, Eugenia (Nia) Georges, Greg Taylor, Thomas Verny, Debra Pascali Bonaro, and Elizabeth Davis for their invaluable contributions to the improvement of this book. We also thank Greg Taylor for his willingness to allow us to create and publish this new, abridged, and improved version of our much longer book, *The Power of Ritual*, published by Daily Grail Press in 2016, and Marion Berghahn of Berghahn Books for being willing to publish it.

Introduction

WHAT IS RITUAL?

Its Definition and Characteristics

⁓𝕸☉

As Glenna began the opening conjuration of the ritual, a silence fell over the circle. Through the castings and chargings of the circle, through the invocation of the Goddess, it grew, and as Albion and Loik and Joaquin Murietta hammered out a dancing rhythm on their drums, as we whirled in a double sunwise ring, that silence swelled into waves of unseen lightness, flooding our circle, washing about our shoulders, breaking over our heads. Afterwards we wandered about the gardens, laughing and clowning, drunk on the very air itself, babbling to each other: it worked!
                                                    —Margot Adler, *Drawing Down the Moon*

A common misconception in the industrialized world holds ritual to be something that goes on in more primitive societies, while we, in our scientific enlightenment, lead rational, non-ritualistic lives. But the facts are otherwise. All human cultures, including our own, use ritual as the physical and metaphysical means for dealing with everyday life and the mystery and unpredictability of the physical, psychological, social, and cosmic realms. Ritual plays significant roles in the social behaviors of most animal species— its pervasiveness in human life reflects ancient biological programming that allows members of a species to communicate and coordinate their lives through behavioral symbols.

What is ritual? What elements does it consist of—what characteristics constitute its anatomy? What does it do and how does it work? What do animal and human rituals share in common? Why does human ritual often produce an experience of the sacred, spiritual, and supernatural? And why does it just as often work toward secular, practical ends? Why does ritual constitute what anthropologists call a *cultural universal* (meaning that it is found in every culture and society)? Where does its power come from, and how can societies and individuals tap that power?

We will address these questions from an anthropological point of view that integrates biological, psychological, neurological, sociocultural, and spiritual perspectives on ritual. Anthropology is the study of humans in their myriad manifestations. It includes comparisons of human and animal behaviors, and studies ranging from the fossilized bones and habitats of our ancestors that provide clues about human evolution (called physical anthropology), to the ruins of ancient societies (archaeology), to the development of languages across cultures (linguistic anthropology), to the complexities of historical or contemporary cultures (cultural anthropology)—and many other subfields of these.

For the past century and a half, cultural anthropologists have left the familiar surroundings of their own homelands to study other cultures and to try to make sense of them in terms that non-members can understand. In every culture they have studied—including their own—anthropologists have encountered rituals. These range from the ritualized daily behaviors of an individual to the group dynamics of a crowd, from the simple prayers of a family sitting down to eat to a Jewish Passover Seder to lavish large-scale ceremonies like feasts and seasonal holidays. And today we can speak even of global rituals in which billions of people across the planet participate in the same experience at the same time, including, for examples, the celebrations marking the dawning of the Third Millennium, the funeral of Princess Diana, the wedding of Kate Middleton to Prince William, the Olympic Games and football's (soccer's) World Cup, and, very specific to the United States, the large-scale rituals performed to honor the dead of 9/11 and to commemorate the deeply felt national experience of being attacked on homeland soil (for the first time since the British attack in 1812).

Many of the individual elements of these rituals seem incomprehensible at first glance. Why, for example, do the So people of Uganda have a ritual in which they smear themselves with gray clay and march around in formation waving their walking sticks in the air? Why does a Catholic priest wear long white robes? Why do shamans dance ecstatically for hours to "heal their community," and why are their practices remarkably similar around the world? Why have some of the ancient spiritual healing rituals of shamans been adopted by modern educated professionals? Why is it important to perform the rituals of your religion—if you have one? Why do actors, before performing a play, often gather together in a circle and chant?

Often it is only after months or years of fieldwork that the anthropologist manages to figure out the meanings of such practices. Yet anthropologists have found that this effort to "decode" the rituals of other cultures—and their own—is always worth the struggle, for such rituals often embody the most essential elements of the culture. Rituals are performances in which cultures—and individuals—describe and display their deepest values and beliefs. Performing these rituals is a part of human nature and biology that is deeply embedded in genetic evolution.

During the 20th and early 21st centuries, anthropologists have made enormous strides in understanding ritual, and ethologists (scientists who study animal behavior) have expanded our knowledge about the broad evolutionary basis of ritual through studies of other species of social animals. Yet much of what these scholars have written about ritual is highly technical and its implications are inaccessible to the general public. This book synthesizes a myriad of anthropological and ethological discoveries about ritual in what we hope is a straightforward and useful format. Its purpose is to explain ritual to people who use it, to people who are interested in it, and to students engaged in its study, and most definitely not to explicate the multiple and complex theories that anthropologists have developed about ritual over time. This book is not about ritual theory but about ritual itself—what it is, what it can do, how it works, what makes it powerful, what makes it dangerous, and most of all, what makes it useful to contemporary humans.

We also intend this book to serve students of various social sciences—especially anthropology, sociology, comparative religion, religious studies, political science, and others—as a comprehensive textbook, a single source that can complement and draw together the myriad of articles and bewildering tomes professors presently use to teach about ritual. For the general public, our principal purposes in writing this book are to: (1) help our readers to understand why so many people feel the need for rituals and what exactly they are doing when they create or participate in rituals (we include an Appendix on "How to Create and Perform an Effective Stage 4 Ritual"); (2) explain why, when people try to change ritualized behaviors (their own or those of others), they may discover that it is harder to accomplish than they imagined; and (3) draw public attention to ritual's power and potential to be used both for good and for ill—what William Sax (2010) called *the efficacy of ritual*. Public awareness of ritual tends to focus on its positive aspects, but the shadow side of ritual is as powerful as the light. Ritual may be used for the good of individuals, communities, and even corporations, as well as manipulated by politicians, religious and cult leaders, and others to sway people's perceptions, emotions, and behaviors in harmful ways.

Animal and Human Ritual as Behavioral Coordination and Communication

We recognize when an animal is on alert by its taut body posture because when we are on alert, ours is in much the same state. An elephant troop forms a protective circle around a female giving birth, just as do medical or midwifery teams and family and friends. Baby bears mimic the battles of their elders in play just as human children do. The alpha gorilla beats his chest, the male stag vies for a female's attention by stomping on the ground to challenge his rival, the guy in the bar flashes his cash when paying the bill while glaring at his potential rival. Similar behaviors in other animals shed light on the underlying causes and functions of human ritual, helping us to see how those behaviors are linked to basic brain functions.

Ritual addresses an adaptive problem encountered by all species: how to coordinate the actions of individuals into collective, socially coherent and coordinated patterns. All large-brained social animals exhibit ritualized behaviors (Schechner 1993: 229). Studies have shown that both the social play of animals and human rituals are formats for instilling and developing altruism—a requisite for cementing social bonds (see Chick 2008). At times, individual desires and behaviors must be superseded in order for group activities to be coordinated. This coordination requires controlling the information transmitted among members of the same species, and the meanings of that information. Studies of ritualistic behaviors in non-human animals indicate their fundamental importance in communication—these ritualistic display signals were selected through evolution to enable members of animal groups to provide information to each other. Animals and birds use often complex rituals in order to warn each other of danger or prepare themselves to mate—rituals we call "foreplay" when humans are concerned (see Spomer 1996 for North American herd animals; Léveillé 2007 for birds).

Animal rituals are techniques for both communicating and coordinating behavior. Ethologists have called these animal rituals *fixed action patterns*, because they are basically instinctual and once begun, are usually carried out to completion. Animal ritual displays are a type of fixed action pattern known as "intention movements"—in this case, actions that signal a readiness for certain activities (e.g., a set of movements preparing birds for flight or for mating). These stereotyped, patterned, and repetitive bodily movements or sounds communicate basic messages and synchronize cognitive processes and movements across individual participants to coordinate the behavior of the group (d'Aquili, Laughlin, and McManus 1979: 156; W. J. Smith 1979, 1990; Salzen 2010).

Humans also manifest fixed action patterns—like sucking, grasping, crawling, and walking—that are genetically "wired-in" to our body's organization.

In other words, animals and humans alike have the capacity to *ritualize* behaviors—to learn to sequence one behavior after another to get something done (see d'Aquili, Laughlin and McManus 1979: 28–41; Bell 1997: 80–81). As among animals, ritual in humans serves a primary biological function in facilitating coordinated group action. For example, the formalized displays of animals are continued in the nonverbal communication—body language (Rowlands 2006)—of humans, such as behaviors for greeting and challenging others. Animal uses of ritual to establish, maintain, and recognize differences in social status—like that of the alpha female or male—also remain prevalent in humans, who find ritual essential to asserting and maintaining social roles or "face" (see Goffman and Best 2005).

Since participation in ritual requires coordination of individual processes with group patterns, *ritual serves biologically as a mechanism for socialization.* Ceremonial rituals found in all human societies are analogous to certain animal behaviors and displays, from gatherings of wolf packs to the seasonal migratory patterns of birds. Ritual is fundamental to the adaptation of all big-brained social animals, and we humans inherited our ritual proclivities from our pre-human animal past. Indeed, ritual is so integral to human social and cognitive evolution that, as Tom Driver (1991: 10) wrote, "to study humanity is to study ritual." Concordantly, Ronald Grimes (1996a: 1) notes that "Ritual is one of the oldest human activities—often considered as important as eating, sex, and shelter," and asks: "Why has it persisted so long? Why does every attempt to suppress it result in creating it anew? What makes ritual seems at once so foundational that even the animals do it and so superfluous that Protestants once imagined they could dispense with it altogether?" Popular conceptions often generally characterize rituals as ineffective, repetitive, meaningless actions or as merely symbolic statements that produce no results in the world—as just "habits," "customs," or "traditions." Yet on the contrary, as we will show throughout this book, rituals can be instrumental, producing effects at multiple levels. Understanding ritual requires perspectives that address the multiple instrumental dimensions of its effects; we will provide these perspectives in the following pages.

Our Definition of Ritual

There are many, many definitions of ritual from which one may choose (see Bell 1992; Grimes 1990, 2014: 193–94). There are also many views on the nature, functions, meaning, and efficacy of ritual in anthropology (see Handelman 1998:10–11; Snoek 2006). Most anthropologists concentrate upon the role of ritual in religion (e.g., Stewart and Strathern 2014), for many of the rituals we anthropologists encounter involve magic and the supernatural (spirits, gods, ancestors, ghosts, etc.). But in this book, we include the secular, nonreligious use of ritual.

We will use a definition that Robbie developed ([1992] 2003a: 8): "a ritual is a patterned, repetitive, and symbolic enactment of cultural (or individual) beliefs and values." Since Robbie's formulation is a foundational concept for our book, we now consider each of its components.

Patterning, Repetition, and Symbolism: Coordination and Communication

A quick run-through of events that have long been called rituals in both the scholarly and popular lexicons immediately makes obvious the reasons why we say that patterning and repetition are two of the definitive characteristics of ritual. Events consensually labeled rituals include, among many others: church services, parades and processions, greetings and farewells, folk dances, pilgrimages, certain types of healing, bar and bat mitzvahs, graduations, initiation ceremonies, and presidential inaugurations. We think the reader will grant us that everything on this list is immediately recognizable as ritual and also as highly structured behavior that entails a distinct pattern. One recognizes a parade as different from normal traffic on the street because of the distinctive pattern of the parade—a pattern that repeats itself over and over in the various groupings that constitute the parade, from the bands that march by to the clowns and the floats.

Normal traffic on the street is also patterned and repetitive of course—most of cultural life is (see Schechner 1993). This is where the third adjective in the definition comes in: ritual is patterned, repetitive, and *symbolic* behavior. This notion of "symbolic" emphasizes that ritual is a form of communication (Rothenbuhler 2006; Senft and Basso 2009). Normal traffic on the street does not symbolize or communicate anything in particular. People on the road generally are not trying to make a statement by driving— they just want to get where they are going. The instrumental goal—getting there—is the most important reason for driving. A parade, on the other hand, is intentionally designed to be symbolic. Through parades, communities enact and display their values and celebrate their unity and diversity. Thus, parades are rituals: patterned, repetitive, and symbolic enactments that communicate cultural beliefs and values.

But wait, you say! When people drive, they are not just driving, they are also making symbolic statements. The kind of car they drive and the way they drive convey messages to others about the kind of people they are, their socioeconomic status, and so forth. And the endless flow of traffic on city streets is powerfully symbolic of the "rat race" of technocratic life.[1] So right away, as we try to define ritual, we are confronted with a problem that has plagued all those who have tried to write about and explain ritual: it is often hard to separate ritual from everyday life.

Clearly a church, mosque, or temple service is a ritual—it is patterned, repetitive, and highly symbolic—but in some ways so is an ordinary conversation. Conversations generally observe rules for turntaking, employ repetitive elements, begin with greeting formulas and close with formulaic farewells, stipulate appropriate social space, and can symbolize many things (Tannen 2005). Everyday acts like doing the laundry, cooking a meal, and getting dressed in the morning can also be patterned, repetitive, and symbolic. This fact reflects the deeply embedded nature of ritual within human behavior. Human behavior is ritualized at many different levels, some of which are shared with other animals, like grooming and greeting rituals and the sequencing of everyday activities. But humans have ritual behaviors that are unique to humans, and reflect the different adaptive needs of human communities. Consequently, understanding ritual requires that we distinguish among different forms of ritual behavior.

We suggest that ritual should not be thought of as something fixed, concrete, and discrete, but rather can most usefully be understood as existing on a *spectrum* from loosely patterned and thinly symbolic (like conversation) at one end, to highly patterned and densely symbolic (like a Catholic mass or a presidential inauguration) at the other. Human greetings ("Hi, how are you?" "I'm good, you?") and conversations are ritualized in mundane forms similar to those seen in other animals, while we also engage in behavioral routines that are organized into very complex fixed patterns such as the Mass, which uses formal ritual to evoke a human relationship with the cosmos. Conversations, daily routines, and the Mass can all be productively analyzed as ritual. But to understand why the Catholic Mass is more of a ritual than a conversation is, we must recognize the bases underlying the spectrum of ritual behaviors.

To recap, ritual can usefully be thought of as existing on a spectrum that ranges from simple patterned and repetitive behavior, like habitually getting dressed the same way every morning, to complex patterned and repetitive behaviors, like participation in a Mass. The symbolic meanings attached to and conveyed by the ritual increase toward the complex end of the scale. Yet there is some meaning in every ritualized act. When you get dressed every day, the clothes you choose to wear will reflect your individuality and personality and some of your values (are you wearing pure cotton or polyester?) When you habitually brush and floss your teeth, you are symbolically enacting your personal value on good dental hygiene. Putting on a uniform will symbolically show that you are part of a certain profession and therefore must act a certain way. Exchanging that uniform for regular clothes symbolizes that you are off-duty and therefore free to act as you like. But there is a great deal more meaning in the Catholic Mass that has taken many pages of written text to fully describe (see, e.g., Murphy 1979). To understand what both simple and complex rituals share in common, as well as what distinguishes them, requires that human ritual behavior be placed in comparative perspective, related to the behaviors of other animals, as we have seen above.

Rituals as Enactments of Beliefs and Values

Again, *a ritual is a patterned, repetitive, and symbolic enactment of cultural (or individual) beliefs and values.* We place "individual" in parentheses to indicate that most rituals are developed at the level of social groups, but it is also quite common for families and individuals to develop idiosyncratic and personal rituals that have meaning to them, like making an annual pilgrimage, saying daily prayers before a meal or at an altar, or taking your child for a walk by the river every day, complete with peanut butter and jelly sandwiches (thereby enacting the high value you place on the parent-child relationship) (see Sherman and Sherman 1990: 95–100; Feinstein and Krippner 2009). Yet on the whole, and to put it most simply, rituals most often enact cultural beliefs and values, establishing linkages among beliefs, values, and behaviors (see Handelman 1998). Anthropologists figured out this relationship of ritual to beliefs and values a long time ago, and for a century now have been using ritual to gain insights into understanding a given culture or sub-cultural social group. (A "sub-culture" is a group that has social, economic, ethnic, or other traits distinctive enough to distinguish it from others within the same overall culture or society.) If you study their rituals in a search for their meaning, you will arrive at the most important and deeply held beliefs and values of that culture or group.

In most cases, cultural rituals are inherently conservative—in other words, because rituals enact and display a culture's most basic beliefs and values, they also serve as mechanisms for transmitting and thus reinforcing and preserving those beliefs and values. Thus rituals usually work to enhance social cohesion, as their primary purpose in most cases is to align the behavior, values, and belief system of the individual with those of the group. *The more a belief system is enacted through ritual, the stronger it is. The less it is enacted, the weaker it becomes.* That's why your minister (if you have one) so often exhorts you to come to church every Sunday—and prayer group or Bible study every Wednesday night. If you stop going—if you cease to enact the rituals of your religion—over time your religion will have less and less meaning and significant attachments for you. Now we will move on to the specific characteristics that make ritual what it is and provide it with its performative power.

The Characteristics/Anatomy of Ritual and the Contents of This Book

Here we present and examine eight major characteristics of ritual that are integral to its myriad roles in human cultural life and central to the way it wields its power. These characteristics constitute what we call an *anatomy of ritual* (see also Grimes 2014). They include:

1. the use of symbols to convey a ritual's messages;
2. a cognitive matrix (belief system) from which ritual emerges;
3. rhythm, repetition and redundancy: ritual drivers;
4. the use of tools, techniques, and technologies to accomplish ritual's multiple goals;
5. the framing of ritual performances;
6. the order and formality that often separates ritual from everyday life, identifying it as ritual;
7. the sense of inviolability and inevitability that rituals can generate;
8. the acting, stylization, and staging that often give ritual its elements of high drama, the fact that it is performed and that it often intensifies toward a climax.

Not all rituals exhibit each of these characteristics; however, they are all salient features of ritual in general, all part of the anatomy of ritual and its capacity as a powerful communicative form. Understanding these characteristics of ritual—in other words, deconstructing its anatomy—is essential to understanding how it accomplishes its work in the world. So the early chapters of this book address these eight characteristics and how they work inside the human brain.

Chapter 1, on symbolism and ritual, describes the organization of the human brain and shows how the symbols through which rituals work "penetrate" to different areas of the brain, accomplishing their effects by entraining (synchronizing) physical sensation, emotion, meaning, and intellect. We also describe "core symbols" and how to interpret them, and give some entertaining and illustrative examples of symbolic interpretation, including Darth Vader, an Indigenous ancestor named Naro, and a contemporary debate among midwives over a kettle and what it symbolized for them.

Chapter 2 describes some of the cognitive matrices/belief systems that rituals enact, display, and transmit to their participants, including myths and paradigms. We use as examples the Navajo origin myth of Changing Woman, dream incubation, and what Robbie calls "the technocratic, humanistic, and holistic paradigms of medicine." We describe the human *cognitive imperative* to know and understand the world we live in, the *cycle of meaning* that cultures develop to meet that cognitive imperative, and the ways in which rituals make that cycle of meaning come alive—feel real—for its participants.

Chapter 3 focuses on the varying relationships of myths, paradigms, and other belief systems to reality and truth, explaining that these belief systems, while only partial pictures of larger realities, serve to "true" those pictures—to make them reflect enough of reality to ensure that the cultures that create and live through them will be able to function effectively in the world. We describe the differences among "sensate," "idealistic," and "ideational" cultures and how these different cultural types enact their beliefs and values through ritual, how they may use ritual to accommodate themselves to cultural and environmental change—and how, if they don't, they may be unable to adapt to such change. The Native American Sun Dance and the US space program provide examples here.

Chapter 4 points out the wide range of rhythmic and repetitive stimuli—called *ritual drivers*—through which rituals act on the human body and consciousness and analyzes their neurological effects. We describe states and "warps" of consciousness and how information is transferred between them, "monophasic" and "polyphasic" cultures (can you already guess what we mean by these terms?), and how ritual can "drive," or control, states of consciousness among its participants. We look at "portals" as doorways to alternative states of consciousness, and ask and answer the question, "Why are ritual drivers so compelling?"

Chapter 5 describes some of the many techniques and technologies used in ritual performances that enable ritual to do its work in the world and in the human brain and body. We ask: How do technologies serve as implements of ritual practice, and how on earth did the ritual diviner find the purloined pots? What is "spooky causation," and how can ritual serve as a vehicle for "divine inspiration" and "psychic power"? And how, and in what ways, can the ancient technique called "ritual" manifest itself in the contemporary high-tech and virtual worlds?

Chapter 6 illustrates the ways in which ritual is framed—set apart from ordinary life, the order and formality that characterize ritual performances, and the sense of inviolability and inevitability they work to establish. We describe physical and non-physical ritual frames in terms of energy and power, and the meaning, purpose, and power of shrines and altars of all types and kinds. Questions of why order and formality matter so much to the anatomy and effectiveness of ritual are answered through examples from the Trobriand Islands, the experiences of Bolivian tin miners (which will resonate for miners and factory workers of all types and in all countries), and from contemporary obstetricians, who use ritual in entirely predictable and formalized ways to control the process of birth. And we ask, how can the "ritual train" lead a young woman who really does not want to get married to go through the ceremony anyway? What happens when someone chooses to "break the ritual frame," purposefully disrupting the ritual? And how does the "ludic" dimension of ritual—play and laughter—manage not to break the ritual frame, but only enhance it, thus making it more powerful?

In this chapter, we also describe the altered state of consciousness called "flow," making it clear that flow most often happens inside of a clearly delineated ritual frame—*the stronger the ritual, the deeper the sense of flow*—an experience so powerful that some people change their lives in an effort to achieve more of that experience. This chapter also describes how rituals enhance courage, enabling humans to do what they could not do without the sense that the rituals they perform will somehow see them successfully through the dangers they face. Finally, this chapter acknowledges that while rituals do have some degree of power (when believed in by the participants and performed correctly according to the participants), they are not all-powerful and they sometimes—or often—do not work, meaning that they do not accomplish the symbolic and/or instrumental work in the world that they were intended by their leaders and/or participants to do. So, we ask in this chapter, *what happens when rituals fail?*

In subsequent chapters, we focus on the effects that ritual can have on its participants and the multiple roles ritual plays in social and individual life. These include, among others:

- facilitating daily living
- transmitting knowledge
- acquiring information
- transforming individual consciousness
- engendering and solidifying belief
- maintaining religious vitality
- enhancing courage
- effecting healing
- cohering communities
- initiating individuals into new social groups or new ways of being
- preserving the status quo in a given society
- and, paradoxically, effecting social change

These uses of ritual are evident in many domains of social life everywhere. Particularly emphasized in this book are the roles of ritual in the domains of community, business, sports, religion, the military, spirituality movements, cult conversion, technomedicine, and holistic healing. We have filled each chapter with examples of our points from both traditional and modern societies and from countries all over the world.

In Chapter 7, we integrate our earlier descriptions of the anatomy of ritual into a focus on how ritual is *performed*—the acting, stylization, and staging that characterize ritual performances, their climactic nature, and the roles that charismatic ritual leaders, from cult leaders to priests to politicians, play in making these performances effective through generating emotional buildup and catharsis and achieving psychological transformation in their participants. No matter what the end goal is, very similar rituals are used to achieve that goal.

In Chapter 8, we investigate "4 Stages of Cognition" and the roles that ritual plays in each Stage. We make a clear distinction between rigid and fluid ways of thinking, delineate the 4 Stages of Cognition, and more or less equate them with their anthropological equivalents. We explain each of these 4 Stages of Cognition in relation to each other, and demonstrate how ritual can be employed to reinforce each way of thinking, and to reduce many kinds of stress by solidly grounding individuals in their belief system and worldview, giving them a sense of safety and stability in an uncertain world, and preventing them from regressing into "Substage"—in other words, from "losing it" and taking out their stress on others.

In Chapter 9, we address ritual's paradoxical roles: as noted above, ritual can work both to preserve the status quo and to effect social change. We provide examples of ritual failure and ritual success in both endeavors, and discuss various cultural revitalization movements—some of which failed to achieve social change, and some of which succeeded or are in the process of succeeding. We examine the contemporary invention of ritual by holistic obstetricians in Brazil and by Herb Kelleher, the founder of Southwest Airlines, who intentionally created a consciously alternative corporate culture that was long hailed as an exemplar of how to run a successful business.

In Chapter 10, we describe what it is like to design and carry out your own ceremonial rituals, and give examples of how such contrived affairs either work well, or don't, from memorial ceremonies to weddings to puberty rites and "dream incubation." And in our Conclusion, we sum up our findings and leave you with room for further thinking about ritual, how it can work in the world and in your brain/body, and how you might use it for the most positive possible effects in your own life.

In the pages that follow, we will stick mostly to standard English, but will ask our readers to bear with us as we introduce (as we have already started doing above) a few anthropological terms, perspectives, and concepts that we find particularly useful for talking about and understanding ritual—what it is, how it works, and why.

Ritual is a complex subject—the anthropological writings on it could fill a library. And as we have seen, its cultural uses are myriad. Ritual is a powerful didactic and socializing tool, but often its power and influence go unrecognized because most people are not generally aware of its inner workings. To grasp these inner workings is to have a choice in our response to the rituals that permeate our daily lives.

Note

1. Robbie (Davis-Floyd [1992] 2008, 2018a, 2022) has long defined a *technocracy* as a capitalistic, hierarchical, bureaucratic, and (still) patriarchal society organized around an ideology of progress via the development of ever-higher technologies and the global flow of information through those technologies.

Chapter 1

SYMBOLISM IN RITUAL

Ritual's primary characteristic is that it has effects on individuals by sending messages through symbols. (Please note that symbols don't actually "send" messages—rather, people perceive meaning in symbols, in ways that may be similar or may differ individually, culturally, historically, etc. Saying that "symbols send messages" is a convenient shorthand we will use throughout this book.) A *symbol* is an object, form, idea, or action that "stands for something else," providing a source of cultural—or individual—meaning.

Symbols are *multivocal*—that is, many meanings can be combined and expressed in a single symbol (Deacon 1997; Donald 2001). For example, think about how many different things are symbolized by a cross. This one simple object can connote Christ's death, an action that itself conveys the central message of Christianity: the potential redemption and salvation of humankind through the acceptance of Jesus Christ as "our Lord and Savior." A cross can also connote a person's identification with Christianity, while its style and design can indicate one specific Christian sect or group. A cross placed on the wall in someone's home indicates that this is a Christian household; a cross placed in a public space can be a political statement; a burning cross in someone's yard sends a hate message. These are only a few of the multiple messages this one symbol can send. It sends other messages in other cultures: in various shamanic traditions, the cross is a symbol of connection and transition where two dimensions meet at the center (the axis), which constitutes a symbolic threshold of transition—a portal—between those two dimensions.

Symbols serve as "vehicles for conception" (Geertz 1973). Claude Lévi-Strauss (1995) has said that symbols are "goods to think with." Another useful way of thinking about symbols is as *vehicles for communication*. All symbols carry messages that can be received by the interpretive frameworks of the perceivers. The ease with which symbols evoke broad interpretive processes is what makes them so effective in communication and so essential to the processes and efficacy of ritual.

Symbols Are Brain Talk

Symbols are the elements of what we call the *symbolic process*—the process by which the brain makes sense of what it perceives. The symbolic process is shorthand for how the cells of our nervous system interact in such an automatic and rapid way that we are barely aware of the difference between seeing something like the lines on this page and the meaning we attach to the lines as words, concepts, images, and thoughts. The reason why this linking of image and meaning is so rapid and natural is that symbolic interpretation is an innate human potential that unfolds naturally through environmental exposure and socialization. We have inherited this facility not just as humans, but more generally as a consequence of being animals with brains. All animals with brains operate similarly. Honeybees and dogs and chimpanzees all have this in common—their brains make sense of the world by way of the symbolic process.

You may well ask then, if all animals with brains operate via the symbolic process, does that mean all animals with brains have culture? If this question did occur to you, then welcome to anthropology! Authorities have been arguing over this issue for decades. The answer of course depends on how you define culture. If you define it broadly enough, you will likely acknowledge that some of the big-brained social animals, such as arctic wolves, African elephants, bottlenose dolphins, and chimpanzees have rudimentary cultures. We suggest that you read Frans de Waal's and Frans Lantings's wonderful book *Bonobo: The Forgotten Ape* (1997) and decide for yourself about the Bonobo chimpanzee, one of our closest biological relatives among surviving apes. What we can say for sure, as we did above, is that many nonhuman animals have rituals—patterned, repetitive, and symbolic performances that communicate important messages to others.

The outcome of symbolic processing is relatively stable and recurring across time, especially in adult humans and other animals. Similar stimuli evoke the same symbolic interpretation time after time. (For example, consider the effect that the Nazi swastika has on Jews, and many others, still today.) The neural structures that mediate symbols and meanings—and that mediate each and every moment of experience—are linked across our billions of brain cells and their trillions of interconnections. These structures are made up of circuits—an organization of cells that come together to form a *neural network*—in this case, the network mediating symbols and their meaning.

Different parts of our brain interpret different dimensions of symbols. As you may know, the cortex of the brain is divided into two hemispheres, the left and the right, that talk to each other across major neural tracts such as the corpus callosum. Straightforward verbal messages (like "pigs are pink") are decoded and analyzed in the left hemisphere of the brain, so we can choose whether or not to believe them ("I know better; pigs can be dark or light brown, black and white, black, or white—they are certainly not all pink!"). In contrast, nonverbal symbols are received by the right hemisphere of the brain, where they are interpreted as a *gestalt* (a whole) (see Table 1.1). In other words, instead of being intellectually analyzed, *a symbol's message will be felt in its totality through the body, the emotions, and the intuitive faculty of the mind.* For example, when a Marine on deployment is required to keep his rifle with him at all times, even in the bathroom, he *in-corporates* its symbolic meanings—literally taking them into his psyche through the physical senses of his body. (Contrary to the popular notion, Marines do not sleep with their rifles.) Of course, the whole brain takes part in all brain functions—it is important to keep in mind that the division between the functions of the hemisphere is not absolute but a matter of degree and complementarity of function or of relative dominance.

Table 1.1. The Two Sides of the Human Brain (Frontal Cortex). Table created by authors.

Left Hemisphere Functions	Right Hemisphere Functions
analytic—dissects, segregates, categorizes, evaluates	synthetic—receives the gestalt, the whole
either/or logic, linear thinking	poetic, metaphoric, analogic
emphasizes differences, discontinuities	stresses similarities, relationships
works things through	creates A-HA! experiences
verbal	musical, pictorial, general semantics
speech	gestures, tone of voice
temporal (watches clock)	spatial
linear	holistic
intellectual, rational	emotional
individual more likely to be conscious of its functions	individual less likely to be conscious of its functions

Please note: This Table is oversimplified because the whole brain operates in all brain functions, yet the Table is still generally useful in terms of brain hemispheric predominance.

The fact that symbolic messages are generally physically and emotionally experienced, rather than being intellectually analyzed, means that *ritual participants are often unconscious of the powerful symbolic messages they are receiving.* Some of these happenings are only unconscious because we are not paying attention to them at the moment—like driving a car while thinking about something else. We can become conscious of our driving in an instant if need be. (There are other things that happen at an unconscious level that are not so easy to become aware of—such as what our liver is doing at the moment or how our skin is processing vitamin D when we are out in the sun.) The brain often processes symbols at deeper levels of the unconscious, as when we may find ourselves profoundly moved by watching a flag flying high without even thinking about the fact that the flag is a symbol or knowing why it is affecting us in that way. Many people watching Princess Diana's funeral—or the wedding of her son William to Kate Middleton—were uncertain as to why they were so profoundly moved by the death—or marriage—of people they had never met. They would not have been interested had these people not been royals, for royals tap into deep, widely shared archetypes of the Leader, King, or Queen. (In Jungian terms, an *archetype* is a collectively inherited unconscious idea, pattern of thought, image, etc., that is universally present in individual psyches.) This is symbolic processing at its most powerful and unconscious level. It is safe to say that almost all of the symbolism affecting us is operating in part at an unconscious level.

For a more detailed example, consider a woman in early labor walking into a typical hospital and being asked to sit in a wheelchair for transport to the labor ward. She knows that she is quite capable of walking there by herself and may understand that the purpose of the wheelchair is simply to protect the hospital from liability should she fall, and that it is used in this way for all women in labor so has nothing in particular to do with her as an individual. Nevertheless, a wheelchair is a powerful symbol of disability. To sit down and be wheeled is to convey the impression that one is disabled and weak. The laboring woman may know intellectually that she is not disabled, but she will be physically and emotionally sensing the impression of disability simply through sitting in the wheelchair. And when others—the nurses, the partner, and family or friends who accompany her—look at her, they will see not an autonomous woman but a woman in a wheelchair who appears to be disabled, a perception that may soon translate into subtle changes in the ways they talk to and treat her (Davis-Floyd [1992] 2003a: 77–78).

And there is a further layer of symbolic meaning that accompanies sitting in a wheelchair instead of walking upright—in the metaphorical systems of Western cultures, *up is good* and *down is bad* (Lakoff and Johnson 1980). To be "up" means to be on top of things, in control; to be "down" means to be subordinate to, not in control, lower on the totem pole. Interactionally, everyone else is now "up," and the laboring woman is "down"—a double whammy.

Significantly, no one stops to consider the fact that they are all receiving powerful symbolic messages that the woman in labor is disabled, not in control, and lower down on the interactional hierarchy than everyone else. These symbolic messages are received unconsciously: they are not thought about, they are simply experienced. Thus their effect is all the more powerful because the participants do not have a choice about what they feel. They don't stop to warn themselves not to treat the woman differently just because she is in a wheelchair; rather, they may start treating her differently without realizing it. If she goes from the wheelchair to the hospital bed, these impressions of disability will be intensified, for once she is wearing a hospital gown and lying in a hospital bed, she will look like any other hospital patient. Since most patients are sick, weak, and unable to care for themselves, she will appear to be the same. These symbolic impressions of illness and weakness will influence how this laboring woman is viewed and thus treated by her caregivers and friends from the very first moments of her hospital stay.

Robbie experienced another dramatic example of how powerful a symbol of illness the hospital gown and plastic bracelet can be when a friend of hers was suddenly discharged from the hospital two days after an appendectomy. He had thought he would be spending another day, when the doctor suddenly decided that he was fine and could go home. One moment, sitting in his hospital bed, wearing a hospital gown, he appeared, felt, and acted weak and ill. But as he shed the gown, cut off the bracelet, took a shower, and put on his street clothes (which of course symbolize normality in relation to the abnormality of the hospital gown), he started to appear and act normal. By the time they left, he was feeling normal as well, and could hardly believe that only an hour before he had felt and acted weak and ill.

The Core, Emotional, and Cortical Brains

Understanding how the brain works is fundamental—indeed, essential—to understanding the power of ritual and how its anatomy works to achieve that power. The human brain and its symbol-making capacity are characterized by both the complementary right and left hemisphere processes illustrated above, and by a hierarchy of other information-processing capacities that emerged, complexified, and reorganized over the course of evolution. The human capacity to have experiences, be conscious, process information and meaning, and know the world is based on different brain strata. For the sake of clarity, and using straightforward terms, we will talk about how the brain functions at three levels of structure:

- the *core brain,* which mediates bodily regulation, metabolism, physical and psychological arousal, instinct, etc.;
- the *emotional brain* (often thought of as the *limbic* brain), which mediates emotional states;
- the *cortical brain,* which mediates imagination, thought, modulation or control of emotion, planning, etc.

These three levels of the brain used to be called by brain scientists the "reptilian," "paleomammalian," and "neomammalian" brains, because to some extent, we humans share the lower levels of neural structure—the core and emotional brains—with other animals; their functions underlie the similarities in patterns of human behavior with those found in other vertebrates, including reptiles, birds, and mammals. These lower brain systems were reworked and elaborated in the human brain over the course of our evolution, yet their propensity for the ritualization of behavior has remained. These three brain strata each play roles in different kinds of experience and information processing that can be both elicited and mediated through ritual processes.

Integration of the Three Levels of the Brain

These three levels of brain activity—the core brain, the emotional brain, and the cortical brain—are not stacked up like three pancakes, as brain scientists used to believe. All the layers of the brain are interconnected, and connections between different areas and levels of the brain are reciprocal—information is exchanged in various directions. The different areas and levels of the brain talk to each other in the service of a holistic and effective response to the environment. If one area of the brain is destroyed by disease, injury, or surgery, the entire brain tries to reorganize itself to take over the functions of the damaged tissues. In the healthy brain, the pre-frontal, or cerebral, cortex—the front one-third of the *neocortex,* which is the largest and evolutionarily most recent portion of the cortical brain and the site of most of the higher brain functions—will often exercise control over our emotional brain so that we don't "lose it" in a confrontation. The core brain will modulate our arousal, awareness, and instinctive reactions relative to possible dangers or opportunities perceived in the environment. Each area performs its function in relation to the other areas of the brain that, operating together, can all be involved in learning, the transmission of culture, problem-solving, planning, imagining, conversing, and so forth.

A central aspect of this expressive and communication system is manifested in symbolism. Rituals, through their manipulation of symbols, play a fundamental role in manipulating and managing these expressive processes. *The great power of ritual stems in part from its ability to engage all levels of the brain, and thus control—or at least maximally mediate—the experiences of its participants.*

The core brain is primarily responsible for instinct, impulses, compulsions, and obsessions, and for regulating them in our daily behavioral routines, basic forms of survival behavior, and social cooperation and integration. The emotional brain in turn generates emotions and influences behavior with subjective information and feelings. Its emotional intelligence gives rise to the basic dynamics that underlie everyday social behavior and the tone of social interactions. These lower brain centers provide non-verbal communication—body language, facial expressions, posture, and gestures. Non-verbal awareness and emotional dynamics are generally unconscious, cut off from conscious awareness because of the domination of the left-hemisphere- and language-based cultural rules of the neocortex. In other words, our thoughts and behaviors, as well as our sense of wellbeing, require the coordination of many different kinds of competing information and motivations, processed in a simultaneous and parallel fashion all over the brain.

Again, most of us are unaware of this brain-wide integration of functions because conscious awareness is typically focused on the activities of the left hemisphere. Nevertheless, the intuitions, emotions, and unconscious decision-making processes of the right hemisphere, and those arising from the lower brain systems, contribute fundamental operations linked to the neocortex's higher cognitive processes. The lower brain processes provide our sense of self, the emotional dynamics of our relationships with others, the felt meanings we associate with self and others, and our convictions of certainty about feeling and beliefs. These lower brain dynamics can also produce emotional conflicts that we may repress to facilitate social adaptation. (Sometimes these repressed conflicts express themselves physiologically as various types of illness or pain—for example, a sore throat can result from not expressing something important [like emotional pain], a skin rash from repressed anger.)

One of the functions of ritual (and of the altered states of consciousness rituals can produce) is to integrate processes normally managed by the lower brain centers with the analytical power of the neocortex. Through the power of symbols that "penetrate" all levels of the brain (see below), ritual can tap into the lower brain systems, integrating their physiological, instinctual, and emotional subjectivity with the abstract systems of the neocortex. In other words, ritual can be used to bring unconscious processes that have been repressed and automatized (e.g., unconscious destructive habits or feelings) into consciousness.

Many psychotherapists, for example, use ritualized techniques to facilitate this kind of integration, such as guided visualization—a process in which the therapist has a client imagine a series of events, often in the form of a story. (For Robbie's integrative experience of highly ritualized EMDR therapy, see Chapter 7.) For another example, some psychiatrists working with substance abuse among Native Americans have prescribed participation in sweat lodge rituals, Native American Church peyote rituals, and the Sun Dance ritual, and have found all of these ritual treatments to be sound and effective with certain individuals because of the emotional release and psychological catharsis they can generate for members of those cultures—and sometimes for non-members as well.

It is important to note that the power of ritual to affect the human brain can also be employed in extremely negative and destructive ways that include hazing and brainwashing, to name only two (see Smith 1993). The cultures of prisons and other total institutions (such as hospitals, asylums, nursing homes; see Goffman 1961) may be built around a series of ritualized ways in which the authorities regularly abuse the inmates without feeling guilty about it, because "that's the way it's done around here." This is what we call the "shadow side" of ritual—it can be manipulated just as effectively for ill as for good.

The Power of Symbols

The power of ritual depends in large part upon the power of symbols. The brain is in a sense an organ of symbolism, for it operates in virtually every moment of consciousness to wed images with meanings in the manner described above.

How Symbols Work

The power of symbols derives from their operation on the whole body to bring about transformations in perception and experience. Earlier, we defined a symbol as an object, idea, or action that "stands for something else," providing a source of multiple meanings. But it is more precise to say that the term "symbolizing" *refers to the process by which an object or an event out in the world is attributed meaning within our brains.* Our brains—which extend throughout our bodies via our central nervous systems—are actively involved in producing the meaning of various things and happenings in our experiences. If something is a symbol to us, it is because a whole network of associations has become attached to that something. Key symbols incorporated into a ritual will evoke a pattern of associations that are manipulated within our psyches in response to the sequential placement of the symbols within the ritual.

The cultural world is full of powerful symbols—flags display love of country, a Jaguar displays the owner's wealth and taste in cars, a cross on top of a building clearly tells us that it is a church. Even our perception of a simple chair is loaded with symbolism. We know (if we are from a culture that utilizes chairs) that the object is fundamentally something to be sat upon. But there are chairs, and there are chairs. The chair's shape and materials convey messages about the wealth and status of its owner or the place where it should be used, and so forth. It may be a comfortable armchair, a royal throne, a cheap Wal-Mart camp chair, or a valuable 18th-century Chippendale. The sensory object we take to be a chair is the "symbol" and the cognitive associations we attribute to that object—"chairness," "wheelchair-ness," "antique-ness," and so forth—are the "meaning" of the symbol for us. The cognitive associations we make with the object function to extend and elaborate its meaning for us.

We are reminded of the story that anthropologist Marcel Griaule (1965) told about himself while he was doing fieldwork among the Dogon in Mali, West Africa. After years of visiting the Dogon, Griaule welcomed the decision the elders finally made to assign one of their number to instruct him on the "real truth" of things. They appointed the blind shaman Ogotemmeli to teach him about Dogon cosmology and myth. Ogotemmeli upended a grain basket, stuck an arrow in the bottom, and used the stairstepped form of the basket to organize all the various animals and plants according to native categories. All of the leopards were on this step and all the elephants on that step, and so on. At one point, quite confused, Griaule asked Ogotemmeli how it was possible to put so many animals on a step. Thinking his student quite dense, the old shaman replied that didn't Griaule understand that these were all *symbols* and that you could put an endless number of symbols on a step? The Dogon, as well as other traditional peoples, understand the role of symbols in revealing and representing the elements and relations operating in the world around them.

Symbolic Penetration

The way that something outside of our body—a wheelchair, a bar/bat mitzvah, a photo, a song—links up to a set of meanings inside our body is what we call *penetration*. The more we understand how symbols can "penetrate" us, the more fully we will come to understand why rituals are so powerful. ("Symbolic penetration" is a term that has nothing to do with sexual penetration, so please don't think of it that way!) The term actually refers to how cells and organs interact within our body as they assimilate/are penetrated by the symbol's message.

A special kind of fulfilling "penetration" occurs when we communicate with other people in certain ways. For instance, we may feel a lot of love for someone and send them a card on Valentine's Day. The card is a symbol expressing our loving feelings toward that person, and we hope that they will "get the message" when they receive the card—"getting the message" of course requires the kind of penetration we desire. For many, Christmas activities revolve around the ritual exchange of gifts that may have profound significance for both the giver and receiver. Gifts in such circumstances are powerful symbols of the kind of relationship between giver and the receiver. The symbolism of the gifts may penetrate us deeply, reinforcing or even

Figure 1.1. An astronaut planting the US flag on the moon—an act with little instrumental value but laden with powerful symbolic meaning. What does this image symbolize for you? Wikimedia Commons, public domain.

enhancing a sense of bonding. Or the opposite may occur—an inappropriate gift may penetrate us with the message "This person does not understand me at all!"

Sometimes we actively work to achieve symbolic penetration in other people. If we get angry at others, we expect our histrionics to "get inside" and "push their buttons" to emotionally affect them. We want them to understand and perhaps feel what we are feeling, so we speak loudly, make angry sounds, and manipulate our body language in order to "get through" (penetrate). Or we express love in very clear ways that we hope will penetrate our beloved so that she or he really "gets it" and assimilates the full extent of our love.

Whether a particular symbolic object or event is external to our body, as in the case of the wheelchair, or internal, as in the imagery of a dream, hallucination, or fantasy, the image becomes a symbol when it connects to its meaning from our memory and within our experience. We may have never seen a particular wheelchair before, and yet we know it for what it is—a wheelchair, with all that "wheelchair-ness" implies for us. The symbol "out there" has penetrated and evoked its meaning inside our mind and body.

As previously mentioned, Charlie lived for a time with a tribe of East African people called the So, who were, at that time, terrified of hospitals, because the hospital was "the place where people go to die." Why? It turned out that hospital staff, insensitive to local cultural norms, required women to remove their neck rings when they were admitted into a ward. But in the So culture of that era, the only time a woman's neck rings were taken off was when she died—hence the automatic and symbolic So association of hospital admission with death.

Socialization and Ritual Symbolic Penetration

The power of symbolic penetration is also based in processes of socialization that link cultural symbols with individual physiological responses. In this way, ritual is able under certain circumstances to reveal previously repressed psychodynamics and to channel emotions of fear and anxiety in socially useful ways.

Human development involves the *entrainment*—the synchronization—of neurons into circuits and networks that mediate experiences and can be elicited by symbolic stimuli. Socialization results in making physiological responses to symbols automatic and habitual: an adult frowns; recognizing the meaning of this symbol, the child's skin prickles; she feels a flash of fear; and to alleviate that fear, she alters her behavior. These mental effects upon physiology are an inherent aspect of development, as symbolic meanings increasingly elicit physiological responses in a child over time. In other words, the child's initial innate organization of neural networks is reconfigured over time by learning to understand symbolic processes and their associated cultural patterns of interpretation and response.

Symbolic processes are obviously fundamental to the development of experience; they "tune" the central nervous system, entraining/synchronizing the relationships between action, emotion, and cognition. Human perception is in its most fundamental form a symbolic process that allows us to interpret present stimuli in terms of our previous experiences. (In order for a single frown to immediately cause a child to alter her behavior, she must have previously experienced overt negative sanctions that were preceded by frowns; thus she learns to associate the frown with the sanctions that will result if she does not respond to the frown.) Again, experience, development, and socialization involve entrainment—the linking or synchronizing of brain neurons into networks—through adaptation to the environment, including the family and cultural environment. During a child's development, neurophysiological circuits form in response to repetitive social stimuli.

So that we are on the same page here, let's look at how neurons work. The brain is a "community of cells" (Laughlin, McManus, and d'Aquili 1990: 34), by which we mean that our brain is like a vast human community in which the neurons and "support" cells are living organisms that organize themselves at both local (circuits, networks) and higher, more complex levels (interactions across hemispheres and up and down the neural hierarchy), and that communicate among themselves. Neural cells have the capacity of *synaptic plasticity*—that is, the ability of the system of synapses involved in memory storage to change and grow. Neurons are very special cells that communicate by "reaching out" and touching each other (neurons that touch other neurons are called *interneurons*) and other tissue cells, like those that make up muscles and other organs. This "reaching out" develops over time into more and more complex neural structures.

The point at which one neuron touches another in a circuit is called a *synapse*—a point of connection between nerve cells where one cell can influence the activity of another cell. Synapses can exist between the tip of a cell's *axon* (an appendage reaching off the body of a nerve cell like a thread-like tentacle of a squid) and a *dendrite* (a smaller appendage, kind of like a strand or strands of hair growing out of the body of the nerve cell). The axon communicates with the dendrite by releasing tiny bubbles of a chemical messenger (called a *neurotransmitter*) across a tiny gap (the *synaptic junction*) between the transmitting cell and the receiving cell. Synaptic plasticity is the ability of the cell to change the quality and properties of this biochemical communication.

It might help a bit to realize that there exist more synapses in your brain than there are stars in all the galaxies in the known universe! This multiplicity of synapses is the secret to the human brain's profound complexity. Within the dynamic, ever-changing structure of all these synapses are stored all our memories. In light of our later discussion of the importance of sleep and dreaming for the efficacy of certain rituals, we note here the important role sleep plays in potentiating, storing, associating, changing, and developing the synaptic organizations that mediate our memories.

Communication between symbolic stimuli coming in through the senses and the deep structures of memory and emotional/physiological association—*symbolic penetration*—occurs by way of cells influencing each other synaptically through a series of circuits that carry and alter information from the periphery of the body into the central nervous system and its networks, and then perhaps outward again, conducting commands from these deep structures to the muscles and organs that mediate behavior and metabolism. Thus, ritual can influence biological processes by the manipulation and placement of symbols. Through symbols and the systems of meaning (like myths, paradigms, and other types of belief systems) that underlie them, *ritual bridges levels of the brain, entraining various neurocognitive structures through the associative linkages symbols provide.*

In other words, the ritual process integrates the neural networks of the conscious mind with those of the lower brain structures, which are not normally accessible to consciousness. The ritual use of symbolic associations *entrains* physiological processes involved in basic emotions, social attachments, needs of the self, and senses of comfort, security, and certainty, providing catharses for fears, anxieties, and other psychodynamic processes by altering those psychological processes mediated by lower and older brain centers. For instance, smells may operate to evoke strong memories. Thus, in many cultures, olfactory stimuli (such as incense) are specifically used in rituals to establish and then evoke such memories and integrate them with the conscious experiences people have during ritual participation.

Symbolic penetration via ritual performance can in fact evoke healing processes within our bodies because it operates on these brain structures, mediating and transforming them, often outside of awareness. For instance, it has been shown experimentally that if a sick or injured person visualizes his or her injury or illness (e.g., cancer) as the site of a battle between opponents—say, a pack of white dogs against dark demons—in which the "good guys" eventually defeat the "bad guys," there is a corresponding increase in the population of immune system cells at the actual site of the illness or injury (see Weil and Rossman 2006). As we shall see in Chapter 7, this use of visualization—or "guided imagery"—for the purpose of healing is fundamental to shamanic healing systems all over the globe.

The power of particular symbols and messages to penetrate differs widely. Abstract cognitive symbols that are easily recognized and understood by the prefrontal cortex may seem the most powerful, but they do not necessarily penetrate to the lower brain systems that drive emotions, metabolism, or behaviors. For instance, we may receive lots of symbolic messages about what to do to maximize health (e.g., "smoking is dangerous," "just say no" to drugs), and we may agree with and accept those messages at the cognitive level. But then there is the issue of actually acting on those messages. As much as we intellectually accept the message, it may not penetrate to the lower brain systems. Conversely, these lower brain systems can send messages that penetrate "up" to the various cortical systems and have profound effects upon our behavior and emotions, even if the neocortex does not rationally accept them.

For example, we might continue to smoke or do drugs because our lower brain system desires pleasure, stress release, or the security of fitting into a peer group, or we are subject to a chemically based addiction. Or we might carry into adulthood an irrational fear of clowns stemming from a childhood trauma involving a clown—a trauma deeply embedded in the limbic system (emotional brain) that continues to affect our emotional responses and behaviors. The objects of our desire or our trauma (a cigarette, a packet of heroin, or a billboard showing a clown) work as symbols that immediately penetrate to those lower brain levels, evoking the desire to smoke or take drugs or reviving the fear we felt as children. Because the wiring of the brain is mostly bottom-up (from the lower, more primitive areas to the neocortex), rather than top-down, the messages evoked from the lower emotional or behavioral levels of the brain can be very compelling. Our best intentions (like stopping smoking or doing drugs) may go unful-filled because the higher brain cannot easily force its message onto the lower brain systems. Similarly, irrational fears may persist in spite of the person knowing that they are irrational because the powerful ascending messages from the lower brain easily overwhelm the rational cortical messages.

Ritual is a technique that helps humans reinforce the upward penetration of messages from deep in the brain. Messages that begin in the neocortex may be more easily ignored by the emotional brain than are the powerful, survival-oriented messages ascending from the lower brain centers. Rituals engage and manipulate these older systems in order to enhance the upward penetration of the symbolic messages they send. The negative side of this upward penetration can include ongoing habitual/ritual smoking or drug use. One of the positive sides is that rituals help humans to overcome our instinctive, lower-brain "fight, flight, or freeze" responses to danger and engage instead in cooperative behaviors that protect and enhance the wellbeing of the group.

Soldiers, for example, are put through complex ritual programs—called "basic training"—full of all sorts of physically strenuous ordeals that alter the natural human tendency to avoid life-threatening situations, replacing it instead with feelings of group cohesion and the ability to engage head-on in battle (see Chapter 7 on rites of passage). Police trainees go through similar programs, as do firefighters, emergency medical technicians, airline pilots, and members of other professions who often have to face dangerous situations that might cause them to flee or "freeze" if they were not ritually socialized to fight.

The point we wish to emphasize here is that individuals can consciously use symbols to affect their own lower brain centers: for instance, to heal themselves or to reduce or eliminate their anxieties and fears. And societies can use collective rituals, which link symbols with patterned behavior, to affect the lower parts of the brains of multiple individuals—for example, to train them to be soldiers or to reinforce their society's values and beliefs, instilled in them by socialization, usually from a very early age.

Core Symbols

At the very center of the symbolism through which rituals work lie what may be called a society's *core symbols*. Whereas most of the symbols used in people's everyday interaction and communication are not really recognized as symbols per se, a society's core symbols are perceived as such by most people in that society. A national flag, the Presidential Seal, the Statue of Liberty, the Eiffel Tower, the Christian cross, the Jewish Star of David, a corporation's logo—all of these are core symbols that incorporate a great deal of meaning and significance for the people who value them, as well as for people outside the society who see the core symbol as representing the nation, religion, or corporate group. The US flag may be reverenced by some and vilified by others, such as Iranians, Palestinians, and the Taliban, because the core symbol and the people that symbol evokes often become cognitively equated. Thus the core symbol may be the focus of devotion, identification, and activity for a given group.

For example, among the Navajo of the US Southwest, the corn plant is at the same time a major staple crop and a powerful symbol of the people's worldview. The corn stalk is for the Navajo what the "World Tree" or "Vision Serpent" was for the Ancient Maya and the Tree of Life is for practitioners of Kabbalah. Within the core symbol of the corn plant, the Navajo may read the relations between the levels of reality—the underworld, this world, and the sky—as well as the four sacred directions and all the sacred things that are revered by the people.

Likewise, high technology is a core symbol of technocratic societies. Like corn for the Navajo, in a technocracy, high technology is simultaneously a major economic driver, an essential element of daily life, and a powerful symbol of the technocratic worldview, which centers around an ideology of progress through the development of high technologies and the control over nature and daily life that these technologies provide (Davis-Floyd 1994, [1992] 2003a, 2022). High technology represents the ongoing fulfillment of that ideological mandate, and thus its pervasive presence is a constant reassurance that we are achieving our cultural goals.

We can better understand the role of core symbols in ritual by looking at some of the properties of core symbols:

1. *Core symbols are pervasive.* These symbols pervade most domains of life, involving both the sacred and the everyday. Just as corn is the most common food resource of the Navajo, so too does the corn plant remind people of the major elements of their religious life. Just as high-tech products are pervasive in US life, so too do they remind people of their overall faith in the benefits and goals promised and often achieved by technology.

2. *Core symbols may be archetypal in origin.* Symbols may derive from and represent the deep levels of the human psyche. To recap from above, the term "archetype" comes from the work of Carl G. Jung (1964), who defined an *archetype* as a collectively inherited unconscious idea, pattern of thought, image, etc., that is universally present in individual psyches. Jung recognized that certain symbols seem to have universal occurrence and appeal. Their universality suggests that their meaning is "hard-wired" into the human brain by way of genetic inheritance. In Jung's sense, archetypes are encoded in the human brain as the result of hundreds of generations of species-typical experience. Hence, symbols like Gods or Goddesses, the Leader, or King or Queen, the Hero or Heroine, the Trickster (a supernatural figure appearing in various guises and typically engaging in mischievous activities, important in the folklore and mythology of many traditional peoples), the "changeling" (a human able to change into other forms), the "Ancients," and the Under-, Middle-, and Upper-Worlds are considered by many students of mythology to be images generated by the human mind to reflect its own essential nature—a nature that gets projected out onto the world in mythical stories, artifacts, sacred landscapes, and ritual performances. Such archetypes play significant roles in modern technocracies—for example, we exhibit an archetypal fascination with royals (kings, queens, princes, and princesses), with God(s) and Goddesses, heroes and heroines, with ancient peoples (think of Troy), with changelings (such as werewolves,

humans transformed into vampires, "meta-humans," and cyborg trans-formers), and with the "upper world" long recognized by traditional shamans as we reach toward "the heavens" by exploring outer space.

3. *Core symbols often link individual identity with that of "others" in one's social group.* People often display their group membership, and represent themselves to themselves and to others, through their group's core symbols. Doctors may wear a white coat and sling a stethoscope around their necks to indicate their status as doctors. A student from Canada might stitch a maple leaf to his or her backpack to identify as a Canadian. In Israel, the kind of yarmulke (*kippah*) men wear can signify their membership in a particular religious sect or that they are non-religious, secular Jews. When young people from certain North American Plains Indian cultures reach puberty, they go on a vision quest, during which one of the culture's repertoire of sacred beings may appear to them and give them instructions and perhaps signal their life's career. Thereafter, they identify themselves with that sacred entity and thus with the mythology associated with the entity.

4. *Core symbols lie at the very center of nationalism and work to bind the homeland together.* Patriotism and cultural identity are really a set of emotionally charged beliefs organized around a set of core symbols that, for the people involved, signify their group identity. Often this feeling of membership is linked to the land itself. For example, being born on their native land is a core value for the Inuit of Northern Quebec (see Epoo et al. 2021)—so much so that they put a great deal of work into building their own maternity units and training Inuit midwives, in order to stop the Canadian government's practice of flying pregnant Inuit women to southern Canadian cities to give birth alone in hospitals. Thus they have "re-matriated" birth back to the land they value so highly—and despite the fact that these maternity units in the Nunavik region have no cesarean capabilities; it takes two-to-eight hours to reach a medical facility where a cesarean can be performed. Collectively, the Inuit of Nunavik decided to take this risk, considering it more important to re-matriate birth back to the land. (Surprising to many, over the 30 years or so of this re-matriation, the Inuit birth outcomes have been excellent—even better than those for the country as a whole [Epoo et al. 2021].)

And for many thousands of years, people have been projecting their cultural identity upon nature to produce "sacred landscapes" (see Devereux 1992, 1996). Many know of the famous Stonehenge on the Salisbury Plain in England, which dates back to around 4000 BCE. But few realize that this great structure was made from stones weighing 5 tons or more each that were quarried and transported from as far as

130 miles away by rafts and rollers, forming part of a gigantic structure of earthworks found over much of Neolithic England. Obviously, their Neolithic constructors considered it tremendously important to modify their natural environment in these meaningful ways. (The problem is that today we no longer know just what that meaning was to those ancient people. When the once-living belief-and-meaning system of a given society is completely lost to time, it is very difficult, often impossible, to reconstruct it.)

Within these symbolically pregnant landscapes, ritual performances have been played out in which the mythological events that were the people's origins are enacted. From the beginnings of human prehistory, people have bound themselves together by linking core symbols, landscapes, and rituals in a deeply emotional package of significance. And still today, various groups such as Wiccans and other pagans perform rituals at Stonehenge to enact and display their particular beliefs and values as connected to the earth and to the Ancients (who may be thought of by such groups as Priestesses or Druids who held the keys to long-lost magic), and as vivified—given special meaning—by using that sacred site as an altar and a ritual "frame" (see Chapter 6).

5. *Core symbols reveal the hidden forces operating in the world.* Core symbols often operate to evoke an epiphany—that is, the realization of normally hidden forces or the existence of sacred beings. The Catholic priest performing a Mass will wear raiment that is essentially designed after the street clothes of Romans living at the time of Christ. The raiment is worn over the priest's everyday street clothes, thus symbolically binding the time of Christ with our own time and expressing the timelessness of Christ's message of love and salvation to the congregation. The Iroquois people in the Northeastern United States carry out healing ceremonies in which the spirit that causes the disease is invoked to cure the disease. The spirit is revealed by way of healers wearing grotesque masks representing the normally invisible face of the disease-causing spirit. Likewise, high-tech diagnostic machines like CT scanners, ultrasound machines, and X-ray machines can peer deep into the human body, making the hidden manifest. Symbolically speaking, there is little difference between the hidden spirit embodied in the mask and the hidden tumor revealed on the radiographic film—both facilitate decision-making and action in the world by revealing the operation of mysterious forces.

6. *Core symbols are "pregnant with meaning."* As we have seen, symbols are rich in cognitive, emotional, and instinctive (cortical, emotional, and core brain) associations that are readily accessed in the presence of the symbols—this is the power of symbolic penetration. Often the field of

meaning and the emotional loading of a set of symbols grows ever greater during the course of one's life, as a result of repeated participation in rituals in which the symbolism is presented, renewed, and reinforced.

For many people, the sight of McDonald's "golden arches" is sufficient to evoke hunger and memories of tasty meals while traveling down the nation's highways, and to cause them to take the exit and pull up to the order stand. What is interesting here is that the "golden arches" are not really golden, they are yellow. McDonald's, in a brilliant advertising move, chose to label them "golden"—a term that of course symbolizes so much more that is appealing to hungry people than "yellow" ever could—"golden arches" symbolize both great value and an invitation into heaven itself. In a sense, all of one's memory associations of McDonald's, whether positive or negative, are linked to and evoked by the symbol of the "golden" arches. Far beyond a mere desire to eat a Big Mac, the arches may penetrate to exciting and happy memories of childhood, parents, and special outings for some, while evoking negative associations with junk fast food and the obesity problem in the United States for others.

In the same way, a prayer rug can both evoke Islam and the meanings of Mecca (such rugs are laid out facing Mecca) and serve as a sacred space for prayer, or it can evoke fear of Muslim jihadists in others, just as a burka can evoke a sense of safety and protection in the Muslim women who wear it, yet for Westerners it can symbolize women's oppression by the Muslim patriarchy.

7. *Core symbols are multivocal.* Symbols used in rituals often speak with many voices that penetrate to the core brain and contain many layers of meaning that engage the cortical brain. So much more than a piece of cloth, a nation's or a state's flag evokes homeland, patriotism, the history of the nation or state, province, or region it represents, the values of its people, and on and on. An electronic fetal monitoring machine, which Robbie has interpreted as the primary symbol of hospital birth (Davis-Floyd [1992] 2003a, 2022), also speaks with many voices, promising to provide full information on the strength of the laboring mother's contractions and the condition of the fetal heart rate, representing the vast corporation that created it and all of the technological know-how that went into making it, and giving hospital practitioners and women a sense of psychological, emotional, and instinctive trust in the information it provides. (For more on the electronic fetal monitor and its ritual functions, see Chapters 5 and 7). Levels of symbolic meaning and penetration range from the most primitive instinctive and emotional reactions to highly elaborate intellectual understandings of the symbols and their interrelations.

Interpreting Core Symbolism

Perhaps by now you can see why anthropologists find it a challenge to interpret the meaning of ritual performances: full understanding of the multiple layers of meaning enacted in rituals often requires years of participant observation, and sometimes official training in those rituals, to appreciate their nuances. This necessity of experience is why anthropologists studying various cultures depend so heavily both on participating in rituals as much as they can and on talking to people who understand and can communicate the meaning of the ritual.

The So of East Africa, Their "Gray Goop," and Charlie's Efforts to Understand Its Symbolic Meaning

During Charlie's ethnographic field experience among the East African So people, he experienced the difficulty of understanding the deep symbolic associations evoked by rituals. One morning early in his stay in So Land, he awoke upon hearing a loud commotion down the hill from where he had pitched his tent. He bounded out of his sleeping bag, jumped into his clothes, and ran down the hill to see what was happening—just in time to see a large group of tribesmen and women lining up in front of a fellow who was slapping some gray goop across each person's chest in turn. Charlie joined the line and in turn received a swatch of gray goop across his chest. When everybody had been marked with the gray goop, they all lined up in military fashion and began to march back and forth. At the end of each march people would stop and raise their sticks up in the air and yell something unintelligible (to Charlie) to the sky. They did this about three times and then suddenly the event was finished, the company disbanded, and everyone went their own way.

Charlie was thrilled of course! He knew that he had just participated in his first So ritual. (Anthropologists simply love such stuff.) He sat right down and recorded what he had experienced and observed in meticulous detail. But then it dawned on him that he had no idea whatsoever as to what purpose or meaning to attach to the ritual he had just undergone. (What Charlie wrote down was what anthropologist Clifford Geertz [1973] called a "thin description"—a simple description of what took place, lacking any kind of interpretation.) It took nine months of further research before he could safely say that he understood what the people were up to on that sunny day—an activity that had taken less than 30 minutes to complete. What he eventually learned (here comes what Geertz called a "thick description"—one that layers in the meaning of the event) was that the gray goop was clay from a sacred place in the local creek that was believed to protect each participant from evil. The march was a procedure prescribed by the shamans to exorcise the evil spirits that were causing the people an inordinate incidence of disease. (The So were experiencing the second year of what would eventually prove to be a devastating ten-year drought period in that part of Africa.)

Charlie's research challenge was to learn enough about the language and lore of the So people to comprehend the meanings associated with disease, walking sticks, gray clay, the sky, the earth, the cardinal directions—in fact the entire cosmology of a people who had lived in that area of the world for countless generations. His learning process involved questioning people who were very shy about talking to outsiders about their religious beliefs. The So had experienced several generations of Christian and Muslim missionaries who had been telling them that they were pagans and that their beliefs and practices were wrong-headed. Even when Charlie had hung around long enough to make friends, it was difficult for him to get his mind around a worldview that put the mountain homelands of the So at the center of reality, and to think in terms of dead ancestors as mediators between God and the earth. And of course, there are aspects of the So comprehension of reality and disease that Charlie never came to understand. Thus his interpretations of that ritual and other aspects of the So way of life have to be considered partial at best. In other words, Charlie's understanding of So core symbolism is incomplete, as it must be for any outsider to a full-blown ritual tradition.

Understanding and Acting on Core Symbolism: Michael Winkelman and the Messenger Mice

Our colleague Michael Winkelman, a pre-eminent anthropologist of shamanism, adds to our understanding of core symbolism through the following report (personal communication 2011). Although Michael intellectually recognized the importance of participating in rituals in order to understand the relevance and application of ritual elements, at first he did not understand that the practical aspects (as opposed to the intellectual aspects) of this participation could only be known through participating. For example, he understood that animals were fundamental to shamanic ideology, practice, and behaviors. But reading about the importance of animal relationships and identity provided little insight into how animals actually come to play a role in shamanic practice. Most people think very little of the actual animals (or their representations) that intersect our daily lives, and few people look for significance in those encounters. But, says Michael, once the shamanic path opens an awareness of the importance of animal powers, an awareness of their presence in everyday life expands.

This awareness then allows the understanding that animals can act as messengers and guides for human behavior.

For example, on two occasions when Michael was thinking that he would "speak his mind" by telling others what he thought on an important issue, mice unexpectedly showed up at his feet in unlikely places—on a path outside of a conference meeting room and outside of a phone booth on a crowded street. These mice were behaving unusually—not scurrying off and hiding but standing squarely in his path, undeterred by his presence in spite of him nearly stepping on them! Without his experientially based shamanic training and perspective, Michael would most likely have seen no meaning at all in the presence of these tiny creatures. Yet because of that perspective, he interpreted these mice as "messengers" encouraging timidity rather than a forceful outspokenness. This interpretation affected his behavior—he refrained from speaking and thereby, as it turned out, saved himself a great deal of trouble that quite likely would have descended upon him if he had.

In the terms we have been using in this chapter, the mouse-as-symbolic messenger penetrated all three levels of Michael's brain in complex ways that produced certain responses. In his neocortex, his previous cultural learning and experiences had led to certain associations/meanings about mice and what they represent in their demeanor and behavior. Furthermore, his understanding of shamanic beliefs regarding the significance of animals appearing unexpectedly had long existed because of his years of studying and analyzing shamanism in various cultures. His experiential participation in shamanic activities had evoked many emotional responses about the importance of animals as bearers of significant personal messages. At the deeper, core level of his brain, his participation in shamanic rituals and altered states of consciousness had entrained shamanic practices with instinctive sensations of peace and security, and special significance. The appearance of the mice penetrated through all brain strata to produce a profound difference in his behavior: he physically sensed, emotionally felt, and intellectually understood the importance and significance of the symbolic message conveyed by the presence of the mice in such unlikely places, and acted accordingly, to apparent great benefit.

Understanding and Interpreting Core Symbolism: Robbie and the Bonobo

Robbie had a similarly evocative experience with a bonobo. She was participating in a shamanic workshop in a hotel, during which the leader—a contemporary shaman—asked the participants to visualize their "power animal," and then to get up and dance with that animal and ask him or her what they could learn. Robbie was unable to visualize anything, but she got up and started dancing anyway. Suddenly she found herself dancing with an (imagined) female bonobo. They just danced and laughed for a while. Then when Robbie asked for the lesson, the bonobo laughed again and said, "*You* need to learn to be more like *me!*" Familiar with bonobo culture and customs from her readings, Robbie took that to mean that she should learn to stop "living in my head so much" and to be more playful, more social, and more comfortable with her own sexuality—as bonobos are well-known to be. In our terms here, the symbolism of the bonobo penetrated deep into Robbie's brain, and she changed her lifestyle accordingly, to great benefits in many ways, which we leave our readers to imagine!

Examples of Symbolic Interpretation

In order to better appreciate the importance of lived experience in the process of interpreting ritual symbolism, we offer below a few more examples of symbolic penetration and how it works.

Confrontation with the Quintessence of Evil

Some years ago, one of Charlie's students, Ray Robertson, studied the phenomenon of the science fiction (SF) convention from the perspective of the anthropology of religion. An avid science fiction reader, he quickly immersed himself in the culture of SF "fandom" and attended many SF conventions ("cons") to see what they were all about. He found that the SF fans who attend these cons are typically members of a community of SF aficionados who share a culture of understanding pertaining to the world around them, including personal identity, sexual mores, political values, attitudes about various scientific theories and enterprises, and so on.

For fandom, the SF con is essentially a complex ritual during which many of these values and attitudes are acted out in the form of role-playing, games, and costumed pageantry. Many SF fans come to the cons dressed as characters from various SF novels, movies, and TV series. For example, *Star Trek* devotees (known as Trekkies or Trekkers) attend Trekker cons dressed as their favorite *Star Trek* characters. There are contests for the best costumes and much role-playing. A great deal of revelry takes place during the cons, especially at night. And there is sufficient "suspension of disbelief" about the role-playing that one can easily lose track of the normal world outside the hotel or conference center.

Well into his research, Robertson invited Charlie to a local SF con being held in a major hotel. During the evening, the two friends were wandering down a corridor, deep in conversation about some arcane theoretical issue and oblivious of their surroundings. They turned the corner in the corridor and suddenly came face-to-face with a huge six-and-a-half-foot Darth Vader striding down the hall toward them. Dressed all in black with flowing robes and black mask and helmet, the apparition seemed to have stepped right off the silver screen and into their lives. Both Robertson and Charlie independently had the same experience. They stopped abruptly and froze where they stood, and for a moment normal everyday reality was suspended. They were suddenly part of the *Star Wars* mythos and were facing the very quintessence of evil himself—the actual living, breathing Darth Vader. The next moment, the fan wearing the costume passed them and said, "Good day!"—and the spell was broken. But the experience left both anthropologists speechless and then intensely awestruck at the power of the SF con ritual environment to so alter their perceptions that the fictional Darth Vader had become totally real to them, if only for a moment. Moreover, for both, the experience became part of the meaning of the Darth Vader character ever after. In other words, in our terms in this chapter, their experience of the symbol powerfully, if temporarily, penetrated their psyches and altered their perceptions of reality.

Naro's Unhappy Resting Place

When Charlie and his family moved into their more permanent location on the lovely green slopes of Mount Moroto among the So people of Karamoja District, Uganda, little did they know that just outside the thorn fence that demarcated their compound, a drama of significance was unfolding in the earth. Old grandmother Naro was becoming restive and was posing a serious threat to her lineage—a hole was opening in the earth where Naro had been buried some years before. People passing by were becoming increasingly concerned about the fact that the hole seemed to be expanding almost daily. There was much discussion about this phenomenon.

Among the So, when young men, women, and children die, their bodies are taken into the bush where they are left in a sitting position under a tree. But when an important elder man or woman dies, a crypt is dug in the ground, topped with a log cover and buried under earth and stones. A great deal of ceremony attends the burying of important dead, for their patronage is desired in the afterworld. Moreover, the living are concerned that the person's ghost not come back to disturb them. Old Naro was one such important elder, and it was increasingly clear to her fellow tribesmen from the gradually widening hole in the top of her gravesite that she was displeased in some way. People became very anxious that the old woman might be signaling that she was dissatisfied and unhappy. And if things were to go on unchecked, Naro might claim the life of someone else in her lineage, as she might be lonely and want someone from her family to join her.

It was finally decided that something had to be done about the situation. Preparations were made, resources were gathered, and important people were called together. On the appointed day, the elders gathered at the site of the grave and began a lengthy ceremony (a ceremony is constituted by a series of rituals) during which they carefully cleaned out the top of the grave, ritually slaughtered a goat, cooked food (including the goat) for everyone to eat, offered libations of beer and tobacco to Naro, and then filled in the opening with stones until a cairn was formed over the grave. Much relieved, the people from her lineage then settled down to consume the goat meat and other foods and to chat about everyday matters.

For Charlie, it was truly remarkable to perceive the effect the ritual had upon Naro's lineage mates—the alleviation of their anxiety was palpable. The rite seemed to stand as a kind of buffer between the living and their anxiety about death and the potentially dangerous intentions of the departed. (As we will further show below, *ritual often stands as a buffer between cognition and chaos*.) And by being a part of the process, Charlie became very aware of the power of ritual to alleviate fear and suffering by (symbolically) removing a perceived deadly threat.

The Great Kettle Debate

After over a decade of studying and "hanging out" with midwives during the 1990s and early 2000s, Robbie became involved in an interesting group discussion about the symbolic meaning of a particular gift. The midwifery group leaders wanted to honor one of their members, the world-famous midwife Ina May Gaskin, and were debating what kind of gift would be most appropriate. They were thinking about giving her a big black kettle— a powerful cultural symbol not only of hearth and home in olden times, but also, for these particular midwives, of their desire to harken back to and reinterpret the cultural meanings attached to the European "witches" of the medieval and Renaissance periods. Their re-interpretation (which stemmed in part from a highly influential booklet written by Barbara Ehrenreich and Deirdre English in 1973 entitled *Witches, Midwives, and Nurses*) was that these "witches" were really wise women and healers who traced their roots to Druidic and other pagan traditions. Such women were often intentionally misrepresented by Inquisitors and others as devil-worshippers (and for other reasons too complex to explore here—see the book mentioned above) and thus were heavily and unjustly persecuted during the European witch hunts (from the late 1400s to the 1700s). Black iron kettles, or cauldrons, have for hundreds of years been symbols of witches stirring up their brews, but have more recently become, for many women, symbols of female healers, good "witches" (wise women) who used such kettles to brew herbs and healing remedies, and who discovered many of the medicines we still use today, from chamomile tea for stomach pains to foxglove (its active ingredient is digitalis) to regulate the heart. Many of the midwives in the group thought a kettle would make an ideal gift, as the honoree was an herbalist herself.

But a problem arose. There were a number of Christians in this midwifery group who were deeply offended by the symbolic association of kettle >> cauldron >> witch, and adamantly opposed such a gift. In the end, the group decided to gift their honoree with a pressure cooker, which still evokes hearth and home but is far more symbolically neutral—in other words, far less culturally loaded—than a black kettle could ever be. (Ina May was very happy with the pressure cooker and still uses it to this day.)

Summary: The Power of Symbols

The primary characteristic of ritual is that it works through symbols that are employed throughout the ritual performance. Symbols convey complex, multivocal cultural meanings. They operate both consciously and unconsciously because they can penetrate the levels or strata of the brain (core, emotional, and cortical), and consequently work to integrate instinctive, emotional, imaginative, and intellectual responses with the cultural messages they send. Part of the power of symbols derives from the fact that we can experience their messages with our bodies and emotions; we may or may not be intellectually aware of their penetration but may simply *feel* their effects.

The above examples illustrate the expressive and evocative power of symbols, their multivocality, and the importance of lived experience in symbolic interpretation. A regular guy dressed up as Darth Vader can express the individual's identification with *Star Wars* and can evoke in total strangers the experience of actually encountering this embodiment of evil. This is not merely an intellectual or cognitive experience but a *felt* experience involving psychological, emotional, instinctive (all brain levels), and physiological reactions. A collapsing grave can evoke perceptions of a dead ancestor's displeasure, strike fear into a whole social group, and cause that group to enact a ritual to express their concern for that ancestor and fulfill their need to restore the cosmic order. For some midwives, a black kettle can evoke centuries of stereotyping and persecution and the need to reinterpret their conceptual heritage, while at the same time conveying the powers of evil witches and the devil for others. Each of these symbols is capable of penetrating individual consciousness and evoking strong instinctive (core brain) and emotional (emotional brain) reactions in accordance with the system of beliefs it expresses. Core cultural symbols like a national flag or the Christian cross evoke deep emotions and link individual identity with that of a group. In the following chapter, we will more closely examine the role of symbols in the myths, paradigms, and other types of belief systems that rituals enact.

Chapter 2

THE COGNITIVE MATRIX OF RITUAL
Belief Systems, Myths, and Paradigms

A matrix (from the Latin *mater*, "mother"), like a womb, is something from within which something else emerges. Rituals are never arbitrary; they emerge from within the belief system of a group or individual, and their primary purpose, generally speaking, is to enact and transmit that belief system into the psyches of their participants, aligning their individual beliefs and values with those of the group. Each symbolic message contained within a given ritual manifests one or more underlying cultural beliefs or values (Handelman 1998). Sometimes these beliefs are explicitly held, as is generally the case with religion: devout religious members know what they believe and can articulate those beliefs more or less clearly. But often the beliefs and values that ritual enacts are unconsciously held. In other words, people can ritually enact beliefs and values that they may not consciously know they hold or can be socialized through ritual into accepting beliefs and values they may not even wish to hold (see McCauley and Lawson 2002).

There is no necessary link between myth and ritual—they are not two sides of the same coin. It is very true that myth and ritual are often entangled, yet it is possible to have myth without ritual, and vice versa. And it is possible to have a "belief system" without myths—or paradigms—underlying it, but rather a system of core values that are encoded in that belief system. In fact, Oxford English Dictionary defines a "belief system" as "a set of principles or tenets which together form the basis of a religion, philosophy, or moral code."[1] Herein we use "belief system" as a larger concept that can encompass myths and paradigms yet be more than those.

As previously noted, because the belief system of a culture may be enacted through ritual, analysis of ritual can lead directly to a profound understanding of that belief system and any myths that encapsulate it. For this reason, anthropologists have often focused on interpreting the rituals of a given culture, including their own, as a primary "way in" to understanding the culture. For example, Lloyd Warner's (1959) analysis of Memorial Day—which he called "An American Sacred Ceremony"—as a means of celebrating the unity of the nation in the face of its ethnic diversity provides important insights into US life. For another example, Peter Metcalf and Richard Huntington (1991) showed that a close understanding of a people's handling of death and performance of mortuary rituals can tell us a lot about the people's values, moral beliefs, and worldview. Thus, in a sense, all mythically rich rituals can reveal the innermost collective desires of a people—goals they may not actually measure up to in everyday life, but often get closer to the more often the relevant rituals are performed.

This chapter examines the cognitive matrices—belief systems—within which ritual produces its extraordinary power over human consciousness. We look at the relationships of ritual to myth in traditional societies, to myths and paradigms in modern societies, and to belief systems in general. Just as one can say that ritual enacts cultural or individual beliefs and values, so also can one say that *rituals enact myths,* that *rituals enact paradigms,* and that *rituals enact belief systems.* All of these are *systems of meaning.* A "paradigm" is a model that provides a template for reality, consisting of a set of cohesive and internally consistent principles, beliefs, tenets, or guidelines for action, whereas a "myth" is a story that does much the same, only not so explicitly. As do myths, paradigms integrate different levels of experience, meaning, and explanation. We sum up this relationship as the *myth-ritual, paradigm-ritual,* or *belief system-ritual complex.*

A word about language here: as we discuss the belief system/myth/paradigm-ritual complex, we will often use the labels "traditional" and "modern" to refer to the differences between small-scale societies with long histories and well-elaborated mythologies, as opposed to the larger and more diffuse national, regional, and ethnic groups that constitute contemporary society in its rich diversity. This traditional/modern dichotomy is not rigid. Today's traditional or Indigenous societies are as "contemporary" as are the planet's nation-states. Traditional groups of people are still in touch with their cultural heritage—a heritage that may span tens and even hundreds of generations. In later chapters, we will show how some of the thousands of traditional societies that continue to exist creatively manipulate myth and ritual to eclectically combine the traditional and the modern in ways that preserve their cultural integrity, while enabling them to move more or less fluidly in the contemporary world. (And thousands of traditional societies that were unable to achieve such integration have died out.) Contemporary societies also encompass many entirely new groups, from gangs to "urban tribes" that quickly generate and adopt specific belief and value systems and create rituals that enact them—such as a particular type of "handshake"— hand and arm movements—that indicate group membership. Cults and new religious sects often appear; their leaders construct cosmologies with attendant myths, rituals, and other "invented traditions." Today's traditional societies are increasingly embedded in many aspects of the globalized, modern world, and what we say about "traditional societies" often applies just as strongly to many recently formed contemporary groups.

The Cognitive Imperative and the Cycle of Meaning

Humans have a drive to understand—a *cognitive imperative*—to order the world into significant elements and events and unify them into a systematic cognitive whole. Myths, paradigms, and other belief systems not based on myths or paradigms play fundamental roles in the cognitive imperative, defining boundaries, revealing and imputing causes, and organizing human experience in order to remove uncertainty (Rappaport 1991: 21) and buffer against existential anxieties (Atran 2002). This cognitive imperative for understanding the world is often achieved through the use of ritual to assimilate the novelty and variety presented in daily life within a familiar cognitive structure. Ritual provides meaningful explanations by limiting relevant information and reducing uncertainty by synchronizing/entraining neural processes within each person and across individuals. Ceremonial rituals are a special and more dramatic type of human ritual embedded in a cognitive matrix of meanings often associated with myth. Myth plays a vital role in providing conceptual integration, particularly for those events that humans find to be unpredictable and inexplicable by any other means.

Members of traditional societies tend to ground their understandings of the world and themselves in a specific mythic cosmology, the elements of which have been passed down from generation to generation. Many subcultural groups within contemporary societies, from religious sects and cults to various virtual communities, do the same, although there may be less time depth to their cultural heritage. By *cosmology*, we mean that people conceive of the world as:

1. a totality, which is
2. made up of everything in existence as parts of that totality, and

3. all the parts are causally entangled and interact in a systemic way, such that
4. the existence of the totality depends upon all the parts interacting and mutually influencing each other and the totality.
5. Much or most of the totality, as well as essential aspects and causal interactions of all the parts, are hidden from normal sensory perception.

We must emphasize here that there is a distinct difference between a worldview and a cosmology. Everyone has a *worldview*, by which we mean a person or group's collective conception or philosophy of the world they live in. And that worldview may or may not be based in a particular mythic or paradigmatic model; it may be based on a belief system, such as that of a gang, an urban tribe, a family, or an individual, and thus not be cosmological in scope. While it is true that modern scientists use the term *cosmology* to refer to the systemic properties of our universe, from an anthropological point of view, they are actually describing a kind of quasi-cosmology, or simply a worldview that applies strictly to science, not the true cosmology of a people who go about their daily lives with an intimate understanding of and participation in the world-as-cosmos—an understanding that many of us living in contemporary societies do not have. In order to be a true cosmology in the anthropological sense, a people's worldview must be understood intuitively as a living system within the context of the people's everyday *lifeworld*—that is, within their everyday lived experience.

The Huichol people of northern Mexico say, "To be Huichol is to be sacred," thereby expressing their sense of their lifeworld as intimately bound up with their cosmology (Myerhoff 1974). Their cosmological understanding is not merely intellectual, *it is lived*—in other words, their cosmology is *instantiated* in their everyday experience of life ("instantiate" as we are using it here means to vivify something by making it real in lived experience, as in "heroes instantiate ideals").

Many of us living in modern technocratic societies have in common with the Huichol that we too understand that what we do in our daily lives impacts the planetary ecology. It could be said that many of us have a (spiritual or non-spiritual) cosmology that starts with the Big Bang and extends to the idea that everything is interconnected—as we will further discuss in Chapter 5. Ever since the famous 1969 Apollo 11 "earthrise" photograph began to percolate throughout our collective consciousness, many of us have understood how very fragile our "life layer" is and how easily we can damage it. This understanding accelerated efforts to protect the environment and to stop the vast levels of pollution our industries have been producing. It is no coincidence that in the wake of that photo, the United States Environmental Protection Agency was proposed by President Richard Nixon and came into existence on December 2,1970. We now watch our energy consumption, seek new and renewable energy resources, recycle basic materials, clean up messes, spills, and waterways, and (sometimes) penalize those who continue to foul our life layer. Debates about the extent to which human activities endanger the planet are always in the news these days. Discussions, points of view, and policy debates about industrial influences on the Climate Crisis are embedded in contemporary consciousness. Meanwhile, a growing number of "green" groups—groups of environmentalists concerned with stopping the destruction of the planet's ecosystem—are using efficacious collective rituals to repetitively make their points (see Grimes 2014).

Thus many people, whether traditional or modern, intuitively grasp that what they do in their daily lives impacts upon the totality of existence, and that what happens in the world as a whole impinges on their daily lives. (This interconnectedness has been instantiated in the coronavirus pandemic, which is still ongoing in most countries as we write [January 2022] [see Ali and Davis-Floyd 2022].) In technocratic societies with their materialistic worldview, the understanding of human-environment interaction tends to be a secular one. In more traditional societies where there is no separation of church and state, of religion and daily reality, people tell a consistent story about the nature of reality, and they experience reality through that story, in a feedback loop that we call the *cycle of meaning*.

An Example of Mythic Interpretation: The Navajo Origin Myth

Charlie has spent many years living with and studying the Navajo people of the US Southwest, who live in a land they conceive to be sacred. Navajoland (or as the Navajo themselves say, *Diné Bikéyah*, "the Land of the People") is demarcated by four sacred mountains and a central "place of emergence." The people know about the origin of this sacred land and its People by way of stories that are passed down from generation to generation—stories that anthropologists call "myths" or "origin stories." (Myths can also be explanatory stories that do not deal specifically with origins.) These stories paint various pictures of the origin of the present world, just as the different gospels of the New Testament tell the stories of Jesus from different points of view.

According to these Navajo origin stories, there existed several past worlds, beginning with the darkest and then proceeding through various colors until the contemporary world—some of Charlie's Navajo friends call our present world the "Glitter World" because of all the colors in it. Each subsequent world evolved out of the previous world in a state of disastrous chaos. Various mythological beings climbed out of the last world into this world at the "place of emergence" and commenced creating all the beings that inhabit the present Glitter World. But this process was neither straightforward nor easy, for various factors produced all sorts of aberrations in the forms of monsters and other disruptions of the beautiful and harmonious relations among beings.

Seeing this reawakening of chaos, the Holy People (spirit beings) decided to get involved and placed the baby Changing Woman, wrapped in a cradle, on the top of one of the central mountains to be discovered by Talking God (a male), who then turned the infant over to First Man and First Woman (both being primary gods) to raise. The First Couple did such a miraculous job of raising Changing Woman that she reached puberty in just 12 days. With her first menstruation, harmonious fertility was renewed in the world. The central ceremonial ritual of the Navajo, called the Blessing Way, became a celebration of Changing Woman's renewal of the earth and of her subsequent mating with the Sun, which produced the hero twins, Monster Slayer and Born for Water. They went on many adventures and ended up killing most of the monsters that were infesting the earth. Once the earth was safe, Changing Woman created human beings, who then took over the world while the Holy People chose to retire to being the invisible essences of things in the Glitter World. Changing Woman herself became the cycle of existence, the climatological seasons, the phases of life, the cycle of day and night. She is for the Navajo the Earth Mother, the quintessence of fertility, the source of natural laws and movement, the perfect coordination of the male and female principles in the cosmos and here on earth. (There are many versions of this Navajo origin myth; see, for examples, McNeley 1981; Farella 1984.)

From this story, we can see that the cosmology of the Navajo, and thus their whole mythopoeic symbolic system, are part of a living, instantiated system of meaning for people born and raised in this traditional culture. In addition to describing the origins of the present world, this myth portrays the two sides of the coin of change—on one side harmony and beauty, on the other disharmony and ugliness. It also tells that most of the really important dynamics of origin are invisible to normal perception. The Holy People are real to the Navajo, though they, by their own choice, have faded into the background of essential forces behind events. As well, the story reinforces the understanding that the life cycle of people and other beings is natural and lawful—that we are born, mature, age, and die. For the Navajo, this life cycle is as true for whole worlds as it is for the People.

By living with the People and listening to how they use these stories in their everyday lives, as Charlie has done, the anthropologist as outsider can come to more or less understand how many Navajo people interpret the significance of this myth/origin story for those daily lives. When we experience how a people utilize their stories—where, when, and under what conditions the stories are unpacked and remembered, told, or referred to—then we begin to intuit the range of contexts within which people are informed by the stories. And as we will see below, one of the most common contexts within which myths like Changing Woman become real for people is ritual enactment.

The cosmology and its symbolic representations as depicted in a myth like the one about Changing Woman are part of a people's lifeworld, and in living in accordance with its meanings and the memory of its motifs, relations, and events, the cosmology is instantiated—animated and reinforced within each person's consciousness. The fundamental assumptions of traditional cosmologies are rarely fully articulated by the members of that society. Rather, most people unselfconsciously and uncritically accept and participate in the worldview they inherit from their culture, interpreting their real-life experiences in terms of that worldview—again, in a feedback loop that instantiates the cosmology in individual experience and thus appears to confirm its truth.

For instance, Charlie found that the So people he lived with in Uganda would not enter a deep pool of water to either swim or wash themselves. They believed that pools are infested with a spirit called a *tegwech* that can attack a person and cause them to sicken and die. Children are taught from a young age to be afraid of these pools. They do not think about the *tegwech*, they just take their existence for granted. And as it turns out, the pools in question were in fact infested with *bilharzia*, the "liver fluke," which causes schistosomiasis, a disease with precisely the same symptoms as a *tegwech* attack. Likewise, rural Pakistani children are warned not to wear their shoes in bed because if they do, a *Balla*—a snake—will crawl up and bite them. A Pakistani anthropologist named Inayat Ali (2022) figured out that the Balla was a culturally intuited metaphor for the dirt and germs that can be carried on shoes. In such ways, people can align their stories with their lived realities.

Another Example of Mythic Interpretation: Dream Incubation

Consider the not uncommon phenomenon of "dream incubation" (see Laughlin 2011). A culture—such as the Australian Aborigines or the Papago Native Americans in the US Southwest—may believe that while one is asleep, one's soul can depart from the body and fly around and learn much. So a member of such a culture, who might want to discover something important, might use ritual to induce lucid dreams and actually experience himself as a consciousness flying free of his body and having spiritually significant adventures. For that individual, this experience both instantiates the belief system (makes it "come alive" in his personal experience) and appears to confirm its truth. For the moment, we will beg the question of whether or not the information people are able to attain in this way has any basis in "reality"—we will take this question up again in Chapter 7 when we discuss ritual and transpersonal experiences. Here we note that the "belief systems," "cosmologies," "myths," and "paradigms" we discuss often overlap and are all encompassed within the term "belief system." Most importantly, they have a "heuristic" or practical nature—meaning that they enable us to cognize the world around us and thus to move confidently within it.

Traditional cosmologies tend to be conservative and enduring. They resist radical changes in knowledge, for the principal functions of a traditional society's worldview are to organize their experiences of the world and to assure a complementarity of experience for the society's members. In contrast to science, which (ideally) seeks to discover the truth about the world, *the cycle of meaning* in traditional societies—and in many contemporary religious groups—*reflects the desire to imbue ordinary experience with meaning.* That is, the cognitive processes of the human brain usually work to associate what people perceive at the moment with patterns of meaning stored in their memories, rather than to either acquire new information about the world, or empirically test theories about the world.

The Myth/Paradigm/Ritual Complex

Myths and Paradigms

At the very center of a traditional society's symbolic system may be found a complex of myth and ritual from which other media (art, drama, games) derive their primary inspiration. Our definition of myth is broad, going beyond the usual anthropological definition of a myth as an "origin story": as our Foreword author Betty Sue Flowers (personal communication 2011) states, "a myth is a story that organizes experience through telling something explicitly about meaning—where we're going, where we came from, or who we are." Myths in all societies are primarily concerned with: (1) making sense of the world and giving it meaning; and (2) transmitting cosmological knowledge upon which the existence and well-being of the people depend.

Myths do many things for people, from inspiring to severely limiting imagination and possibility. Myths charter the cultural world, laying out the blueprints for many of society's most basic categories and institutions. Consider the myth of *Genesis*, which charters at least four of the world's major religions (Judaism, Islam, Christianity, and Ba'hai) and has been formative in the development of many cultures, either generically or from the proselytizing efforts of missionaries. The early part of the Genesis story lays out a series of basic binary oppositions in terms of which people in many cultures still organize their experience: God created the world, dividing the heavens from the earth, day from night, dark from light, the waters from the land. Later on, in (one telling of) the story, God creates man, and then woman. She violates God's orders and eats from the tree of knowledge, bringing God's wrath upon them both and causing them to be cast out of the Garden. That part of the story has served in many cultures as a charter for and justification of patriarchy and the exploitation and domination of women by men.

And here we can see clearly the partial relationship between myth and historical reality. From an anthropological viewpoint, as Robbie figured out, *the story of Adam and Eve being cast out of the Garden is a metaphorical way of addressing the transition from hunting and gathering to agriculture.* Hunting-gathering was the subsistence strategy that sustained the human species for more than 200,000 years; agriculture only arose around 10,000 years ago. As anthropologists who have worked with the few remaining hunter-gatherer societies discovered, even in harsh environments like the Kalahari Desert of Southern Africa, getting enough food through gathering plants and hunting animals only took an average of around three to five hours a day, leaving plenty of time for other activities like games, storytelling, and dancing. But agriculture was extremely labor-intensive, requiring eight to ten hours per day of hard labor. So the transition from living off the bounty of the land through hunting and gathering, to working the fields by the "sweat of one's brow," was in overall effect getting "cast out of the Garden."

This encapsulation of historical events into one story is a characteristic feature of myths: they often collapse thousands of years of history into one story that sums up, or encapsulates, major lifestyle transitions. Today most anthropologists conclude that agriculture was a consequence of a rise in the populations of various hunting-gathering groups at the end of the last Ice Age 12,000 years ago, leading to a depletion in natural resources and forcing people to move into less bountiful areas, making intentional food production a necessary adaptation. We suggest that this environmentally forced adaptation was encoded and encapsulated in the myth (origin story) of Genesis, which provided a divine explanation for the forced transition. Unfortunately for women, the story was told, and eventually written down around the sixth or 7th century BCE, by men in a form that blamed women for getting us "cast out of the Garden," setting in place thousands of years of patriarchal blame of women for the problems that actually faced human societies in general. (We should note here that Genesis as a creation narrative also worked toward the Jewish goal of establishing only one true God. Judaism is a monotheistic religion that opposed the polytheistic creation stories of Babylon, Israel's historical enemy, and other surrounding societies.)

A much more recent example of this forced transition from hunting/gathering to agriculture comes from the Huichol, who were hunter-gatherers until the Spanish conquest of Mexico gradually pushed them out of their desert home around San Luis Potosí and into the Sierra Madre mountain range of northern Mexico, where they had to grow maize to survive. This transition took over a century to complete. As Barbara Myerhoff (1974) showed, the Huichol, who had always gathered peyote (an hallucinogenic plant) in the desert for their religious ceremonies and had hunted deer, created new myths over time that wove the deer, the maize, and the peyote into a rich symbolic system that gave meaning to their new agricultural life by linking past and present into one cohesive picture.

We can contrast this successful transition made by the Huichol, who, again, had 100 years to accommodate their myths and rituals to their new agricultural reality, with the much less successful transition of a Ugandan tribal people known as the Ik. When the government of Uganda arbitrarily decided to turn the forested region in which they had hunted, gathered, and possibly also farmed for centuries into a game and hunting preserve for European tourists, the Ik were forcibly and suddenly relocated to another region in which farming was their only subsistence option. Given this massive and rapid change in their lifeworld, the Ik had no time to gradually develop a new cycle of meaning integrating their old and new realities as the Huichol had done. With the traditional myths and rituals that had made their previous existence now rendered meaningless, the Ik experienced a tragic cultural disintegration—their longstanding traditional culture simply fell apart (Tainter 2006; Turnbull 1972, 1978). People ceased to help others, and many children and elderly simply starved, as the food distributed by the government was generally confiscated by the strongest young men, who often refused to share it. While Turnbull's conclusions about the Ik and their implications for "human nature" have been heavily critiqued by other scholars (Beidelman 1973; Heine 1985), they remain a compelling example of the need for a strong enough match between a people's lifeworld and their cycle of meaning to enable, beyond mere survival, a culturally ordered and satisfying life. The Ik lost their cycle of meaning, which had been part and parcel of their forest life, and therefore became unable to cope in any organized way in a now-meaningless environment. (By now, decades later, the 10,000 or so Ik appear to have re-couped and re-grouped into a relatively stable and rapidly modernizing agricultural society.)

In addition to encapsulating history and generating meaning, myths/origin stories can also create a moral order to situations faced by people in their daily lives, like the story of Moses and the Ten Commandments. Myths can also offer explanations for various phenomena and catastrophes that help people make sense of nonsensical events, and operate as a storage bank for culturally important information. Among New Guinea and other seafaring peoples of the Pacific, myths tell the story of epic sea voyages that, when enacted by modern seamen, proved to be templates for carrying out safe and successful ventures.

The Myth-Ritual Complex and Human Development

There are two other important functions of myth we need to address here, for we are not just interested in myth as a repository or template for culture, but rather in how myth is enacted in ritual. Those two functions are: (1) transmitting socially important vicarious experience; and (2) aligning individual conceptual systems with socially valued experience (Faiola 2002; Sias, Lambie, and Foster 2006). In other words, myth is a primary mechanism for developing and maintaining what sociologist Émile Durkheim ([1912] 1995) called the "collective consciousness" fundamental to a people's religion and cosmology. Important domains of social experience are recorded in stories containing vivid imagery, so that the listener can imagine and internalize, say, the adventures of heroes or sacred beings as if they were living in the present. (For example, Robbie's grandson Jax believes more firmly in his ability to climb the playground bars when he is wearing his Spiderman T-shirt and cap!)

Moreover, the didactic quality of myth—the fact that mythological stories are told over and over to all members of the group with the explicit intent of teaching a group's cosmology or religion—assures that everyone shares the same body of core symbols and the sacred context in which the symbols apply. For instance, it is impossible to be a Christian without knowing the stories of Jesus' miraculous birth and of how He died on the cross to redeem the sins of humankind and to offer the possibility of eternal salvation.

As Durkheim emphasized, the reality expressed in myth is not merely a figment of somebody's imagination, *but is reality itself imagined.* In other words, *through their myths, people collectively imagine reality, and then they live in the collective reality they have imagined.* For example, thousands of years ago, the Australian aborigines imagined that when their bodies die, their spirits go to live in the Dreamtime, an alternate reality that surrounds and sometimes links with ordinary reality. Since that time, they have lived in the reality they imagined—their experience of life is permeated with experiences of entering Dreamtime in dreaming and in trance. And the geographic landscape they traverse is dotted with sacred sites that serve as portals between this reality and Dreamtime, where for example the souls of the ancestors are understood to be able to cross over and enter the body of a woman, making her pregnant. Cosmology is manifested in experience, and experience both confirms and further elaborates cosmology in an ongoing cycle of meaning.

Joseph Campbell (1986: xxiii) recognized myth's role in ensuring that the development of each member's consciousness proceeds in a way that maintains a collective understanding of reality. Take for example the attitudes and practices pertaining to the Navajo role of warrior. According to Navajo Indigenous psychology, the normal healthy human being lives in an ongoing balance between "male" and "female" properties. But in the development of a warrior, who must face combat and come into intimate contact with the dead and dying, the "male" principle is accentuated during training—as indeed it is in modern military training. But unlike in military culture, the Navajo consider the off-balance nature of warriorhood, though useful when needed, to be disharmonious, dangerous, and unhealthy. When warriors returned from battle, they were (and sometimes still are—the Navajo still have warriors/soldiers who fight in the US Armed Services) put through rituals designed to re-establish the balance between "male" and "female" psychological properties before they were allowed to fully return to family and community. We suggest here that if all contemporary soldiers were put through this sort of ritual re-integration, their incidence of post-traumatic stress disorder (PTSD) might be much lower and their re-assimilation into society would likely be much smoother.

While it is easiest to see and to analyze these primary roles of myth in small-scale traditional societies, it is important to understand that myths also play a similar critical role in today's modern world, not only in the highly specific cosmologies of small religious groups, but also in the more diffuse cosmologies of larger cultures and nation-states. Part of the capacity for mythic thinking is hard-wired into the human brain. There is no human culture without myth—we have long known that myth is a cultural universal (Hocart 1915)—and the societies of the contemporary world are no exception. Myths as origin stories still form the basis of all religions and are foundational for many nations, cultures, and ethnic groups. (Consider for example the 1999 war in Kosovo, which had much to do with the mythological importance of that region to the Serbs.) And many archetypal and ancient myths, like the hero's journey or the apocalypse, still provide the basis for contemporary expressive forms, including painting, literature, movies, and even computer games.

Yet some of our most important cultural myths are unarticulated. For example, Robbie has written elsewhere (Davis-Floyd [1992] 2003a, 2018a, 2022) about a central organizing myth of US society, which she calls the *myth of technological transcendence*—the story we tell ourselves that through technology, we will ultimately transcend the limitations of nature. (This myth meets Flower's definition of a myth as "a story that organizes experience through telling something explicitly about meaning—*where we're going,* where we came from, or who we are." The myth of technological transcendence enables us to face the problems presented by our untrammeled technological development with relative equanimity, even when the dangers presented, such as those increasingly generated by the Climate Crisis, are grave.

Ultimately we believe, because we have to in order to live in the world with confidence, that the problems we have generated with technology will not lead to doom for humanity, but *will be solved with more technology.* This "myth of technological transcendence" is recounted in multiple forms in numerous futuristic movies, from *Star Wars* to *The Matrix* to the Pixar film *Wall-e* (which depicts a future in which the Earth becomes so polluted that its remaining humans flee the planet in a giant spaceship, returning many generations later when the Earth has regenerated and is capable of growing things once again).

Our faith in this myth of technological transcendence is extreme, and we enact that faith daily via the promise of new, environmentally friendly technologies, the development of biotechnologies and research into the human genome, and through the billions of dollars we pour into the high-tech development of cancer treatments and research, even as we continue to pollute our environment and our food and get cancer as a result! Here we can see clearly another of the primary functions of myth, which is to enable a people to replace the conceptual fuzziness of an uncertain future with the hope and certainty that humanity (in the future, through technology) will prevail. Such certainty (at that time, through the belief that they were God's chosen people) got the ancient Hebrews through their period of wandering in the desert (the myth/origin story has this wandering lasting some four decades), and lets us contemporary citizens sleep at night instead of lying awake wondering what "on earth" might happen if too many glaciers melt and huge areas of land are consumed by the rising, polluted seas.

Ritual as Mythic Enactment: The Navajo *Kinaalda* Ceremony

Durkheim's realization that "myth is reality imagined" is an important one, for it separates our discussion from the naïve views of modern people who think that mythic stories are just "primitive nonsense." Indeed, anthropologists have shown that people's symbolic systems are very often grounded in reality, for the events described in myth, as we have seen with Genesis, often encapsulate historical events they have experienced and codify adaptive knowledge they have gained over generations, and perhaps centuries or millennia. In addition, myths provide a way of making visible what is hidden in the world.

The Navajo, as we have seen above, hold that all perceivable things in the world have invisible aspects that are imagined as "Holy People." For example, there are the Mountain People, the Star People, the River People, the Rain

People, the Corn People, and more. For sophisticated Navajo thinkers, the Holy People are anthropomorphized symbols that stand for the invisible and vital element within all things, and which traditional Navajo philosophy equates with "Wind" (*nilch'I*). Individuals also have such a hidden dimension, called "the Wind within one" (*nilch'I hwii"siziinii*) (see McNeley 1981). All these Winds are really part of the one and all-encompassing Holy Wind. Winds are never distinct unattached entities, and energy always flows in and out of even the most enduring objects. (Wind comes and goes from the human body through the breath, cowlicks in the hair, finger and toe tip swirls, the belly button, etc.) The choice of "wind" as the central metaphor is an explicit recognition, common to many cultures on the planet, that there are forces that, just like moving air, normally cannot be observed save by inference from their effects. We see again the powerful role of symbolism in putting a face upon the invisible but efficacious forces that play out in human affairs.

In order to see how myth can be enacted in ritual, let us return to the Navajo origin myth briefly described above, which tells the story of the birth and development of Changing Woman. In that story, we mentioned that Changing Woman grew into womanhood and had her first menstruation. The Holy People wanted to mark the importance of her fertility, and to that end, created a puberty ceremony for Changing Woman they called *Kinaalda* (taken from the verb that means "to menstruate for the first time"). All the Holy People showed up to celebrate Changing Woman's *Kinaalda* and sang songs and created ritual acts so that the offspring that she brought into the world would be beautiful and wholesome. During the ceremony, Salt Woman painted Changing Woman the color of white shell and gave her another name, White Shell Woman. The people gathered around and combed Changing Woman's hair and molded her body so that she would grow into a fine form. Then at dawn one morning, she raced toward the sun and back again where she ground corn and did other things that mature women have to do, such as cooking and distributing corn pollen. During the process of the ceremony (again, a "ceremony" is constituted by a series of rituals), Changing Woman not only went through the motions of enacting *Kinaalda*, she literally became *Kinaalda*. In other words, the ceremonial activities evoked the maturation potential within Changing Woman and set the course of her future development so that she became the quintessence of womanhood. Only then was she prepared to bear healthy, wholesome children.

Ever since, all Navajo girls are strongly encouraged go through *Kinaalda* at the time of their first menses. While still young, they become prepared by their mothers and other women for their great day. They are taught that they will attain important powers when they come of age and must comply with certain restrictions in order to protect others from those powers. When the joyous day arrives, the girls follow in the footsteps of Changing Woman, and repeat all of the ritual acts that the myth records for Changing Woman's *Kinaalda*. Many people significant to the young girl participate in the four-day ceremony. Her family members have their responsibilities—many of them will take part in activities like the race toward the sun that the girl must undergo. As a consequence, the pubescent girl is taught to identify with Changing Woman within a thoroughly social and thoroughly embodied context. One aspect of the power of the Navajo *Kinaalda* ritual is that it incorporates many of the core symbols of Navajo cosmology. In Chapter 1, we mentioned that a major function of core cultural symbols is to reveal the hidden dimensions of the world. Myth encapsulates core symbols and weaves them into stories that further explicate these hidden dimensions.

The essential point to emphasize here is the process of instantiation (the embodiment of an idea in experience). The enactment of this most central myth of Navajo cosmology sets up young women to actually experience themselves as *Kinaalda*, as Changing Woman. Thus through myth and its concomitant rituals, an experience of significant growth and change lived by the individual is designed to become cognitively and experientially linked to the most important elements of the Navajo worldview. The naïve outside observer might call it "a set-up," for it is doubtful that all young girls in fact experience this identification with Changing Woman, and through Changing Woman to the vital processes operating in the cosmology. But a sufficient number of Navajo girls do still experience this connection, particularly when they have been adequately prepared for years in advance. In all likelihood, a higher proportion of girls had this experience in olden times than at present, when there has been a significant drop in active participation in the traditional religious system—indicating its eventual end, for as we have previously noted, when members of a culture or religious group cease to enact its essential rituals on a regular basis, those rituals and their symbolic expressions of cultural belief will cease to carry meaning.

And yet, we note here with a certain irony that this "race toward the sun" lives on in its fairly recent and very postmodern incorporation into contemporary Wiccan puberty rituals for girls. At the end of their puberty festival, organized by their parents, young girls raised as Wiccans will race with their mothers down the beach toward the sun. At some point, the exhausted mother will stop, while the young girl races on—a lovely symbolic expression of her youth and its accompanying athletic prowess, and of her own "moving on" process as she develops into adolescence and later adulthood (see Hill 1998).

Ritual as Paradigmatic Enactment

Myths in traditional societies are stories—they have characters, a plot, and a beginning, a middle, and an end (thoroughly analyzed by Claude Lévi-Strauss 1963, 1995, 2012, 2021; see also Deliège 2004; Wilcken 2010). In today's world, where mythological stories have ceased to have meaning for many people, paradigms have come to provide the structures within which people think and take action. Like myths, paradigms provide order and cohesiveness to the lifeworld, but they are not explicitly formulated into stories. For example, there has been discussion for well over three decades of a "paradigm shift" in business, from the old industrial paradigm to the new paradigm of the information society. The old and the new paradigms are not expressed as stories; rather, they are best described as a list of tenets—principles and guidelines.

Like the mythological systems of traditional societies, paradigms play a central role in the cycle of meaning for many individuals and groups in technocratic societies; they serve as the interpretive screens through which people who espouse a given paradigm will filter their perceptions of reality. Philosopher Thomas Kuhn (2012) famously demonstrated the profound effect paradigms have on scientific research—each time a scientific paradigm shifts, new possibilities are opened up while others close down. Just as a fish cannot see outside of the water it swims in, so an individual operating within a paradigm is subject to the illusion that the paradigm represents the

Table 2.1. The Old and New Paradigms of Business. Table created by authors; see also Kaufman 2019.

Old Paradigm of Business	New Paradigm of Business
hierarchical, linear, top-down	lateral, webbed, networking
"my way or the highway"	input from each individual valued
fixed, rigid, compartmentalized	flexible, responsive
each player sees and takes responsibility only for parts	each player sees and takes responsibility for the systemic whole
aggressive, competitive (win-lose)	cooperative, partnership-oriented (win-win)
product-oriented, process irrelevant	the process is the product
short-term gain	long-range view
manipulation and domination of nature	symbiosis with nature, stewardship
closed system (*tries to make reality conform to its dictates*)	open system (*responds to what is*)

whole of reality. But no paradigm actually does. All models of reality, no matter how complex, are bound to leave out some aspects of the "reality" they are attempting to model. Many paradigms come to constitute relatively closed conceptual systems that discount, explain away, or exclude incompatible information, regardless of its potential validity within another paradigm. Because paradigms create the parameters of thought, individuals who cannot "think beyond" the bounds of a given paradigm are often trapped within the limitations that all paradigms exhibit. (When people say "think outside the box," they generally mean "think outside of the paradigm within which you have been operating.") For Kuhn showed that, far from being an accurate model of reality, *the most a paradigm can be is a set of beliefs about the nature of an ultimately unknowable, transcendental universe.*

The limitations of paradigms are counterbalanced by their advantages: like myths, paradigms provide clear conceptual models that facilitate one's actions in the world. In acting not only as models of, but also as templates for, "reality," paradigms enable us to behave in organized ways, to take actions that make sense under a given set of principles. "To paradigm," if you will, is to create the world through the picture we paint of it. We then can live as cultural beings in the organized and coherent paradigmatic world we have created. And one primary way in which we accomplish that is by enacting our paradigms—or our individual or group belief systems—in ritual.

The corporate world, for example, was and still is full of rituals that enact and thus reinforce the old paradigm of business, including rigidly followed behavioral pre- and proscriptions (what clothes to wear, whom you can talk to, and where and when), assembly lines designed for efficiency that do not take the experience of the worker into account, and hierarchical meetings in which the chain of command is overtly or subtly reinforced. Those who seek to accomplish a "paradigm shift" within a given company fail if their retooling does not address the rituals, visible and invisible, that keep the old paradigm in effect. For, as we will discuss in detail in Chapter 9, *if you want to change the paradigm, you must change the rituals first.*

The Technocratic, Humanistic, and Holistic Paradigms of Medicine and Their Enactments in Ritual

Again, myths are explicit stories, whereas paradigms are implicit sets of principles and beliefs—in other words, while myths are spelled out in actual stories, paradigms are simply cohesive sets of beliefs that are not explicitly spelled out in stories. Thus it is easier to see how rituals enact myths than it is to see how rituals enact paradigms. To illustrate the latter, we will take three contrasting paradigms of health care and describe the differences in the rituals that enact each one. Our examples here come from what Robbie (Davis-Floyd 2001, 2018 a; Davis-Floyd and Cheyney 2022) has described as the *technocratic, humanistic,* and *holistic paradigms of medicine.* The technocratic paradigm defines the body as a machine, postulates the separation of mind and body, views the patient as an object, and charters an alienated, depersonalized physician-patient relationship (e.g., referring to a patient as "the gall bladder in Room 212" or "the cesarean in 313"). The humanistic paradigm defines the body as an organism, stresses the connection of mind and body, views the patient as a relational subject, and stresses the importance of a personalized relationship between patient and practitioner—which can be a source of healing in itself. The holistic model of medicine defines the body as an energy field, insists that body, mind, and spirit are one, and views the patient and practitioner as part of one unified energy field so that each can affect the other, for better or for worse (See Table 2.2).

The technocratic paradigm of medicine is hegemonic in most US hospitals—in fact, in most hospitals in high resource countries[2]—and is daily enacted through numerous rituals that are usually viewed not as rituals, but as "necessary" procedures of "traditional" biomedical care, as we will further detail below.

Here we illustrate our point about how rituals enact paradigms through one small but revealing example. Imagine a woman going into a doctor's office for a pelvic exam. In a technocratic practice, she is ushered into a usually cold room, told to take off her clothes and put on a paper gown (a symbol, need we say of what?), and asked to lie down on a high table with her bare feet up in cold metal stirrups. The doctor enters, accompanied by the nurse, walks to the end of the table, and greets her while looking down at her genitals. With few words of preparation or explanation, he inserts his gloved hand into her vagina to examine her. If she tightens up in alarm or fear, he orders her to relax and if she does not, he forces his way in until he obtains the information he seeks.

In a humanistic practice, the doctor enters the room to chat with the patient while she is still in her street clothes (a symbol of her status as an autonomous individual). He/she asks the patient about her concerns around this visit and anything else that may be on her mind. After this conversation, he asks her to undress as he leaves the room. The cold metal stirrups are covered with soft socks or pads. During the exam, the doctor explains what he is doing and checks with the woman to make sure she is feeling OK. If she tightens her muscles in alarm, he immediately withdraws his hand and talks to her about what is causing her to close up. If she is truly distressed, he helps her sit up, speaks reassuring words, and promises not to continue with the exam until she is ready. He talks with her about

Table 2.2. The Technocratic, Humanistic, and Holistic Models of Medicine Compared. Table derived from Davis-Floyd (2018a) with the permission of Waveland Press.

The Technocratic Model	The Humanistic (Biopsychosocial) Model	The Holistic Model
1. Mind/body separation	1. Mind-body connection	1. Oneness of bodymindspirit
2. The body as machine	2. The body as an organism	2. The body as an energy system interlinked with other energy systems
3. The patient as object	3. The patient as relational subject	3. Healing the whole person in whole-life context
4. Alienation of practitioner from patient	4. Connection and caring between practitioner and patient	4. Essential unity of practitioner and client
5. Diagnosis and treatment from the outside in (use of high technologies for diagnosis; curing disease, repairing dysfunction)	5. Diagnosis and healing from the outside in and from the inside out (combining technological diagnosis with active listening)	5. Diagnosis and healing primarily from the inside out (reliance on intuition, intuitive diagnosis; may include use of high technologies but not total reliance on them)
6. Hierarchical organization and standardization of care	6. Balance between the needs of the institution and the individual	6. Lateral, networking organizational structure that facilitates individualization of care
7. Authority and responsibility inherent in practitioner, not patient	7. Information, decision making, and responsibility shared between patient and practitioner	7. Authority and responsibility inherent in each individual
8. Supervaluation of science and technology	8. Science and technology counterbalanced with humanism	8. Science and technology placed at the service of the individual
9. Aggressive intervention with emphasis on short-term results	9. A long-term focus on disease prevention	9. A long-term focus on creating and maintaining health and wellbeing
10. Death as defeat	10. Death as an acceptable outcome	10. Death as a step in a process
11. A profit-driven system	11. Compassion-driven care	11. Healing as the focus
12. Intolerance of other modalities	12. Open-mindedness toward other modalities	12. Embrace of multiple healing modalities
Basic underlying principle: separation	Basic underlying principles: balance and connection	Basic underlying principles: connection and integration
Type of thinking: unimodal, left-brained, linear	Type of thinking: bimodal	Type of thinking: fluid, multimodal, right-brained, holistic

her past—was she sexually abused at some point?—and will recommend counseling or perhaps a support group.

In the first scenario, the doctor is enacting the beliefs and values of the technocratic paradigm of medicine—the body is a machine, time is of the essence, information is important, his status is higher than hers, the coldness of the metal on her feet is irrelevant, as are her experience of the exam and their relationship. In the second scenario, the doctor is enacting the values of humanism: status is not relevant, relationship is; body and mind are connected; if her muscles tense in fear, there is a good reason, most likely having to do with past sexual abuse, or simple, momentary fear that can easily be addressed. Obtaining needed information from a pelvic exam is not as immediately important as addressing the woman's emotional state and not repeating or adding to trauma related to past abuses.

In each case, the procedures are ritualistic: they are patterned and repetitive (being ushered into the examining room, being told to put on the gown, lying down on the table with legs spread, etc.). They are also symbolic: in the technocratic case, the white coat of the doctor contrasts with the naked genitals of the patient, and he is "up" and she is "down," both literally and interactionally. In the humanistic case, the white coat of the doctor is paralleled to some degree by the clothing of the patient during their first conversation, which takes place eye to eye, on a much more equal level. The pad over the stirrup sends the symbolic message that her experience matters, a message that is heavily reinforced if the doctor stops the exam to accommodate the woman's needs. There is no explicit myth being told here, but there are two implicit paradigms being acted out. The technocratic practitioner may not think much about what he is doing—he may simply be enacting the beliefs and values he was taught in medical school and residency, without awareness of the paradigm underlying them. The humanistic practitioner, in contrast, will very likely be aware that he is "doing it differently"—his choice to enact the values of humanism in his medical practice will usually be a very conscious one because it is alternative to the norm. In both cases, it is through ritual that each practitioner enacts and displays—and thus reinforces—the values that he or she holds.

In contrast, in a fully holistic practice, a homebirth midwife would be performing any necessary vaginal exams in the mother's home, both dressed in regular clothes, on the mother's own bed (see Cheyney 2011). The mother and the midwife would likely spend an hour or so talking about any concerns the mother has, reinforcing their pre-existing relationship. The midwife would proceed with the exam ever-so-gently and immediately share with the mother any information she is obtaining as she is feeling it with her gloved fingers. The midwife would be sensitive to the mother's energy and to the energy field established between them, and would be quick to address the mother's reactions and feelings, as the mother would also be sensitive to the midwife and trust in both her expertise and their relationship. The midwife would also encourage the mother to be sensitive to her baby's energy, to talk to her baby, touch her belly a lot, and send love to that baby all during pregnancy and during the labor and birth process. In this situation, we find less actual ritual and more actual, interactive communication between client and practitioner, because (in contrast to the technocratic and humanistic models), this holistic belief system is explicitly spelled out in numerous publications (for example, see Table 2.2 above, which has been published in many places at various times by Robbie (Davis-Floyd 2001, 2003a, 2018a; 2022) and by others, and on homebirth midwives' websites, and is enacted between midwife and mother in explicit conversations, relationships, and caring touch.

Summary: The Human Need to Understand

Human beings universally seek to understand local events by referencing a more global worldview. This quest for meaning is met in part by the belief system/myth/paradigm/ritual complex, which provides socially shared representations of personal and external realities. This interaction between the universal and the personal has the very great advantage of patterning personal knowledge and behavior to the immediate circumstances of the environment, while often retaining a cosmic outlook. The tension between archetypal (deeply unconscious) and local ways of knowing can be resolved, at least to some extent, by the concerted, meaningful activity of ritual performance.

Notes

1. "Belief system." *Lexico.com*. Retrieved 22 November 2021 from https://www.lexico.com/definition/belief_system.
2. In low resource countries, the older industrial model of medicine, which tends to work in assembly-line ways, still prevails because low resource hospitals generally do not have the high technologies that facilitate and characterize the application of the technocratic model.

Chapter 3

BELIEF SYSTEMS, MYTHS, PARADIGMS, RITUALS, AND THE PROCESS OF TRUING

~ℬ℠❍

Myths and the Process of Truing

The belief system/myth/paradigm/ritual complex must be grounded to reality in at least three important ways: (1) through the direct intuitive grasp of the order of reality; (2) through regulating the development of individual consciousness along socially collective paths; (3) through enactments in the world that have real effects and consequences. Let us now bear down a bit more on this question of "reality-grounding." Earlier we made the distinction between the quest for meaning typical of traditional cycles of meaning and the scientific quest for truth. We did not mean to imply that the system of meaning that people strive to bring alive in everyday experience is untrue in any fundamental way. Far from it! Religious beliefs and doctrines are not often the product of logical thought (Atran 2002) (though they are likely to have their own internal logic). The creative imagination represented in a living symbolic system nonetheless operates to "true" the collective consciousness of a people to achieve integration within a culturally consensual story that assuages anxieties and fears, keeping the interpretation of experience closer to the actual nature of reality than rational thought alone is able to do.

"To rationalize" is to make up unreasonable reasons to seek to validate one's acts and opinions; whereas "rational thought" generally means having or exercising reason, sound judgment, or good sense. Yet rational thought can take the form of logical chains that lead one further and further away from reality—we all know how easy it is to "rationalize" an action that we know is wrong. While our rational faculties can easily lead us astray from the essential nature of things, genuine myth rarely does, because the symbols and metaphors encapsulated in myth usually derive from an individual or group's intuitive grasp of some essential aspects of the cosmos. As a consequence of this intuitive grasp, myths may under some circumstances be more "real" than are purely rational accounts of reality. We now want to develop a better understanding of how this relative accuracy of myth is achieved and how it works its way through ritual performance.

According to the dictionary, the word "true" means that one's statement is consistent with the facts, is in agreement with reality, represents things as they really are, or matches the cultural description of the way things are. The root of "true" means "telling the truth" in the sense that what one says is without intentional deceit and is consistent with reality as the culture (or individual) understands it. The root also refers to agreement about an act or statement with some standard, rule, or pattern. The connotation is that the statement is as it should be—it is "correct." Used as a verb, instead of as a noun or adjective, the word "true" implies a physical activity. When a carpenter refers to "truing a wall," it means that the wall is accurate as measured relative to plumb line or a level—the connotation here is that of an activity that makes something "true." And when a bicycle mechanic fixes a warped wheel, it is known as "truing the wheel." One may "true" something by adjusting or shaping it into accurate conformation with a pattern or plan. To "prove something true" is to verify it in relation to something else. And once upon a time, a tool that was used to true something was called a "truer."

Myth operates as a *truer of cognition* (Campbell 1986, 1988). From now on we want to use the terms "truing" and "truer" in this very special sense. That is, *"truing" refers specifically to the inherent ability of the brain to produce an experiential world that conforms to the reality of the environment well enough to enable survival and adequate functioning.* The role of "truing" in adaptation is essential. During the countless generations of human evolution, failure to model the world accurately enough to successfully move around in it resulted in death and a continuous selection against distortions of experienced reality. For instance, if a group of people live in a desert with only one oasis, but continue to mythically imagine that desert to be full of oases because it once was, then their inherited cultural belief system will not "true" them to the environment they live in, and must be changed if that group is to survive.

Yet some of the most complex and important cognitions that go on in our brains is of the intuitive and imagining kind. Indeed, were all of our cognition to be carried out within our conscious, rational minds, our consciousness would be quickly overwhelmed with information. This potential information overload is why most of the associations we make are handled within our unconscious faculties. Intuition and imagination develop early in childhood, before linguistically organized conceptual facilities. The production of metaphorical associations, so fundamental to the structure of mythology, is present in and typical of the thought of very young children.

For example, children might associate Mommy with the family car because the car is blue and Mommy is wearing a blue dress. Or they might associate Daddy with the game of checkers because he wears checkered tweed jackets. This process is fundamental to "totemic" thinking—one clan associates itself with an eagle because its members saw an eagle flying during an important clan ceremony, while another associates itself with a wombat—much as sports teams in many countries adopt totems relevant in their locations. Think about the sports teams in your locale—what totems have they adopted, and why?

Truing and the Brain

The human brain does not begin its life as a "blank slate." On the contrary, the neural structures that develop through childhood to eventually become the adult brain have their beginning in rudimentary, genetically programmed circuits of neural cells, many of which are present in a baby before birth. These initial structures of the brain produce the highly organized world of experience of the late-term fetus and infant, and lay the foundation for all that comes next.

The exact nature of the initial structural makeup of each individual person varies, as do the specifics of individuals' development over their lifetimes. Likewise, the developmental course of the initial structures of each person's brain varies depending upon the history, environment, and social dynamics of the group's culture and the individual's (culturally rooted) personality. These are based in the underlying initial structural origin of the imagery, organization, and thematic motifs that are definitive of myth, and that we recognize to be cross-culturally similar, even when festooned with culturally distinct surface material. For instance, the "changeling" in myths from various cultures may feature a human character becoming variously a tiger, hyena, wolf, bat, or killer whale, depending upon the local fauna and the values of a people. Yet the structure of the changeling remains the same—the notion that a human being can mysteriously change into an animal or other sort of creature, usually a carnivore of some kind. US pop culture, now gone global, is full of such stories—vampires, witches, daemons, werewolves, "meta-humans," and cyborg transformers abound in comic books and novels, TV series, and movies. These long-standing mythologies regarding human changelings both challenge and reinforce our understandings of what it means to be human—or not—and raise questions such as: what exactly is the relationship of humans to other species? And are we limited to our humanity, or can we become more than human? (See for examples Robbie's edited collection *Birthing Techno-Sapiens: Human-Technology Co-Evolution and the Future of Reproduction* [Davis-Floyd 2021].)

The plasticity of our human brains ensures that we are not completely driven by our archetypal "hard-wired" programming. We have flexible brains that can re-order themselves when we confront new challenges. Our brains are capable of coming up with wonderfully new ways of doing things. We are able to learn and to express to others what we have learned. Yet the similarities of all human brains—their core, emotional, and cortical structures—ensure that aspects encoded deep in our core brains—archetypal aspects—can enable us to have shared experiences and understandings, even when we come from extremely different cultures.

For example, Charlie was fascinated to see that when Tibetan Buddhist lamas first encountered Navajo shamans back in the 1970s, they found that they were kindred spirits, for they shared much of the same spiritual knowledge—including elements of archetypal cosmology such as unitary beingness (a sense of totality, or of the oneness of everything with everything else), the illusory nature of the physical body, the relations between wholeness and health, and so on. As is the case with the culture's cycle of meaning, the experiences arising relative to the archetypal cosmology act to both confirm the "truth" of the cosmology and to bring it alive.

For instance, it is easy for many of us to identify with the knight or fair lady on a quest to find the Holy Grail and with their adventures while trying to find their way through the dark forest with its terrifying monsters and challenges—as shown, for example, in the movie *The Princess Bride* and in the Harry Potter books and movie series. The Quest myth encodes for many humans, women and men alike, a developmentally important message—that each of us must confront our own unconscious if we are to grow. If we are to access the great wisdom symbolized by "the Grail"—or the trophy Harry won that sent him straight to "he who must not be named," Lord Voldemort—we may ultimately find it within ourselves, as Harry did. For example, in his confrontations with Voldemort and in his creation of his "Patronus," he had to dig deep down into his core brain and integrate all his brain levels to find the necessary intuition, courage, and wisdom to accomplish that feat. And it was Indiana Jones's father, not the hero himself, who received "illumination" when he drank from the Holy Grail, which he had been pursuing for most of his life.

Thus, a society's mythology may be multi-developmental. The mythology may be so organized that it can effectively potentiate the progressive growth of archetypal neurocognitive structures at different stages of maturation. Some mythologies are actually arranged in multiple layers of narrative and interpretation, each subsequent and more complex layer given to the initiate when they are considered to be developmentally ready to receive that new layer. The Navajo explicitly recognize multiple levels of understanding of their mythic traditions—levels that range from the earliest childhood "just-so" stories (like how the turtle got its shell; see Fontes and Fontes 2001) to the understandings of the most advanced shamans.

Another example is offered by anthropologist Dan Jorgensen (1980) from the Telefolmin people of the South Pacific. The Telefolmin have a system of myth that is structured into at least ten layers. The first layer is that told to young children in the form of many short "just-so" stories about things like how the pig got its curly tail. As the children grow, they are initiated into more advanced versions of the stories. These stories are fewer in number and longer. By the time an adult is receiving initiation, the cycle of myths takes on the form of a single saga that takes days to tell. Moreover, the messages encoded in the myths become more and more advanced with each ascending level of initiation. This advancing over time has been the strategy of many Western mystery schools—simply google "Western mystery schools" for information about their many, varied, and often fascinating programs of initiation and spiritual development (see also Snoek 2014 on Masonic initiations).

Truing, Intuition, and Action in the World

Take for example the (now widely spread around the globe) myth (explanatory story) of Santa Claus. Children whose parents socialize them into that myth and its ensuing rituals of gift giving and receiving tend to believe it until they reach a certain age when, due to their peers or to their own understanding of "reality," they cease to believe yet continue to engage in the fantasy, because they know their parents want them to and because believing in Santa Claus is fun and enables them to write that letter to Santa, now intended for their parents. Such children have matured beyond literal belief in the myth of Santa Claus, yet they understand that their pretended continuation of belief invites instantiation in the lived moment of Christmas morning when their presents will "magically" (and ritually) appear—thereby "truing" their now-imaginary belief in Santa Claus to reality. And parents who continue to live inside that myth with their children find an almost magical re-instantiation of their own childhood

Christmas rituals as they work to "true" their children's belief in the magic of Christmas. Such parents know the value of magic and belief enacted in ritual, and work hard to give that gift to their children, because they know deep-down that both magic and gift-giving are intrinsically good. A sense of the magical works to enhance children's imaginative abilities, and gift-giving works to enhance relationships. Ok, we know that a huge consumer industry has evolved from all this ritualized gift giving—and we applaud that industry for the massive ritual benefits it facilitates. At the same time, we note and regret the extreme systemic differentiations in access to those ritual benefits, which are fully available to the middle- and upper-classes but not so much to the poor and marginalized, who must often struggle to instantiate the Santa Claus myth for their children—a myth that is not trued to their economic realities, whereas it is trued to the socioeconomic realities of the wealthier segments of society.

Truing and Culture: Sensate, Ideational, and Idealistic Cultures

Cultures privilege knowledge in different ways. Some cultures emphasize knowing in the archetypal, mythological way, while others emphasize knowing in the local, empirical sense—a phenomenon particularly evident in the way societies orchestrate how their children learn. *Sensate cultures* are those that privilege local ways of knowing over knowing in the more archetypal cosmological mode. Sensate cultures, like that of the ancient Romans and our own contemporary technocracies, produce populations that are off-balance toward a materialistic, secular, empirical understanding of the world. Because they are way off balance, sensate cultures will, over the course of generations, tend to compensate by swinging back toward a more balanced view, in which knowledge derived from the local mode becomes integrated with knowledge arising from the development of mythological archetypal structures; Pitirim Sorokin (1957, 1962) called these more balanced systems *idealistic cultures.*

This pendulum swing back to a more idealistic balance seems to be happening to some extent in Euroamerican culture at the present time, which has long been sensate but seems to be developing an increasing tolerance for mysticism. It is in the balanced idealistic cultures (such as the ones we have described above), as well as the more extreme *ideational cultures,* that a corpus of mythological tradition forms a living core of knowledge. It is fair to say that most of the several thousand traditional cultures (some of which consist of only a few thousand people) currently co-existing on the planet lie along the scale from the middle (idealistic) to the ideational extreme.

From the point of view of people living in an extremely ideational culture, what we might consider "mystical" knowledge or experience is not mystical at all—it is simply "the way things are." The human brain is structurally prepared to apprehend the mysteries of archetypal cosmology, but we have been conditioned by our sensate cultural upbringing not to do so; thus we often must apply effort and specific ritual techniques to produce mystical experiences.

One of the characteristics of a sensate culture is that it will tend not to reverence a living mythology, while a society way out on the ideational pole will relate everything of importance back to the culture's core mythology with its mysteries. Examples include traditional Australian Aboriginal societies, whose members, as previously mentioned, relate features and events in their modern homeland back to *Tjukuba*—the "Dreamtime"—the period before the human age when gigantic mythological characters like Python and Poisonous Snake left indelible marks on the sacred landscape. Other examples include Pagan Goddess/Gaia worshippers and the previously mentioned New Agers, many of whom live their contemporary lives in that same intimate accord with the mysteries of the hidden, relating many of their experiences to past lives, present dreams, and/or meditative experiences of the mystical, including communing with spirits and angels. Another example is the millions of faith-full Christians whose lifeworlds are permeated with their mystical connection to God, Jesus, and the Holy Spirit, and the Muslims who live their lives in deep connection to Allah and enact that connection in their five-times-daily prayer rituals.

Clearly, in the midst of the generally sensate contemporary technocracy, many millions choose to live in the midst of the mystical. People living "in the midst of the mystical" may see God/Allah, guardian angels, and/or various forces of spirit "moving in mysterious ways" throughout their lives. Thus, again, although contemporary technocracies are generally sensate cultures, millions of those among them live in ideational worlds—a fact that may, over time, lead to a culture-wide pendulum swing. Such a swing may become essential—were we all to live in greater connection with "Gaia/Mother Earth," we would stop the behaviors that are generating the Climate Crisis.

Rituals provide fundamental means for linking our current experience of the world with the fundamental mechanisms for knowing reality holistically, a "truing" that can give one a sense of coherence, meaning and personal integration. Thus it is no accident that in our intensely sensate contemporary technocracy, we are experiencing a dramatic resurgence of charismatic religious groups and of holistic, spiritually oriented forms of healing and health care. By 1993, one-third of all US citizens used some form of holistic or alternative health care (Eisenberg et al. 1993); today, more people do than don't. The World Health Organization estimates that 65–80% of the global population uses holistic naturopathic medicine as a primary form of health care. And US citizens make more visits to holistic health care providers (some 600 million a year) than to MDs and spend more money out-of-pocket to do so—about $30 billion a year by recent estimates (Neddermeyer 2020).

Thus we can see that around the world and in the United States, holistic, energy-based modalities like homeopathy, Reiki, acupuncture and acupressure, reflexology, Shiatsu, breath therapy, and many others are increasingly utilized by a US public disillusioned with the limitations of the sensate, mechanistic, technomedical approach. Their rapid growth, like the growth of charismatic religious groups, demonstrates the pendulum swing that US society is undergoing as we seek to counterbalance the imbalance of our sensate lives by moving back toward more idealistic, and perhaps eventually more ideational, cultural forms.

Myth, Truing, Quantum Physics, and the Origin of Our Universe

We have explained how myth operates to provide a sense of coherence, to "true" individual conceptual systems and experiences to the world around them. And we have just seen how even members of sensate technocratic societies often "true" their mythologies to their lifeworlds and live inside of those mythologies. (Remember that anthropologically calling something a "myth" does not mean that it is not true.) Truing our mental models of reality occurs in both the holistic (the intuitive grasp of the systemic properties upon which the universe operates) and the empirical (practical) styles. Truing is accomplished in part through familiarization with sacred or explanatory stories and through their enactments in ritual, both of which are directed at revealing the often hidden, but nonetheless real (to people and groups), nature of the cosmology in which people's lives are embedded. And, just as with the Navajo notion of Holy Wind, most traditional and contemporary spiritual cosmologies have ways of accounting for the energetic and causative aspects of the cosmos—from God to some kind of equally energetic, mystical, universal force.

In our own cultural history, science has gone a long way in supplanting the truing function of the traditional myth-ritual complex. For a couple of centuries or more, the picture science has painted of the universe has been mechanical and based on Newtonian principles. However, with the 20th century advent of quantum physics, science has begun to portray the universe in ways that look more and more like that of a traditional holistic and archetypal cosmology. Scientists are coming to understand the universe as a vast sea of energy in which everything is awash (see Bohm 1980; Prigogine 1980; Meadows and Wright 2008; von Bertalanffy 2015; Thurner and Klimek 2015) and all things are fundamentally interconnected. According to Charlie and Sheila Richardson (1986: 412), "The lack of systems consciousness is the single greatest danger to this planet ... The emergence of systems consciousness may prove pivotal to our future."

The ideational paradigm of systems theory can take us to an extreme of difference from conventional sensate understandings of reality, as is clearly illustrated in some excerpts from Larry Dossey's (1982) chart of the primary differences between the conventional/Newtonian sensate view and the systems approach (see Table 3.1).

Table 3.1. A Spacetime Model of Birth, Life, Health, and Death. Excerpted and adapted with permission from Dossey (1982: 148–49).

Conventional View	Systems Theory View
The body is an object, localized to a specific space.	The body is not an object and cannot be localized in space.
The body is an isolated, self-contained unit.	The body is in dynamic relationship with the universe and with all other bodies through actual physical exchange—"the *biodance*."
The body is comprised of individual building blocks, the atoms.	"Building blocks" and atoms are inaccurate descriptions, since all particles can only be understood in relation to all other particles.
Birth and death are demarcations at the poles of life.	No demarcations in time exist.
Time flows.	The flow of time is a psychological, not a natural event. No physical experiment has ever detected the flow of time.
The matter that comprises the body is an absolute.	Nothing of the body's matter is absolute. All matter, and space and time, are relative.
Disease is molecular misbehavior and is thus an objective affair.	Objective theory is an illusion. Intervention in nature, as well as scrutiny of all types, changes what is observed. Observers cannot separate themselves from the outcome of the observation, so that objectivity in its pure sense is an impossibility.
Disease is a body affair.	The influence of consciousness on the physical processes occurring in the body obliterates this distinction.

Ideational systems theory has fascinating parallels in other cultures. For example, this systems account of the universe looks a lot like the Navajo notion of Holy Wind, which is for the Navajo the essential energy foundation and hidden inner nature of all things. Indeed, the notion of a quantum sea of energy is a motif repeated in many of the world's cosmologies. Anthropologist Carol Laderman (1991) found similar wind-related cosmological views among the traditional Malay of rural Malaysia, as did Barbara Tedlock (2005) in her study of female shamans in various countries, who are much more likely to use "wind" and "breath" for healing than the hallucinogens favored by their male counterparts. Also, in some schools of Buddhism, the domain of ultimate transcendence and causation is the *alaya-vijnana*. The *alaya* is a domain of pure, non-dual awareness beyond all distinctions. Other great mystical traditions have similar interpretations of this holistic sea of energy. The Kabbalah teaches us that material existence extrudes from the subtle, non-dual, and divine realm of *Binah* and *Chokmah*, the higher centers of the Tree of Life.

This Tree of Life can be viewed as archetypal—common in all human experience. In fact, it may be the most primal of all archetypes, as all humans gestate inside a womb. The fetal side of the placenta, which the fetus can see (babies can see inside the womb, as light filters through), looks like a tree with branches.

Robbie once witnessed a presentation in which the speaker showed this placental Tree of Life, then compared it to many slides of artwork depicting an actual tree with a snake wound around it, and suggesting, quite aptly, that the snake represents the umbilical cord, which can indeed become wrapped around itself or around the fetus like a snake (especially when the fetus is quite small and is swimming around in the vast space of the womb), and which the fetus can see and even play with. (For example, when Robbie asked her two-year-old daughter Peyton, "Do you remember what you did while you were inside me?" Peyton replied, "I rested my head on a pillow [the placenta] and I played with a snake!") Thus this "Tree of Life" image is part of universal human experience and therefore found in artwork all over the world, most especially in "Garden of Eden" art. We leave our readers to imagine how they might now re-interpret the "snake" in Genesis and thus the archetypal meaning of that origin story.

Returning to our subject of the holistic quantum energy sea, on January 18, 2013, Robbie attended a talk given by the popular physicist Brian Greene (see Greene 2003, 2004, 2005, 2011, 2021), a proponent of string theory and the notion of parallel universes. The Paramount Theater in Austin, Texas, where he gave that talk was completely sold out to an audience of enthusiastic fans, many of whom were New Agers, as we discuss above. During the question-and-answer session at the end, Robbie had such a pressing question that she stood up to catch Greene's attention instead of just raising her hand like everyone else. It worked.

Her question was: "Where did the stuff that was in the original Big Bang come from?" Dr. Greene said that it was a great question, the fundamental question. His answer was first, that he didn't know (well of course he didn't—some questions are simply unanswerable, yet beg to be asked anyway). Yet then he went deeper to speculate about "nothing versus something," noting that "nothing"—the absence of space, time, matter, energy, everything—might be an unstable state that requires "something."

Later, at the very end of the session, Robbie opened her big mouth again, and asked if he might talk about God? Negative hoots, yells, and catcalls arose immediately arose from the audience—we suppose they thought Robbie was a Christian fundamentalist (who would be an anathema to that audience). Greene responded that he was simply too tired to address that question, to great audience approval. Unsatisfied, Robbie wrote an email to Dr. Greene, from which we excerpt the following:

> You were saying that you would be talking on Facebook and Twitter about lots of things, so I yelled out "Talk about God!"—not meaning for you to try to answer the question right then, just suggesting that you address the subject via your social media. I had no chance to explain why I asked the question—I almost didn't because belief in God is a matter of faith and you (and I) are all about science. But if you follow science all the way back to the Big Bang, or to millions of Big Bangs, you get to the question (if you think about religion at all), is there a God (or many) and were the ingredients in the Big Bang, "God"? That would imply that the ingredients in the Big Bang included a consciousness.
>
> I'm particularly interested in this question right now because I'm coauthoring (with Dr. Charles Laughlin, a neuroanthropologist) a book on ritual. In that book, we discuss how peoples enact and transmit their mythological/cosmological belief systems through ritual. In the section where we discuss the belief system of the Navajo, we note that their mythological system holds that First Man and First Woman gave birth to Changing Woman, who grew up rapidly and then created the world. A literal-minded reviewer asked, "But where did First Man and First Woman come from?"
>
> All such belief systems that I as a cultural anthropologist know about postulate that there was something before there was the something we know—something was there before the world we live in existed, and those somethings—gods, beings, monsters, whatever—created this world. (I'm sure you've heard the "turtles all the way down" story!) Rationally oriented Westerners tend to dismiss all such stories as "primitive nonsense," yet they are all explanatory models that postulate something coming from something that preceded it, just as three of the major world religions (Judaism, Christianity, Islam) postulate via *Genesis* that God preceded the world and created it—just as scientists postulate that first there was all this condensed energy and matter,

which then exploded in the Big Bang. They are all on a parallel, as far as I can see, in terms of being very similar types of explanatory frameworks.

It's just that *science* leads us to the Big Bang, and not myth. Yet science cannot answer my question above, so you could not. There is an ancient Hindu myth which says something like "God breathed out, and the stars and galaxies went flying." Possibly that reflects an intuitive understanding of the Big Bang, thousands of years before the theory of the Big Bang was generated—a way of saying that there had to be something from which everything else came. Possibly the Navajo myth of First Man and First Woman, and all other such myths, reflect that same intuitive understanding that *everything came out of something*. Possibly humans hold that intuitive understanding because we are a part of our fully interconnected universe and our brains are "hard-wired" to know that in some archetypal way. So it might be entirely rational and reasonable that we construct these explanatory models because in some way, we "sense" the fundamental truth underlying all of them.

Perhaps any feedback you might care to give could include an answer to this question: Does God form any part of your own explanatory framework? Full disclosure on my part: My own answer would be sometimes yes, when I'm desperate for something to believe in, and sometimes no, when I'm able to live with total ambiguity. I just can't get past my question about where the ingredients in the Big Bang came from without at least imagining a God, since I can't find any other answer—yet even that one is extremely unsatisfactory—if it *was* God who created the Big Bang and thus the universe, then where did God come from? Same issue!

Robbie received no response from Dr. Greene, yet the questions—and their implications for the archetypal answers humans come up with to explain why we are here and why our world and our universe exist—remain. Even eminent physicists, in the end, can do no better than "primitive" peoples— they all end up saying that there was something, or someone(s), out of which everything else came.

How the Cycle of Meaning Operates: The Sun Dance and the American Space Program

As we previously described, there are significant differences between mythic and paradigmatic matrices (belief systems). The most important are that modern paradigms are neither narrated in traditional story form, nor are they necessarily informed from the deep psychological foundations of archetypal cosmology. Modern paradigms are nonetheless coherent and operate, as do myths, as templates for action. Both myths and paradigms must remain to some extent current (trued to their current circumstances), or they will drop away or be replaced.

Let us explore two more examples of cognitive matrices, one from a traditional mythical system and the other from a modern paradigmatic system, with a view to better understanding the cycle of meaning operating via both instantiation and *interpretation*—for how one interprets the meaning of a ritual has everything to do with what that ritual means to them.

The Sun Dance: Instantiation, Interpretation, Ritual, and the Mythic Matrix

For the mythic matrix, almost any traditional system would do as an example. Take for instance the Plains Indian Sun Dance. The Sioux people of the US plains have been quite innovative in their borrowing and reorganization of cultural materials—an essential quality of a cycle of meaning that helps keep it "trued" to changing realities. During the 18th century, the Sioux incorporated horses (introduced into the Americas by the invading Spaniards) into their stock of resources, a strategic borrowing that radically changed their patterns of subsistence and political relations—and that also set the stage for borrowing cosmological and religious elements from both Spanish and other horse cultures, and reorganizing them into what became in the 19th century the Sun Dance religion. Elements centered upon corn and fertility were reorganized as befitted a migratory, hunting-gathering people who were now more concerned with buffalo, deer, and other game than with gathering activities (J. Jorgensen 1972). Because hunting was now more important than gathering, male hunters became more highly valued, while still retaining their traditional role as warriors. Hence, traditional roles were adjusted to true them to the changes in means of subsistence.

During the Sun Dance, an annual festival, young male warriors would be tied to a pole by a lengthy cord passed through their pectoral muscles. The youths undergoing the ritual would walk and dance toward and away from the pole—the ritual center—straining on the rope until their flesh tore and they were free from the tether. The torn flesh would be treated and would eventually produce scars that were symbols of courage, prowess and fortitude—qualities greatly valued by the Sioux.

The US government forbade the practice of the Sun Dance in the 1880s, but it was reestablished years later in a new form—one that is practiced today. The more modern, peace-oriented version of the Sun Dance once again "trued" its intentions to the new demands of reservation life, and now emphasizes performing purification practices (like sweat lodge ceremonies) and dietary taboos prior to the ceremony, and then spending days dancing around a pole upon which the symbol of Buffalo, Eagle, or some other religious icon is attached. Eventually the dancer may enter a trance in which visions occur that reveal to the young man his life purpose.

Thinking about those changes in terms of the cycle of meaning, we can see that the worldview of Plains Indians altered considerably over the years. Once the Sioux were confined to a reservation, the role of the hunter/warrior diminished, while the role of farming once again increased in importance, and therefore the role of the Sun Dance as a ceremony of defiance of incursions by the dominant Euroamerican culture dwindled. And yet the core symbols of Sioux cosmology remained, including Buffalo, the Sun, the importance of the high god *Wakan Tanka,* and so on.

The Sun Dance ritual itself has all along been directed at evoking visions and other alternative states of consciousness. The extraordinary states of consciousness many dancers experience bring the normally hidden aspects of the cosmology alive and thus instantiate (generate lived experiences of) the values and core symbols (Sun, Buffalo, etc.) of the people's cosmology. Yet, as the Sun Dance has changed over the generations, the form and significance of its elements—their instantiation and interpretation—have shifted as the spiritual and healing needs of the people have changed. So flexible has the Sun Dance become that it has spread beyond the confines of Sioux culture to many other Native American societies, and remains a very viable cosmological-ritual performance today, for it is easily modified to true/align the cosmology of the people to local conditions.

NASA's Space Program: Instantiation, Interpretation, Ritual, and the Paradigmatic Matrix

In 1960, President John F. Kennedy expressed a vision that was later instantiated—"send a man to the moon and return him to Earth within this decade." That vision galvanized the US space program into intensive action that resulted in the culmination of that vision. As NASA developed into a major institution, receiving billions of dollars from the federal government to help make that vision a reality, its members developed a culture organized around achieving Kennedy's goal. "Making it to the moon" before anyone else developed US technological capabilities, leading to the inevitable cultural interpretation that "the US is Number One in the world" in terms of technological prowess and global superiority and leadership.

Yet once we had succeeded in making it to the moon via the Apollo program, our national priorities for further space exploration and leadership were suddenly unclear. We had made it to the moon, several times—what were we supposed to do now? The answer that NASA came up with was to build the shuttles and the international space station—a mission now accomplished.

During Robbie's four years of conducting oral history interviews with some of NASA's pioneers,[1] it became clear to Robbie that they had "lost their way," in a sense, after the moon trips ended. They had built their entire culture and the vision that led that culture under Kennedy's mandate. The NASA culture that achieved that goal was based on the core value of "doing it yourself." The corporate rituals of this early NASA culture were minimal. Bosses would overturn trash cans and sit on them next to the desks of their young, bright employees to check in on their progress and hear their many ideas. One phone call to the right person could result in the building of a major facility to test a round rocket, for example—it was all about networking, and not at all about hierarchy.

That lateral, horizontal, networked early NASA culture got us to the moon—yet getting there led to the establishment of massive facilities and a massive bureaucracy. No longer would one phone call suffice, no longer could NASA engineers build what they designed on their own with financial support only from NASA. It became all about "outsourcing"— limiting NASA's former primary role in technology development in order to give government contracts to outside agencies that would do the work themselves. A single phone call was replaced with file drawers full of the paperwork that the federal government now required. Immediate "instantiation" of ideas was replaced by too much "interpretation" of those ideas by the recently created federal bureaucracy. Some of the most creative engineers and designers left in frustration. Others carried on and ended up facing the *Challenger* disaster, which, as Robbie learned in her interviews, was the clear result of that very same bureaucracy. As we know, it was the frozen O-rings that caused the disaster. But why was the *Challenger* launched under extreme cold weather temperatures? And more pertinently, why did the O-rings exist in the first place?

Because of the rituals of the bureaucracy! Once NASA employees were no longer allowed to build rockets on their own, bids had to be taken from competing companies. The obvious thing would have been to build solid rockets all in one piece, with no O-rings to join the separated parts. But that would have meant going with the one company that was close enough to Cape Canaveral to get those huge rockets there in one piece. Having to "contract out" (i.e., ritualize) the bids for building those rockets meant having to accept a cheaper bid from a company far away, which would have to build the rockets in two pieces in order to be able to transport them to Florida, and to use O-rings to reconnect them. Ritual government protocol was followed, the cheaper bid was accepted, the O-rings were used, they froze in the cold weather, and the *Challenger* exploded.

And what about the decision-making process that allowed the *Challenger* to launch when it should have remained grounded on that too-cold morning? Again, it is a very sad story of conflicting corporate cultures that pitted the engineers, who insistently warned that the O-rings might fail in freezing temperatures, against the administrators who just wanted to "go for it" because everyone was there watching—the thrilling and very public ritual of launch was already in process, and they just followed that "ritual train." *Challenger* was scheduled to be launched around 4 a.m. The engineers wanted to let the sun rise and warm up the launch site to about noon that day. Yet a major senior NASA meeting/ritual of intensification was planned for Washington DC, later that same morning and would have to be canceled if the launch were postponed (Kenneth J. Cox, personal communication, April 21, 2012)—so the administrators prevailed and the ritual train proceeded (see Chapter 6 on "ritual inviolability and inevitability"). Launching the *Challenger* was supposed to be a successful ritual performance and mass celebration of US core values on technological innovation, prowess, and supremacy. Yet because of major dysfunctions within NASA's core culture and in NASA's cultural/ritual relationships with government employees and contractors, that planned mass ritual celebration turned into a massive and heart-rending disaster.

Returning to instantiation and interpretation, we can see how the instantiated belief in the supremacy of the US space program led to the initial idea for the *Challenger* launch and to the idea that for the first time, a US space shuttle was so safe that it could carry an ordinary citizen, schoolteacher Christa McAuliffe, into space along with the trained astronauts (whose training included the constant warning of the possibility of crisis and even death). From a US-centric point of view, the ideal outcome of the *Challenger* launch would have been to re-instantiate US core values on technological supremacy and additionally instantiate the access of an ordinary citizen to the highest technological achievement of the United States and to re-interpret, and thus "true," the United States of America as Number One in the world.

We can see how ritualized (as in, affected by corporate culture and ritualized hierarchies and policies) miscommunications and the resulting *mis*interpretations led to the *Challenger* disaster. As noted above, entrenched and ritualized hierarchies did not characterize the early years of NASA and did not get us to the moon. Yet the later bureaucratization of NASA did lead to massive, ritualized dysfunction and straight to the *Challenger* disaster. And NASA learned from that experience, restructured its corporate hierarchies and communication systems accordingly, and went on to accomplish many more successful shuttle journeys (although another shuttle was lost in 2003). The International Space Station continues to reflect and embody the positive results of international collaboration and successful communication and to symbolize what one united world can accomplish beyond its planetary boundaries.

Summary: The Human Need to Know

Humans exhibit a universal need to know about and to understand the world they live in, and so they develop explanatory frameworks—myths and paradigms, and the belief systems that often encompass those myths and paradigms—to fulfill that need. Knowledge and understanding are adaptive strategies that have been evolutionarily selected for over hundreds of thousands of years. If our systems of knowledge—our cultures and their mythic or paradigmatic matrices and belief systems—were not adaptively accurate enough for us to survive, were not sufficiently "trued" to the world we live in, we would simply die off as a species.

And indeed we might, if we do not true our actions to the multiple environmental crises that our actions have caused. The cultural (and individual) rituals we perform enable us to express and enact the understandings of the world that we develop, in the moment and over time. The role of ritual in truing knowledge and understanding is fundamental to adapting the belief system, paradigm, or cosmology of the culture to sufficiently match/true it to actual circumstances. The adaptive changes in the Sun Dance ritual trued Sioux culture to the realities of a peaceful, agricultural reservation life, as opposed to the warrior, hunting, nomadic lifestyle they had previously engaged in. The rituals changed as the circumstances changed. Yet as we saw with the *Challenger* disaster, when the circumstances changed (the unexpected freezing weather), the rituals did not, thereby failing to true plans and expectations to the new reality. Rather, the administrators tried to force reality to be as they wanted it to be. This ever-present possibility of "truing-gone-wrong" underscores how the knowledge and understandings of a group must be kept more or less current—more or less trued—with the daily experience of people on the ground (Hüsken 2007). Otherwise, ritual fails by imposing the enactment of a world as we want to force it to be instead of an enactment of the world as it (more or less) is.

Note

1. See Davis-Floyd, Cox, and White (2012, 2022) for abridged versions of some of these interviews, and www.davis-floyd.com for the full texts. Robbie conducted that research because she is fascinated by the US space program and its instantiation of "the myth of technological transcendence."

Chapter 4

Ritual Drivers
Generating and Controlling States of Consciousness

—⚮☉

What is it about the elements that make up ritual that are so physiologically, psychologically, and socially compelling and meaningful? That is the question we want to explore now. In order to do so, we have to understand how the symbolism and repetitive behaviors embedded in ritual operate to influence—to "penetrate"—the consciousness of participants. We begin by examining "states of consciousness" and how they can be changed from one state to another very quickly, or over time.

States and Warps of Consciousness

As all of us will no doubt agree, our consciousness does not remain the same from one moment to the next but is forever changing. Yet we cognize categories of experience as distinct from each other: for example, we may say we are "awake," "stoned," "drunk," "depressed," "dreaming," "excited," "exhausted," "angry," "out-of-body," "playing," etc. These cognized and labeled categories of experience, and their underlying neurocognitive structures, are what anthropologists and others call *states of consciousness* (SOCs). When we refer to SOCs other than those that occur in waking consciousness, we often speak of *alternative, or altered, states of consciousness* (ASCs), like dreaming, trance, hypnosis, getting high on drugs, and so forth.

Any SOC is produced by a distinctive organization of brain activity. The organization of our brain when we are happy is not the same as when we are sad. Moreover, in order for one SOC to be transformed into another SOC, the underlying neuronal structures of the brain must reorganize themselves. This reorganization usually happens in the blink of an eye. Almost instantly, we can experience a change in SOC from being on the phone with someone to becoming absorbed in a TV program, from feeling very sad to experiencing happiness, or from our usual busy SOC to deep meditation. The points of experiential and neurophysiological transition between states of consciousness are what we call *warps of consciousness* (WOCs or warps). The really important thing to remember about WOCs is that although they happen very rapidly compared to the longer duration of SOCs, they are crucial because the precise organization of warps can determine the organization and the qualities of the subsequent SOC. WOCs generally happen unconsciously, so we tend to be unaware of the warp processes that alter our SOCs. For example, the warp that produces the onset of sleeping may last for only a few seconds, yet its brief activity can determine the quality of the dream states that follow it (see Molino 2000).

Sometimes activities in one SOC can influence experiences had in another SOC. In order for this to happen, memories of the activities in one SOC (say, being "awake") are retained across the warp and thus can inform experiences had in another SOC (say a "dream"). To illustrate, one evening Robbie had a talk with her 20-year-old daughter Peyton about how much her 16-year-old son Jason had changed in the last few years. And just before she went to sleep that night, Robbie glanced at a photo of her children riding on a merry-go-round when they were little. Not surprisingly, her subsequent dreams centered on vivid flashbacks to Jason's childhood. Upon waking, Robbie remembered the conversation and the photo, and thus understood what induced the WOC that led to her dreams.

WOCs are crucial in the transformation between SOCs, for if the society—or the individual—can control the warp, it can control subsequent states of consciousness and the experiences that may arise in those states. To accomplish this *warp control*, the memory of what occurs in one SOC must be retained across the warp and into the subsequent SOC (Laughlin et al. 1986). So if you want to make sense of your dreams, you might want to try to be aware of what you are thinking about just before you fall asleep.

Now we turn to a description of ritual drivers, which are recurrent elements in ritual that have strong and predictable effects on participants—that *drive* the penetration of the ritual's symbolic messages. We will describe two different kinds of ritual drivers: *extrinsic drivers* that depend upon stimuli outside a person's body (drumming, flickering flames, the use of an icon like a mandala, the electronic fetal monitor in childbirth) and *intrinsic drivers* that are initiated from within the person's body (fasting, breathing techniques, meditation).

Types of Ritual Drivers and Examples of How They Work

For maximum effectiveness, either within or across SOCs, a ritual will concentrate on sending one basic set of messages that will be rhythmically repeated using different procedures and various codes. What is repeated in ritual can include the occasion for its performance, such as an event that happens every year at the same time; its content; the form the ritual takes into which this content is slotted; or any combination of these. This redundancy enhances ritual's efficacy in communicating whatever messages it is designed to send. As anthropologist Robert Redfield (1962) pointed out, the Maya farmer who hears the shaman chant the names of the gods 20 times in one hour, several times a day, is not likely to forget them!

Rhythm has long been recognized by anthropologists as a key feature of ritual. Rhythmic, repetitive stimuli affect the human central nervous system, generating a high degree of arousal, emotion, imagery, cognition, and movement, synchronizing/entraining these processes among the various participants (Chapple 1970). This process of entrainment may be experienced as a loss of self-consciousness and a feeling of *flow* (see Chapter 6). Ritual entrainment can lead to transpersonal bonding—a sense of the unity and oneness of the group.

Rhythm and music are powerful "ritual drivers." You may have experienced this power at rock concerts—as the audience begins to entrain with the rhythms of the music, the huge auditorium may suddenly seem to shrink and be suffused with shared energy; you no longer feel yourself to be just one individual, but an integral part of a pulsating, organic whole. In *Drumming at the Edge of Magic* (1990), Mickey Hart, then-drummer for the Grateful Dead, described it this way: "Sometimes I felt that we were becoming a big noisy animal that made music when it breathed." The same entrainment and sense of oneness characterize many church, mosque, and other types of religious services. For example, when the congregation sings together, their neural rhythms entrain both with each other and with the religious messages conveyed during the service and by the hymn. In many societies, and especially in cults and religions, rituals are used to influence people's experience by specific design. Rhythm and its ensuing neural entrainment are powerful, and savvy pastors and cult leaders (like the notorious Jim Jones and David Koresh) include large doses of them in the services they design.

The *ritual drivers* that can produce such neural entrainment are many and varied. They include, among others: drumming, chanting, running, singing, dancing, mantras, meditation, privations and painful ordeals, hazing, isolation, sensory deprivation, and drugs. The power of ritual depends in part upon the ability of these drivers to produce alterations in consciousness by penetrating into and triggering the metabolic and neural processes that can produce the desired experience.

Let us consider how mantras operate as drivers. For example, the simplest element in a more complex mantra like OM MANE PADME HUM, the famous Buddhist mantra of compassion, is the "seed syllable" (or *bīja*; see Pabongka Rinpoche 2006). For a ritual practitioner, the seed syllables OM and HUM are initially given dictionary-like definitions. OM

Table 4.1. Types of Intrinsic Drivers Used in the Ritual Production of Experience. Table created by Charles D. Laughlin.

Intrinsic Drivers	Examples
Breathing exercises	Buddhist meditation
Breath therapy	Holotropic breathwork
Chanting	Hindu and Buddhist mantras; shouting and doing "the chop" at baseball games; chanting as one during a religious or spiritual event
Visualization	Tibetan "arising" yoga
Vision quest	Plains Indian initiations
Dream incubation	Ancient Greeks; Tsimshian shamanism
Active imagination	Jungian psychotherapy
High fever	Iroquois Handsome Lake movement; Tsimshian shamanism
Circadian rhythms	Biofeedback techniques for stress reduction
Fasting	Purification for Sun Dance; annual purge among some alternative healing practitioners; the Muslim month of Ramadan
Physical exertion	Long distance running; Tibetan trance-running
Fatigue	Use of exhausting exercise
Physical deprivation, sleep deprivation	Navajo all-night sing
Sexual abstinence	Many monastic traditions
Sensory deprivation	Kogi shamans raised in caves
Concentration	Navajo stargazing; Zen koan meditation
Directed intention	Tibetan *wang kur*
Seclusion	Tsimshian shamans; Benedictine monastic tradition

may be defined as "the original sound of the universe," or "the name of God," but this is only an exoteric tag historically associated with the sound and with the sign (e.g., the Chinese character 唵) denoting the sound. The real esoteric meaning(s) of OM are the experiences evoked by repetition of the syllable. If you were to play around with repeating OM (pronounced "aouuwmmm"), you would find that making the sound causes physical vibrations in your body and that the vibrations move around. If you also contrast the OM vibrations with those produced by the HUM (usually pronounced "hunggg" or "hummm") seed syllable, you would feel that the vibrations in your body are quite different. In fact, the entire mantra, OM MANE PADME HUM, causes a myriad of physical vibrations in your body, repeating a pattern over and over again. A serious devotee of mantra yoga will tell you that eventually certain experiences may arise as a consequence of doing mantra work, and those experiences are the esoteric meaning(s) of the mantra (Paul 2004). We will return to a discussion of mantra (singular: mantrum) in Chapter 10.

As previously noted, there are essentially two different kinds of ritual drivers: *extrinsic drivers* that depend upon stimuli outside a person's body (drumming, flickering flames, the use of an icon like a mandala, the electronic fetal monitor in childbirth—see below), and *intrinsic drivers* that are initiated from within the person's body (fasting, breathing techniques, meditation). Tables 4.1 and 4.2 list some examples of both kinds.

Ritual Drivers at Work: The Ancient Juǀ'hoansi Trance Dance and Contemporary Breath Therapy

The Juǀ'hoansi of the Kalahari region of Namibia and Botswana (formerly called the !Kung Bushmen—theirs is a click language; the "ǀ'" represents a particular kind of click, as does the "!") have an ancient tradition called by outside observers the "trance dance" and by the people themselves the "healing dance," which employs both extrinsic and intrinsic drivers. Katz (1982) and Katz, Biesele, and St. Denis (1997) have documented the process through which the Juǀ'hoansi generate a powerful ASC in the dancers. While the women of the group clap in complex rhythms, male and sometimes female healers dance around a fire, often for hours. The clapping is an extrinsic driver, and its effects are enhanced by two intrinsic drivers—the stomping of the dancers and their heavy breathing. The healers say that as they dance, a healing energy that they call *nǀum* begins to rise up inside them, eventually boiling over and spilling out of their hands, which they lay on other members of their community to transmit that energy to them for all kinds of healing purposes.

Table 4.2. Types of Extrinsic Drivers Used in the Ritual Production of Experience. Table created by Charles D. Laughlin.

Extrinsic Drivers	Examples
Rhythm:	
dancing	Ju|'hoansi *n/um* dance; US "raves"
drumming	Tsimshian healing rituals; fife and drum
Marching events	Fourth of July or 'Macy's' Thanksgiving Parades in the United States
Group chanting	The "wave" at US sports events
Flickering light	Peaceful "trance" around the campfire at night
Psychotropic drugs	Ingestion of *ebene* by Yanomamo shamans
Imagery:	
art	Navajo sandpainting; Tibetan *tankas*; acid rock concert "liquid emulsions"
Skrying	Shaman's "mirror"; crystal gazing
Kasina	Buddhist 10 meditations
Mnemonics/reminders	Tsimshian power songs; national anthems
Ordeal:	
scary task	Firewalking; snake handling; drinking poison
pain	Plains Indian vision quest ordeals; college fraternity "hazing" rituals
sweat bath	Plains Indian Sun Dance sweat lodge
Performance	Tibetan *cham* dances; Wagnerian Ring Cycle
Bloodletting	Maya ritual bloodletting; bloodletting in obsolete Western medicine
Continuous electronic fetal monitoring	Women giving birth in hospitals all over the high-resource world

Rhythmic heavy breathing—the principal intrinsic driver employed by the Ju|'hoansi in this dance—can produce profound ASCs on its own, as many practitioners of the healing technique called "breath therapy" have found. Originally called "rebirthing" because its first practitioners used it to re-experience their own births in order to heal any traumas arising from their experiences of being born, and to help their clients do the same, breath therapy involves focused deep breathing, usually under the tutelage of an experienced breath therapist (see Ray 1983; Star 1986). After an initial 20-minute period of intentional, connected breathing—meaning that one breath is immediately, consciously followed by the next, without the usual pause in-between—the people undergoing this process often find that they are in a profoundly altered state of consciousness in which it is possible to "go anywhere" in memory in order to relive a given event or series of events in her life. The rationale behind breath therapy holds that individuals who have undergone deeply traumatic events like a terrible accident or some form of sexual abuse often cannot remember exactly what happened to them. As long as the memory remains blocked, these individuals may find themselves unable to move forward in certain areas of their lives. The idea is to consciously re-experience the trauma, this time in a safe context, and to scream or sob out pain and anguish until the emotional blockage is released. There is no drumming or other stimulus. Many people find breath therapy to be extremely effective.

In this type of ritualized therapy, just as in the "trance dance," rhythmic breathing is the principal driver that produces the altered state, augmented by verbal suggestions from the facilitator to follow one's breath, focus on a particular memory fragment, and trust that the person is safe and it's okay to let the memories come. Similarly, Eye Movement Desensitization and Reprocessing (EMDR) therapy often utilizes electronic drivers—buzzers in both hands and sometimes a light pattern that flashes to the right and to the left, while the hand buzzers emit their buzz concomitantly. These synchronized stimuli easily facilitate brain hemisphere integration across the corpus callosum and a mildly altered state of consciousness that can facilitate access to the desired memory or cognitive process, often to great psychotherapeutic effect. (See Chapter 7 for a description of Robbie's extremely effective EMDR experience.)

Percussion and Transition: One Student's Intentional Use of Ritual Drivers

Across cultures, rhythm, whether established through an intrinsic driver like deep breathing or through extrinsic artifacts like drums, is utilized to induce particular SOCs and their accompanying experiences. Anthropologist Rodney Needham was the first to document this strong cross-cultural connection between *percussion* and *transition*. And Michael Harner's popular book *The Way of the Shaman* ([1980] 1990) offers a percussive formula that any individual can use for entering a trance state. For individuals who do not have access to a drum, Harner recommends tape recording rhythmic drumming with a spoon on a book and playing it back at high volume.

Some years ago, when Robbie was teaching medical anthropology at Rice University in Houston, one of her students asked if he could do his term paper on shamanic trance and healing, with an experiential focus. Skeptical, Robbie insisted that he complement his experiential work with a hefty bibliography on shamanism across cultures, to which he agreed. Near the end of the semester, settling down at home with a large stack of term papers, Robbie found herself searching the pile for this student's paper, curious to know the outcome of his research. When she found it and started reading, she nearly fell out of her chair, and she learned a lot about how to create an effective combination of extrinsic and intrinsic ritual drivers to induce an altered state.

This student, whom we will call John, had begun the experiential part of his research by doing as Harner suggested: drumming on a book with a spoon and taping the sound. Then he laid in his bed and listened to the tape, but did not experience any significant shift in consciousness. The next day and the day after, he tried listening for longer and longer periods, still without success. Worried about making the deadline for the paper, he decided to escalate his use of ritual drivers in order to generate as much sensory and cognitive engagement as possible. He thought that employing some core symbols of shamanism might help him generate the experience he sought. His research had taught him that shamanic religions are usually highly *chthonic*—grounded in the earth. So first he paid attention to setting, exploring the Rice campus and the nearby park until he found a secluded spot under some bushes where, lying down, he felt a sense of privacy and connection to the earth and its living creatures. Then he employed a traditional intrinsic shamanic driver—he fasted for three days, so that when he began his experiment he would already be in an ASC. He hoped that the combination of extrinsic (drumming, the proper setting) and intrinsic (fasting) drivers would allow him to experience a shamanic journey to the Underworld. On the third day of his fast, with tape recorder in hand, John walked to the park, laid down under the bushes, and turned on the tape.

The results were dramatic. He soon entered a deep trance state in which he perceived, to his surprise, a portal on the horizon of his consciousness that led, not to the expected Underworld, but to what shamans sometimes call the "Middle World." He passed through this portal into a strange realm where he had all kinds of adventures, meeting animal helpers and others along the way. Eventually, many hours later, he traveled back through the portal and came out of his ASC astonished, shaken, and delighted that at last he would have something exciting to write about in the experiential section of his paper!

A week or so later, John became aware that one of his friends was having severe emotional difficulties that were impeding her ability to complete her semester's work. He offered to help and she gladly accepted. So he again fasted, took his tape recorder into the bushes, and laid down, this time inviting her to lie down with him and put her head on his shoulder. Holding her tightly, he again journeyed into the Middle World, where he learned about the sources of her malaise and worked with his animal helpers to heal her spirit. After that experience, her emotional difficulties vanished, and she successfully completed her semester.

John had these experiences in the context of an academic course that was certainly not intended to induce ASCs in its students, so he had no larger cognitive matrix within which to pursue his shamanic work. Robbie suggested that he look for a teacher, someone who could provide such a matrix, but after that semester Robbie and John lost touch and she does not know if he went any further. The failure of John's early efforts to enter trance with the aid of only one driver—the tape of him drumming on a book with a spoon—shows us that one simple driver is often not sufficient to induce an altered state; rather, a combination of drivers, which in John's case included a core symbol (the earth), fasting, and rhythmic percussion, proved essential to inducing the ASC he sought.

Electronic Fetal Monitoring as an Extrinsic Ritual Driver

And now we come to the last line on our chart above, the one that most of our readers will not immediately recognize as an actual "ritual driver"—continuous electronic monitoring of the laboring woman's contractions and her baby's heartbeat via hooking the mother up to a sophisticated machine complete with computer screen, called the electronic fetal monitor (EFM) in the United States and cardiotocography (CTG) in the UK and other European countries. To recap from Chapter 1, symbols work through the emotions. The EFM is the most powerful symbol of the rituals of hospital birth—it epitomizes our technocratic core values on high technology and the flow of information through machines. In most US hospitals, the entire labor experience is organized around the monitor. Stuck in bed tethered to the EFM and numbed by her epidural, the mother (along with the father, family, and nursing staff) is left with little to do but stare at the monitor and get kind of hypnotized by those glowing wavy lines rhythmically moving up, down, and sideways as contractions come and go and the fetal heartbeat speeds up and slows down. The following quotations from two of Robbie's interlocutors for her first book (Davis-Floyd [1992] 2003a, 2022) illustrate the symbolic "mapping-on" process generated by this powerful extrinsic ritual driver. From a nurse: "I know it's irrational, but as soon as I put a woman on the monitor, I get afraid to take her off of it because I get the feeling that the machine is keeping the baby's heart beating." From a mother: "As soon as I got hooked up to the monitor, no one even looked at me anymore, they just stared at the machine. And pretty soon I started staring at it too, and then I got the feeling that *it* was having the baby, and not me."

The machine, in other words, becomes more than an instrumental means of checking on the wellbeing of the mother and the baby; it conceptually takes over the birth experience, mapping its meaning—which is that the birthing body is a potentially dysfunctional machine that cannot give birth safely without high-tech monitoring and surveillance—onto the mother's and her attendants' interpretations of her birth experience. (See Chapter 5 and Davis-Floyd [1992] 2003a, 2018d; 2022 for an analysis of the EFM as a ritual technology and its instrumental effects.)

Ritual and Warp Control

When a society wishes to exercise control over the recurrence, quality, and attributes of a particular SOC, it will tend to ritualize the individual's activity before and, if possible, during the warp preceding the SOC. Thus ritual takes on the function of "warp controller." For example, so important is the moment before sleeping to determining the quality of dreaming that Tibetan dream yogis learn to control the warp and are thus able to exercise considerable control over the experiences they have during dreaming. Charlie was a long-time practitioner of this brand of dream yoga and has written descriptions of his experiences (Laughlin 2011). Tibetan yogis are able to *incubate* (give form to) their dreams via practices carried out just prior to and while entering sleep. For another example, in church the minister lifts his hands and asks the audience to bow their heads—a WOC that produces, in devout members, a conditioned transition to the state of consciousness called "prayer." True prayer is not just a series of gestures (kneeling, bowing the head, clasping the hands together in supplication), but is a distinct ASC in which the participant is more open to directly experiencing the sublime.

Because ritual plays such an important role in warp control, anthropologists working in various cultures have to learn to recognize shifts in SOCs in their hosts and ascertain what, if any, ritual activity has generated the shift. However, when dealing with complex religious practices, one must be aware that while a certain ritual activity may be a necessary condition for an intended experience, it is likely not a sufficient condition—there may be other ingredients required to evoke the intended experience. As Robbie's student John discovered, one may repeat the attempt many times without reaching the intended goal—especially when that goal is an ASC and/or an important realization—because one or several of the requisites for the intended experience may be absent. It is not uncommon for practitioners to have to repeat a ritual activity numerous times, and sometimes for years, before the intended experience arises.

This is often the case with practitioners of the newer version of the Sun Dance ritual described in the preceding chapter. Participants may have to repeat the four days of dancing annually for years before the ultimate mystical experience occurs for them. The mere use of drivers, even multiple drivers, does not ensure that the desired SOC will be obtained. Often the problem is internal—the ritual practitioner may need to develop a certain level of inner tranquility, for example, or to cultivate a state of receptiveness, or to drop all expectations or self-consciousness.

In addition, because experience develops over the course of life, rituals may be repeated over the course of years with the experiences intended by the guide or teacher changing in order to be appropriate to the maturational stage of the practitioner. Some rituals may be appropriate for puberty (see Chapter 10), and other rituals may be appropriate for women during pregnancy and childbirth (such as Blessingways and baby showers), and still others, such as "croning" ceremonies and retirement parties, for advancement into elderhood. Thus it is common for "life crisis" rituals to be designed with the age and maturity level of the practitioners in mind. And sometimes there is no precise design—profoundly significant ASCs can suddenly and unexpectedly arise, even when the ritual context is loose and unstructured.

For example, Robbie chose to give birth to her second child at home. For her, labor and birth were more than painful physiological processes— they were profoundly significant emotional, psychological, and spiritual experiences as well. So the house had a sacred air about it, and labor felt both deeply physical and deeply holy to her as it proceeded. Near the end, Robbie, who had been laboring in a hot tub, got out to walk around for a while. Entering her bedroom, she noticed that the bed had been freshly made by her midwives with her favorite sheets and quilt. It looked so inviting that she dove in, face down. And then, in her words, "a miracle" happened:

> With my face buried in the quilt, which shielded me from external stimuli, I went deep inside myself. I realized that for almost three days I had been singing with the contractions, dancing with the contractions, breathing with the contractions—in other words, I had been trying to *do something* about the contractions. That maintained a separation between the contractions, the pain they caused, and me. Suddenly, and without any pre-plan, I said to the pain, "OK, I surrender. Take me, I'm yours!" Instantly I, body and soul, became the pain, and once there was no more separation between me and the pain, there was no more pain! There was only oneness.

Like John lying under the bushes, Robbie had powerful core symbols around her that aligned her cognitively with her own perceptions of labor and birth as sacred—her home, her family, her midwives and friends, candles, and a "psychosphere" (Jones 2009) of love. In her case, the rhythmic drivers were the contractions of labor, which had at this point been going on for almost three days (intermittently for the first two, when she was in "latent" labor—"active" labor is recognized as starting at 6 cm of cervical dilation). The WOC was diving down into the bed, which had been ritually made up by the midwives to receive Robbie and her newborn after birth. The bed was beautiful, pristine, and to Robbie constituted the inner sanctum of her family life. It was the place where her children were conceived, where she read bedtime stories to her daughter Peyton, and where she cried out her sorrows and meditated upon her joys. Diving onto that bed in the midst of heavy labor felt to Robbie like diving into the inner sanctum of her own consciousness. Removed from visual connection with the outside world, that warp moment, suffused with ritual significance, took her into an unexpected and fully unified state of consciousness—Nirvana—one that monks in monasteries may take decades to attain, as Charlie has illustrated above. Of course, the monks who work so hard and long to attain this SOC are usually able to enter it at will, and/or are experienced in the use of the ritual drivers that help them attain it; for Robbie, it was a one-time, life-altering, gift.

Monophasic and Polyphasic Cultures

Many societies integrate knowledge gleaned from awareness of events encountered in all states of consciousness within a single worldview. We saw in the preceding chapter that ideational and idealistic cultures manifest this kind of cosmological worldview. In these cultures, *all states of consciousness are of relevance to the people's understanding of themselves and their reality.* We might say that such cultures are more or less *polyphasic* relative to the range of alternative SOCs—ASCs—that human beings are capable of attaining and paying attention to. We are using the word "polyphasic" to describe idealistic and ideational cultures that incorporate multiple states of consciousness into their lifeworlds and worldviews. Indeed, it is likely that prior to some point in human prehistory, virtually all human societies were more or less polyphasic (see Lewis-Williams and Pearce 2004).

For example, it is considered important among Tibetan Buddhists, at least for active practitioners, to be as aware as possible in all states of consciousness, whether they are "awake" or "asleep" from our Western point of view. Practitioners of dream yoga are sometimes taught to wander around while they are awake telling themselves that they are dreaming, and while they are dreaming to tell themselves that they are awake. The intention is to transform the stream of consciousness so that their awareness will be well-balanced between SOCs.

In contrast, modern Euroamerican societies and other sensate cultures typically give credence only to experiences they have in what people consider to be "normal" waking states—that is, in the SOCs oriented primarily toward the external world. Sensate cultures maintain the view that reality is the world that is present to the senses during normal waking states of consciousness—that is, the reality of the table is the object as it appears to our senses and nothing more. Thus, the kind of intense attention given by Tibetan Buddhists to their dream life makes little sense to the average sensate Euroamerican. After all, sleeping is what we do when we are tired and wish to "zone out" and refresh ourselves. Moreover, we conceptually distinguish among feelings, thoughts, and actions in a way that those living in polyphasic cultures rarely do. We tend to distinguish between feeling and intuitive stuff, which we often don't take seriously, and the serious stuff of "work." Thus we might say that we Euroamericans live in a relatively *mono-phasic* culture. Sensate, monophasic cultures are characterized by a marked concern for the world as presented to the senses and are all about material values, with relatively less concern for inner growth, spiritual development, and balance among SOCs.

Anthropologists who have been raised in monophasic cultures, and who find themselves working in polyphasic cultures, may have a hard time learning how to access other SOCs, especially ASCs. But if they don't do so, they will miss precisely those experiences that inform and enrich the worldview of their hosts—and the experiences that are intended by their host's interstate rituals that drive the transition between SOCs. Such anthropologists may discover that they are experientially out-of-sync with the host culture in two obvious situations. One such situation is when they are out of touch with their dream life while doing fieldwork among a society whose members routinely track their dream experiences, and consider dreaming to be a substantial source of knowledge about themselves and the spiritual world. The other situation is when the polyphasic worldview of the host society is enriched with experiences had while participating in rituals or drug-induced "trips" generally unavailable to the researcher.

In polyphasic societies, commonly-held beliefs in spirits and animistic objects tend to be grounded in direct experience of "other-than-human persons" (Hallowell 2002: 20) in dreams, visions, trance states, drug-induced ASCs, and so forth. People in polyphasic societies consider what they experience in *all* SOCs to be "real" in some sense. They may know, for instance, that there are ghosts because they see ghosts, interact with, and communicate with ghosts. While belief in supernatural agencies and beings may seem counterintuitive to a sensate Westerner, they are simply experienced reality among ideational, polyphasic peoples (see Edith Turner [1996] on this crucial issue).

Sometimes learning to access the SOCs considered important in a polyphasic culture can be quite daunting. For instance, the healer/sorcerer shamans among the Indigenous Yanomami living in the rain forests of Venezuela and Brazil ingest a powerful hallucinogenic substance sometimes called *ebene* (*Virola* species, related to nutmeg) which allows them to access the *hekura* (spirit beings) that inhabit the normally invisible spirit world. When they take the drug, they unite with their *hekura* and then are able to fly to distant places and see things and get things done, such as detecting the cause of an illness or resolving a spirit-being dispute that is affecting tribal members. The shamans are able to use the *hekura* both to heal their fellow group members and to kill their enemies.

Two Polyphasic Experiences: Napoleon Chagnon and Robbie

Anthropologist Napoleon Chagnon, who lived among the Yanomami (aka Yanomamo) for years, had learned a great deal about their cosmology and had witnessed the shamans using the sacred green powder many times but had resisted taking the drug himself. Only when certain political conditions pressured him into accepting the drug did he try it. He took the *ebene* under the supervision of the shamans and had an ecstatic experience during which he felt light and floaty, danced, sang, and chanted, and invited the *hekura* to enter him, reproducing the ritual activities he had witnessed the shamans perform so many times. In the end, he fell exhausted into a hammock and reflected upon the considerable differences between Yanomamo religion and Euroamerican Christianity.

The thing to keep in mind here is that while the anthropologist in this case exhibited great courage in trying out the drug (very painful to ingest, as it is a powder that is forcefully blown up one's nostril and has the initial effect of making one extremely nauseous), he only did it once. And in doing it once he was already quite unusual among his peers, for most anthropologists shy away from taking powerful hallucinogens. Yet the Yanomami shamans take the drug, sometimes on a daily basis, over the course of years. It is unclear from Chagnon's report whether he actually perceived any *hekura*, and he certainly did not experience the at-oneness with the *hekura* that allowed his shaman hosts to fly around and "eat the souls" of their enemies. His experiences with *ebene* were actually quite limited, for there is, of course, a developmental aspect to learning how to use drugs in this way. To our knowledge, very few anthropologists have ever had that experience and written about it, much less taken the drug on a regular basis long enough for the physiological systems producing the shamanic experience to develop. Being raised in a society that is so extremely monophasic places severe limitations on the kinds of experiences the anthropologist is open to in the field among a people who, like the Yanomamo, live in a polyphasic universe.

Among many modern people in South America and elsewhere, ayahuasca—a psychoactive brew used as a traditional spiritual medicine in ceremonies among the Indigenous peoples of the Amazon basin—is considered sacred and is taken in special ceremonies among certain spiritual groups, or subcultures, that have their own cosmologies, mostly based on their polyphasic experiences of the ASCs generated by drinking small amounts of ayahuasca. They take these experiences quite seriously and seek to learn from them, usually guided by group leaders who help them interpret such experiences in terms of their cosmology. Upon Robbie's return to Brazil a few months after the death of her daughter Peyton in 2000, a special ayahuasca ceremony was held for her and her friends—who were Brazilian holistic obstetricians (see Davis-Floyd and Georges 2018)—in a beautiful round white temple with a thatched roof somewhere in a jungle. As the ceremony began, Robbie says:

> We all lined up and got our little plastic cups of the brew—which they made themselves, then returned to our places and, on a signal from one of the group leaders, drank the ayahuasca together. Then we sat and listened to classical music in an atmosphere of sacredness for a time. After a while, the group members started to ask questions of the leaders, which I didn't understand as I don't speak Portuguese, so I just enjoyed my own private experience. At first, I experienced myself as a tiny being who dove down into a crystal glass full of the liquid ayahuasca brew that spiraled at the bottom, spinning me out into an ocean that to me represented the quantum sea—the totality and interconnectedness of everything.
>
> Once I emerged back into my comfy chair, in contrast to the deep seriousness of the rest of the group, I suddenly started to remember all of the funny things that had happened since Peyton had died—and there were many! So for four whole hours, while everyone else remained very, very serious, I (quietly) laughed my head off. When I looked at the group leaders to see if that was okay, I saw them smiling at me and nodding approval.
>
> Meanwhile, my obstetrician friend Ric, who was being sued for a maternal death that was not his fault, was outside puking his guts out—as often happens after you drink this highly hallucinogenic brew. Apparently, he needed to release his fears and sense of persecution, while I needed to rediscover some of the many joys and happy moments I had experienced after Peyton died. These highly ritualized, polyphasic experiences were transformative in very good

ways for both of us, teaching both Ric and me that the drug "trips" we both had always been so afraid of could be very good things after all—although, like Chagnon, I felt that this one-time experience was quite enough for me, and it did give me an appreciation of the value of that kind of ASC—and sort of made me wish that I lived in a polyphasic culture where ASCs are normal parts of daily life, as there is so much we generally sensate people could learn from them.

Transferring Information across States of Consciousness

As Robbie infers, states of consciousness organized around the inner life of the polyphasic individual are frequently ignored, repressed, negatively sanctioned, considered pathological, or otherwise derided as "irrational" and "mystical" by sensate people raised in monophasic cultures. Experiences in alternative SOCs/ASCs may be lost or compartmentalized in memory when the individual has no intellectual framework for making sense of the experience in normal waking consciousness. Memory of experiences in an ASC (a dream, a trance, a vision, an intuition about the divine reality lying behind the world of appearances) may be lost to another SOC (our baseline state of being "awake") due to a radical transformation of the warp between SOCs. This kind of radical transformation occurs in the brain when the neural systems producing experience change rapidly and totally during the warp from one SOC to another—as happens for most Euroamericans when they "fall asleep." Thus, we are often unable to organize our experience of altered states in terms that our waking brains can understand.

Some experimental evidence from sleep labs suggests that if we can retain even a minimal amount of cognitive organization as we move through the warp from the ASC to our normal waking state, we can integrate at least parts of the altered SOC into our memories. That is why people who are trying to become more conscious of their dreams often write down whatever they remember immediately upon awakening—a technique that can help to lead to "lucid dreaming." Fragmented memories of ASCs tend to be common in societies that do not have ritualized methods for transferring memories across warps nor a culturally transmitted, polyphasic worldview. Living in a monophasic culture commonly constitutes an impediment to the transfer of memory or information from one SOC to another—for example, from waking to dreaming or vice versa—because the process of symbolic penetration cannot operate as freely across WOCs between SOCs. Rituals that in a polyphasic culture may easily penetrate into, for example, dreams, have less effect in sensate, monophasic cultures whose members routinely ignore or disattend their dreams.

Ritual and the Control of States of Consciousness

Now that we better understand SOCs (states of consciousness) and WOCs (warps of consciousness), we can return to ritual drivers more fully informed, and can begin to understand the influence of these drivers in terms of the hierarchy of neurocognitive functionings affected by ritual stimuli. The entire neuroendocrine system ("neuro-" refers to the nervous system per se, and "endocrine" refers to the body's system of glands and hormones) may be driven "from the top down," so to speak, by means of symbolic penetration. This kind of ritual driving occurs very commonly in our everyday lives, for example through symbols we encounter that penetrate our consciousness from outside. Robbie vividly remembers the shock she felt upon exiting a New York City subway station to find herself facing the street where her daughter Peyton had lived. The street sign symbol penetrated her consciousness, evoking Robbie's memories of Peyton's life in New York—the life she had just before she died. Needless to say, Robbie "lost it" for a few moments until the friends she was with helped to ritually calm her down with hugs, understanding, and love.

Also, symbolic activity mediated by the brain's cortex may be driven from the "bottom-up" by lower neurological, metabolic, and endocrine activities. This kind of driving also occurs commonly in our everyday lives—for example, when we have a core brain instinct or intuition so strong that we actually act on it, such as when a doctor suddenly intuits and acts on a solution to a patient's problem, despite the fact that his intuition does not correlate with objective test results. He will explain to his colleagues that he just had "a gut feeling"—an instinct. This doctor "drove" his higher order cognitive and emotional systems "from the bottom up"—the core brain.

Rituals employ both top-down and bottom-up drivers to effect alterations in SOCs. Fasting or the use of psychotropic drugs (bottom-up drivers) may be paired with drumming or sensory deprivation (top-down drivers) to produce a distinct ASC intended by those who designed the ritual. Indeed, one may find that a complex ritual contains an *orchestra of drivers,* the combined effects of which may result in a range of ASCs over time.

Theatrical performances are a type of ritual that may involve music, special effects, historical and archetypal symbolism, activity or passivity of the audience, and so on, to influence the audiences' state of consciousness by fully engaging them in the performance; such complete engagement involves the well-known "willing suspension of disbelief" so that both the audience and the actors live in the world created by the performance, for as long as it lasts.

Theatrical performances are only one of many forms of complex rituals in which we can trace the impacts of drivers. Rock concerts, political rallies, sports, and religious or spiritual services are all forms of ritual in which we can isolate and analyze systems of embedded drivers that influence the SOCs of participants and audiences. Rock concerts often blend heavy repetitive rhythms, flashing lights, pyrotechnics, dancing, "moshing," and sometimes psychotropic drugs (e.g., "ecstasy") into a distinct state of consciousness that is avidly sought by fans of that kind of entertainment. We note here, with curiosity, that the word "entertain" literally means "to hold someone in a particular state"—in this case a state of enjoyment and flow. A rock concert—or a sports event—then may be understood as a complex ritual that integrates a number of drivers in such a way that participants are "transported" into and maintained for a period of time in a desired and enjoyable ASC.

Games are a ritualized form of play that is organized into roles and rules. In many cultures, games have important religious significance; for example, the *Rājasūya* dice game in Indian cosmology (Handelman and Shulman 1997: 61–68), or the Apache Indian moccasin game (Reagan 1904). Sports are a very important form of *secular* ritual. Whole-hearted involvement in sports may produce a special sense of "fun" or elation. Among professional sports players, this sense of pleasure or ecstasy may be part and parcel of a particular SOC required for peak proficiency, as we explore later on.

Ritual drivers may be relatively extreme, like fasting for days or running to exhaustion, or may be quite subtle, like chanting a mantra inside your head, depending on the intended effects upon consciousness. In fact, in many of the world's mystical traditions, the deeper the level of consciousness that one is trying to reach or master, the more extreme or blatant may be the array of ritual drivers involved in evoking the state. By the same token, as the practitioner becomes "higher" or more mature—as his or her neural networks develop to a certain point—the range of drivers may become more and more subtle until a point in development is reached when the practitioner is able to reach a desired and very subtle ASC with little effort of will and without any apparent reliance upon external drivers. There is a legendary story about the time when the Buddha held up a flower in the presence of his students, and that simple action caused one of his students, named Kassapa, to fully awaken to "the essence of mind." The flower was a symbolic driver that triggered a revolutionary transformation in Kassapa's consciousness. This is a case par excellence of a very subtle extrinsic driver having a profound effect upon the recipient, who had already reached a higher or more mature level of the Buddha's teachings and needed only a very subtle driver for a profound transformation in consciousness.

Portals as Ritual Drivers into Multiple Realities

Important to our depictions of the characteristics and power of ritual is to remember that the cosmologies of traditional peoples are typically "multiple-reality" or polyphasic worldviews. That is, many peoples today (and in the past) believe that reality consists of a system of several worlds, sometimes stacked one upon the other. For instance, the Tukano Indians, who live in the rain forests of the Amazon basin in South America, divide the universe into three realms—the upper world (celestial), the intermediate world (earth), and the underworld (paradise) (Reichel-Dolmatoff 1971). The sun is believed to travel a path along the Milky Way through the upper world, shedding its light upon the earth during its passage, and then through the underworld during the night. The creator god lives in the underworld and sends the divine blessing of energy to the people of earth through the flow of this daily solar cycle. Smoke is believed to unite the heavens and the earth.

This cosmic scheme is not merely a conceptual invention. Rather, it is the sense that shamans in many cultures have made over the ages of visions they have had during periods of intense concentration and from the use of hallucinogens. They experience moving from realm to realm via the smoke of fires. In a vastly simpler way, we could light a candle in a cathedral in memory of a loved one, and feel more connected to that loved one through the channel opened between dimensions by the flame and the smoke it produces, which travels upward and transforms into cosmic ether, (hopefully) carrying our messages of love and remembrance to the spirit of the departed.

For the Tukano and many other polyphasic cultures, individuals may have to access the different realms—the multiple realities—in order to maintain a balance, to correct an imbalance, or to heal the sick. Sometimes shamans will use meditation devices to aid them in moving from one realm to another—a process of transforming SOCs called *portalling*. A meditation object used to alter the SOC of a shaman or practitioner is called a *portalling device*. Portalling devices operate as a threshold, a *limen*—a passageway or tunnel through which the consciousness of a practitioner may pass to an alternative world. These devices are really symbols, and the experience of portalling is actually a form of symbolic penetration that can produce a massive transformation in the organization of the neurocognitive structures mediating experience. Many different kinds of objects may be used to portal, including crystals and other gemstones, mandalas, cave mouths, "bulls-eye" concentric circles, labyrinths, and skrying bowls—sacred vessels filled with water, mercury, liquid lead, or other fluid and reflective materials—like the one the Lady Galadriel of Lothlórien used to show Frodo Baggins and Samwise Gamgee their possible futures in the *Lord of the Rings* saga.

Mirrors are among the most common types of portalling devices. Reflective pools, skrying bowls, polished metal objects, and the like can be used as meditation objects that have a potentially powerful evocative influence on the state of mind of the meditator. It is no coincidence that Lewis Carroll has Alice enter the strange mystical world of her adventures by stepping though a mirror. We move from one room to another through doorways; a meditative "doorway" is uniquely suggestive to a receptive mind of moving between inner spaces. Note the contemporary practice of the husband carrying his new bride over the threshold, which he often does even if they have been living there together for years! Actually marrying still remains a powerful and meaningful rite of passage for contemporary citizens of technocracies—we remain ritualistic, just as we humans have always been (see Grimes 2002).

One of the basic foundational practices (*ngon-dro*) in Tibetan Tantric Buddhist practice is the *dkyil-'kyor* or "mandala practice," which has to do with meditating on a portalling device. The practice involves repetitively constructing and destroying a mandala of heaped rice on top of a polished, translucent mirrored surface. The mirror (the *sa-gzhi*, which looks like a metal bowl made of silver or copper turned upside down) is held in one hand while the other hand constructs a mandala of rice and then sweeps the mirror clean of the rice. This practice is done over and over while repeating an appropriate mantra. For some practitioners, this mirror meditation can be extremely powerful, for it invites visions and dreams that have to do with (from the Buddhist point of view) the illusory nature of the world.

Charlie undertook the mandala offering practice during the early days of his exploration of Tibetan Buddhism. He finished one hundred thousand repetitions of this practice during solitary meditation retreats. (Upon reading this statement for the first time, Robbie asked via email, "Seriously? 100,000 repetitions??" and Charlie replied, "Yes!") He used a round shaving mirror glued to a tea saucer and a large bowl of rice that had been stained yellow with food coloring. (See Laughlin, McManus and d'Aquili (1990: 328) for a more detailed description of these experiments.) Over and over, for five one-hour sessions a day for weeks, Charlie would take up a handful of rice from the large bowl in his lap and construct a mandala on the mirror—a mandala is a circular form with four cardinal points and a center. He would then offer the completed mandala up to the guru he visualized above his head, and then wipe the mirror clean—all the while repeating a mantrum that he had been taught. At night Charlie would have lucid dreams of the mirror becoming a portal or a three-dimensional mandala-like form. The mirror would become a colorful tunnel down which he would fly, entering various dreamscapes and having various adventures. In one such dream, the rice grains became yellow flowers that sprang out of a circular mirror and emitted great energy. At other times, the mirror would become a body of water or some other symbolic transformation. Charlie had hundreds of such experiences, which obviously were evoked by the repetitive action of constructing and deconstructing the rice edifice on the mirror. In our present terms, the rice and the mirror operated as extrinsic drivers, while the repetition of the mantrum acted as an intrinsic driver, all slotted in a certain order within the context of the "mandala offering" ritual.

Another set of experiments further underscores the power of ritual drivers to produce spiritually salient experiences, even without a cultural context for them. This time Charlie joined forces with his friend and colleague John Cove to help John explore the possible esoteric significance of what is termed the "shaman's mirror." John had spent years working with the Tsimshian and other Indigenous peoples of the Northwest Coast of Canada and was fascinated by their shamanic traditions. During his fieldwork, John encountered the phenomenon of the mirror. The shaman's mirror can take various forms, but the particular one Charlie and John were interested in is made of slate and is commonly found in the graves associated with shamans.

As these objects were no longer in use among the contemporary Tsimshian people, Charlie and John decided that the only way they could find out how they had been used by the shamans of the past was to try them out for themselves. They manufactured their own mirrors from black slate roofing tiles, and made them to conform exactly to some of the real objects they found in museums. These look something like small paddles with one side ground down slightly so that it is concave, or spoon-shaped. They also incorporate a curious feature—a small notch at the top of the mirror. When John and Charlie wetted the concave side with water, it became very like a hand mirror. Held horizontally as the water evaporated, the reflective "portal" would shrink down to a dot and then disappear. At first they could see their faces in the mirror, but as the reflective circle got smaller and smaller, a tunneling effect was produced: their attention to their faces changed to attention to a tunnel, and they were drawn into the portal. It was like being poised on a threshold, quite able to pass over into another realm of experience or return to the normal state—quite literally a "liminal" state of mind. If you concentrate on your face in just the right way, the curious little notch at the top of the mirror causes a split representation of your face—a common motif used in Tsimshian art to represent supernatural beings.

Given that the Tsimshian shaman's mirror is no longer used in this way, John and Charlie really had no ritual context within which to interpret the experiments with the slate "mirror." Nonetheless, their experiments demonstrated the robust effects of ritual drivers, even bereft of their traditional context. And undoubtedly, as in the case of the Tibetan practice, the shaman's mirror was used repetitively and within the context of some now-lost spiritual practice, intent, and cycle of meaning. Yet we can only speculate as to the "places" the mirror would take the ancient Tsimshian shamans.

What we do know from research on other systems of meditation is that over time, experienced practitioners become quite adept at controlling the experiences they have "on the other side" of the portal. In ideational, polyphasic cultures, people who become adept at traveling to spiritual realms are frequently perceived as accruing great power. To touch the sacred or the numinous, to be in the presence of the divine, to be able to intervene between this world and the other worlds—all this leaves its mark on the practitioner, who may gain high status for skill in accessing power and using it for the good of the community. And every time a shaman or a practitioner accesses the spiritual domain, they give evidence of the existence of such places and reinforce the society's belief in its polyphasic cosmology. It is fascinating and curious that the more contemporary quantum physicists delve into the dynamics of the universe, the more they seem to share this polyphasic view of multiple realities and dimensions, at least at the theoretical level, and the more common become multidimensional pictures of the nature of scientific cosmology. Quantum physicists like Brian Greene now quite blithely speak of the "10th dimension," parallel universes, superstrings, and more (see Chapter 3; Baggott 2020).

The key to understanding just how the mind is able to access these normally hidden domains is to understand the power of ritual drivers to evoke WOCs and subsequent SOCs. Portals invite the liminal—they suggest to the mind an alternative view, and may evoke a WOC resulting in novel—even amazing—experiences. In a very real sense, portalling devices are doorways precisely because they symbolically penetrate to the brain structures that mediate experience and cause them to radically reorganize themselves.

Whether immediate or delayed, to go through the tunnel between the realms is to experience the radical transformation of one's own brain-state. And just as with a physical doorway, one may have to "knock" repeatedly upon the portal before one experiences entry. Diligence in the ritual repetition of drivers may eventually be rewarded by the experiences they are devised to activate—perhaps one of the meanings behind the esoteric promise "knock and it shall be opened unto you" in the Bible (Matthew 7:7). Ritual drivers often only work upon the mind and body when conditions are auspicious—when the ambience is appropriate and the individual is fully able to concentrate. Repetition of the rituals and their drivers assures a greater chance that the intended experiences will occur. Ritual repetition lays the foundations for completing the cycle of meaning because it enables people to become more masterful at interpreting the experiences that ritual evokes in terms of their society's worldview.

Why Are Ritual Drivers So Compelling?

The power of ritual is in part the power of drivers, alone and in concert with other ritual elements, to compel/drive experience. Whether or not you think of yourself as patriotic, hearing your national anthem sung at a sports event may still cause you to experience a certain unbidden *frisson* (a sudden sensation of excitement; a shudder of emotion) or even tears. This emotional reaction reflects the power of ritual drivers to penetrate into and influence the physical processes that mediate experience.

The effects that particular drivers have upon people are often very specific and predictable. Take for example "the blues." The curious thing about the blues is that while the lyrics are usually about suffering, pain, and loss, the effect of the music (for those who are "into" to that genre) is to produce joy and even ecstasy. This effect is produced by the characteristic rhythms and syncopation that constitute the structure of the music. Indeed, the blues may be interpreted both biologically and socially as rituals for the transformation of depression and despair into happiness and joy. Considering that the historical roots of the genre called "the blues" lie in the terrible conditions of Black slaves and sharecroppers on southern US plantations, the invention of the blues as a rite of emotional transformation was really quite ingenious. The music would be played at Sunday socials and in "juke" joints (both are ritual venues) throughout the US South, and when paired with imbibing alcohol and dancing, had a predictably cathartic effect upon a much downtrodden people.

Thus, some drivers compel experience by manipulating the internal biorhythms of the body, while others (like fasting and purging) manipulate metabolism. Hot steam produced in sweat lodge ceremonies operates directly on the dynamics of the body's autonomic system. Even systematic, excruciating pain applied during ritual ordeals like the Sun Dance has the predictable effect of producing visions in ASCs—that is the goal and the point of these ritual ordeals. (Intentional torture, in contrast, has no goal beyond the infliction of pain to obtain information or simply to cause intense suffering.) Orchestrating a balance among the use and organization of ritual drivers and other more cognitive materials like symbolically rich stories and lore can act to guide participants into, through, and out of a predictable and profoundly mind-altering experience.

Summary: SOCS, WOCS, and Ritual Drivers

Rhythmic drivers, used repetitively, are core elements of the anatomy, or characteristics, of ritual. There are many different types of drivers, and they share important roles in producing warps of consciousness (WOCs) that can lead to altered states of consciousness (ASCs). A central feature of both intrinsic and extrinsic drivers is their ability to produce coherent, highly synchronized neural activities in various areas and levels of the brain. Cultures differ in the importance they give to this alteration of consciousness, ranging from polyphasic cultures that recognize, experience, and endorse many states of consciousness (SOCs)—such as dreaming and ASCs, to sensate, monophasic cultures that only value the normal waking state of consciousness. In polyphasic (ideational, idealistic) cultures, people are developmentally prepared to take advantage of WOCs and the experiences of multiple realities they can produce. Certain members of these cultures have developed ways to ritually control the warps that alter consciousness and enhance information transfer back to normal, waking consciousness. Such experiences can instantiate a people's cycle of meaning, can enhance social cohesion and health by establishing connections between the conscious mind and the usually unconscious processes of the lower brain systems, and can also produce life-altering and life-enhancing ways of thinking and being. Taking full advantage of SOCs and WOCs remains an option for individuals living in sensate, technocratic societies to employ the power of ritual toward individual and group psychological and psychic development—and perhaps, in time, for cultural and societal evolution toward more humanistic and holistic, and ideational and polyphasic, ways of thinking and living, which, again, will become essential if we are to stop the sensate, monophasic behaviors that are generating the Climate Crisis and move toward a polyphasic "Gaia consciousness." This kind of consciousness must include Indigenous ideas of *planetary health*, which focus on the harmonious interconnections of the planet, the environment, and human beings.[1]

Note

1. See https://www.planetaryhealthalliance.org/planetary-health.

Chapter 5

RITUAL TECHNIQUES AND TECHNOLOGIES

You are now almost halfway through this book (if you have been reading the chapters in sequence). At this point, we wish to remind you of our definition of a "ritual" as *a patterned, repetitive, and symbolic enactment of cultural (or individual) beliefs and values.* We also wish to remind you of what we consider to be the eight primary characteristics of ritual—*the anatomy of ritual*—that the chapters you have been reading have addressed. Again, they include:

1. the use of symbols to convey a ritual's messages;
2. a cognitive matrix (belief system) from which ritual emerges;
3. rhythm, repetition, and redundancy: ritual drivers;
4. the use of tools, techniques, and technologies to accomplish ritual's multiple goals;
5. the framing of ritual performances;
6. the order and formality that separates ritual from everyday life, identifying it *as ritual;*
7. the sense of inviolability and inevitability that rituals can generate;
8. the acting, stylization, and staging that often give ritual its elements of high drama, the fact that it is *performed* and that it often intensifies toward a climax.

Just to keep everything in context, we note to you here that this particular chapter focuses on characteristic #4: ritual's use of techniques and technologies to accomplish its multiple goals, including its instrumental ones—the goals of achieving specific, often dramatic, effects and results in people's lives.

Ritual Technique and Technology: Divination and Intent

Ritual often operates as a kind of technology (Wallace 1966: 71). People carry out rituals not just to do things in a traditional fashion or to express symbolic meanings. Ritual has utility *utility* and *instrumentality*—which means getting things done in the world, as well as providing the means to do so.

For instance, people often perform rituals that are designed to obtain information. They may carry out a *divination* in order to find out where they are likely to find game to hunt, when the rains will fall, if their enemies might attack in the near future, to discover something that happened in the past—such as who committed a crime or perhaps what event in childhood might have produced the illness a patient is suffering from today. People also perform rituals and rites with the intent of increasing the quantity of game animals or the crop yield; to exorcize evil spirits that might be causing problems for living people; to make the rains come or stop—as Don Lucio, a Mexican shaman and weather-worker with whom Robbie had worked—often did (see Preface.)

In fact, after Robbie and her then-husband Robert went through Don Lucio's elaborate initiation process, he trained them in weather-working rituals. When, back at home in Austin, Texas, they tried out these ritual techniques to stop a major storm, they worked so well that Robbie and Robert "freaked out"—they did not wish to carry the burden of such responsibility, so they never did it again. This often happens to anthropologists who learn such techniques as part of their ethnographic research, yet refuse to use them precisely because they do not wish to carry this burden of responsibility. Here we celebrate the courage and fortitude of those who do and simply mention this weather-working as an example of how ritual can in fact have efficacy and instrumentality in the world, including affecting the weather.

The primary shaman of the Mescalero Apaches in the US Southwest, a man named Bernard (now deceased), also had this power to stop or start the rain—and to call down thunder and lightning—as described to Robbie by Claire (Ginger) Farrer (personal communication, 2011, now also deceased), who lived with and studied the Mescalero for many years (see Farrer 1991, 2010) and often witnessed Bernard doing these things. Yet she never published this information for fear of being thought "nuts" by sensate scholars—although many other anthropologists have experienced similar polyphasic events. A BBC crew actually filmed Bernard calling down thunder and lightning out of a clear blue sky, then realized they could not use the film because people would think they had altered it. In general, people living in sensate cultures do not tend to believe evidence from ideational cultures like the Mescalero, who—at least during the time of Farrer's fieldwork (the 1970s and 1980s)—lived in a polyphasic world where their cycle of meaning was constantly instantiated in their everyday lives.

Rituals of Divination: The Purloined Pots

An occasion during Charlie's time with the So illustrates how a divination ritual can discover important information. As mentioned in Chapter 1, when Charlie and his family arrived among the So in East Africa, his hosts were experiencing a serious drought, and food resources were very scarce for a period of some months. Charlie and his wife Elizabeth ended up feeding all the children who needed food on a daily basis. Every midday, they prepared huge pots of porridge for any children and pregnant women who showed up. But one morning, they discovered that the gigantic aluminum pots that they used to make the porridge, and that would be nearly impossible to replace, had been stolen. Searches by Charlie and his So friends came to naught.

Finally, one of Charlie's So friends suggested that a famous Turkana (a tribe of people who live in Kenya, to the east of the So) diviner, who happened to be visiting relatives living on the mountain, could be consulted to find out where the pots might be. Having no confidence whatever in divination, but delighted at the prospect of watching a diviner "do his thing," Charlie consented. The next day at the appointed time, a wizened old man came to Charlie's compound and commenced throwing his sandals on the ground over and over and reading the patterns they made in the dirt. Finally he stated the obvious: the pots had indeed been stolen. All those present agreed that this was the case. Then he threw the sandals some more and said that the pots were no longer on the mountain. More sandal tossing, and then the old man said that the pots were now located outside the house of someone in a particular neighborhood in the town of Moroto, the district capital at the base of Moroto Mountain where the So live. "Now that's more like it!" thought Charlie, and he gave the old man his fee and thanked him profusely for having taken the trouble to help the So children in their plight.

Charlie gathered some of his young warrior friends into the Land Rover, drove to the specified neighborhood, and within minutes spotted the purloined pots stacked on the side of a hut in the village. When told that the pots had been stolen, the woman of the house said that she had bought them in good faith from two young So men. Charlie compensated her for the money she had spent and returned to So with the pots just in time to prepare the porridge for the hungry kids. The information gleaned from the divination had proven to be both accurate and very fruitful.

Of course, the interesting question is how the ritual specialist—the Turkana diviner—had known just where the pots were located. Did he read their whereabouts in the patterns made by the sandals, kind of like reading tea leaves? Or did he have prior knowledge about the theft of the pots, or just a good hunch as to who had stolen them and who had bought them? We will return to this question later on, for it suggests some interesting aspects of *ritual as technology*—as anthropologist Anthony Wallace noted (1966: 108), there is likely no society on Earth, including modern urban society, in which some people do not practice divination. People in even sensate, monophasic societies flip coins to make decisions and consult palm and Tarot readers to find out about the future. But first we want to provide clarity on what ritual techniques are and in what ways ritual can operate as technology.

Ritual Techniques and Technologies

Ritual is a form of symbolically rich technique that frequently incorporates technologies to effect its goals—for example, the alleviation of suffering (healing rituals that include the use of herbs); the accessing of divine power and guidance (rituals of invocation and divination using sandals, dice, tea leaves, Tarot cards, or other "random event generators"); reinforcing group identity (patriotic ceremonies using flags, icons, and regalia); or the acknowledgment of a new social status such as gang initiation—a rite of passage that often includes going through an intense hazing process, getting a tattoo, and committing a crime. The techniques of the ritual specialist may be augmented by physical objects, such as the instrument that engraves the tattoo, just as the technique of the artisan is extended by the use of chisels or looms. In cases of illness, the healer perceives the patient through the medium of the technology—in traditional cultures, smudging, rattling, making sand paintings; in high-tech hospitals, x-rays, EEG printouts, vital sign monitors, CT and PET scans, and EFMs (electronic fetal monitors). In modern technomedical hospitals, the patient may experience alienation when the medical specialists appear to be more oriented toward the information on computer screens than upon the patient as a person.

The technical augmentation of human abilities may apply at the group level. Let us return to the example of the Navajo healing ritual that we introduced in the preceding chapter. What we did not mention there is that a traditional healing ceremony (a "sing") can only be held either inside or around a traditional Navajo house called a "hogan"—a five-sided, eight-sided, or round hut made of wood, mud, rocks, or more recently, brick or concrete. Today, a majority of Navajo people no longer actually live in hogans, but rather in more modern styles of buildings like ranch-style houses, row houses, and mobile homes. Yet a healer will not consider holding a "sing" unless the family sponsoring the event owns or builds a hogan, because the myths and other texts that stipulate the techniques for symbolic healing also stipulate that it must be performed in a hogan constructed in the proper way.

All of the different Navajo ceremonies, or "sings," are applied when the balance, the state of *hozho*/beauty, is disrupted. Central to many of these healing sings is a point during which an ill person is placed in the middle of a mandala, called "dry paintings" by the Navajo and "sand paintings" by others, which symbolically represents the return of the patient to a state of beauty and balance. The "sand painting" is meticulously drawn using different colored ground rocks, not sand, on the floor of a hogan. The hogan is built with its one entrance pointed East, the direction that Changing Woman comes from—all mandalas in Navajo sand paintings likewise are open toward the east. The sand painting is oriented correctly vis-à-vis the hogan, and the hogan is oriented within the sacred homeland of the Navajo, demarcated by the four sacred mountains. Thus the hogan is correctly oriented to the cosmos. By placing the patient in the middle of the mandala, which is in the middle of the hogan, which in turn is, for the patient, the center of the cosmos, beauty—the natural state of being—is symbolically accomplished.

Also, when people enter the hogan for ceremonial activities during the sing, they sit along the walls according to their gender, age, and status. Thus, people become arranged properly relative to each other, relative to the sand painting and the ill person lying on it, relative to the hogan, which is relative to the homeland, and is ultimately relative to the entire cosmos— all of this simply because of the physical structure of the hogan. So you can see that the traditional hogan provides for the Navajo a kind of ritual technology with great cosmological significance and efficacy in organizing social relations, activities, and symbolism during a sacred ceremony.

In this way, the hogan is no different, say, than the synagogue is for Jews, the mosque for Muslims, and the church or cathedral for Christians. All are architectural forms of ritual technology. Within these edifices, people move and relate to each other in highly formalized and socially meaningful ways that reveal much about the social processes being expressed in the rituals that occur therein.

Ritual Reinforces an Instrumental Lifeworld

Virtually all rituals involve technique and technology. And the techniques and technologies thereby employed influence each participant's lifeworld. But just how these are conceived to cause things to happen will vary significantly, depending upon the worldview of the culture in question. People living in sensate/monophasic cultures may interpret causation in materialistic ways, while people living in ideational/polyphasic cultures may see causation in mystical terms.

Let us return for a moment to the mysterious case of the Turkana diviner and the purloined pots described above. We ended the story by mentioning that the real question was, how are we to interpret the fact that the old diviner appeared to know exactly where to find the pots? There are at least three explanations that have been put forward to account for this kind of phenomenon:

1. *Prior knowledge.* The diviner anticipates the question that will be asked and quietly obtains the requisite knowledge through social networking. They then present the knowledge during the ritual divination, thus powerfully reinforcing cultural belief in the efficacy of divination. This anticipation would have the advantage in some cases of the knowledge becoming public in a ritual situation in which none of the diviner's informants could be blamed or negatively sanctioned.

2. *Divine inspiration.* The diviner uses "random event generator" techniques, like throwing sandals, bones, dice, stirring tea leaves, shuffling a deck of cards, and so forth, to invite the intercession of the spirits or the gods in answering the question through divine inspiration. The answer is read in the pattern produced by the random event generator. A genuine diviner lineage will likely transmit a system of interpretation of patterns from master to apprentice. In this sense, the diviner is acting as a medium between the mundane world of everyday life and the divine realm (Rock, Thorsteinsson, and Tressoldi 2014). The divine will is read in the patterns produced by the actions of the diviner.

3. *A vehicle for psychic powers or magical causation.* The diviner is someone who has a special gift. They are able to access information through noncausal links to events distant in time and space. The information comes in a dream, vision, or intuition that may or may not be projected by the diviner upon the patterns made by a random event generator. In other words, the diviner appears to "read" the information in the patterns made by the sandals, but is actually projecting information gleaned through more subtle psychic powers.

Ritual and Prior Knowledge

If you are like most people reading this book, you were raised in a sensate culture and will likely be inclined toward the first explanation—that the diviner had known what he was going to be asked and had prior knowledge gleaned from gossip going around the day before. But actually, we have no way of knowing how the old man came by his information, and if we assume the prior knowledge scenario, we would be guilty of projecting our own cultural views on a very alien (to us) situation.

We do know of other situations in which prior or consensual knowledge becomes publicly available and then apparently justified in ritual. Take for example the ritual use of masks in West Africa. Among some of the peoples living in Liberia, political control was long publicly held by a group of chiefs and a council of elder males (Harley 1950). But their real power at that time rested in the fact they were members of the *poro* secret society, which every young man had to join at puberty. The *poro* society in turn was controlled by a hierarchy of elders. When the very most important elders died, the society had highly stylized death masks carved for them from wood. These allowed the dead members to continue as though they were still attending society functions and could be addressed through the medium of the mask when being appealed to for intercession with the ancestors.

Also, judges in these societies sat masked and robed, and spoke in falsetto voices so they could remain publicly anonymous. The mask was a technological artifact that represented the face of a great forest demon. Some chiefs had a mask of the forest spirits that was handed down with the office. When important issues were raised, the chief and elders met in the forest at night and discussed the issue thoroughly. Then they brought out the mask and reviewed the issue for the mask/spirit. Addressing the mask, they would say something like: "If the cowrie shells we toss fall up, you agree with us, if they fall down, you disagree." Four shells were then thrown, and the decision of the mask spirit was supposed to be final and binding. (It was well known, however, that some chiefs learned to manipulate the shells so they would always fall the way they wanted them to.)

It is not too much of an exaggeration to say that ritual technologies and techniques such as consulting spirits through the medium of masks (consulting is the technique, the mask is the technology) are open to all sorts of influences. At least in some cases, as Scott Atran (2002) has shown, the outcome of the consultation puts the stamp of divine approval upon the decisions made in very worldly councils. The decisions and actions of those in power are perceived to be in sync with the wills of the ancestors, spirits, and gods. In a sense, these kinds of divinatory rituals are a sort of ritual theater for acting out upon a public stage the proper relations and functions generally expected of leaders. So from this point of view, the old Turkana diviner may have given voice to commonly shared knowledge, but in a forum in which no one could accuse anyone of snitching.

Ritual as Divine Inspiration

But what of the alternative explanations for the old Turkana's divination? In order to comprehend how people might use a "random event generator" like sandal-tossing to divine important information, we have to note that for many people, "random chance" has no real meaning in their lifeworlds. Rather, "chance" is a term we in the contemporary technocracy apply to outcomes and decisions that more traditionally oriented peoples would consider as having been made by supernatural forces. If we flip a coin to resolve some indecision, Western science would tell us we are randomizing the outcome—that is, there is an equal chance that one outcome (represented by "heads") will happen over the alternative outcome ("tails"). But for many, to toss a coin is to invite divine intervention—to ask the spirit realm or the universe to make the decision for us.

To build a chance element into a game, for instance, is for most people not a simple matter of removing rational strategy from the game, but actually inviting decisions to be made by the spirits. In other words, games of strategy like chess and games of chance like poker or dice could be just two different modes of assigning the locus of decision-making. In a game of strategy, the outcome is determined by our own skill in planning moves, but in a game of "chance," we are giving up the decision-making "to the gods," to God, to "fate," or to "the universe." Actually, we members of sensate cultures are not that distant from this kind of attribution. How many gamblers carry a "lucky" piece with them when they go to the casino, how many Catholics cross themselves when facing a potentially dangerous situation?

Games of chance in some traditional societies are actually played as divining rituals, and their members pay close attention to the outcome for signs of important divine intervention. Random event generators like cards and dice, sandals and bones are often ritual technologies used to invite divine intervention into problems and decision-making. There is certainly an element of this kind of invitation when some of us consult a Tarot card reader in order to clear up conflicts and ambiguities in our lives. A serious Tarot reader is intentionally using the cards to invoke the divine realm in informing the clients about their questions and uncertainties.

Thus, ritual technologies may operate as random event generators that may be perceived to remove ambiguity and uncertainty by inviting information and decision-making from divine beings or mysterious forces. Ritual technologies can be used both as ways of randomizing the outcomes and as means for getting things done—reaching a decision or divining the will of the divine beings that are perceived to be the "real" power behind events.

Ritual as a Technique for Enhancing Psychic Power: Magical Causation

The two above explanations of the old Turkana's divinatory skill are more acceptable to the Western sensate mind than is the final alternative—that ritual technologies such as sandals and Tarot cards are vehicles for application of psychic powers and "magical causation." And yet there are many cultures that hold this kind of dynamic as not only possible but also as primary. All of the meditation systems of the East—Hindu yoga, Theravaden Buddhism, Tibetan Tantric Buddhism, and more—recognize the arising of psychic powers as a byproduct of spiritual practices aided by using techniques and technologies such as elaborate sand paintings portraying mandalas, or the rice bowl and mirror Charlie used to construct his mandalas those 100,000 times. Australian Aborigines say that in the dreaming state, their ritual techniques allow them to fly to places and do things at a distance.

From this perspective, with respect to ritual's potential enhancement of psychic powers and "magical" thinking, the old Turkana diviner might have been "remotely viewing" the purloined pots, giving voice to an internal image or intuition that he received while staring at the sandals. We simply do not know, for we do not have the data to decide among the three possible explanations we outlined above. The lesson for us is that from the traditional cultural point of view, the first explanation—prior knowledge—does not exhaust the possibilities, and that we have to be sensitive to the biases built into our own sensate cultural conditioning when trying to understand the full extent of the multiple possibilities inherent in ritual, including those of enhancing psychic power and magical causation.

For most of us living in sensate, monophasic cultures, the problem we have with this view of magical causation is that it is outside of our lifeworlds. We are taught in our culture and in our schools that in order to cause something to happen, there must be some mechanical connection between the causal event and the caused event, like one billiard ball striking another and causing the second ball to move. The idea that the first billiard ball could cause the second billiard ball to move without ever touching it—so-called *causation-at-a-distance*, or *magical causation*—is alien to our thinking.

And yet this very sort of thinking underlies many of the "magical" rites performed by traditional peoples, and is perhaps inherent in some of the ritual acts we experience in our own religious life. What else would one call the act of transubstantiation of the bread and the wine into the body and blood of Christ in the Eucharist but magic? Christians today would tend to eschew the term "magic" and speak perhaps of "divine intervention," but Christians living in the Middle Ages would have found no problem using the term "magic," for their cosmology was very different from ours today (see Huizinga [1919] 1996).

Although there is no scientific evidence showing that prayer—a type of magical causation—works, many individuals do experience that their prayers are answered. And certainly, prayers do work for those who pray; according to Phil Zuckerman (2019: 1):

> Prayer can be a solid source of self-soothing and self-comfort when one is experiencing pain, coping with loss, or dealing with traumatic circumstances. Prayer can also be of benefit as a form of concentrated mental motivation for achieving personal goals. Prayer can also help people focus on the well-being of others. And, of course, when one finds oneself in a hopeless or helpless situation, with no real options, no clear solution, and no actionable form of alleviation, then prayer is something to engage in to—at the very least—make one feel like one is doing at least *something* in the face of dire circumstances. Clearly, people pray because it makes them feel better, or makes them feel hope, or makes them feel love, or makes them feel just a welcomed hair shy of being utterly powerless. So, concerning all of the above, it can be said that prayer works [for the people who are praying].

Robbie suggests that well-meaning prayers are a way of sending "positive energy"—they may work or they may not, yet they do no harm, and, as noted in the quote above, they provide a way for individuals to try, in ritual fashion, to make a positive difference. So, every time Robbie hears the sirens of an ambulance or a fire truck, she prays for the people for whom those vehicles are rolling. It's the only thing she can do; it might help or it might not. But at least she is feeling and sending compassion, caring, and love, and that act produces endorphins in Robbie's body, so at the very least, her prayers for others are helping her! She is very aware that her prayers for others are selfish in this very personal sense, in spite of the fact that she is trying to act selflessly. Sending positive energy in whatever form can never do harm, and might just possibly be of help.

In similar fashion, if a baby is born and does not immediately breathe, many midwives will start neonatal resuscitation (in which all midwives are thoroughly trained) while at the same time asking the parents to "call the baby" as part of their repertoire of ritualized techniques to get the baby to breathe. Their underlying belief in doing so—its "thick" description—is that the spirit or soul of the baby might be hesitant to come into the world and need encouragement to make that decision. Certainly, "calling the baby" does no harm and has the positive effect of empowering the parents to play a role in this life-or-death situation. And, if in fact the spirit does exist and is hesitating, it might respond to the call. Many midwives and some neonatologists have experiences in which the baby begins to breathe as soon as the parents call their baby; thus "calling the baby" has been incorporated as an instrumental neonatal resuscitation technique into many midwifery training programs—but not into neonatology or pediatric programs, as sensate physicians generally have little room in their worldviews for something as mystical and abstract as "spirit" or "soul."

Ritual Instrumentality: Spooky Causation in Modern Science

To further understand notions of ritual instrumentality and causation, we need to reflect upon developments in quantum physics, which incorporates really "spooky" causation as well. There is, for example, a phenomenon called "the Einstein, Podolsky, Rosen effect" (aka "the EPR system"). In a 1935 thought experiment, these three famous physicists modeled that once two parts or particles of a quantum system are separated, they remain connected and continue to act as a correlated unity no matter how far they travel from each other. EPR-type systems also confound commonsense notions of local causation, for there exists no clear mechanism by which the two parts can "interact" at a distance. Since that time, numerous experiments have upheld the EPR effect and have thus disconfirmed to some extent the "local" causation assumptions of the more commonsense and classical Newtonian view (Selleri 1988).

Robbie's Spooky Quantum Physics Story: Peyton, the Dallas-Ft. Worth Airport, and a Spontaneous Ritual Performance

This "spooky" quantum physics conclusion—that two particles, once interlinked and then separated in space and time, remain connected and continue to act as a correlated entity (meaning, for example, that if one particle changes its spin, the other will too)—had profound meaning for Robbie after the 2000 death (by car accident) of her 20-year-old daughter Peyton. (For a full description of Robbie's experience of her daughter's death, see Davis-Floyd 2003b.) Robbie describes:

> Three months after Peyton's death, I found myself walking the long corridors in the Dallas-Ft. Worth airport on my way to make my flight connection to Brazil, in a daze and sobbing. Suddenly, Peyton showed up in front of me, wearing a pair of blue-jean cutoffs and a blue halter top that I knew well, and walking backwards facing me. Laughing her head off, Peyton said, "Mom, you are sooooo not getting this!" Pointing at me and then at herself and back and forth, then making a circle with her fingers and holding one finger up, she said "Mom, I want you to repeat after me: I am you and you are me and we are One!" So, following her lead, I walked those long airport corridors facing

Peyton, making the same hand gestures, and repeating aloud in wonder, "I am you and you are me and we are One."

Of course I got weird looks from the people around me, and of course my rational mind was racing like crazy: "No P-Pey, we are NOT One. I gave birth to you, I raised you, yet you were so much more than I ever could be—I am not you and you are not me, you are your own very special, very separate self!" while at the same time, my rational mind was also thinking, "Yet quantum physics says that if two interlinked particles are separated in time and space, a change in the spin of one can effect the same change in the spin of the other … so maybe it's possible …"

And while this dialogue between me and myself is going on in my head, Peyton is still laughing and insisting that I continue to make those back-and-forth pointing hand movements and continue to repeat, "I am you and you are me and we are One." All the way to the gate—a very long way. And when I arrived at the gate, she, still grinning, vanished.

I was assigned a bulkhead seat, with plenty of room in front of me. After the plane took off, Peyton showed up again, still smiling, and made me do the hand gestures and the words four more times, and then, slanting her hand horizontally, she made a circle with her thumb and forefinger, with the other fingers splayed out, and held it out in front of her, then moved it to her heart.

I knew that Peyton had been fluent in American Sign Language (ASL)— she had volunteered at the Austin School for the Deaf—so I figured that last gesture was some kind of "sign"—and so, trusting, I just waited to find out its meaning. Months later, I received an invitation in the mail to a dinner for bereaved parents hosted by our marvelous local counseling group, called "For the Love of Christi." Well, I received those invitations every month and usually tossed them, but this particular one was *glowing*. I could barely let it out of my hands for long enough to tape it onto the fridge.

Of course, this time I accepted the invitation and attended the dinner. Scanning the room, I saw a group of people signing to each other with a translator, who was also clearly hearing. Tentatively, I approached, and found the courage to show the sign P had made to the translator and to ask him what it meant? He said with a huge smile that the sign was shorthand for "spirit," and that when she held it to her heart, she was saying "My spirit lives in your heart!" (He also showed me the longhand sign for "spirit," which involves more movement.)

I could not speak. Instead, I found a place to sit down, and simply sobbed from the intense feelings of both sorrow and joy that I was experiencing. My daughter was dead, and yet she was alive in some way and had communicated with me with the goal of teaching/showing me that her spirit lives in my heart!

At the time, if anyone had suggested to me that this vision, this marvelous Peyton apparition in the DFW airport, might be simply the product of my own imagination, my psychic longing for my dead daughter to be alive and in my presence again, I would have gotten furious. For me at that time, only three months after her death, seeing her in that airport was absolute proof positive that her spirit was still alive and well somewhere, somehow. I *needed* to believe that in order to survive.

Now, over 20 years after her death, I can admit the possibility that perhaps I simply manifested her to myself to fulfill my then-desperate need to see her once again. Yet, says my rational mind, I don't know ASL and never have, so how could I possibly have imagined the sign for "spirit"? I know that I could never have imagined that sign—yet I also know that occasionally I dream in other languages that seem very real in my dreams. I fly in my dreams some-times. I live whole novels that I never could actually write—spy stories, action adventures, romances, historical novels—I dream them all in vivid detail. So could I have tapped some deep knowledge in myself to come up with those "visions" of Peyton in the airport, including the ASL sign—gifts from myself to myself? Or did/does her spirit actually live and manifest itself to me?

I *choose to believe* that Peyton's spirit does live, and did choose to show up for her grieving mother (as she has on other occasions, too many to recount in this book). My point here is that *belief follows emotion*. We generally do not intellectually choose our beliefs; rather, we tend to believe what we emotion-ally experience as "true." I, very emotionally, experienced Peyton's spirit as true and real, and I'm just like the rest of us—*my beliefs follow my emotions*. So I believe that she is alive and well and happy, dancing around the universe as she danced so excellently in life. I really have no choice—my sorrow would be greater if I could not believe that she is still alive somewhere, somehow, in some form.

Isn't that a lot like what religion and ritual are all about? We humans need to make sense of our suffering—we need to believe that the bad things that happen to us happen for good reasons. And the rituals that ritual designers (which any of us can become) create can show all the rest of us that they do—our rituals can vivify for us that life has meaning even in death.

Perhaps now you will understand why I have so much passion for under-standing ritual and explaining this human cultural universal to others as Charlie and I seek to do in this book. Although sometimes ritual performance and ensuing belief have cost me dearly (e.g., when I was a participant in a cult—see Chapter 7), different kinds of ritual performance and ensuing belief in the cycle of meaning I created for myself around Peyton's death did finally enable me to heal, as I show in the Preface to this volume.

I affirm that even spontaneous rituals that happen in sudden, unexpected visions of dead loved ones (like the hand ritual that Peyton made me do throughout that long airport walk, and like the EMDR healing I experienced at Sierra Tucson nine years later—see Chapter 7) can be extremely instrumen-tal for healing!

Taking a deep breath, we now return to our point about "spooky causa-tion" in modern science—Robbie's section above is intended to serve as an example of how the same intuitions pop up in quantum physics as well as in traditional ideas of causal relations.

The Technologies of Ritual Practice as Dependent on Context

All human cultures are technological to some extent, whether they make their living by hunting and gathering, by growing crops, by fishing, or by working in factories and offices. The techniques and technologies people bring to bear in solving problems and getting things done are integral to the ways they experience and interpret their lifeworlds—to their cycles of meaning. Thus far we have emphasized rituals as techniques for getting things done. Yet we also need to pay some attention to rituals as *contexts* for the use of technologies.

We have already given numerous examples of the uses of ritual technologies, showing how sandals, masks, mirrors, a wheelchair, an IV drip, the electronic fetal monitor, a flag, a cross, a stalk of corn, a person dressed as Darth Vader, can all act as ritual technologies *within their ritual contexts.* Navajo sand painting, prayer sticks, rattles, and other ritual paraphernalia gain their significance within both the physical relations of the hogan and from the hogan outward to the sacred homeland and thence to the cosmos. Yet outside of their ritual contexts, a stalk of corn is just for eating, prayer sticks can just be mildly interesting museum artifacts, and the EFM is just a machine without the symbolic meanings attached to it within its ritual context—the hospital room containing the laboring woman, her partner, and her care providers.

Despite evidence of the importance of context for the effective use of modern medicines—much of this evidence includes the importance of the "placebo" effect—medical practice today downplays this crucial ritual aspect to healing (but see Benedetti 2008). Situating medicines and other ritual technologies within an appropriate ritual context is all-important for maximizing their effects regarding healing and other purposes. Nevertheless, most contemporary physicians choose to ignore the shamanic role that many patients wish to impute to them—they would never think, for example, of asking the parents to "call the baby" as they start resuscitation—and reject out-of-hand the conscious and deliberate performance of non-medical, shamanic healing rituals such as chants or prayers, choosing to rely on the (unconsciously ritualistic) performance of medical procedures instead.

And yet, when a renowned traditional Mexican midwife and healer, Doña Enriqueta (Queta) Contreras, came to Austin to conduct a healing retreat at the request of Mexican-Americans who wanted to "get in touch with their roots," she was also allowed to perform healing ceremonies in the rooms of some hospital patients, who then rapidly got well. Was that just coincidence, or was it magical causation? Or was it that Doña Queta and those patients lived within the same cycle of meaning, so that the healing rituals she performed easily penetrated their brain strata, mapping the symbols in the rituals onto their psyches and thereby entraining their neuronal networks to effect healing? Certainly, Doña Queta transformed the hospital rooms into ritual contexts for her type of healing via the power of her presence (she is extremely charismatic), and via the techniques and technologies of the ancient ritual practice of smudging with slow-burning sage. This practice is believed by Doña Queta and her patients—and many others, even in sensate societies—to ritually cleanse and purify both the atmosphere of the room and the bodies within it.[1]

Thus, as we have shown, the context in which we encounter any ritual implement will certainly influence how the object works on us. A cross viewed in the midst of a Mass has a different impact than a cross worn around a friend's neck or a cross brandished to protect herself by the heroine of a vampire movie. Context always conditions both perception and interpretation and hence is always a factor in the practitioner's instrumentality. A mirror used to evoke the mandala offering in Tibetan meditation does not carry the same meaning as when that same mirror is used to shave with or to apply lipstick, because the context is different. A mask may be viewed as merely a prop in a theater production or as the physical dwelling place of a powerful spirit. And how one views the mask will condition how one treats it and uses it. There are Northwest Coast Indian masks in the collection of the Canadian Museum of Civilization that are still considered by First Nations peoples to be repositories of powerful spirits. Every once in a while, a contingent of shamans visits the collection to ritually "feed" the masks—ritual technologies, like prayer sticks, that most visitors to the museum think of as only physical objects to be seen and then ignored.

Often the technologies used in rituals (such as burning sage) have actual physical properties that are part of their overall utility. Mirrors do indeed reflect light and allow you to see your face. The stethoscope is not only a medical icon/symbol, it actually lets the physician hear the sounds of your heart. The electronic fetal monitor does record the mother's uterine contractions and the fetal heartbeat. The sandals used in divination can also be worn on the feet. Moreover, we know from the study of ethnobotany that many, if not most, of the herbs used by traditional shamans actually do have biochemical properties that prove efficacious—our readers can find hundreds of them on the shelves of Whole Foods and other such stores (bringing up more issues involving the exploitation of traditional peoples and their knowledge and resources than we can begin to address here). And of course, all the psychotropic plants and concoctions used by traditional peoples to alter the SOCs of ritual practitioners are known to have biochemically induced hallucinatory effects (see Schultes and Hofmann 1980; Devereux 2008).

A caveat: Much of the power of ritual implements has more to do with the features of their symbolic design than their inherent physical properties—a fact most clearly demonstrated in the use of art in ritual. Art can involve practical use—or as anthropologist Alfred Gell (1998) called it, "art as agency" can be used to get things done within specific ritual contexts. Gell pointed to the artistic technologies used by some peoples to influence the minds of other people, especially their trading partners or enemies. Gell (1992: 40–67) called this use of art the "technology of enchantment." Just as when putting a child to bed is made easier if "the bed in question has sheets and pillowcase richly embellished with space-ships, dinosaurs, or even polka dots, be they sufficiently jolly and attractive" (Gell 1992: 74), so too does the trading expedition tend to go better when one dazzles one's trading partner with magical symbolism at the very beginning. Thus the Trobriand Islanders of Melanesia in the South Pacific, who (to this day) go on lengthy, dangerous trading expeditions in huge ocean-going canoes, have intricate prow boards carved and painted with magical symbols so that the first thing their trading partners see coming over the horizon at them is a phalanx of beautiful, magical images that have the effect of demoralizing them and making them more compliant in the economic transactions to come.

In the same vein, 19th-century warriors from the Marquesan Islands in the Polynesian Archipelago used to decorate their bodies and shields with intricate and highly abstract symbolism designed to work on the psychology of their enemies. The intent was to directly cause lack of morale, loss of confidence, and confusion because of the magical significance of these dazzling motifs. In a certain sense, the Marquesan's intent was little different from that of the Scots regiments who went into battle during World War II to the haunting (and to their enemies, terrifying) strains of the bagpipe. Marquesan body tattoos and Scots bagpipes are examples of ritual "technologies of enchantment" designed to affect their enemies' mind-states. Even weapons may have this dazzling, psychological effect—for example, common knowledge in military history holds that the use of rocketry by the British during the Napoleonic Wars generally caused more terror in the enemy than actual physical destruction.

Hi-Tech and Virtual Rituals

It is clear from what we have said about instrumental realism that the invention of ever more complex technologies in our contemporary world must impact the nature of human interaction in general and ritual in particular. In our Introduction, we alluded to the remarkable effects that

Princess Diana's funeral and her son's wedding to Kate Middleton had upon millions of people who neither knew these royals personally nor were physically present in London for the events. Nevertheless, people viewing these events on their television, computer, or tablet screens all over the world likely had the sense of having participated in the ceremonies—of having in some way been "present" and "participating" in the ritual. And in a psychological sense, these people *were* present, for they were experiencing what we call a *virtual ritual* (see Kapferer 2004; Grimes et al. 2011). By "virtual ritual," we mean that most of the elements of ritual are operating in the experience of the participants, except for the intimacy of actual physical presence.

Examples of virtual rituals abound in modern life (see Goethals 2003; Wagner 2012; Grimes 2014). People become involved in and are influenced by such televised events as football, soccer, and ice hockey games, televangelist religious programs and church services, real life court cases, parliamentary and legislative debates, and more. People become even more interactive in ritual dramas on the internet when they participate in MUDs, blogs, and online real-time computer games (see Goethals 2003).

Hi-tech virtual rituals may be extremely effective, for much of the sensory experiences triggered by the images on the television, laptop, iPad, or smartphone are very close to the experiences we would have if physically present at the event. Because our technologies tend to withdraw from our awareness when they are working efficiently, what is left in our consciousness is the event—the ritual itself.

The more interactive the technology allows us to be, the more our illusory sense of reality is heightened. Viewing a televised sports event and listening to a concert broadcast over the radio are fairly passive activities. But on the internet, even these relatively passive virtual rituals can be intensified and instantiated by interactive websites. The sense of interaction with either real or virtual persons is crucial to the sense of virtual participation. We have all had the experience of talking with a distant loved one over the phone or via computer for so long that the virtual conversation slips into being very real. Indeed, we may call the loved one repeatedly in order to reinforce that sense of virtual closeness—especially nowadays when we are communicating via Skype, Zoom, or WhatsApp, and can actually see images of each other during our conversations. The more intimate the interaction over the phone or the computer, the greater the sense of shared relationship—understanding here that a conversation may range from being a formal exchange of information to actually making virtual love with each other (having "phone sex"). Intimate conversations via technological media amount to very simple virtual rituals—in this case, virtual rites of intensification.

Summary: Ritual Technique and Technology

All ritual is technique, and most rituals are also technologized—we experience them not just through activity but also through physical, technological objects. Modern rituals often involve high technology, and thus express the changes in a society's technology just as they enact changes in its members' core values. Modern electronics have even made "virtual" rituals possible. Video games provide an outlet for both conscious and unconscious feelings and proclivities, while at the same time conditioning players to an underlying set of rules of virtual behavior. The games make certain virtual technologies (swords, light sabers, healing potions, communications technologies) available to the player and exclude other alternative technologies, all the while limiting what players can do with these objects and what actions they can take while utilizing them. Just so with the old Turkana diviner and the purloined pots!

Note

1. Research has shown that burning sage—a healing practice that in some countries dates back thousands of years—removes 94 percent of bacteria from the air within a confined space, along with viruses, taking about an hour to work and often lasting for up to 30 days (see Nautiyal, Chauhan, and Nene 2007).

Chapter 6

RITUAL FRAMING, ORDER, AND FORMALITY
How Ritual Generates a Sense of Inevitability and Inviolability

Ritual Framing

Ritual framing constitutes a major part of the anatomy of ritual. On our ritual spectrum, formal rituals differ greatly from everyday ritualizations. One of formal ritual's primary characteristics is that it is framed—set apart from the realm of the everyday, in a special building, room, or specially marked space, and/or held at a special time. Order and formality intensify this sense of set-apartness, and are the dominant modes in this type of ritual. You know you are in the presence of formal ritual when things are no longer casual but precise, when order matters, when the feeling is formal—that is, when you have to start paying special attention to your body movements to be sure you are behaving appropriately, as in church or at a formal dinner ("formal" means "attention to form").

A formal dining room with the table fully set indicates that a highly elaborate dinner ritual is about to take place. The dining room, or the space around the dinner table in open floor plans, serves as a frame, setting this ritual apart from everyday life. The kitchen, by way of contrast, while often also a ritual space, is one of multiple functions—food is prepared there as well as eaten. So dinners at a kitchen table are culturally marked as more casual than dinners in a dining room—the frame is less clearly demarcated and the ritual is concomitantly more diffuse. We do not mean to imply that the boundaries of a ritual frame are always precise. What is critical to framing ritual is the intention to generate a sense of formality and thus an intensification of the ritual via the framing—for example, moving the questioning of crime suspects into an interrogation room instead of simply querying them on the street.

The significance of the ritual frame became most evident to Robbie while she was working in the early 1990s with the previously mentioned Mexican *curandero*, shaman, and weatherworker Don Lucio, who performed ceremonies every year in a grotto on the side of the volcano Iztaccihuatl to pray for a good harvest during planting time and to give thanks for the harvest after it was gathered in (*"to everything, there is a season"*). It bothered Don Lucio that there was no clear demarcation of the grotto from the open field in front of it because there was no clarity about where the ritual space ended and began. So he had his followers construct a wooden portal through which all had to pass to enter the special space—the grotto—which could now be defined as sacred because it had been formally separated from the world of the profane. On the field side of the portal, casual conversation and movement were appropriate. But a few inches away, on the grotto side of the portal, one had to stand up straight, keep one's eyes focused on the altar built into the side of the grotto, refrain from speaking to others, and do whatever the other participants in the ritual were doing—silently listen to Don Lucio pray and chant and do so along with him at the appropriate times. One's spatial relationship to the ritual frame, in other words, determined the kind of behavior that was appropriate.

Physical and Non-Physical Frames

Ritual frames can be physical or non-physical. Physical frames include such devices as church or temple sanctuaries, Navajo hogans, sacred caves or grottos like the one shown above, auditoriums, theaters, concert halls, stadiums, the garden patio adorned by the ivy-covered wedding arch, and so forth—and, for virtual rituals, the plastic frame around the TV or computer screen. Such architectural frames keep the ritual contained within a demarcated space and are symbolically loaded with expectations and rules for what kind of behavior is expected and appropriate in that particular space. These rules or expectations facilitate the work of ritual, as they predispose people entering those spaces to behave in ritually appropriate ways and thus to begin to enter the psychological mindset the ritual is constructed to generate. The mere act of entering an obviously ritualistic space can constitute a sort of ritual—once inside the frame, people will alter their behavior accordingly even if they do not plan to actually participate in a full-fledged ritual performance.

Imagine that you are sightseeing in a European or Mexican city and you decide to visit the local cathedral. As you walk up the steps, you start scanning the interior for signs that a service is in progress, so you can avoid disrupting it. Perhaps you cover, or uncover, your head, depending on the local rules and your self-identified gender. If there is a service in progress, you will probably enter to the side, and try to scan the interior as unobtrusively as possible. If there is no service, you likely will enter in the middle, so as to obtain the most complete view of the interior, and walk directly down the central aisle. But you will at the same time be scanning for people kneeling in prayer, and will respectfully keep your distance from them. Here you are encountering a smaller ritual frame.

A person kneeling in prayer inside a church, or even on the street, constitutes a *ritual microcosm*—the space immediately around the praying person, or people, is perceived by themselves and by others as sacred and inviolable, as is the ritual space created when someone kneels to propose marriage, even in a restaurant or on the street. People engaged in performing rituals, with or without technological accoutrements, often generate what Charlie and Robbie like to think of as *invisible lines of energy running around the space they inhabit*. Other people walking by will notice this non-physical ritual frame and will generally go out of their way to avoid breaking or violating it. Sacred icons, art, and altars can generate a similar kind of non-physical frame. In their presence, you keep a respectful distance, you do not touch the icon or altar, and you behave in relatively formalized ways until you move outside of the frame.

This sense of the sublime can arise anywhere, really—it does not require the physical presence of a sacred building (hogan, tipi, pyramid, church, mosque, temple, etc.), but only the sense of an aura—an energetic frame—around someone or some event, triggered by ritual elements. Suppose we go on a picnic and there is great merriment and boisterous fun going on while the table is set for the feast. Once all are seated, someone says, "Let us pray" and holds out their hands to their neighbors, a circle is formed, all play ceases, and everyone bows their heads while a prayer is recited. The ritual words and the forming of the circle are sufficient for many to have the sense of a holy event, a sacred space and time in which there are strict rules of behavior and attitude (Grimes 2007). In the Islamic world, daily activities cease with the call to prayer five times a day. The devout Muslim is expected to stop what he is doing, roll out his prayer rug, and do prostrations toward the sacred city of Mecca. The rugs may have woven into them sacred symbols, including portals of one sort or another. The call to prayer and the act of praying constitute a ritual and a frame within which the sense of the sublime may arise, depending upon the proficiency of the practitioner.

Theater history was made in 1972 when the famed British director Peter Brook took a troupe of his actors (including Helen Mirren and Yoshi Oida) on an adventure to sub-Saharan Africa (Heilpern 1999). Over the course of months and more than 8000 miles, the troupe set up shop in tiny villages and marketplaces. They would lay down a carpet in the village and do their performances upon it. They found that the villagers would sometimes insist upon doing their own performances, which were frequently more interesting than those of the professional actors. The only rule was that when one stepped onto the carpet, one had to act a part in the ongoing, unfolding play. The carpet became the ritual frame, and surprisingly, many of the African villagers, unfamiliar with European stage productions, nonetheless quickly got into the act. They seemed to intuit the notion of the carpet as a ritual space that required of them extraordinary psychology and action. On the carpet, you were in the play; off the carpet, you were not.

Ritual Frames: Energy and Power

Those who participate fully in a ritual, either within or outside of a physical frame, will often describe a sense of spiritual "power" that may surround and enter/penetrate them during the ritual. You may be wondering by now if we are speaking metaphorically about the "energy" generated by ritual, or if we think that energy is in some sense real. Quantum physicists will say that all physical objects are "peaks of coherence in the energy sea." In other words, all physical objects, all matter, are coalescences of energy—everything and everyone is energized out of the quantum sea. One of the implications of this view is that we humans are normally aware of only a tiny fraction of the energies that envelop us. Other animals are clearly able to perceive energies we are unable to. Just prior to an earthquake, animals on a farm or in a zoo may act strangely and exhibit agitation for no perceivable (to us humans) reason. Certain fish in the ocean perceive electromagnetic energies that humans cannot without the aid of technology. Sea turtles and many migratory birds sense electromagnetic forces we are only able to measure through technological means (such as compasses).

Thus far, we have been speaking of the "power of ritual" in the sense that rituals done properly can be extremely efficacious. But there is this other sense in which the term "power" is used by traditional peoples—the access to normally invisible, but perhaps real energies that may be tapped through ritual means, and that may be used for specific purposes.

Framing is essential to the efficacy of ritual because the energy that ritual generates (whether physical, psychological, psychic, or metaphorical) is much more palpable when it is contained within a defined space (see Driver

2006). And when ritual spaces are permanent, like churches, temples, and hogans, the energy of every ritual ever performed in that space lingers and can be sensed when one enters. Such places are thought of by the cultural groups who use them as *power spots, power centers,* or *power places.* As we have mentioned, simply entering such a place is often enough to generate a strong sense of ritual participation.

This pattern of perception and behavior has an ancient history, as Paul Devereux (1992, 1996, 2010) described. Devereux has traced the sacred landscape frame all over the planet and into very ancient times. Common to these many traditions seems to be recognition of power places as sources of spiritual energy and guidance. Thus shrines like the one on Mount Parnassus in Ancient Greece where the Oracle of Delphi (a real woman, replaced by another carefully selected by priests when the previous one died) gave her prophesies, and Stonehenge in ancient England were often constructed on these power sites. Fascinatingly, sometimes high on botanical plants or toxic fumes that rose from the earth in that sacred place, the Oracle was believed to enter into a trance in which she channeled the god Apollo to foretell the future.

Modern folks too are able to sense such power. Years ago, Robbie had the good fortune to visit a church in the small English village of Isleham where, she had learned, a number of her ancestors were buried. To her surprise, she discovered that they were buried not in the graveyard outside, but inside the church, in crypts on top of which rest their marble effigies. The earliest crypt is dated 1484. Standing alone inside the church, Robbie got goose-bumps thinking of the long and tenuous chain of life events that led over the centuries and across an ocean from their genes to her birth in 1951. Had they lived or died differently, she—and her children and her son's children—would not exist. And here she was, in the very church where these people had knelt in prayer, joined hands in marriage, and baptized their children—and who were now her ancestors. The energy traces of these ritual lives seemed to Robbie to "shimmer in the air" as she reached out to touch the cold marble of the stone effigies of her direct ancestors. Moved to her core, and wanting both to honor her sense of connection to these ancestors and to leave her own ritual trace to mingle with theirs in that sacred space, she lifted her arms and sang a hymn of praise.

Inside that ritual frame, this act seemed to make perfect sense; once outside, Robbie felt embarrassed and hoped no one had heard—*because behavior that is appropriate in a ritually framed space is generally not appropriate in the everyday world.* We tend to react negatively to preachers yelling their ritualistic words on the street corner or in the park, yet positively to a preacher standing at his podium in a church. What works within a ritual frame usually does not work outside of it.

As previously noted for a picnic prayer, physical ritual frames can be generated not only by the landscape and by technological artifacts, but also by human bodies. Have you ever stood or sat with others in a circle and clasped hands? When you did, you were participating in creating a ritual frame. People who often use this technique to create ritual frames are generally aware of the *power of framing*—in other words, of the energy generated and contained within the frame. If an individual has to leave the circle—break the frame—they will generally back out slowly and make sure to pull together the two hands of the other participants on either side until they clasp to minimize the "energy rupture." Members of various Wiccan communities often create sacred circles as part of their ritualizing. At the conclusion of the ritual, they will likely say "The circle is open but unbroken!" to indicate that although the ritual is over, the energy it generated will live on for its participants, forming threads of connection and continuity between each of them and the ritual they collectively performed.

The Meaning and Power of Shrines and Altars

The smaller the frame, the more focused and intense can be the energy generated by the ritual performed within it. Frames work like lenses in their capacity to focus attention and energies. Altars are particularly important ritual frames. Because they are small in size (compared to the church, the temple, or the rooms in which altars are constructed) and visually compelling, they are effective focal points for focusing energy around various phenomena, from religious icons to secular mementos. Many people create "shrines"—specific spaces in homes and other places that reflect and display their beliefs and values. These shrines are not necessarily religious foci, but spaces that are pregnant with meaning for the people who create them—shelves holding small statues and other artifacts and mementos sacred to them, a cabinet with souvenir spoon collections reflecting their travels, collections of family photographs on tables and pianos, various objects grouped together on mantelpieces, a wall full of framed diplomas and certificates. All such shrines, whether sacred or secular, draw the eye and trigger memories that enhance the meaning of the shrine.

Religious altars are a special category of shrine that have very special efficacy. Before his death, Don Julio (a *compadre* of Don Lucio) and his family lived in a village in central Mexico in a small house with one large room containing the family dining table, the double bed in which Don Julio and his wife slept, and the family living area with sofa and TV. At the far end of that room, near the door, was an altar that took up a whole wall of the room. The altar consisted of a large blue table covered with a flowered plastic tablecloth, on top of which rested statuettes of various Catholic saints, flickering candles in tall glass candle holders, dried flower arrangements, and paper cards depicting still other saints. In the middle of the table, toward the back, stood a tall wooden cross. On the wall above the table, and on either side of the cross, hung multiple pictures of Jesus, the Virgin of Guadalupe, and still more saints. Fresh flowers and baskets of bread as offerings adorned the lower part of the altar. If family members, or visitors, happened to pass within three feet of that altar, they had to kneel down and cross themselves before they could go on. The altar, in other words, defined the space around it as ritual frame in which certain behaviors were appropriate and others, like normal conversation, were not.

The power and utility of altars became evident to Robbie in February 1993. All day she felt out of sorts, as if something were missing or dreadfully wrong, but she couldn't put her finger on exactly what. Arriving home in the late afternoon, she happened to glance at the calendar on the fridge, and realized that it was February 7, the day on which, 20 years ago, her father had suddenly and unexpectedly died. Twenty years! (Regarding important anniversaries, we Westerners tend to think in terms of decades because of the structure of our numerical system.) Robbie was overwhelmed with a need to mark the occasion in some way. Without forethought, she moved about the house gathering up mementos of her father, Walter Gray Davis: two large photos of him riding his palomino stallion on the small ranch he had owned in Wyoming, his cowboy boots with the elaborate stitching and the silver inlay over the heels and toes, the scrapbook containing photos and newspaper articles describing his work as an independent oil operator in Wyoming in the 1950s and 1960s, the cocky green felt hat with the red feather he had so often worn when he served as ringmaster at horse shows in San Antonio, Texas, after his retirement from the oil business. Robbie found herself carefully arranging all these mementos on a table next to a wall, on which she hung the two large photos. She scrounged for candles, placed them, and lit them. Then she sat on the floor, stared at the altar, and sobbed for an hour, flooded with the memories of her father's strong presence, his wit, his characteristic East Texas accent ("Ah cain't hep it!"), his strong and steady arms around her on his stallion, Casanova, as they galloped like the wind when she was a small child, his anger over a boyfriend he didn't like when she was 16, his joy over her marriage at 19 to a man he did like, his untimely death when she was 23. After a while it almost seemed as if her father Walter were physically present with Robbie—she could see the tweed checks of his favorite jacket, feel its rough texture, smell his Old Spice aftershave, revel once again in the ruddiness of his cheeks and the twinkle in his grey-blue eyes.

When Robbie's children Peyton and Jason came home from school sometime later, they found Robbie sitting on the floor in front of her makeshift altar and smiling through her tears. She nestled them close and began to tell them stories of their grandfather, who had died long before they were born. She explained every artifact she had placed on the altar and its place and meaning in her father's life, so that her children could have some sense of the life and personality of the grandfather they had never known. And at the next school Costume Day—a ritual that allows participants to play with other identities—Jason chose to dress up as a cowboy, because that was the identity he had gleaned from the photos of his grandfather Walter on his stallion.

As this story makes clear, even simple, makeshift home altars can serve as powerful focal points or portals, helping us to focus energy and attention on the symbolic meaning of the artifacts we place upon them, and taking us into the world being symbolized. Thus, as Robbie experienced, altars can make the elements they represent a stronger part of everyday life, open lines of communication between dimensions, and help people achieve emotional catharsis around specific events. Through creating such sacred spaces in our homes, we demonstrate, honor, and more deeply align ourselves with what we consider to be some of the most important aspects of our families and ourselves. Look around your home: what altars have you created, and what do they mean to you?

In contrast, degree and award certificates hung in professional spaces (offices, restaurants) are generally placed there as symbols of the competence of the professional in question, not so much about the expression of values through ritual as about exhibition, showmanship, and proof of professionalism. Yet many professionals also choose to create small "altars" in their offices or cubicles displaying photos of family and friends as a way of interlinking their professional and private lives, and often also as a powerful reminder of why they are working so hard—for their loved ones.

For another take on altars, Buddhists in Thailand, Bali, and Myanmar believe that certain spirits can cause people travail if they are not given gifts and other ritual observances. Hence they will place a small temple or "spirit house" on their property, usually on a small pedestal, where the spirits can gather and be ritually "fed" with daily offerings, believing that this practice keeps the spirits from gathering in the person's restaurant, business, or home. Tourists visiting these countries often marvel at the beauty and intricacy of these spirit houses, while Buddhists will often pause to bow and pray to the spirits before entering the establishment. Robbie saw many such spirit houses during a visit to Bali, and was consistently impressed by the fresh flower petals that appeared on each one of them every morning (see Figure 6.1). Few Westerners would go to such daily trouble to honor the

Figure 6.1. Balinese spirit houses awaiting their morning decoration with flowers. © Robbie Davis-Floyd, 2018.

deceased! The ritual motif of *propitiation* (acting to evoke divine favor) is widespread across the world's cultures, where the forces of the spirit world are considered to be both dangerous and helpful, depending upon how they are approached and placated.

Formality, Order, and a Sense of Inviolability and Inevitability: Ritual's "Cranking Gears"

The Trobriand Islanders: Fishing, Canoes, and Cranking Gears

One of the first anthropologists to actually participate within the culture he was studying, Bronisław Malinowski, lived among the Trobriand Islanders for over a year and published some of his work in a book called *The Sexual Life of Savages* (1925)—a brilliant title, given that he was writing for a generally Victorian culture whose members could not officially deal with their own sexuality but who would be thrilled to read about "savages" who "obviously" had nothing to do with the august members of Victorian society, hence a book that provided free vicarious enjoyment and lots of book sales! Most of Malinowski's book was straightforward ethnography—how the

Trobriand Islanders lived, what they ate, their customs, rituals, economic exchange systems, and so on. Only one chapter—indeed a most lascivious one—dealt with their sexual customs. Much of his book in fact dealt with the Trobrianders' rituals in relation to obtaining food. He noted that the lagoon they enjoyed was placid and full of fish, albeit small ones, and they often put their small canoes into that lagoon, as the fishing was easy—yet the yield was always as small as the fish that lived there—enough to feed a family for a day or two.

Much greater rewards awaited in the deep ocean—huge fish that could feed a family for a week or more. Yet the dangers were significant—one large wave could collapse the small boat, and sharks were ever-present. So, how to gain the courage to fish in the deep, rewarding, yet dangerous and fearful ocean? The Trobriand ritual response was to create an altar on the beach containing symbolic artifacts, and then to chant the names of the gods in a particular sequence for an hour or so. This ritual action, at least in their minds, would ensure that the gods would respond by keeping them safe during their dangerous ventures. They could engage the gods with the ritual, thus (hopefully) binding them to respond.

Likewise, when the Trobrianders built those large ocean-going dugout canoes, knowing that sea voyages were very perilous (many such expeditions never returned), they performed an elaborate series of rituals during the construction of the canoes to make them impervious to calamity and protect those aboard. These ritual ingredients of construction were for them as utilitarian as the physical construction of the canoes, and each ritual had to occur in its proper sequence in order for it to protect the boat and its crew.

In other words, ritual technology can (be perceived to) have cosmological efficacy. These ritual technologies and performances served for the Trobrianders like cranking gears serve for machines—you set the little gear in motion with your careful ritual performance, and get the psychological and very comforting feeling that cranking the little gear will set a larger process in motion—you do your part, then the gods will be obliged to do theirs.

Bolivian Tin Miners and Danger: The Devil Is in the Details

Another excellent example of using ritual to generate a sense of inevitability comes from the work of anthropologist June Nash (1979, 1992), who studied Bolivian tin miners with the profound question, "How do you gain the courage to go down so deep into hot and potentially explosive mines every single working day?" The answer she discovered was that the miners conceived of the mines as the "Devil's territory," so they worked hard to make the Devil their friend. They coded him as *Tio* (Uncle) and left offerings of coca leaves, candy, gum, and cash to him on altars at the entrance of every mine shaft. In our terms, the miners acted to engage that little gear and give them the courage to go down into what they conceived as "Hell." You give a gift to the Devil, then the Devil is obligated to protect you.

But what happened when eventually there was a major mine explosion and dozens of their colleagues died? Did these miners then throw away their belief system, reinterpreting it as unreal and useless? No, of course not! The fault was theirs, for they obviously had failed to properly perform the rituals. Some miners had failed to leave appropriate offerings (ritual symbols and technologies) at the altars, had failed to invoke and honor Tio sufficiently, so he was angry! The solution: *intensify ritual performance.* In this case, that meant holding a huge community feast, sacrificing a llama and cooking its meat, and building a huge altar on which to offer the llama meat and many other delectable foods so that the spirit of the devil could consume the spirits of the food. Then the community consumed the "leftovers" and held dances and prayer ceremonies in honor of Tio—and of course, the mine company having taken some care, it would be months or years before another such disaster, so of course the ritual would appear to have worked to accomplish its instrumental end. With the Devil appeased, the cranking gear function of the altar offerings was restored in the miners' perceptions, and they could once again enter the mines with a feeling of safety and new carefulness in giving the Devil his due, so that he would not become angry again.

Contemporary Obstetricians and Danger: The Power Is in the Rituals

We find another, very powerful use of ritual's cranking gears in the many ritualized procedures that contemporary obstetricians utilize to keep their fear of the natural birth process and its many unpredictabilities at bay. In previous chapters, we mentioned the ritual uses of the electronic fetal monitor—a powerful symbol that speaks with many voices, providing information on the strength of the laboring mother's contractions and the condition of the fetal heart rate, representing the vast corporation that created it and all of the technological know-how that went into making it, symbolizing our technocratic cultural value on high technologies, and often giving both laboring people and their care providers a sense of psychological and emotional trust in the information it provides. (Reviewer Henci Goer aptly suggested that the EFM is a "high-tech divination tool masquerading as a diagnostic evaluation.") In Chapter 2, we described the technocratic, humanistic, and holistic models of medicine, noting that the dominant, hegemonic technocratic paradigm metaphorizes the body as a machine and the female body as an inherently defective machine (after all, this model/paradigm has its beginnings in the already-patriarchal Western Europe during its industrialization phase), and birth as an inherently dysfunctional process that can go wrong at any point. Since its inception, as Robbie points out (Davis-Floyd [1992] 2003a, 2022), Western obstetrics has always been all about controlling the chaotic and therefore "dangerous" process of labor and birth.

From the moment a laboring woman enters a hospital to give birth, the staff begins the "cranking gear" process of transforming a healthy laboring woman into a patient whose body is now under ritual technological surveillance and control. As in all initiatory rites of passage, the woman is stripped of her individual identity—her own clothes are removed and she is dressed in a hospital gown and put into a hospital bed, symbolizing her "patient" status. An IV (intravenous line) is inserted—a symbolic representation of the umbilical cord—the woman is now dependent on the institution for her "lifeblood." If she is still in the early stage of labor, Pitocin will likely be administered through that IV to speed up her labor. In many US hospitals (and indeed in most hospitals around the world), she will be deprived of food and drink—well, she is "hydrated" through the IV—yet hunger can make her weak and unable to face the medically termed "trial of labor" that she is now enduring. The common use of Pitocin to hasten birth has been shown to interfere with normal physiologic labor and can play a detrimental role in the so-called "cascade of interventions"—the cranking gears or ritual train—in the labor process.

This cascade continues with our laboring mother asking for pain relief and receiving an epidural (in resource-poor countries, the mother will often have to endure the intense pain of the Pitocin-induced contractions with no pain relief at all). The epidural will usually take the pain away, yet if given too early (before six centimeters of dilation), it can slow labor, necessitating an increase in her Pitocin drip. Of course, she will now be hooked up to the electronic fetal monitor, because that is hospital protocol (reinforced by insurance company requirements).

While mountains of scientific evidence show that women in labor should be up and moving around (movement assists fetal descent, the effectiveness of contractions, and cervical dilation), even if the woman knows that evidence, she will find herself in bed tethered to the monitor and the IV, with nothing to do (she is no longer in pain) but stare at the monitor and measure her own labor progress according to its vacillating lines and beeps. She will receive regular (and often painful) vaginal "checks" to make sure that her cervix is dilating "on time" (at the rate of 1 cm per hour). If it is, she will go on to give birth vaginally. If it is not, her Pitocin drip will be increased, the now back-to-back induced contractions will likely cause the baby to go into fetal distress, she will end up with a cesarean section (as 32 percent of US women currently do), and she will thank her obstetrician for saving her baby's life—usually never realizing that the "cascade of interventions," the ritual train—that she experienced were *the cause* of the baby's distress.

Robbie (Davis-Floyd [1992] 2003a, 2022) explains and analyzes this powerful ritual process in detail, likening it to damming up a river to keep it from flooding. Because none of these "standard obstetrical procedures" have any scientific basis or actual medical efficacy in (what otherwise would likely have been) normal births, in her effort to understand why such practices have become so routine for so many decades, Robbie concluded that these routine practices serve as rituals that enact and display our core cultural values on the supremacy of high technology and our profound cultural fear of untrammeled nature. She wrote:

> If we stop a moment now, to see in our mind's eye the visual and kinesthetic images that a laboring woman will be experiencing—herself in a bed, in a hospital gown, staring up at an IV pole, bag, and cord on one side, and a big, whirring machine on the other, and down at a steel bed and a huge belt encircling her waist—we can see that her entire visual field is conveying one overwhelming perceptual message about our culture's deepest beliefs and values: technology is supreme, and you are utterly dependent upon it and the institutions that control and dispense it. (Davis-Floyd [1992] 2003a: 109)[1]

The technocratically trained obstetricians Robbie has interviewed over her 30 years of research on childbirth, midwifery, and obstetrics seemed to have learned little from their attendance at normal, unproblematic births. But they learned a lot from the fetal deaths and maternal hemorrhages they all experienced. These are extremely rare in high resource settings, yet they carry such a powerful emotional charge that the obstetricians who experience them will do absolutely anything to avoid experiencing them again (see Davis-Floyd 1987, [1992] 2003a, 2018b; Davis-Floyd and St. John 1998). Like the Trobriand Islanders and the Bolivian tin miners we described above, contemporary obstetricians depend on their technological rituals to engage those cranking gears to carry them through danger to safety. Not once did a technocratic obstetrician interlocutor of Robbie's ever say that perhaps the problem happened *because* of the interventions they performed. On the contrary, they consistently expressed the belief that if they had only performed more rituals—administered Pitocin sooner, done the cesarean sooner—the mother or baby would not have died. So great is their belief in the efficacy of the rituals they routinely perform that *they always believe that intensifying their ritual performance would have saved them and their patients from danger.*

This belief is belied by the excellent outcomes achieved by US homebirth midwives with their non-interventive approach (see Cheyney 2011; Cheyney et al. 2014), and by the holistic obstetricians of Brazil (Davis-Floyd and Georges 2018)—all of whom re-ritualize birth in humanistic ways by acting on the scientific evidence in favor of facilitating and supporting the normal, physiologic process of birth. They stop performing technocratic-model interventions/rituals in favor of developing rituals that enact the humanistic and holistic paradigms (described in Chapter 2).

Inviolability and Inevitability: "The Ritual Train"

The exaggerated precision and careful adherence to form and pattern that set ritual apart from more casual modes of social interaction work to establish an atmosphere that feels inviolate and an order that feels inevitable. One would find it hard to imagine, for example, stopping a graduation ceremony, interrupting the Pledge of Allegiance, standing up in the middle of a church service to argue with the minister, or walking out of the hospital in mid-labor. Participants understand that the sequence of events is laid out and will proceed as planned; interruptions are generally neither permitted nor thinkable. As we have previously mentioned, this unstoppability of ritual has been likened to getting on a train—once it starts moving, you can't get off.

Think of a graduation ceremony, a wedding, a Presidential inauguration. Once the graduates begin their procession, once the bridesmaids start walking down the aisle, once the orchestra begins to play, there is consensual agreement among all participants that things must proceed as planned and no individual would dream of trying to stop the ritual progression, except in the case of a dire emergency like an earthquake, a bomb, or a fire. How often have you sat all the way through a ceremony or performance (or a boring lecture) you desperately wanted to leave, yet you did not wish to break the ritual frame? And if you do dare to disrupt the ritual by leaving, you do so bending at the waist, as if to make yourself as small and invisible as possible. This body language, while completely useless in making you take up less space, at least symbolically communicates to others that you are sorry to be so disruptive, letting them know that you respect the ritual norms and rules even as you violate them by leaving.

An Unwanted Wedding and an Unnecessary Cesarean: Getting Stuck on the Ritual Train

Robbie's first experience of this sense of inevitability that ritual can generate occurred when she was 18 and her boyfriend proposed marriage. She was a senior in high school, and he a senior in college. It all seemed so romantic at the time! She accepted. She knew she was perhaps too young to be making this commitment, so she set a wedding date a year into the future, thinking that during her first year of college, if she so desired, she could change her mind at any time. But she was completely unprepared for the ritualistic sequence of events that then began to unfold. Once the date was set, her mother and mother-in-law-to-be flew into action. They reserved the church and the minister, the country club for the rehearsal dinner and the hotel banquet room for the wedding reception, which was to be a seated formal dinner complete with an orchestra for dinner entertainment and dancing. Within months, the wedding invitations were ordered, the bridesmaids' dresses picked, and Robbie increasingly began to feel that she was indeed on a moving train and could not get off. By the time she started to realize that she was making a mistake, she found herself completely unable to stop the sequence of events that had been started. So she got married in spite of her doubts, and four years later, got divorced. From this experience, Robbie learned firsthand about the power of ritual, and that it takes tremendous strength of character to stop a ritual process once it has started—a strength she did not have at the age of 19.

Nineteen-year-old girls are not the only ones who find themselves unable to stop the ritual juggernaut. Even middle-aged and mature medical practitioners can find themselves highly susceptible to the sense of inevitability generated by ritual. Consider the following story told to Robbie by midwife Sister Morningstar:

> A family practice physician in my home state, who herself had had a home birth, found herself faced with a pregnant patient whose baby was breech (bottom instead of head first). Since obstetrical protocols prescribe cesarean section for breech, surgery was scheduled for Elaine at 38 weeks. [Full term is 40 weeks; the physician did not want her patient to go into labor, so the operation was scheduled well in advance of her due date, but within what was then considered to be the safety zone.]
>
> On the morning of the surgery, the doctor found herself full of doubt about its appropriateness. Her intuition told her it should be stopped, but the patient was already being prepped—in other words, the ritual process was already in motion. After the epidural was administered and Elaine was on the operating table, the physician checked the baby again and found that it was no longer in the breech position—it had turned. Thus there was no reason to perform the cesarean.
>
> Yet with the patient prepped and ready, surrounded by an expectant medical staff, the doctor found herself saying "Why don't we get on with this? We can have this baby out in fifteen minutes." Acquiescing, the patient signed the papers and the operation proceeded as scheduled. In spite of repeated ultrasounds, it turned out that the age of the baby had been severely overestimated: the newborn was only thirty-two weeks old—dangerously premature—and had to be flown out to the nearest neonatal intensive care unit (NICU). (Sister Morningstar, personal correspondence, Oct12, 2002)

Such events are common in contemporary medicine. Once a ritualized sequence of events like an elaborate testing procedure or an operation has been started, people start behaving in stylized, choreographed, pre-sequenced ways, and it becomes very difficult to stop the process, even when you know that you should.

Breaking Frame: The Purposeful Disruption of Ritual

This sense of inevitability that characterizes a ritual's progression is enhanced by the sense of inviolability generated by the ritual frame. At a friend's wedding, you may have been casually chatting with one of the bridesmaids outside the sanctuary before the ceremony began, but you wouldn't dream of trying to talk to her while she is walking down the aisle. As we previously noted, once established, there is a clear sense among the participants that *the ritual frame must not be broken.* Children generally learn this rule at their parents' knees—they have no sense of the existence of ritual frames until their parents instill such a sense in them by constant admonishments not to make noise or interrupt—in other words, not to "break the frame." The sense of inviolability that ritual can generate means that some of the most interesting and exciting behaviors humans can perform involve violating or "breaking" ritual frames. The stronger the frame, the greater the charge you get—and everyone else gets—when you break it. Many movies climax with the breaking of a ritual frame—the jilted suitor zooms into the church on a motorcycle and stops the wedding, the graduation ceremony is stopped just before the unworthy candidate is awarded his diploma. And new religions are often started by religious reformers who deliberately break the ritual frames of the older one.

Consider Jesus, who generated a new religion in part by smashing the categories and ritual frames of the older religion, Judaism. According to the Christian Bible, Jesus overturned tables in the sacred temple, violated the Jewish rule of not working on Saturday (the Sabbath), and commanded his disciples to drink his "blood" when any form of consumption of blood was expressly prohibited in Judaism. Perhaps he intuitively understood that when you break a ritual frame, you release the energy that it has been holding it in place and if you are quick, you can grab that energy and turn it to your own purposes, which Jesus and many other creators of new religions have proven most adept at doing.

For another instance, there once lived a Seneca Indian named Handsome Lake (1735–1815) who was an alcoholic and, as a consequence of his drinking, became very ill. During his illness, he received a series of visions. Upon recovery, he began to preach lessons based upon those visions and eventually transformed the religion of the entire Six Nation Iroquois Confederacy, melding the traditional *Haudenosaunee* religious beliefs with a new and more up-to-date system meant to revitalize their culture in the context of colonization by Europeans (Wallace 1969). That religion, the Code of Handsome Lake, is practiced to this very day. It grew out of a previous religious system that had become incapable of handling the new conditions imposed by the European interlopers—of "truing" the older religion's beliefs and practice to the new reality. The new system incorporated proper responses, moral perspectives, and interpretations appropriate ("trued") to the new times.

The Ludic Dimension of Ritual: Enhancing the Energy through Laughter

In spite of their serious formality, rituals often intentionally incorporate an intensely ludic (playful) dimension. In some cultures, like the Mescalero Apache of New Mexico, during their most sacred ceremonies, a clown mimics and mocks the singers as they perform the ritual acts in the required sequence, while the watching participants laugh uproariously at the clown's antics. The Mescalero do not feel that their laughter decreases the sacredness of the event, but rather increases it through the revitalizing energy that laughter brings to the culture's most deeply held beliefs.

A parallel can be found in the rodeo clown (see Handelman 1998). Rodeo bull riders ritually display the manly heroic virtues that their subculture holds dear; the clowns whose task it is to divert the bulls while entertaining the audience mock those manly traits, even as they themselves exemplify them. When Don Lucio and his group held their annual ceremonies to bring the rains and give thanks for the harvest, there always came a much-anticipated moment when the chanting and the praying ceased, bottles of orange soda pop mysteriously began to appear in people's hands, and those in the know started to smile. Suddenly, at a signal from Don Lucio, those holding the pop bottles began to shake them vigorously, then pop off the lids and spray the assembled multitude while everyone ran around laughing and screaming and trying either to escape the spray or to obtain a bottle themselves so they could spray others.

Robbie experienced the ludic/playful dimension of ritual for the first time during her very fun attendance at Camp Cimarroncita in New Mexico when she was ten years old. With all campers gathered in the large Kiva (a big room designed for plays, dances, group meetings, etc.), the counselors instructed the campers to get down on their knees and chant the following phrase: "OWA TA GOO SIAM." And then, chuckling to themselves under their hands, they waited to see when we would "get it." True believers all, at that young age, we dutifully chanted the supposed mantrum over and over, lifting and lowering our arms to the floor as instructed—thinking that we were actually performing some kind of sacred Native American ritual and duly excited. (Charlie had the same experience in Boy Scout camp.) We are not going to tell you what that chant was actually about—repeat the "mantrum" for yourselves until you get it too, and then laugh your head off, as we did when we got that we had been totally "had"!

Often the ludic, or playful, dimension of ritual is reserved for the very end, when for example university graduates simultaneously throw their caps high into the air, yelling and cheering. Robbie had a very different experience when she attended the May 2000 graduation ceremonies for Yale University. The elegant old buildings surrounding the huge courtyard provided a beautiful frame for what Robbie expected to be a serious and austere ceremony. The long procession of black-robed-and-capped undergraduates and the multicolored robes and capes of the faculty did nothing to alter this expectation. But then the graduate students began to enter the courtyard. The Divinity students all had gold tinsel halos tacked to their black caps. The Forestry students had long green ferns growing out of their caps and trailing down to the ground. Little plastic balloon globes bobbed above the caps of the Earth Science students, while old-fashioned white nurses' caps with little red stripes were tacked onto the black graduation caps of the nursing student graduates.

Nor was the students' employment of the ludic dimension mitigated by the commencement of the ceremony. Throughout the proceedings, even during the formal speeches, huge inflatable balls were periodically tossed about, balloons were batted from row to row, and occasionally various graduates would rise and shoot off cans of a ribbon-like substance that arced over the group, forming temporary and very colorful rainbows in the air.

Intrigued, Robbie asked some Yale faculty members why they tolerated this behavior, and was told that after years of intense work, the students who completed that work were fully entitled to play! And of course, the students' play had high entertainment value, bringing life and celebration to what might otherwise have been a dry and dull ceremony. In other words, the Yale faculty and student body shared a belief in the value of play and celebration, and mutually delighted in its enactment during their graduation ceremony. And the audience benefited as well, as the energy thus generated was tremendous, and everyone left "on a high," as one student quite aptly expressed it.

Play and fun can form essential ingredients in the anatomy and power of ritual. They lighten up the seriousness, evoke laughter, and release tension and stress, all by generating the production of endorphins in our brains. Remember, *ritual is very much about affecting and effecting emotions.* When you experience fun and joy during an otherwise serious ritual, your emotions, and thus your perceptions and beliefs, will be all the more engaged, and you will be all the more open to internalizing the messages of the rituals you are experiencing—a good thing when you actually want to internalize those messages, and not so great when you don't.

Framing and Flow

Ritual behaviors, when they are effective—when they work—can help the individual enter a state of consciousness that psychologist Mihaly Csikszentmihalyi (1975) has called *flow*. The flow state is one in which there is no inhibition, repression, fear, or hesitation. Flow is the experience of fully "letting go" into the action, which in turn results in creativity and happiness. According to renowned anthropologist Victor Turner (1979: 154):

> Flow is the holistic sensation present when we act with total involvement, a state in which action follows action according to an internal logic, with no conscious intervention on our part. Flow is experienced in play and sport, in artistic performance and religious ritual. There is no dualism in flow... Flow is made possible by a centering of attention on a limited stimulus field, by means of bracketing, framing, and often a set of rules. There is a loss of ego, the self becomes irrelevant ... Flow is an inner state so enjoyable that people sometimes forsake a comfortable life for its sake.

Flow occurs when the central nervous system is totally involved in an act or course of action. There is no interference by alternative systems in the body. Metabolic, motor, emotional, and cognitive-imaging systems are all entrained (synchronized) in a single, unitary, and unfolding ritual activity.

The role of ritual in generating flow experience is pivotal. If it is a social ritual, flow may arise when the central nervous systems of participants fully entrain with each other and with the movement of the ritual—in other words, when they enter a mutually shared ASC (altered state of consciousness). Time seems to slow down, all participants act as one (think of a rock concert, a mosh, a spiral dance, the entire congregation of a Baptist church praying with arms uplifted, the free flow of play in children's ritualized games, or even the altered state you enter when playing a video game and become so engrossed that you feel part of that virtual reality and win, time after time). All that is required aside from the ritual action itself is intense and single-minded attention. When attention (please note: attention = energy—*when you "pay attention" to something, you focus your energy on it*) is powerful enough, all impediments to flow disappear. The basketball player or the long-distance runner—or any athlete—may also experience this flow, as do birthing women who are not interfered with during labor and thus can fully immerse themselves in the physiologically induced flow-state of normal labor and birth—which many midwives call "laborland."

One of Charlie's dear friends was the late Major League baseball pitcher Frank "Tug" McGraw, who often spoke of entering a "sweet spot in time" while on the mound, during which he simply could not miss. If something happened to disrupt this state of mind, then his performance would fall apart. He said that his manager could tell when Tug lost the sweet spot—the ASC of flow—and would pull him off the mound and replace him.

Artists often enter a state of flow while writing, painting, dancing, singing, or sculpting; their mind-states are inextricably associated with "setting loose" the creative muse. This also can happen with scholars and writers. For example, Robbie often enters a state of flow while totally immersed in writing; it feels like her brain is connected to her computer through her fingers. In that flow state, time does indeed seem to stop and the words simply come. Hours can fly by without her noticing. (Yet that sense of flow gets broken when Robbie has to stop to look up references and page numbers, etc., taking her out of "the zone.") When sleeping, she sometimes dreams about the chapters that are up for working on and returns to them with renewed energy within what she experiences as the sacred ritual frame of her small-but-beautiful office.

Because flow is the natural outcome of total concentration and focus, meditators of all religious persuasions experience from time to time a state of intense bliss or ecstasy. The ecstatic bliss achieved during flow can be transportive to other realms of being and is often an ASC in which permanent alterations in personality and self-understanding can take place. Hence, this kind of experience is frequently one of the goals of religious (and other types of) ritual—to transport the mind of the practitioner from one SOC to another through flow. This transportive effect is fundamental to religious initiations, as well as to the application of many traditional healing rituals. Ritual evocation of certain flow experiences can transform the balance of autonomic functions and other factors and literally transform, even heal, ritual practitioners and participants—just as Doña Queta most likely did in those hospital rooms.

Ritual Order: Enhancing Courage and Confidence

The courage- and confidence-enhancing function of ritual is as pervasive in the contemporary world as it always was in the past. It is especially obvious among obstetricians, as described above, and in sports—as when the pitcher turns his cap sideways and eats pancakes before every game, because the first time he did that, he pitched a no-hitter, and doing it again gives him the feeling that he has started those cranking gears in motion and they will carry him safely through the pitfalls of the game.

The Need for Awareness in the Performance of Ritual

The following story demonstrates the importance of awareness in the deployment of ritual. Back in 1988, US figure skater Debi Thomas was positioned to win an Olympic gold medal. She was in first place, and all she had left to do was the last, long figure-skating performance. Every time she had gone onto the ice, the TV cameras had shown her skating over to her coach before her performance. He would give her a quick pep talk, she would hold out her hands, he would slap her ten, and she would skate off and do a terrific job. This last time, she skated over to her coach, he gave her a quick pep talk, and she held out her hands for him to slap her ten, but he missed and their fingers glanced off of each other—their hands did not connect. In other words, the ritual sequence was not completed, the small gear was not fully cranked. She skated off, fell twice, and won a bronze medal instead of the expected gold. The moral of this story: *if you are going to use ritual to enhance your courage and increase your chances of success, it is wise to be conscious about your use of ritual and to be sure that you complete the process fully and properly, so that small gear will engage the larger cosmic (or psychological) gear and your desired outcome will result.*

Watching the 2012 London Olympics, Robbie was fascinated to see another very clear example of the intentional "cranking gear" use of ritual to enhance performance in the pre-performance rituals enacted by gymnast Daniel Leyva and his stepfather/coach Yin Alvarez. In the seconds before the beginning of each set, Alvarez would tap Daniel on the head, pull swiftly up on his ears, and whisper to him, "Trust your training!" The rituals worked— the gears got engaged, and Leyva won his expected bronze medal in the individual all-arounds.

Obviously, these courage-enhancing ritual "gears" we are talking about are metaphorical, yet performing them can have deep physical and psychological effects. Whether or not there are gods or devils or spirits that can bring one safely through danger in return for ritual chants and offerings, for sure humans have brains; performing rituals in carefully sequenced ways to bring about desired outcomes will affect the neural networks of those brains, as we have shown above. Moreover, rituals may incorporate and bracket decisive acts in such a way that the ritualized behaviors before the decisive act (throwing the ball, skating a program, etc.) influence the act before it is even attempted. Basketball fans may be aware that free-throw masters often prepare to shoot the ball by various, apparently inessential ritual acts before the throw. Experiments carried out by sports anthropologists have shown that interfering with the ritual context of free-throwing will decrease players' accuracy and confidence (Southard and Miracle 1993). The reason for this decrease is that the brain does not behaviorally delimit where ritual behavior stops and decisive action begins. Rather, there is an entire sequence of actions in which the decisive act (actually throwing the ball at the hoop) may be embedded among other sequenced activities that are crucial to the success of the decisive act. Stripped of the planned sequence of ritualized acts, the efficacy of the decisive act is reduced or even eliminated. Continued practice of the decisive acts, when repetitively preceded by the same sequenced activities—like bouncing the ball in a certain way for a certain number of times—results in an entrainment of neural circuits and motor sequences that facilitates carrying out the decisive act (throwing the ball) without the need for planning or thought.

The downside is that, after habituation, changing or correcting the sequence of the ritual is difficult. For instance, it is often far harder for a golf instructor to improve an experienced golfer's swing than to teach a beginner to swing correctly in the first place, just as it is often hard for an obstetrician to change her habituation to the performances of technocratic standard procedures/rituals—even when she has read the evidence and wishes to change. In "The Paradigm Shift of Humanistic and Holistic Obstetricians" (Davis-Floyd and Georges 2018), Robbie and her colleague Eugenia (Nia) Georges describe the difficulties obstetricians who made a paradigm shift encountered as they became aware of and consciously tried to change their habituation to technocratic practices "step by step," as several of them put it. Such major changes in habituation require massive neuronal restructuring, which takes a great deal of time and energy/attention—which of course explains why most obstetricians are not willing to attempt such changes, even when the evidence and their patients tell them they should. It's just so much easier to keep on practicing in the habitual ritual ways that are out-of-awareness because they have already been internalized/habituated to, and generate a sense of confidence in the practitioner.

This confidence-enhancing role played by ritual is even evident in much subtler form in the previously mentioned cultural greeting rituals ("Hello, how are you?" "Good, thanks. You?"). Although such standardized performances may appear trite or insincere to the analytical intellect, they nevertheless perform an important service. The rhythmicity of greeting rituals facilitates rapid entrainment of linguistic and bodily rhythms that is accompanied by a sense of comfort and security—all of which happens before an actual conversation takes place, thus facilitating that conversation.

For example, when a stranger stops you on the street, you may react with fear. But if he is courteous and polite—in other words, if he engages you in the performance of greeting rituals that you recognize as known and familiar—your fear may subside. Through his skillful use of these rituals, he has demonstrated that he shares the same cultural universe as you. This apparent sharing metaphorically suggests that he abides by the same cultural rules and is therefore safe to interact with. You will then tend to relax, and have friendly open feelings toward him (for better or worse, for correct ritual performance does not guarantee honesty, as ritual can easily be manipulated for sinister ends). In this capacity, ritual has for eons served humans well by "greasing the wheels" of their social interactions. Ritual is the symbolic form through which trust between strangers can quickly be established, so that information can be exchanged, the friendship initiated, the business deal closed.

When Rituals Fail

As we have seen, what happens when a mining tunnel collapses in spite of multiple offerings to the devil, or when the obstetrician follows ritual procedure, but the baby dies anyway—in other words, what happens when cranking the (metaphorical) little gear fails to engage the larger one and produce the desired outcome—is *not* that the participants realize it was all nonsense, throw out their belief system, and stop performing the rituals that enact it.

One of the most powerful aspects of the rituals that people design is their flexibility. It is almost always possible to find a reason why the ritual failed, and to assure yourself that if you only perform it right the next time, it is bound to work (see Hüsken 2007). You didn't make the altar right, you skipped a verse or two of the chant, you didn't leave enough coca leaves for the devil—or if *you* did, then it wasn't enough because *other people* didn't, and so the devil is very angry and decides to punish the people for their transgressions. So now, clearly (within the belief system—the cognitive matrix underlying the ritual), restitution must be made so that balance and order can be restored—as when the Bolivian tin miners hold the large ceremony to honor the devil that we described above.

That's the way it almost always is with ritual—if it doesn't work, you don't assume that the belief system underlying it is faulty. Instead you assume that you or others haven't been doing the rituals right—something was out of order, or not done properly—and thus you intensify ritual performance in an attempt to set things right. As previously noted, if an obstetrician experiences a fetal or maternal death, he never assumes that it might be because he performed too many ritualistic interventions into the birth process—instead he always assumes that if he had gone immediately to the very most powerful ritual—a cesarean section—the outcome would have been good. One such ob/gyn of Robbie's acquaintance had a patient whose first baby had died of severe congenital anomalies. He persuaded her to plan a cesarean for her next birth so that he could ensure her a healthy baby! Such is the nature of ritual—we almost always assume that it works, and that if it doesn't, it's not because our belief system from which our rituals stem is wrong, it's because we simply didn't pay enough attention to the proper performance of the rituals (Hüsken 2007).

An extreme example of too much faith in ritual and in the belief system it enacts comes from a 1950s sect Robbie once read about (but can't remember the name of the book), whose members were absolutely convinced that they were in touch with an alien spacecraft whose crew would transport them aboard if they met certain conditions, including the removal of all metal of all kinds from their clothing and teeth. So these cult members removed their metal fillings and cut off their metal zippers, and spent countless hours in backyards filled with believers ready for transport. Incident after incident, year after year, the reason given by the cult leaders for the failure of the ritual was that someone—maybe *you!*—had not fulfilled the conditions and thus had ruined the experience for the entire group. Most of the group members, true believers all, hung in there for over five years before finally concluding that the whole thing had been a massive hoax perpetrated by people who only wanted the life savings they had committed to the enterprise of "space salvation." These types of charismatic cults are quite common (see Lalich 2004).

Another such group, the so-called Heaven's Gate cult, made news in 1997 when the group's founder talked his followers into committing mass suicide. The members apparently believed that they were actually aliens who were waiting for a spaceship that would accompany the comet Hale-Bopp. By killing themselves, they would set their souls free to be transported to the spaceship. They performed all sorts of ritual preparations, including buying matching shoes and dwelling in the dark to simulate the conditions they expected after transportation.

When ritual fails, the most threatening outcome is not the potential results of the failure of that particular ritual, but rather the potential loss of the entire belief system—the entire cycle of meaning—through which a group of people organize their lifeworld. It's one thing for some individuals to die in a fishing accident or a tunnel collapse, and another for an entire social group to come smack up against the question of whether their cosmology is true or false, whether their whole cycle of meaning is valid or not. When individuals lose their worldviews, they often plunge into doubt, depression, and despair. As the world has witnessed over and over again during the last four centuries, cultures die when their belief systems crumble. When ritual fails (see Hüsken 2007 for examples), there are only four possible explanations (that we can imagine): (1) the belief system on which the ritual is based is wrong, and the rituals that enact that belief system are therefore meaningless and invalid; (2) the ritual participants did not perform the rituals correctly; (3) it was the wrong ritual for that particular situation; (4) the lifeworld is so out of whack that one ritual is not enough—the ritual process must be escalated so that the larger balance can be restored.

The consequences of accepting the first alternative are dire and must be avoided as long as possible, because accepting them will mean the dissolution of the group. So in most cases and in most places, for as long as they can, people turn to the other three. They repeat the ritual performances, only more carefully this time, or they try other rituals, or they escalate to a much larger ritual, like sacrificing a llama and holding a community-wide feast—or for many obstetricians worldwide, just do cesareans on almost every mother—cesarean rates around the world have now risen to epidemic proportions, with one in every five women now being delivered by cesarean worldwide.

It is perhaps useful to run through the cycle of meaning model we presented earlier for purposes of the present context: what happens when rituals fail? A worldview generates lore and rituals that are intended to bring about expected outcomes—distinct experiences—that are then interpreted in such a way that they instantiate and confirm the worldview and reinforce the meanings contained in the ritual. But in the cases we describe above, and many others, the expected outcome does not happen—something bad happens instead. The survival of the cycle of meaning depends upon how the people interpret the unexpected outcome, and as we have noted, most societies have built-in explanations for why the ritual did not cause the desired effect.

An evangelical talk show host named Harold Camping prophesied that the Rapture and Judgment Day would happen on May 21, 2011 and that the world would end on October 21, 2011. He based his predictions—not the first he had made in his career—on numerology (the spiritual meaning of numbers). The Rapture, according to some Christian groups, is the point during the End Days at which God will take his Chosen People into Heaven, leaving all the rest to experience the horrors of "the great catastrophe." Well, as the existence of this book and your reading of it will attest, the world did not end in 2011. So you might reasonably think that the evangelist's prophecy would be debunked and his followers scattered to the winds. Not so, for the failures of his predictions were explained away by his having gotten the math wrong, and many people continued to follow his guidance until his death in 2013.

This kind of ritual cult is not limited to Western societies. Indeed, there is a common phenomenon called a "millenarian movement" that has popped up all over the planet at one time or another. *Millenarianism,* loosely defined, is the belief that if the group carries out certain changes and actions, the society will transform itself into a new age. Technically speaking, and as the name implies, some of those groups think in terms of thousand-year cycles. But anthropologists are interested in studying any religious group that predicts fundamental changes in the society and the world if certain practices, usually ritualized ones, are carried out.

For example, a Paiute Indian prophet named Jack Wilson (or *Wovoka*) created the Ghost Dance religion in 1889—a movement that spread throughout many western North American native cultures and will be described in a future chapter. Here we note that an important spinoff was the transformation of the Ghost Dance taken up by the Lakota Sioux, who interpreted the teachings—which were actually peaceful in intent—as bolstering their resistance to the white invaders. They developed the concept of the Ghost Shirt—a symbolic garment thought to be bulletproof. Many of the Lakota who fought and died at the terrible Wounded Knee massacre in 1890 were wearing those shirts. The failure of the shirts to protect those warriors was taken by most as a sign that the teaching was false, and they ceased to believe in it. Their cessation of belief is one more clear indication that sometimes, when rituals fail to work in a very dramatic, perhaps deadly way, people are capable of ceasing to believe in them and the belief system that underlies them.

Summary: Ritual Order and Ritual Failure

Framing, order, and a sense of formality are primary parts of the characteristics and anatomy of ritual that are essential to its efficacy. Ritual spaces and places are generally culturally acknowledged as such, and thus tend to be respected, even by passers-by. Most often, architecture designed to create ritual spaces generates this cultural acknowledgement. Yet invisible lines of energy that are nonetheless felt both by participants and observers can define these spaces and places even when architecture does not do it for them. Shrines and altars created in individual homes can demarcate ritual spaces that constitute the focusing of energy on family religion, beliefs and values, cherished memories, and individual and family accomplishments. Consider the millions of people who have visited the Vietnam Veterans Memorial Wall in Washington, DC, in order to find their relative's name and pay homage to their sacrifice. The wall is a shrine, and its visitors are often in a very real sense worshippers at that shrine and supplicants for the souls of their deceased loved ones.

In the "cranking gear" effect we have described, the Trobriand sea fisherman who makes elaborate offerings and incantations in precise order before embarking into perilous waters believes that, if he does his part correctly, so must the gods of the sea do their part to bring him safely home. For the same reasons, the batter turns his cap backward and clutches his rabbit's foot before he steps up to the plate; the basketball free-thrower engages in sequenced behaviors before throwing. The Bolivian tin miner, before descending into the hot and dangerous mines that he thinks of as the devil's territory, makes an offering of candy or tobacco to the devil so that the devil will be obligated to reciprocate by protecting him. The obstetrician performs a series of standardized ritual procedures that he believes will carry the birth to a safe conclusion. Every one of these ritual performances invokes a sense of inviolability—the ritual must proceed according to prescribed formulas. Laughter and play—the ludic dimensions of ritual—often form important components of this ritual process, generating, via endorphins, a feeling of well-being in the ritual participants.

When ritual fails, its human enactors will tend to intensify ritual performance in an attempt to set the world right via more focused attention on the proper (ordered and formal) performance of ritual. (Please keep in mind that ritual often involves very little neocortical rationality. It is more embedded deep in the core brain than in the rational cortical brain.) As we have shown, when ritual continues to fail, the adaptability and flexibility of the human mind will incorporate this failure, leading eventually to abandonment of the ritual complex and the worldview underlying it. The chaos resulting from the dissolution of a culture's (or an individual's) worldview will be addressed in the following chapters.

Note

1. For full descriptions of the scientific evidence in favor of normal, physiologic birth, go to "Childbirth Connection." Retrieved 15 November 2021 from http://www.childbirthconnection.org/ or "Evidence Based Birth®." Retrieved 15 November 2021 from https://evidencebasedbirth.com/.

Chapter 7

RITUAL AS PERFORMANCE
Generating Emotion, Belief, and Transformation

⁓❦◎

Ritual, Belief, and Emotion

Many cosmopolitan individuals would like to think that they choose their basic beliefs with intellectual caution and precision. But in most cases the opposite is true. Again, *belief follows emotion*—we tend to believe in our heads what we feel in our hearts. In addition, people are far more likely to remember events, and to absorb lessons from those events, if they carry an emotional charge. Ritual, especially formal ritual, can generate that charge—it can focus the emotions on the symbolic messages it presents. Of course, individuals can go through the motions of a ritual—sit through a synagogue service, a Mass, a graduation ceremony—and be unmoved, may not believe in the belief system behind the ritual, indeed may even be bored. But we are speaking here of how rituals work *when* they work.

The focusing process in ritual is enhanced by the rhythmic repetition of the ritual's messages, which will often intensify toward a climax. If the ritual is successful, belief will be generated or enhanced through the symbolic "mapping on" process (described in Chapter 4), in which ritual and its drivers can penetrate the consciousness of the participants and heavily influence or determine their perceptions, emotions, and experiences. And because of the emotions associated with belief, neither the experience nor the belief is likely to be forgotten. This design has proven to be remarkably adaptive throughout our evolution.

Ritual Healing from Soul Loss through an Indigenous Shamanic Ceremony: Juan the Chamula

As a youth, Juan, an Indigenous member of the Chamula in Southern Mexico, had left his family and his culture in Highland Chiapas to work in the coffee plantations in another part of the south of Mexico for many years. Upon his return, he felt alienated from his old associations, did not understand his culture nor share in its worldview, and eventually fell ill. His community was concerned, so they brought the local shaman to see him. The shaman diagnosed Juan as suffering from "soul loss." In his biography about Juan, anthropologist Ricardo Pozas (1962) described the healing ceremony that the shaman performed to cure Juan of soul loss—a long and elaborate series of rituals involving careful placement of ritual artifacts, lots of chanting, prayer, and storytelling, and the sacrifice of a rooster. At the climax of the ceremony, the shaman twisted the neck of the rooster, killing it, and, as Juan later exclaimed, "Suddenly, I felt free!" This experience of ritual healing constituted for Juan an important step in his reintegration into the cultural system he had left years ago and to which he was now returning.

As this example demonstrates, healers can use ritual's ability to generate belief to map their interpretation of the illness into the mind-body of the patient. When these fuse, healing can be achieved, *as the body responds to what the mind now believes.* Another way to describe this phenomenon is as *healing through storytelling*—or what psychologists might call "visualization." The healer tells a story about the illness—in Juan's case, the story was that the warlocks stole his soul to eat it and the shaman sought to trade the soul of the rooster for the return of Juan's soul—and dramatically enacts that story through ritual. The success of the ritual depended on Juan's emotional and psychological identification with the story that the ritual was enacting. Because this resonance did happen in Juan's psyche, he came to experience his illness through the story, or in terms of the story; thus, when the story reached its climax, Juan's body healed as his soul returned. "Soul loss" is still today regarded as a real phenomenon by many contemporary New Age and other types of healers, and the "retrieval of the lost soul" via ritual and visualization is a common psychotherapeutic technique.

Ritual Healing from "Soul Loss" through Contemporary Psychotherapy: Robbie the Anthropologist

Written by Robbie

The activities we engaged in immediately after Peyton's death were frenzied— me flying to Roanoke, where her body still lay in the hospital, to spend hours ritually cleansing her dead body, so lovely even in death. Then nothing but more action in the ensuing days: gathering P's luggage from the wrecked car, coming home to plan a Memorial Service, the most awesome ritual celebration of her life that we could possibly have created. And then another one for her New York friends two weeks later—they planned that one so of course we had to show up—the logistics of getting 12 people to NYC, finding us a place to stay, getting to the Service—the action went on and on, for a very long time. And those rituals *did* work, and they did carry us through for the next weeks and months. Indeed, they carried me for a year, during which I finally got back to work.

Yet all the while, a *huge* part of me stayed frozen on that square foot of carpet in my house where I received the news of Peyton's death from two officers. (If you can't "fight or fly" from something terrible, you "freeze.") And that "me" who froze—well, that was the "me" that I had worked for many years to become—a happy, fulfilled, and self-actualized person who jumped out of bed in the morning to teach her classes or do her research or write her books and articles.[1] Years of therapy had finally enabled me to heal all my childhood and adolescent issues. I was happy, in a great relationship, and full of enthusiasm every day for whatever that day might bring.

That was the "me" who got frozen in place on that square foot of carpet, and the "me" who carried on, doing everything that needed to be done, was a pale and broken reflection of the *me* who used to be. What I called "being frozen," shamans would call "soul loss"—and I agree.

Fast forward nine years to 2009—the "me" who had remained present to life had gone on to write lots of widely read articles and books, to travel the world giving talks, to become a "culture hero" in the childbirth and midwifery movements—yet I was not whole. I had suffered two massive nervous breakdowns in the years after Peyton's death, had recovered more or less (with the help of Lexapro, Klonopin, and psychotherapy for my grief), yet I still felt shattered and broken into pieces—a mere shell of my former self, glued back together in a very tenuous way.

Then came the ultimate meltdown. My arthritic left knee became swollen to the size of a large cantaloupe. I could barely walk. So, surgery with a titanium and plastic knee replacement—I was totally unprepared for the ensuing pain during recovery. And that physical pain, in horrible addition to my emotional grief and agony over Peyton's death and many other really, really bad things that happened to me in the years after she died (including the deaths of several close friends and my house burning down)—well I simply cratered into a totally suicidal depression. And on one terrible night, when I couldn't bear all that pain anymore, I took 11 strong sleeping pills (all I had, fortunately) and wrote myself a note: "I just want to sleep for a very long time and wake up in rehab at Sierra Tucson." And when I did wake up, late the next night, I saw the note, got it that I needed help, called Sierra Tucson, and got on the next plane in a very straightforward effort to survive.

Help! I'm trapped in this horrible place (well, really it is a wonderful place, yet it's horrible to feel trapped *anywhere*)—yet every time I want to check myself out and go home, the question they ritually tell me to ask myself is, "Do you really want to go back to the way it was?" And of course, I did not—it was a place too terrible to go back to. So I fully committed myself to all the healing therapies they had to offer. I *am* an anthropologist, so I interviewed everyone who was leaving (people were always coming and going)—"Did you get what you came for?"—and every single answer was "YES!"

For the first two weeks, I was sure that I would be the only person to leave without getting what I came for, which was to heal from Peyton's death and to find again the happiness I had lost when she died—it seemed an impossible goal!

And then came the turning point—a three-hour session with an EMDR therapist named Maureen. She put buzzers in my hands and had me watch a blue light that went from one side of my vision to the other—when the light went to the right, the right-hand buzzer went off, and vice versa. Once my brain hemispheres were thereby coordinated, I easily entered a very deep ASC. And Maureen helped me put myself right back on that square foot of carpet where I was standing when I received the news of Peyton's death. And that was when I fully understood "shock."

In that instant of hearing the news, I had been shocked out of my mind and also out of my body. The fully shocked part of me—the formerly self-fulfilled, self-actualized part of me—simply froze on that square foot of carpet, while the rest of me went on to do what had to be done. Nine years later, in the safety of the therapist's room, I am standing in front of her/me nine years earlier on that terrible night. I could see me in that moment, frozen in space and time—I could even see the gray dress I had been wearing with the embroidery down the front—and I could see the look on her/my face. I narrated my experience to Maureen. And Maureen said, "Can you move toward her, can you embrace her?"

I could, so I did. I stood with her on that square foot of gray carpet, put my arms around her/me—she was sooooo cold! I hugged her hard and tried to warm her up. Eventually, she opened her eyes and looked at me, and she said, "Oh, I get it, you are *me* from the future! Does it get any better?" Regretfully, I replied, "No, it only gets worse from here. I've lived what you haven't, and I have to tell you the truth—it only gets worse." Then she said, "OK, I don't want to live through what you have—could we just please lie down and die, right here, right now?"

Knowing that this was only a highly ritualized and very safely framed visualization, I agreed. We both lay down together on the floor, arms around each other—at least I had gotten her to move off that square foot of carpet! We stayed like that for a while until I felt her warming up in my arms. And then I said, "You know, *we can't stay here.* We are *not* going to die right now. And I have gone on, while you have stayed here frozen in place. And the *you* that froze was the best of *me*, the best that I was before P died. I NEED YOU. Please, please, let's get up off this floor and go back to my reality, together. I need you to wake up, be alive and alove, and come back inside of me. I lost so much when I lost you—please come home to me."

Well, really she had no other option. So slowly, slowly, we got up off the floor together, arms still wrapped around each other. And then we were standing, and then I started to freak out, and I said to Maureen, "OK I've got her in my arms, we are standing, but still on that carpet—how do we get out of here?"

In a flash of insight, Maureen said, "Do you see any colors around you?" And I looked at the air around us, which had also frozen when she/me froze—and in fact, there *were* colors, amazing and beautiful colors, swirling all around in the molecules of air that were finally unfreezing. I verbalized that to Maureen, and she said "OK, can you use those colors to get your-selves back here?"

And then suddenly Peyton's voice said, "Look up!" And I did, and there was my precious P-Pey, grinning from ear to ear. She squatted down and extended her right hand—colors flew from that hand, and those swirling colors turned into a rainbow that swirled and curled around us, and lifted us, still embracing—and then we were four feet off the carpet, and then 12 or so, and then, higher and higher till we were flying through the air until, BAM!, we landed together on Maureen's soft sofa, and there she/me was, on top of me in a full-body embrace. And Maureen nodded in satisfaction.

And then I said to her/me, "Come inside me, be part of me again—I've missed you and I've needed you so much!" She nodded, then started to melt into me. As her left leg melted into my left leg, she stopped in surprise and said, "What the hell is that?" And I said, "Oh, I failed to mention, we had a total knee replacement—what you are feeling is titanium and plastic—our new knee. It's working well, though it's still painful—can you be OK with that?" And she said, "Whatever!" and continued to melt into me.

Left side complete, she started melting into my right side. As her right hand melted into mine, it felt like pulling on a glove *inside* my hand. And then, encountering the ring on my right ring finger, she stopped in surprise and said, "What is that ring?" And I explained that it had been Peyton's, and she said, "But that's not possible—Peyton never ever wore gold jewelry—silver was her thing!" And I said, "I know, but this ring was there among P's jewelry when it came back to me—the only gold thing— and I put it on my hand, and it fit perfectly, and I've been wearing it ever since. And guess what? Over time I figured out that the four large loops on the ring represent the four times Big Blue [Peyton's Mitsubishi jeep] flipped over, and the flower to the side represents P's spirit flying free, out the side window—I figure that she 'got' what was happening and just flew away before her body skidded down the road. So this ring is a hologram of her death and new life."

And she/me said, "Ooooh, too much information—I'm so very tired!" And I said, "OK honey, just ooze on into the rest of my body, and then lay your heart on mine"—and she did, and then I said "Okay, now just come on into my heart, and then just rest, for as much and as long as you need." And when she entered my heart, she lifted her head for the last time and said, "OH, Peyton is here, right here in your heart!"—just as P had told me in sign language on that airplane in Dallas, and again in a dream. And then she slept. And over the next days, I began to feel whole again—I knew that I had turned the corner in my healing process. I no longer felt so fragile and fragmented, and after many more healing sessions, I left Sierra Tucson no longer suicidal and very glad to be alive and "alove" and returning to wholeness.

Robbie the Anthropologist and Juan the Chamula: Healing from "Soul Loss" across Time, Space, and Culture

Shamans (and others) would call these experiences "soul loss and recovery." Maybe you can kill a rooster to reclaim the part of the soul you lost when you left your community, and maybe you can do a powerful EMDR visualization like the one Robbie just described, with the same result. Robbie is glad that it didn't take a rooster's death to unfreeze the frozen part of her—but it did take a marvelous therapist, a technology-induced ASC—and a very, very safe ritual frame (Maureen's lovely office with its soft sofas and pillows and buzzers and light flashers, and Maureen's loving and comforting presence, all tucked safely inside the protected premises of Sierra Tucson) to bring the part of Robbie that she had lost to shock back home to Robbie's body. Nine years of suffering Peyton's death, nine years of feeling frozen on that square foot of carpet, and suddenly, just like Juan the Chamula, Robbie felt free! Robbie says: "And of course I still miss my daughter, yet not in that desperate, I-can't-live-without-you way. I *am* living without her, and in recovering and re-warming that frozen part of myself, I am finding my way back towards happiness, day by day." (See the Preface for Robbie's description of the final Peyton ritual that ultimately did bring her peace.) The power of ritual performance brought healing to both Juan the Chamula and Robbie the anthropologist, as it has to so many others across human history, in both traditional and contemporary societies.

Western Medicine: A Differing Perspective

Western medicine usually tells a very different sort of story about illness—a story of germs or cancerous cells invading the body. This story too can be marshaled to aid healing: some researchers (see Simonton, Simonton and Creighton 1978; Kingwatsiaq and Pii 2003; Trakhtenberg 2008) have found that teaching people to visualize the invading germs or cancer cells and zap them like the monsters in a video game can powerfully affect their healing process. But all too often in Western medicine, the doctor ignores his shamanic potential for storytelling and ritual healing, expecting a pill or a surgery to do the work (which they often do) without enlisting the healing power of the mind. (Indeed, Robbie's psychiatrist treated her "depression" with anti-depressant drugs for many years. It never occurred to him, or to her, that soul loss might be involved. It took the much more open-minded therapists of Sierra Tucson to go there—and after Robbie's time there, she was able to get off of her antidepressant, because her body was now producing enough serotonin on its own.) Many Western practitioners treat the body as a machine with a mind in it. They fail to comprehend that body and mind are two aspects of the same being. There is more to the mind than just the brain because our nervous system literally goes everywhere. Our whole body is permeated with nerves that constantly transmit messages from the body to the brain and back again. In fact, our central nervous system *is* our brain, extended all over our bodies. This is precisely why the so-called placebo effect is so important in medicine (Benedetti 2008). Over and over, medical scientists have found that *belief in the efficacy of a medicine has a powerful effect on how well that medicine works* in a given patient. And medical anthropologists have found that it does not matter which culture the patient comes from—there is always a placebo effect operating in healing (Moerman 2002a, 2002b). One of the most critical aspects of healing, therefore, is *belief that the medicine or healing technique will work.* We will be clarifying a lot of this information with respect to ritual below, but first let us look at how *affect* (feeling or emotion) itself works.

The Excitation and Relaxation Nervous Systems: Ritual, Flow, and Ecstasy

The affect generated by ritual can do much more than merely emotionally charge a belief. Our brains come equipped with two subsystems, the excitation and the relaxation systems (Gellhorn 1967; Laughlin and Throop 1999). Under normal everyday conditions, these two systems operate alternatively—when one is active, the other is quiescent. But the repetitive stimuli of ritual may actually cause both systems to become active at the same time. Under the right social, environmental, and ritual conditions, this simultaneous activation of both nervous systems can produce an intensely pleasurable, perhaps ecstatic and almost orgasmic sensation (indeed, both subsystems do simultaneously discharge during orgasm).

This ecstatic state occurs in ritual when our physical, emotional, and intellectual experiences of the symbolic messages we are receiving become one (as in the "flow" we described in Chapter 6). The pleasurable feelings may be very brief, experienced only as goose bumps popping out as the banner-bearing choir marches down the aisle on Easter Sunday or a shiver down the spine as you salute your country's flag during a parade. (Many US citizens, especially those who supported the presidential candidate who won the election, report experiencing just such feelings during presidential inaugurations.) It may happen only once during the ritual, or may be repeated at numerous focal points. Or this ecstatic state may be prolonged, as in meditation and religious trance or dance. Here we revisit the quotation that we used at the beginning of this book:

> As Glenna began the opening conjuration of the ritual, a silence fell over the circle. Through the castings and chargings of the circle, through the invocation of the Goddess, it grew, and as Albion and Loik and Joaquin Murietta hammered out a dancing rhythm on their drums, as we whirled in a double sunwise ring, that silence swelled into waves of unseen lightness, flooding our circle, washing about our shoulders, breaking over our heads. Afterwards we wandered about the gardens, laughing and clowning, drunk on the very air itself, babbling to each other: it worked! (Adler 1988: 4)

These ecstatic sensations become experientially associated by ritual participants with the belief system enacted in the ritual. Charismatic Christian groups are filled with the Holy Spirit, !Kung trance-dancers with the boiling energy they call *n/um,* and Wiccans with the energy of the earth and the Goddess, as in the quote above. Concert and opera attendees who entrain with the music and the songs will feel uplifted. Participants chanting slogans like "Four more years!" or "Yes, we can!" or "Make America great again!" or "Build back better!" in political rallies find their ritual "high" in ritually enacted shared belief in a particular candidate. Biological research has established that during such ASCs, high levels of endorphins—natural pain-relieving, pleasure-producing chemicals—flood the central nervous system. This ritually induced experience of ecstasy is one of the most powerful experiences available to humans.

As previously described in our discussion of flow, once you experience this state (especially the prolonged version) during a ritual, you will never forget it, and you are likely to want more. This desire can be a powerful incentive to begin regular attendance at the ritual events that can induce this feeling. The reader should know by now that attaining these feelings entails actual participation in the ritual, not merely sitting around and watching. Full-bodied ritual participation may, for example, involve full attendance at political conventions for days on end and ritual drivers (of which there are plenty at political conventions) like the ones we described in Chapter 4 (see Tables 4.1 and 4.2).

Even an activity like sexual intercourse generally involves beginning with various ritualized behaviors termed "foreplay" before the activity can proceed on to ecstatic bliss. Foreplay is a precursor to sexual intercourse throughout mammalian and bird species, and, generally speaking, the more complex the brain, the more complex the pre-copulatory ritual. Bottlenose dolphins, for instance, have been called the "sexiest animals on the planet" because their bouts of foreplay can go on for hours before copulation actually occurs. For humans, foreplay ritual can be so entraining that it can work even at a physical distance—over a phone or via the internet. So powerful is the urge to feel sexual ecstasy that it pervades the online industry where various forms of erotic and pornographic imagery are big business (see Quayle and Taylor 2003).

From ritualized sexual foreplay to ceremonial performance, ritual's rhythmic repetition, evocative style, and precise manipulation of symbols and sensory stimuli enable shared rituals to focus the emotions of participants on the calculated intensification of their messages (see Chapple and Coon 1942 on "rites of intensification"). We remind you once again that belief follows emotion. Ritual generates intense emotion in humans, even ecstasy, and intense emotion, in turn, generates belief. As we will discuss further below, *the more people's emotions can be engaged through ritual, the more they can be prevented from questioning its messages or examining alternative views.*

Ritual Mechanisms for Engendering Emotion and Belief: Ritual Performance

A major characteristic of ritual—a major part of its anatomy—is that *it is performed.* You cannot fully participate in a ritual by reading about it—you have to *be there,* either in person or through some virtual technology like computers or television. Rituals are embodied (see Bell 1992, 2008), sensory—and thus must be *experienced.* The more compelling the performance of ritual, the more fully its participants will entrain with the symbolic messages the ritual is sending. A major part of ritual's job is to imbue participants with a strong sense of the value, validity, and importance of the belief system being enacted; in so doing, ritual must also work to preclude or re-interpret challenges to that belief system and the social structure it supports.

Ritual can be high drama—its performers often stage it like a play (well indeed, plays originated via ritual performance) that intensifies toward a climax. The more dramatic ritual is, the more effectively it engages the emotions. These qualities enable ritual to command the attention of participants and audience, while at the same time serving to deflect skeptical questioning or the presentation of alternative points of view.

Masters of Ritual: Charisma and Ritual Command

Masters of ritual are thus master performers, from traditional shamans to fundamentalist preachers to the high Priestesses of Wiccan rites to many politicians, presidents, and totalitarian and cult leaders. They have both total command of the belief system being enacted—indeed, they often have a part in creating that belief system—and dramatic, often charismatic, flair. Their effectiveness rests on their ability to entrain groups—to take individuals of disparate backgrounds, rhythms, and beliefs and entrain them into synchronous adherence to one belief system. Adolf Hitler's ability to accomplish this cognitive entrainment through ritual was so profound that within a few years he was able to restructure the symbolic system of an entire nation around the cognitive matrix of German world dominance and Aryan supremacy, represented by two powerful symbols—the swastika, and Hitler himself.

The secret to understanding the power that such a leader can unleash in a population takes us back to the issue of archetypal symbols. The charismatic leader (the guru, the teacher, the tyrant, the pastor, the priestess, the chief, the politician, the president, etc.) is a person whose physical form and behavior penetrate directly into the archetypal King (or leader) in most people's brains, whatever that symbol may be called within any particular language and by any particular culture. The tipoff that the charismatic leader is receiving projected archetypal King or Queen status is the fascination that he/she holds for us—we tend to be fascinated with people and things that trigger archetypes in us.

Hitler was extremely charismatic—people continue to be fascinated by him to this day, especially when watching his speeches. His messages were simplistic, yet he was explicitly operating in a mythopoeic venue with the goal of creating himself as an icon of his country, in which he massively succeeded. Hitler practiced his gestures over and over—he even had a series of pictures taken of himself in different noble poses, and then studied them to discover the best ones to include in his public displays. Germans never saw the "real" Hitler in public, only Hitler playing to the archetype. It is likely that he became possessed by his own King archetype, and that it ended up controlling him. This danger is ever-present in our own unconscious minds, for if we over-identify with an archetype, we can lose our sense of identity and personhood. You might do the same thing vicariously if you over-identify with a leader—you might end up doing things you would never otherwise dream of doing if you lose your character and personality to the charismatic person and his or her message (as Robbie did during her participation in a cult, described in Chapter 7).

Whether the process of over-identification with a charismatic leader is a good thing or bad thing, of course depends on the intentions of the leader. Some charismatic "gurus" do lead people to a wholesome lifestyle and righteous ends. Charlie had the opportunity to meet and spend some time with Martin Luther King when he visited Austin, Texas, during the early days of the civil rights movement there. In a private, one-on-one meeting with Dr. King, Charlie found him to be a warm and friendly—quite a normal—person. Later, Dr. King mounted a stage before several hundred people and, utilizing the ritualized black Baptist preaching style (returning to a simple repetitive phrase over and over, as he did in his famous "I Have a Dream!" speech), he gave a sermon centered on the idea, "We have come a long, long way, and we have a long, long way to go!" At the beginning of Dr. King's talk, the mostly white audience was quiet, welcoming, and polite. By the time the speech was over, the audience members were ecstatic, on their feet, and cheering at the top of their lungs. Dr. King's charisma was an example of the kind of charisma that leads toward positive, life-affirming ends.

Contrast that with the destructive ends of malignant narcissistic leaders like Jim Jones, the head of the Peoples Temple cult, who persuaded more than 900 of his followers to commit mass suicide at Jonestown, Guyana, in 1978. The question always arises, how could so many people be so deluded that they would kill themselves just because Jones told them to do so? The explanation of course is that the charismatic leader is the focus of such intense fascination that everyday commonsense, including the instinct for personal survival, is overcome, and people cease to use their critical faculties, opting instead to let the leader do their thinking for them—a surrender of the intellect that is always potentially dangerous. In dramatic contrast, Mohandas (Mahatma) Gandhi led millions of Indians into freedom from British imperialism without killing anyone and without ever aspiring to or attaining political office.

Ritual's ability to generate belief, and thus cultural consensus—and their mastery of that ability—is a major reason why totalitarian leaders manage to retain control of entire countries. And here looms again the shadow side of ritual—its potential to be exploited for good or ill. *Ritual can be used to open the mind to new ways of thinking or to close the mind around only one way to the exclusion of all others.* Totalitarian dictators, cult leaders, and others exploit the power of ritual to prevent their followers from questioning their messages or examining alternatives. If, through the manipulation of ritual and symbol, a leader can get people to associate him with "the nation" in their minds and emotions, even if they hate him, they will find it difficult to imagine the country without him.

Fidel Castro's longstanding political power in Cuba, for example, was rooted in his symbolic association with that nation—an association that was as deeply rooted in Cuban people's minds and hearts as in the army or the police forces he used to command. It becomes unimaginable to have one without the other, so opposition movements cannot get off the ground. We could say the same for China under Mao (massive posters of him adorned many buildings, schoolchildren were taught to memorize his *Red Book*), Iraq under Saddam Hussein—every family was required to have a picture of him hanging in their homes, just as was every family in North Korea under Kim Jong-il and now his son. Yet obviously change can happen—totalitarian leaders can be overthrown. (We will address ritual's roles in effecting social change in Chapter 9.)

On a much simpler and smaller level, we need to note that parents too can be "masters of ritual"—orchestrating dinner, homework, play time, bath time, story and lullaby time, and bedtime in ways that accustom their children to follow this ritual sequence, get tucked in, and go to sleep without protest (well, most of the time). Many families organize their night lives around such rituals, which enact their family values and beliefs on the importance of shared family time, eating healthy foods, cleanliness, learning to appreciate the magic of stories and song, learning to read and sing—while at the same time leading their children straight to the parents' desired goal—sleep!

Ritual and Emotionally Charged Beliefs

At the risk of oversimplification, we state here that there are two types of belief: those that have no emotional charge attached—such as believing that a particular car is blue—and those that carry a high emotional charge. Rituals are designed to present symbolic material in ways that generate strong emotions.

The reader might naturally wonder who invents rituals in the first place? A very good question, but not one that is easily answered, for when anthropologists go into the field to study social and cultural behavior, the rituals are usually in place, and have existed more or less changed or unchanged over generations. One of Charlie's friends, Father Ronald Murphy, is an expert on the history of the Catholic Mass (see Murphy 1979). He can carry out a Mass from any century over the long history of the Church. Clearly, although that ritual has existed for centuries, it has also continued to change over time. And of course, it is people, acting in concert, who change such rituals. It is very rare to find a ritual that has been created out of whole cloth.

Cult leaders, for example, may create new rituals that enact the new belief system with which they are seeking to "penetrate" the brains of their followers, yet these rituals tend to strongly resemble those of other sects or religions. The more common situation is that a ritual becomes transformed—the symbolic order is changed, bits are added, moved, or removed—so as to alter the message in some way, or to bring the message up to date to "true" it to a changed reality. Yet humans often invent new rituals designed to encompass new realities. For example, there are appropriate ritualized ways to utilize email (such as "Don't use ALL CAPS, as it feels like you are shouting"; "Start your reply message above the one sent to you, not below it"), Facebook, LinkedIn, and others that are in constant development and flux.

Human beliefs are linked to language—they are models of the world that we can *talk about* with each other. Not only are beliefs sharable, they are also performable—expressible through symbolic media and meaningful action. As such, they are part of a society's cosmology and cycle of meaning. Beliefs about the origins of the people, important resources like game, staple crops, water, herbal remedies, and so on are more or less spelled out in the belief system and articulated in rituals. If you ask Navajo people whether they believe it's true that Changing Woman was the mother of the Hero Twins who went to the Sun in order to get the power to fight the monsters, the people will simply reply, "That's what they say!" Referring to the elders, to sacred stories, to the annual ritual cycle, people will say that their beliefs are true because *that's the way it is*—it's what we've been taught and what we have been enacting in our rituals since childhood, thereby learning to incorporate and embody our cultural and social beliefs. Anthropologists Sally Moore and Barbara Myerhoff (1977) suggested that ritual's insistence on repetition and order evokes the perpetual processes of the cosmos, thereby metaphorically implying that the belief system being enacted has the same permanence and legitimacy as the cosmos itself.

One of the most successful systems of ritual that Charlie knows of is the cycle of Easter Masses carried out in the Eastern Orthodox Catholic Church—its liturgy dates back to the 15th century and before (and was not affected by the Vatican II modernization of Roman Catholic rites). Imagine, if you will, the cycle of Masses as they were performed before the discovery of electricity, when, after sundown, literally all the light was gone from your town, church, roads, and home from Friday night to Sunday morning. At a Friday night Mass, the priest would hide the host (the bread or wafer representing the Body of Christ) under his raiment instead of in the sepulcher, walk out of the church, and all lights would be extinguished, to be rekindled on Sunday morning. Imagine the power of the message: with the death of Jesus all of the light disappears from the world, and only returns with His resurrection from death and ascendence to Heaven. The message is powerful to believers—"just as our life is without light, so too is our life without Jesus."

Ritual as a Generator of Collective Effervescence

A person entering into a liturgy might not understand any of it at a conscious level, but because the ritual drivers are often archetypal (fire, light, water, the smoke of incense), they can affect people emotionally whether or not they understand the liturgy. Christian missionaries commonly used embodied participation in church rites to convert "the natives." Some missionaries came to understand that intellectual presentation of the core beliefs and values of Christianity could not work due to language barriers and profound differences in ways of thinking—only embodied ritual performance could work to engender belief and effect conversion. Rather than relying upon rational persuasion or textual presentations, these missionaries relied upon the right-brained, gestaltic association of symbolic material and intense positive emotion during rituals—what the great French sociologist Émile Durkheim (1858–1917) called "collective effervescence": socially shared excitement and other intense emotions (Durkheim [1912] 1995). As their native congregations knelt in prayer, rose to sing, and gazed at the statue of Christ on the cross, the missionaries could better imbue/penetrate them with the meanings of Jesus's life and death, giving them an embodied understanding and a sense of collective effervescence—even in the absence of a shared language. Again, belief follows emotion—by getting native people to emotionally feel the power of Jesus and God, it became much easier to get them to believe.

With little space to elaborate, we note here the massive disruptions of Indigenous societies and the complete loss of their traditional knowledge systems and longstanding environmental adaptations that resulted from the missionaries' work. When those often centuries-old knowledges are not passed on, they die out within one generation.

On a much simpler level, Robbie wants to speak here of ritual as a generator of collective effervescence in terms of her experience with Mexican and Mexican-American ritual performances during the singing of songs, either by *mariachis* or by the group as a whole. Much as Black Americans will ritually murmur or shout phrases of encouragement or affirmation of his messages to the preacher during his sermon or the speaker during his talk, so Mexicans and Mexican-Americans will often offer *el grito* (the yell, or the cry) at appropriate places during a song. Robbie vividly remembers a graduate student paper by her then-fellow student José Limon describing his intense discomfort during such ritual performances. He was an acculturated Mexican-American, raised by a traditional family yet then attended graduate school at the University of Texas Austin; he later went on to become a Full Professor with a distinguished career. As he reported in that grad school paper, he was often coded by his fellow Mexican-Americans as a *bolillo*—a piece of baked bread that is brown on the outside yet white on the inside. So during the performance of traditional songs, he experienced additional pressure to yell *el grito* to show that he was still "brown on the inside"—a huge cultural challenge for this very intellectual scholar. Robbie, a scholar herself yet far more extroverted than José, took such opportunities as a chance to exhibit, as spectacularly as she could, her chosen assimilation into Mexican culture and its songs. While José continually hung back from performing *el grito*, Robbie took every chance she had during songfests to yell it out loud at the top of her voice—*aaayyyayy ahhhhh—ah a ha eee aaayyy!* (for a poor written facsimile of her totally awesome performances of *el grito*—according to her, anyway). And she was always massively applauded by the Mexican or Mexican-American audience for her efforts to show that she "got" their culture and really wanted to participate in it. Robbie certainly experienced collective effervescence as a result of her efforts, and could only hope that her audience did too (or perhaps they were just being kind to an outsider who was trying so hard to fit in).

Raw Ritual Experience and Its Cultural Interpretation

As we have seen, often the generation of belief through ritual includes inducing ASCs that produce powerful transpersonal experiences. Such raw experiences are then interpreted for the individual by ritual leaders in terms that are consonant with the society's or group's worldview. *The experience is raw, and the culture or the individual group leader is ready and willing to impose the appropriate interpretation.* Conversion can happen when ritual produces an extraordinary state of consciousness that then begs for interpretation, and the society (or group, or cult) is usually right there to tell the person what it means, to "code" the experience for them. Keeping in mind the "rule of multiple interpretations"—that is, there is no such thing as an experience amenable to one and only one interpretation—we note nonetheless that *when the society or group structures the ritual to produce an extraordinary experience, it will inevitably also structure the interpretation of that experience.*

Back in the 1960s, Charlie had a friend who came very close to suicide. She was extremely depressed, took drugs, and had the classic tunnel and light "near-death experience." She interpreted this experience as a blessing from Christ and subsequently embraced a "born again" Christian ideology. The experience and her interpretation of it changed her life. However, any experienced Buddhist meditator hearing the description of her raw experience would tend to recognize it as a *samadhi* (absorption) experience that is associated with a particular level of development. In other words, a Christian will interpret such an experience within the Christian cycle of meaning, while a Buddhist will make sense of the same experience within the Buddhist cycle of meaning.

Beauty as a Ritual Mechanism

The claim that "beauty is in the eye of the beholder" certainly has a strong cultural component—aesthetic standards vary widely among and within cultural groups. Nevertheless, it is fair to say that across cultures, the performance of important cultural rituals demands that people dress in their "Sunday best" and employ artifacts that meet the aesthetic standards of the community (see Dissanayake 1992). Trashy, ugly, ordinary things are generally not found in rituals (unless the ritual designer chooses them to be there for particular meanings—in the way that Robbie kept a few pieces of Peyton's smashed jeep Big Blue on her altar for years—she had found them in the grasses beside the highway near the spot where the wreck occurred). Rather, the technologies and the trappings of ritual are usually as beautiful as the members of the social group in question can make them.

For one example, driving through Kingston, Jamaica, on a Sunday morning, Robbie was impressed to see Jamaican citizens emerging from their tiny homes, hovels in some cases (from Robbie's middle-class, US point of view), extremely well-dressed even in the suffocating heat—the men in suits and ties, the women in elegant outfits complete with matching shoes, purses, and hats, the children dressed equally as well (the girls with exquisitely braided hair)—walking in what Robbie perceived as an aesthetic parade to their respective churches in honor of their religious beliefs and in full display of their cultural and community values. When we dress up for a ritual ceremony (going to church or synagogue, attending a funeral or a marriage, etc.), we are making ourselves "special" for the ritual occasion—doing our part to make the occasion beautiful.

Ritual spaces are often made special by enhancing their beauty—churches, synagogues, and mosques are made beautiful to enhance the sense of sacredness they provide (see Figure 7.1). On the individual level, Muslims lay out their beautiful prayer mats no matter where they may be, and some Christians dress up to pray, putting on their best before God and kneeling in a special place that is sacred to them.

Beauty and the Mandala of Perception

If you look carefully at a lot of Muslim prayer mats, you will see that they almost always include geometric designs that are intended to remind the supplicant of Allah. Because Islam forbids icons depicting the figure of Allah or the Prophet, they are represented by patterns that are both beautiful and meaningful to the practitioner. Sometimes a geometric pattern will take the form of a *mandala*—a circular form that has a center and lines that radiate outward from the center to the periphery. Most people perceive mandalas as beautiful. Study the stained-glass windows in a church, which are often mandalic in form—it is highly likely that even if you do not share the belief system they represent, you will nevertheless find them aesthetically appealing. Mandalas are found everywhere in the iconography of peoples and are universal because they are fundamental structures of perception and imagination, and also because they are a kind of shorthand encapsulating beliefs and aesthetics in one economical form. In some more complex mandalic forms, the radians may be construed to be binary oppositions (right vs. left, up vs. down, east vs. west, etc.). Psychodynamically speaking, a mandala may represent the oppositions of aspects of our being, such as giving versus hoarding, love versus hate, proper thoughts versus improper thoughts, and so on.

Cultures will often define their world as a system of opposites that are at the same time part of one great unified whole. For instance, the Navajo conceive of the world as existing as a set of opposites, some of which are given gender attributions—like Mother Earth and Father Sky, Blue Corn Boy and Blue Corn Girl, night animals and day animals, and so forth. We have seen how in their healing ceremonies—their "sings"—the healer will create an intricate mandala on the floor of the hogan using ground stones of various colors. These mandalas are often circular and have oppositional images around a central figure. When done properly, the drawing is magically transformed into a portal through which the Holy People can come and help heal the patient, who is placed in the middle of the mandala. After the ceremony is finished, the drawing is destroyed and the colored ground rocks are swept up and discarded. A traditional Navajo would not dream of keeping a true healing drawing to hang on the wall no matter how beautiful the creation, for to do so would be considered dangerous in the extreme—allowing a non-ritually controlled portal into the spiritual world to remain open. Mandalic forms, however, are not perceived as dangerous in and of themselves because they do not attract the attention of the Holy People. Indeed, the Great Seal of the Navajo Nation is a simplified mandala (not unlike a healing drawing) and represents the masculine principle (the circle of arrowheads pointing outward in defense of the nation) and the feminine principle (the rainbow path of Changing Woman around the four directions, the four sacred mountains defining Navajoland, the important animals and corn plants) (see Figure 7.1.).

Mandalas found in Buddhist iconography specifically depict the inner nature of consciousness and being. Thus, the mandalic forms we encounter in Buddhist architecture (temples, stupas, sacred spaces) are specifically

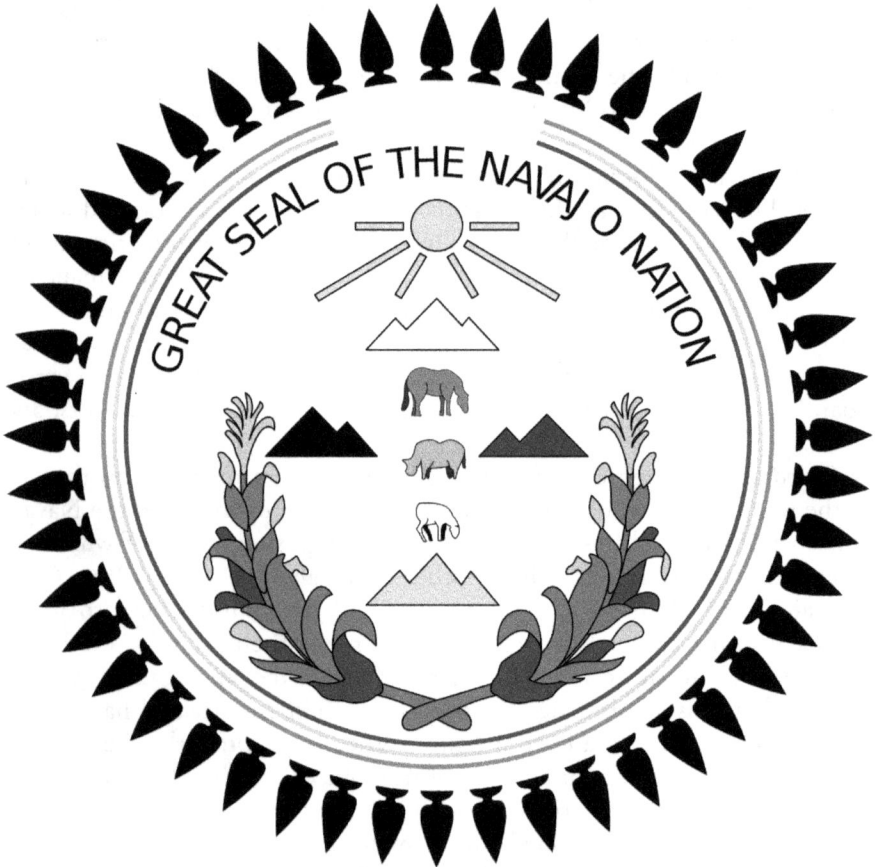

Figure 7.1. The Great Seal of the Navajo Nation. Wikimedia Commons, Creative Commons Attribution-ShareAlike 3.0.

intended to remind us of our true inner nature—a nature that takes the form of oppositions, relations, and the constant struggle of the self for unity. The mandalic nature of perceived space is common throughout the world's religions. When we focus our attention on any altar, then everything else becomes peripheral to that altar, but also constitutes the context or frame of the altar. All the objects, persons and behaviors at or surrounding the altar— all of which take their place within the presentational mandala—must have their assigned meaning and play their part in the sacred drama. As we sit in our pew in a church and gaze at the priest doing his thing at the altar, we see the stained-glass window behind the altar above, the roof arching above to the heavens, the stone or wood floor below, and symbolic objects and persons to the left and right. For those drawn into this ritual world, the effect is to produce a portal into the sublime.

Rites of Passage and Religious Conversions: Transformation through Ritual

The most profoundly transformative of all rituals are initiatory rites of passage and religious indoctrinations (Driver 2006: 61–62).[2] These break down the belief system of the initiate, then rebuild it around the beliefs and values of the group—a process known in religion as a "conversion experience." Whether the individual is converted to Islam, Christianity, Judaism, the Moonies (or any other sect or cult), or initiated into the Marines, the Navy, a terrorist group, or a fraternity or sorority, the ritual process is very much the same.

A *rite of passage* is a series of rituals designed to conduct an individual (or group) from one social state or status to another, thereby effecting transformations both in society's perceptions of the individual and in the individual's perception of themselves (Van Gennep 1966; V. Turner 1969; Grimes 2002).

Ritual's role in rites of passage is fourfold:
1. to give humans a sense of control over natural processes that may be beyond their control by making it appear that natural transformations (e.g., birth, puberty, death) are actually effected (or at least powerfully shaped) by society and serve society's ends (Malinowski 1954);
2. to "fence in" the dangers perceived cross-culturally to be present in transitional periods (when individuals are in-between social categories and therefore call the conceptual reality of those categories into question), while at the same time allowing controlled access to their energizing and revitalizing power (Douglas 1966; Abrahams 1973);

3. to convey, through the emotions and the body, a series of repetitious and unforgettable messages to the initiates concerning the core values of the society into which they are being initiated through the carefully structured manipulation of appropriately representative symbols, and thereby to integrate those values, as well as the basic premises of the belief system on which they are based, into the inmost beings of the initiates (Turner 1967, 1969). As Roger Abrahams (1973: 24) noted, "What distinguishes a full-blown rite from all other ritualized behaviors is the number of central symbols resorted to, and the willingness—indeed the felt necessity—to repeat so often the message of the enactment through these central symbols";

4. to renew and revitalize these values for those conducting, as well as for those participating in or merely watching, the rituals through which these transformations are effected, so that both the perpetuation and the vitality of the belief and value system of the society in question can be assured (Turner 1967, 1969; Geertz 1973; Abrahams 1973).

Rites of passage generally consist of three principal stages, outlined by van Gennep (1966) as: (1) separation of the individuals involved from their preceding social state; (2) a period of transition in which they are neither one thing nor the other; (3) a reintegration phase in which through various rites of incorporation they are absorbed into their new social state. Van Gennep states that these three stages may be of varying degrees of importance, with rites of separation generally emphasized at funerals, and rites of incorporation at weddings.

Yet the most salient feature of all rites of passage is their transitional nature, the fact that they always involve what Victor Turner (1967, 1979) has called "liminality," the stage of being betwixt and between, neither here nor there—no longer part of the old and not yet part of the new (from the Latin word *limen,* which means "threshold"). In the "liminal phase" of initiatory rites of passage, "the ritual subject passes through a realm that has few or none of the attributes of the past or coming state" (1979: 237). Of this liminal phase, Turner (1979: 238–39) writes:

> The passivity of neophytes to their instructors, their malleability, which is increased by submission to ordeal, their reduction to a uniform condition, are signs of the process whereby they are ground down to be fashioned anew and endowed with additional powers to cope with their new station in life... It is the ritual and the esoteric teaching which grows girls and makes men... The arcane knowledge, or "gnosis" obtained in the liminal period is felt to change the inmost nature of the neophyte, impressing him, as a seal impresses wax, with the characteristics of his new state. It is not a mere acquisition of knowledge, but a change in being.

One of the chief characteristics of this liminal or transitional period of any rite of passage is the gradual psychological "opening" of the initiates to profound interior change. In many initiation rites involving major transitions into new social roles, this openness is achieved through rituals designed to break down the initiates' belief system—the internal mental structure of concepts and categories through which they perceive and interpret the world and their relationship to it. Ritual techniques that facilitate this process of cognitive breakdown include *hazing*, the imposition of physical and mental hardships (familiar to participants in military and fraternity [and sometimes sorority] initiation rites), and *strange-making*, making the commonplace strange by juxtaposing it with the unfamiliar (Abrahams 1973). A third such device, *symbolic inversion*, works by metaphorically turning specific elements of the belief system upside-down or inside-out, so that the high is brought low, and the low is raised high, and the world in general is thrown into confusion (Babcock 1978: 13–32):

> As this process is continued over time, the cognitive reality model begins to disintegrate. Learned versions of reality and previously instrumental responses repeatedly fail the initiate. Confusion and disorganization ensue ... introducing a relatively entropic state. At this point the individual should be searching for a way to structure or make sense out of reality, and in terms of the initiation, his search constitutes the launching point for the transformation of identity. (McManus 1979: 239)

The breakdown of their belief systems leaves initiates profoundly open to new learning and to the construction of new categories. Any symbolic messages conveyed to an initiate during this opening process can thus be imprinted on his or her psyche as deeply "as a seal impresses wax" (V. Turner 1979: 239), or "deeply into the bone" as Ronald Grimes (2002) put it. Once broken down, their cognitive structures can then be rebuilt around the beliefs, values, and approved behaviors of the group. (This cognitive de- and re-structuring is not metaphorical—quite literally and physically, the networks of neurons in the brain are broken down and re-organized during intensive initiation rites.)

For example, in the rite of passage of Marine basic training, the initiate's normal patterns of action and thought are turned topsy-turvy. He is *made strange* to himself: his head is shaved, so that he does not even recognize himself in the mirror. He must give up his clothes—those expressions of individual identity and personality—and put on a uniform indistinguishable from that of other initiates. Constant and extremely challenging physical conditioning exercises break down his cognitive structure. Then through repetitive and highly symbolic rituals, such as marching in perfect synchrony, his—or her—physical habits and patterns of thought are literally reorganized into alignment with the basic values, beliefs, and practices of the Marines. In other words, warriors are made, not born.

Cross-culturally, the most prominent type of rites of passage are those dealing with life crises. They accompany what Lloyd Warner (1959: 303) has called:

> the movement of a man [*sic*] through his lifetime, from a fixed placental placement within his mother's womb to his death and ultimate fixed point of his tombstone ... punctuated by a number of critical moments of transition which all societies ritualize and publicly mark with suitable observances to impress the significance of the individual and the group on living members of the community. These are the important times of birth, puberty, marriage, and death.

The sequence of these life-crisis events that Warner uses refers to the baby's birth and not to the *woman's* giving birth nor to *her* transition into motherhood. Thus this sequence reveals a strong male bias that may be one reason for the former general anthropological overlooking of the significance of the rites of childbirth across cultures. Arranged from a female-oriented physiological perspective, the sequence would have to read: birth, puberty, marriage, childbearing, menopause, death.

Ritual and Cognitive Transformation

Transformation for ritual participants can be both mental and physical. It can be external in the eyes of society, and/or internal in the psyche of the participant. Some kind of transformation can be said to occur in all types of ritual along our spectrum. For example, as previously noted, the ritual handshake and "Hi, how are you?" open a previously nonexistent channel of communication between two individuals, resulting in almost immediate entrainment of their bodily rhythms. But ritual's true potential for transformation, of course, goes much deeper than this example, entailing profound possibilities for individual interior change.

Deep transformation for ritual participants occurs when the symbolic messages of ritual fuse with individual emotion and belief, and the individual's entire cognitive structure reorganizes around the newly internalized symbolic complex (as Juan the Chamula's did at the ritual climax of the sacrifice of the rooster, when suddenly he felt "free," and as Robbie's did during her EMDR session). Although this may sound final, as if it could happen only once, it is not. Human neural structures are relatively fluid. As most religious adherents know from experience, belief waxes and wanes, and must be continually reinforced through ritual if it is to retain a significant role in shaping individual cognition and behavior. Each time you attend a religious service or a political rally, you can experience this process anew, diving deeper and deeper into the symbolic constellations of belief of the religious, spiritual, or political system.

Religious and Cult Conversions

Intensive religious and cult indoctrinations can tear apart the prior belief systems of the initiates through prolonged exposure to the beliefs of the new group that results in cognitive breakdown and reorganization (*hazing*), the induction of altered states of consciousness (*strange-making*), the extreme denigration of the initiates, or their exaltation to a place of exaggerated honor and importance in the group (*symbolic inversion*). These tactics can result in a conversion experience in which the entire cognitive structure of the initiate reorganizes itself around the beliefs, values, and approved behaviors of the group. Such religious conversions can evolve slowly, over years of repeated exposure to a given set of beliefs, or can be made to happen very fast.

For example, Mark Galanter (1989), a sociologist studying the Moonies (followers of the Korean evangelist Reverend Sun Myung Moon) found that potential new members were often selected because they were socially isolated, frequently as a result of being new students on a college campus without a strong social network. They were initially recruited by what Galanter called "love-bombing"—showering the potential recruits with multiple messages of appreciation—and thus thrilling and bewildering them and making them want more to entice them to attend a five-day workshop. Fascinatingly, around one-third of those who attended such a workshop (ostensibly offered to explain the religion to interested newcomers) ended up converting—even if their original reason for going was to learn enough about the religion to talk a loved one into getting out!

How could such previously unintended conversions happen? Participants sat through many hours of lectures, during which they were bombarded with an overload of confusing information, resulting in a narrowing of their cognitive abilities (see the following chapter on stages or levels of cognition). Interspersed between lectures were periods of playful fun—volleyball, dancing—during which the newcomers were made to feel wholly important, wholly wanted, wholly loved. Allusions were made to Rev. Moon in connection with the Second Coming of Christ, and it was repeatedly suggested that if the workshop participants were truly blessed, they might see visions of Rev. Moon himself during their regularly scheduled meditation periods. Not surprisingly (due to symbolic penetration), many did. Those who did not sign up after the five-day "workshop" often wanted to, but all had at least one highly significant friend or relative pulling them away.

Robbie's Unwanted Conversion Experience

I am lying on the floor and Steven is above me. "Breathe, breathe," he tells me as he presses on my chest and massages my arms. "I don't want to," I tell him. "This is too hard, it hurts too much. I'll never clear this issue, I can't!" "I am not my negative thoughts," Steven intones. "I am not my negative thoughts," I repeat dutifully. "I am not my negative thoughts—I am unlimited," Steven chants. "I am unlimited," I repeat, over and over. It seems clear that his intention is to get me past my limited notion that I will never heal the emotional pain that led me to request this rebirthing session. His hands press my sternum. "Breathe, breathe," he tells me, again and again. I take one deep breath after another, inhaling as much air as I can get into my lungs and expelling it slowly, completely. Breath after breath, in and out, in a rhythm that opens my psyche and eventually releases the pain in my throat and chest, which seems to float out of my body on the waves of air I expel. Fused as one with the rhythms, Steven breathes with me, urging me to keep repeating "I am unlimited." As my pain floats away and my emotions calm, I feel deeply unified, deeply alive, and wide open.

Turning aside to find his glass of water, Steven muses, almost to himself, "Yeah, you know, it's like the white flame that burns without consuming." The symbol he has just articulated penetrates my consciousness like a wheel of fire. My entire cognitive universe immediately reconstellates around this core symbol, and in an instant, I go from not believing anything the people in this New Age group have been telling me for years to believing it all.

Flying into a rage, I leap from the floor, grab a pillow, and start pounding it against a wall, screaming "Father André, you son of a bitch, you tricked me!" Steven is startled and alarmed. "Damn you!" I scream at him. "How could you do this to me? I didn't choose to believe this stuff, and now it's too late!"

Let us explain. Shortly after the birth of her second child Jason (in 1984), feeling somewhat isolated and overwhelmed by the realities of mothering two young children, Robbie had joined a mother's support group she had been told about that met weekly in a house just down the road. It turned out to be led by a woman named Karen, who had begun to channel a spiritual entity named Father André. Robbie was fascinated—here was the New Age (which was actually "new" back then) happening full force, just a few miles from her house in a conservative, middle-class neighborhood! The anthropologist in her wanted to know more. Plus she was enjoying the companionship of the other mothers, and her older child (Peyton) seemed to enjoy playing with the other kids, for whom activities were always provided.

So she continued her attendance, and as time passed and she got to know other members of this group and their husbands or partners, she began increasingly to utilize the services they offered: massage, Chinese medicine, nutritional counseling, and rebirthing/breath therapy—a major ritual driver (see Chapter 4). Eventually, as Robbie became more familiar with Father André's teachings, she began to request individual counseling sessions with "him," primarily to deal with difficulties she was experiencing in her marriage. But all through this process, Robbie merely "suspended disbelief" in order to gain maximal advantage from the healings and the counseling sessions. She maintained cognitive distance from the belief system of the group, which centered around the core notion of "ascension." Father André taught that just as Jesus Christ had ascended—in this group's words, "had expanded out to become one with all" —so every human being had the potential to do the same. In fact, said Father André, the point of Jesus' ascension was to demonstrate that it could be done and thus encourage others to work toward this ultimate goal.

Members of the group, which was called One World Life Services (OWLS), would occasionally "channel" other entities besides Father André, who recounted remarkable "ascension stories." One was "channeled" from an Indian warrior whose best friend betrayed him by raping his wife. He tracked his betrayer into the desert for three days and finally caught up to him, finding him weak with thirst, hunger, and exhaustion, and unable to fight. Lifting his knife to kill his former friend, the young brave looked into the other man's eyes and, in a profound moment of illumination, knew that they were brothers, indeed, that *all people were one.* In that instant, he "ascended"—became "one with all." Another ascension story, "channeled" by another group member, came from a young Icelandic maiden who was punished for some transgression by being left alone on an ice floe to freeze to death. "As the ship and the sailors who left me there to die sailed off into the distance, my heart reached out to forgive them. With the ice as my support, the wind to empower me, the grey skies to lift me up, I encompassed them with my consciousness and knew that we were one. In love and ecstasy, and without effort, I understood that I was one with all, and so I did not die, but rather ascended."

Robbie found these stories fascinating. She didn't believe them for a second, but she thought they were terrific *stories*—indeed, she intended to record them and to write an article for a folklore journal analyzing what she called "ascension stories" as a New Age storytelling genre. And she had plans to write another article about this New Age group that would analyze its belief and value system and compare it with those of other cults and new religious movements.

But then came the fateful counseling session with Father André, during which he specifically advised that to work on her marital problems, she should do a rebirthing session that week with Steven. Deep into the rebirth, in a deeply altered SOC, Robbie found that Steven's musing about "the white flame that burned without consuming" suddenly, somehow, made all this "nonsense" about ascension make sense. She saw Moses standing before the burning bush that burned but was not consumed, and she understood something essential and profound about energy and eternity that she still has no words to articulate.

As we noted above, such experiences are raw but almost always, the culture or social group is there to interpret them, to tell you what they mean. Steven did not spell it out for her—he did not even have to say "the white flame that burns without consuming indicates that ascension is possible." Robbie had been hanging out with this group for three years at this point, had been hearing their stories and listening to them discuss and work through rebirthing/breath therapy to "clear their issues" in order to achieve ultimate ascension—in the flesh, just like Jesus. So, in a flash, her mind interpreted that raw experience in terms of ascension, and the meaning the symbol of the white flame took on for her was that ascension, like eternity, exists and is possible and can be represented and evoked by the white flame, which exists in perfect balance between producing and consuming—constantly emitting just enough energy to sustain itself without destroying itself or anything else. Had the spiritual context of this group been Christianity, Robbie might have interpreted the "white flame that burns without consuming" as an introduction to Christ Consciousness and promptly become a born-again Christian. Charlie, being a Buddhist, would have interpreted it as a *jhana* experience—a meditative state of absorption (concentration) where the mind becomes unified or absorbed with its object of focus, which can be the breath, a candle flame, a word, and so on. A Jew might have interpreted it in terms of Moses and the Burning Bush. A devout esoteric Kabbalah practitioner might have explained the experience as a *Sephora*—one of the waypoints up and down the tree of life. And so on. Any raw experience of this kind is open to multiple interpretations, and, again, the context within which they take place is always ready to provide an interpretation that fits within its belief system.

In retrospect, what Robbie finds so amazing about this experience is that she knew the instant that it happened that *she had been converted, she did not want to be converted, indeed was furious about it, but it happened anyway!* Without wanting to or choosing to, she went in an instant from not believing to believing, all because, in a state of psychic openness induced by heavy rhythmic breathing (and preceded by three years of exposure to this particular belief system), one core symbol penetrated her consciousness, mapped itself onto her neuronal networks, and changed the way she perceived the world and the meaning of life.

After that intensely transformative experience, Robbie moved ever deeper into the belief system of the group, attending more and more of their weekend seminars, meditation, and rebirthing sessions, and starting herself to "rebirth" others (she got pretty good at it!). During this time, Robbie had more fun and experienced more intimacy and more ecstasy than ever before in her life. She was a full participating member in a community dedicated to healing where she truly felt that she belonged—to such an extent that for a while, she even wanted to move in with them, give them all her money, and put her children in their school as their other members had—the classic reactions of the recently converted.

But in addition to now being a true believer, Robbie was still an anthropologist. She knew she had been "had," as it were, and her intellect never accepted the validity of her conversion experience nor of the belief system into which she had been converted. Most of her being—her emotions, her perceptions, her sensory experiences—resonated with that belief system, but intellectually she understood that it was just one story among many that had been invented by humans, and that ultimately it could be no truer than any other such story.

Nevertheless, it took her six whole months to un-convert herself—with much associated trauma and pain. She was massively assisted in that process by her then-husband, who was adamantly opposed to her participation in OWLS, for obvious and very accurate reasons. OWLS was still in its early stages when Robbie was participating—later, after she withdrew, they did turn into a full-fledged cult, in denial that they were a cult—when Robbie showed them a magazine article about a cult in Dallas, Texas, they responded, "We are nothing like that!" The clearest indication to Robbie that they had turned from a simple group of healers into a full-fledged cult was that after she withdrew and tried to make an appointment with one of the members for massage therapy, he replied, "Father André says that none of us can see you because you are off your path." In other words, the cult members had drawn a clear boundary between who was one of them and who was not.

The ultimate results for those who stayed "on the path" were disastrous—"Father André" told them to burn all their family photos, sell everything they owned, and invest the money in a European pyramid scheme to raise enough capital to build a huge healing center in Hawaii, and move to Europe to make sure the investment would pay off. When the pyramid scheme failed, Father André blamed them for not "clearing all their issues" via constant rebirthing and, of course, told them to intensify their ritual efforts. They lost everything, resulting in homelessness for some of the longest-enduring members—but that is a story for another time. Nevertheless, for many years, Robbie missed that sense of specialness you feel when you believe that only you and a few others *really understand* the meaning and purpose of life—which, as with many cults, included Father André's assurance that their success would create peace in the Middle East.

Conversion Experiences and Ritual Socialization

Robbie's conversion experience was the result of a long, slow socialization process that crystallized suddenly through one powerful core symbol. Yet, as in those Moonie workshops, conversions can also happen much more rapidly. Robbie's conversion experience was very negative for her, as have been the conversion experiences of hostages who experience the well-known "Stockholm syndrome"—identification with their captors and eventual conversion to their belief system (Patricia Hearst is perhaps the most famous example). Yet many others experience very positive conversion experiences, to Christianity, Islam, Ba'hai, Judaism, the Jehovah's Witnesses, Christian Science, Mormonism, and multiple other sects and religions. Many such experiences happen in much the same way as Robbie's—repetitive bombardment over time with symbolic messages and then a sudden flash of opening and acceptance. While the ritual process may remain the same or similar, the final result will depend on whether or not the newly converted individual welcomes the conversion—for example, receiving Jesus Christ into their lives as their personal Savior or realizing that all of the perceptual world is an illusion from the Buddhist point of view—and finds it cause for celebration and positive life transformation.

The successes enjoyed by many religions, sects, and cults that employ such conversion tactics demonstrate the extreme malleability of the human central nervous system. *Under the right conditions, any of us can be made to believe almost anything—and the group engendering the raw experience always stands ready to interpret it their way.* Understanding human susceptibility and the power of ritual to influence belief can leave you free to choose.

Summary: Ritual, Emotion, and Belief

In this chapter, we have described ritual healing from "soul loss" for both Juan the Chamula and Robbie the anthropologist, showing how the sensory manipulation of repetitive and symbolic stimuli facilitated those healings. We have described the excitation and relaxation nervous systems and shown how ritual can cause them both to discharge simultaneously, producing a strong sense of flow and sometimes even ecstasy (which Robbie often experienced during group and individual rebirthing experiences orchestrated by OWLS), which can keep ritual participants coming back for more, as Robbie did. We have described ritual mechanisms for generating emotion and belief, including ritual performance, extrinsic and intrinsic drivers, charisma, beauty, mandalas of perception, ritual socialization, collective effervescence, and ritual drama. We have discussed rites of passage and religious conversions, and have shown how raw individual spiritual experiences can be (and almost always are) interpreted in cultural and religious terms to give them socially shared meaning.

Their rhythmic repetition, evocative style, and precise manipulation of symbols and sensory stimuli enable collective rituals to focus the emotions of participants on the calculated intensification of their messages. Remember, one more time, that belief follows emotion. Ritual generates intense emotion in humans, even ecstasy, and intense emotion, in turn, generates belief. In conclusion, we repeat: *The more people's emotions can be engaged through ritual, the more they can be prevented from questioning its messages or examining alternative views.* Yet please do not misunderstand us here. We applaud and celebrate ritual conversions to belief systems that individuals truly want to hold (when their intellectual faculties are also engaged) because we understand that belief can benefit human beings and add light, even illumination, to our lives. These belief systems, when both ritually effected and consciously welcomed, can bring to us ways of cognizing (thinking about) our lifeworlds that we may well find helpful within the larger scheme of things—a topic that we will discuss at length in the following chapter.

Notes

1. See "Robbie Davis-Floyd." Retrieved 15 November 2021 from http://www.davis-floyd.com/.
2. Some portions of this section are adapted from *Birth as an American Rite of Passage* (Davis-Floyd [1992] 2003a, 2022).

Chapter 8

RITUAL AND THE 4 STAGES OF COGNITION

Cognitive Simplification: How Rituals Speak to the Masses

In any culture, ritual participants will differ from each other both in intellectual ability and in cognitive structure. Individuals of high cognitive complexity may adopt a relative view of reality tolerant of multiple interpretations of a given phenomenon, while individuals with simpler (or simply different) cognitive systems may tend to insist on one and only one correct interpretation (Harvey, Hunt and Schroder 1961; Faiola 2002; Ievers-Landis et al. 2006; Sias, Lambie, and Foster 2006). Straightforward didactic communications must take these differences into account if their messages are to be understood. But *ritual must often work collectively, for the masses.* Ritual overcomes this problem by working to reduce its participants, at least temporarily, to the same cognitive level, at which they will all see the world from within the confines of one cognitive matrix/belief system. Thus we note that *cognitive simplification* generally precedes the conceptual reorganization that accompanies true psychological transformation, as described in the preceding chapter.

The most common technique employed in ritual to accomplish this end is the rhythmically repetitive bombardment of participants with symbolic messages, as also previously described. The advantage of this cognitive reduction of ritual participants to simplified thought is that *only one ritual structure is now sufficient to communicate social or religious norms and values to a wide variety of individuals.* In other words, even complex thinkers can be reduced by ritual to cognitive simplification; thus they may not question the symbolic messages they are internalizing. This process is most clearly visible in the performance of religious rituals such as the Catholic Mass, which can be deeply felt and equally convincing to individuals of all levels of cognitive complexity. (Classic joke: How many Catholics does it take to change a light bulb? Answer: Change? You've got to be kidding!)

Rigid and Fluid Thinking: The 4 Stages of Cognition

To understand how thought may range from very simple to very complex and how ritual may act at all levels of cognition, in this section, we describe "4 Stages of Cognition" and their anthropological equivalents.

Relatively Closed Ways of Thinking: Stages 1 and 2

Stage 1 Thinking

If children grow up in one culture and are exposed for the first 20 or so years of life only to the rhythms, patterns, language, and belief system of that culture, their neural networks will become set in those terms. After that, learning a new language or the norms and values of a different culture or belief system becomes increasingly difficult over time, because integrating new information always requires the formation of entirely new neural pathways in the brain. For a child whose brain is still developing, forming millions of new neural networks every day, that process is effortless; for adults whose neural structures are already largely set, that process requires *enormous amounts of time, energy, and concentrated effort* to create new bridges across the synaptic gaps—new neural networks—between what they already know and what they desire to learn. If you have tried to learn a new language later in life, you will know exactly what we mean.

Individuals who are never required to "think beyond" the belief systems of the cultures or subcultures in which they are raised or trained can over time become resistant to processing new information and can become neurocognitively "rigid" or "concrete" in their thinking—placing them in the cognitive arena of what Harold M. Schroder, Michael J. Driver, and Siegfried Streufert (1967) have called Stage 1 thinking. For Stage 1 thinkers, there is only one possible set of interpretations of reality, and that set of interpretations *is* reality to them; their knowledge system is closed. According to ritual specialist John McManus (1979: 217, 220): "Stage 1 thinkers tend to be oriented toward external standards, authority, and categorical thinking (right/wrong, good/bad) and tend to avoid ambiguity and conflict within the cognitive system ... the adaptive balance is toward assimilating reality to the [person's] own standards, needs, and structure."

Three Types of Stage 1 Thinking: Naïve Realism, Fundamentalism, Fanaticism

Expanding on Schroder, Driver, and Streuferts's (1967) concept of Stage 1 "closed thinking," we here identify three types of Stage 1 thinking in anthropological terms:

1. *Naïve realism*: Anthropologists have long considered a culture based on "naïve realism" to be one in which the people believe that "Our way is the only way there is." Anthropologists have long applied this term to, for example, relatively isolated, small-scale societies whose members, before their massive exposure to Western culture, had no or little notion that other ways even existed. Yet, culturally speaking, naïve realism is more of an anthropological construct than a reality. Humans have always moved around, so cross-cultural contact has been taking place for millennia. Thus, to speak of naïve realism in the sense of small-scale societies that have had very little contact with outsiders is misleading; there are few, if any, such societies left—if, in fact, such societies ever existed. Yet there are many small-scale societies who do have the certainty that "Our way is the only way that matters to us." (And, as we will see just below, many religious groups raise their children to be naïve realists.)

   We must stress that we are not taking any sort of evolutionary perspective here—we reject any notion that naïve realists are less intelligent than others and that the rest of us have "evolved" beyond naïve realism. Both rigid and fluid thinkers exist in every type of society. It is one's degree of *socialization and habituation,* not intelligence, that has the greatest effect on how deeply individuals will internalize the core beliefs of their society or group. And Stage 1 thinkers may find many depths and complexities in delving deeper into their Stage 1 cognitive systems—such as the developmental course of myths that we described above for the Telefolmin people of the South Pacific, who, again, have a system of myth that is structured into at least ten layers, each subsequent and more complex layer given to the initiates when they are considered to be developmentally ready to receive that new layer.

2. *Fundamentalism*: In contrast to naïve realist cultures, whose members tend to have no opinion at all about other ways of life, as those are simply irrelevant to them, fundamentalists have the certainty that "Our way is right and should be the only way for everyone." First called "true believers" by Eric Hoffer (1951), most fundamentalists try hard to shut out all conflicting information, especially from their children,

whom they seek to raise as naïve realists, often by not allowing them to engage with social media or the internet or watch television shows, read books, or attend schools that do not confirm their parents' belief system, worldview, and/or religion's tenets. Fundamentalists usually do not harm others or try to coerce them—rather, they generally just feel sorry for them and often try to proselytize in the hope that they will convert to the one, true way to "save their souls." But their punishment for those who leave the "one true way" can be severe, often involving an extremely traumatizing "shunning" process practiced, for brief examples, by Jehovah's Witnesses, Mormons, some Muslim groups, Orthodox Jews, far-right or far-left politicians, by the members of full-fledged cults (Robbie was shunned by the members of OWLS after she left the group), and by fundamentalist professionals who may shun and bully any colleagues that do not fit inside their paradigmatic box.

3. *Fanaticism:* The profound certainty that "Our way is so right that those who do not adhere to it should be either assimilated or eliminated." Religious and other types of fanatics play increasingly frightening roles in today's world, terrorizing the rest of us with the constant threat of acts designed to bring about an end to the world as we know it and re-create it in the image they seek. Such fanatics, from the medieval Crusaders through the Spanish Inquisition and Hitler's Nazi movement to today's jihadists and other types of terrorists—including white supremacists—often feel justified in torturing, imprisoning, and killing people who are openly opposed to or simply do not share their beliefs, values, and cultural mores. In this contemporary world where people of many colors, beliefs, and cultures live in close proximity, fanatics can be extraordinarily dangerous in their efforts to either coerce or destroy those who do not share their completely closed belief systems.

The Advantages of Stage 1 Thinking

Stage 1 thinking at its best provides individuals and groups with a strong sense of safety, stability, order, and meaning in life. All questions are answered, the rules are clear, and everything is held under tight control. Examples of groups or societies for which this kind of concrete thinking can be adaptive (or at least useful under certain circumstances) include:

1. Small-scale societies living in conditions of relative environmental stability, in which there is little need for individual thinking, because everyone shares the same worldview and it works for everyone because they have sufficient food, shelter, and social satisfaction regarding group activities and social interactions. (Again, there are fewer and fewer such

societies left in the world because modern "development" constantly encroaches against them);

2. Small- or large-scale societies in conditions of high stress or crisis, such as war or environmental disaster, as shared rigid or concrete thinking enables people to join together for concerted action. World War II is a perfect example, while the Vietnam War constitutes a perfect counter-example, as there was little shared concrete thinking about that particular war. Another example is the coronavirus pandemic, during which many people have chosen to follow rigid protocols of self-quarantine, mask wearing, and social/physical distancing;

3. Soldiers (or others) trained to obey orders without question, so that they can immediately respond to those orders (as John McManus [1979: 221] noted: "The army private who is complex and flexible in his thinking may find himself less adapted to rigid, authoritarian army life than his less complex friend");

4. Particular fundamentalist religious groups who live somewhat apart from the rest of society. Examples include Christian, Mormon, Amish, and Hutterite communities in the United States and other countries who seek to raise their children in their religion and worldview only.

We must ask, are these kinds of Stage 1 thinking and learning adaptive in the contemporary world?

Stage 1 Thinking: Maladaptive Manifestations

Closed cognitive structures are vulnerable to at least two types of potentially maladaptive manifestations: (1) fundamentalist and fanatical thinking is often accompanied by intense negative emotion. Indeed, it is commonly the case that closed, rigid, or concrete thinking is a rationalization for or a masking of the real reasons for the belief system: fear, anxiety, loathing, despair, anger—fear that one's cherished belief system might be subsumed by another; anxiety that one's culture or society might be threatened; loathing of those perceived as a threat; despair that the world may be coming to a very bad end because nobody but you and your group knows "the real truth"; anger toward those who don't "get the truth" and about the "unjustness of it all." For example, it is very common for racist and anti-ethnic/immigrant feelings to erupt when the global economy tanks and people are in fear for their jobs. And during the coronavirus pandemic in the United States, many Asian Americans were insulted in public or actually attacked because some misguided Stage 1 thinkers wanted to punish them for the coronavirus because it originated in China—never mind the fact that many of those attacked had never even been to China and/or were not of

Chinese origin. Because they looked "Asian," they were stereotyped as symbols of China and thus of the coronavirus itself. And of course, even if those attacked were Chinese, they certainly were not responsible for bringing the virus to the US.

(2) Closed, concrete thinkers systematically misunderstand information coming at them from a much higher level of cognitive organization. Not only do concrete thinkers oversimplify the information coming at them, they also (often unintentionally) distort it. This distortion is produced by unconscious cognitive structures (neural networks) that lead concrete/rigid thinkers to latch onto and incorporate information that fits into their worldview and to misunderstand or dismiss information that does not—the message heard is not the message sent. For evidence of this kind of processing, one need only track far-right or far-left radio and TV talk shows, where evidence is twisted and distorted through a system of very simplistic assumptions and political beliefs. One senses that behind these views is intense emotion—anger and hatred toward those of a different political or ideological persuasion ("You idiots! Why don't you think as I do—can't you see the real truth?"). The hallmark of such emotionally charged closed, rigid thinking is that no matter how much objective evidence there may be that their views are false, "true believers" persist in holding these views by either ignoring or explaining away all evidence to the contrary. Their mental structures often cannot evaluate or incorporate conflicting information. Putting it another way, they have no neural networks complex enough to process that information because of their intense socialization into one particular worldview—meaning that their neural networks are organized to interpret everything in terms of that one view. (Again, we do not mean to imply that Stage 1 thinkers lack intelligence—they can be extremely intelligent within their own belief systems/worldviews.)

Neural overwhelm has been particularly evidenced by the "information pandemic" or "infodemic" surrounding the coronavirus and the disease it causes, COVID-19. This infodemic/information overwhelm has resulted in multiple rumors and conspiracy theories around the pandemic and has caused many people in many countries to doubt, question, and even refuse to follow the government-imposed preventive measures—which Inayat Ali (2021) has called "rituals of containment." As everyone knows, these include frequent hand washing, mask wearing, physical distancing (we see the term "social distance" as a mistake, as humans are inherently social creatures), and often self-isolation or quarantine. Around the world, many people have given up their previously normative and cherished greeting rituals, such as handshaking, hugging, and kissing on the cheek, showing that global ritual change is possible in the face of an equally global threat.

Stage 2 Thinking: Ethnocentrism

Stage 2 thinking is more flexible than Stage 1 thinking, for it allows for varying views of the same experiences or sets of information, yet tends to favor one view over the others—a type of closed thinking that anthropologists call *ethnocentrism* and that is common to all societies on the globe. Ethnocentric thinkers recognize that other groups and other worldviews can and do legitimately exist, but still insist that "Our way is the best way." Psychological studies suggest that most human beings on the planet are incapable of transcending Stage 2, ethnocentric thought (Schroder 1971; Rest et al. 1999)— the vast majority of us are ethnocentrists at our core.

Ethnocentrism at its most adaptive allows cultural groups facing the prospect of assimilation into another culture to retain their own identities by taking pride in their own traditions, rituals, and mores. Culturally diverse, high-resource societies like contemporary Canada, the EuroZone, and the United States encompass a tremendous variety of ethnic groups. While some members of such ethnic groups (usually first-generation immigrants) work very hard to assimilate—sending their children to English-speaking schools, for example—most of them also work hard to maintain or recreate their culture, or as much as they can of it, by forming ethnic communities—hence we have Chinatowns, Little Italies, and many other such "hoods." Any immigrant family that wants its children to have a sense of cultural continuity will take pains to teach them the language of their culture of origin and to ritualize family life, especially holidays, around their own cultural traditions.

Yet some of the many rituals of ethnicity are extremely minimalist for those who have mostly assimilated into US society and culture. Consider that on March 17 each year, thousands of Irish-Americans may ritually celebrate St. Patrick's Day by wearing green clothing and drinking green beer. For many, this is the sole acknowledgement of their Irish heritage throughout the year.

At its worst and least adaptive, ethnocentrism allows the members of one group to exploit and dominate others while feeling justified in their "superiority." This sense of superiority can be dangerous and result in damage and great harm—as in the transatlantic slave trade that lasted for roughly 300 years, and countless other examples. Unlike fundamentalists and fanatics, ethnocentrists who exploit or harm "others" do not wish to convert them to anything—they generally just want to profit from them in some way.

Again, ethnocentrism at its best simply allows people to value and appreciate their own cultures more than others, while leaving others alone. We repeat that in truth, most of us humans are ethnocentric—because most of us value and appreciate our own cultures and would not choose to live in another one. Yet ethnocentrists are often deeply curious about other societies, other ways of life, and so may travel widely—usually returning home with the sense that "those other places are very interesting, but our way is best." At its worst, ethnocentrism can lead to ethnic cleansing/ genocide, as it often has in many countries. Negative, fear- and anger-based ethnocentrism often arises or intensifies in the wake of economic decline and sociopolitical conflict, usually out of fear that those "others" are taking things away from "us."

Open, Fluid, Ways of Thinking: Stages 3 and 4

Stage 3 Thinking: Cultural Relativism

Schroder, Driver, and Streufert (1967: 102) describe Stage 3 thinking as "complex rules for simultaneously comparing and relating perspectives." In other words, and in dramatic contrast to Stage 1 and 2 thinkers, Stage 3 thinkers are very open. They come to a realization at some point in their lives that every culture and religion has created its own story about the nature and structure of reality, and that no one has the authority to say which story is right. In anthropological terms, we suggest that Stage 3 thinkers are *cultural relativists* who come to see every story about reality as relative to every other story. Nobody has a lock on truth, and every knowledge system must be understood in terms of its own ecological, historical, ideological, and political contexts and must be respected as legitimate in its own right. And all individual behavior must be understood and interpreted within its cultural context.

Many anthropologists are cultural relativists who understand that comparing a given culture with others is the best way to comprehend that culture and its ways, for cross-cultural comparison highlights otherwise invisible aspects of every culture. Certainly, every culture's rituals and the value and belief systems they enact are worth description, interpretation, and understanding. Thus cultural relativism can sound ideal—it entails respect for, appreciation of, and understanding of every story that every culture or religion tells, and of the laws and traditions of each and every society. Such tolerance! No bigotry, no racism, no ethnocentrism, no judgment.

And yet cultural relativism, especially when confused with or equated to *moral relativism*, has severe limitations, as it can and has been used to justify behaviors that are fully acceptable within their cultural context, yet also violate human rights. In some cultures, such as those of rural Pakistan, men are entitled to beat their wives every night just to remind them who is boss (Zakar, Zakar, and Abbas 2016). In some cultures, as we all know from the news media, gay men or adulterous women are stoned to death, torture of prisoners is normal, what outsiders call female genital "mutila-tion" is mandatory, and female fetuses are often aborted due to a higher cultural value on sons, leading to a very skewed population ratio in some countries (Bongaarts and Guilmoto 2015). In most large-scale societies, gender, class, racial, and socioeconomic discrimination are systemic, and environmental pollution is normative, especially when it is profitable in the short term. And in hospitals around the world, most predominantly in low resource countries, treating birthing women with disrespect and abuse is so culturally normative that it has been officially named by those who critique it—*obstetric violence* (see Sadler et al. 2016; Liese et al. 2021[1]). Given that all such practices are part of their cultures, a true cultural relativist would simply seek to understand them within their cultural context, respect-ing the cultural beliefs that lead to such practices. Is that OK? By what standards can cultural relativists say that it is not?

Stage 4 Thinking: Global Humanism

The dilemmas posed by cultural relativism have led to an increased inter-national focus on the development of *global humanism*, which we link to Stage 4 thinking. Schroder, Driver, and Streufert describe Stage 4 thinking as the "generation of complex relationships among rules of comparison" (quoted in McManus 1979: 217). We suggest that Stage 4/global human-ist thinkers recognize the intrinsic integrity and value of every cultural and religious story, every set of customs, beliefs, and the rituals that enact them, yet seek higher standards that can be applied in every context to ensure the *human rights of individuals*, most particularly the poorer and weaker members of society. No one should be beaten, murdered, tortured, raped, abused, or discriminated against in the name of any cause, sociocultural hierarchy, or belief system. Everyone should have access to clean water, good nutrition, effective health care, and fair pay for their work. Daughters should be viewed as intrinsically as valuable as sons.

The higher general standards proposed at the 1985 Women's Conference in Beijing insist that (1) all humans have basic, fundamental rights; (2) women's and children's rights are human rights; and (3) cultural systems that do not recognize or honor basic human rights (as defined by the UN) should be transformed. The challenge of this kind of Stage 4 thinking is to identify, aim for, and help develop "high ethical standards"—*humanistic* standards not based on any one religion or worldview, but on what works to guarantee the rights of all humans to be treated with dignity and respect and to live their lives as best they can without persecution or mistreatment, and without the imposition of the rigid/concrete belief or value system of one group on others. Yet the fact that some Islamic nations have long criticized the 1948 UN Universal Declaration of Human Rights as biased in favor of Western values demonstrates just how hard it is to enumerate rights that everyone in the world can agree on.

Such seemingly desirable goals can often go deeply against the grain of a given culture—as in South Africa during apartheid; as in those cultures whose members believe that uncircumcised women are "unclean" and must be socially excluded; as during the Nazi regime, and many others. Thus global humanists (sometimes also called "universalists") seek to think beyond the limitations of cultural relativism, *searching for universal standards that work for everyone*. They want to validate and legitimate every culture and every individual, while devaluing and discouraging specific cultural practices that hurt people who do not deserve to be hurt in this higher, human rights sense.

Global humanists tend to be acutely aware of the structural inequities that pervade contemporary societies and often do their best to address and work to find solutions for them. Global humanists are also aware that they are on an almost impossible set of missions—how can you work to preserve a culture while also working to change key aspects of it—such as ending the poverty induced by colonialism and the global culture of the capitalistic technocracy, and fostering the births and education of girls and women in nations where they are devalued? Global humanists understand that they must keep their knowledge systems open to new information and engage in bioethical discussion and debate, trying to figure out what works best to preserve everyone's rights without necessarily assuming superiority for any one system.

There is no greater challenge to Stage 1 fundamentalists and fanatics than global humanism—and vice versa. Global humanism says that there can be *many* right ways as long as everyone's individual rights are preserved; fundamentalists and fanatics say there is only *one* right way, and only their leaders and/or their authoritative texts get to decide who has what rights. Fundamentalists and fanatics seek to build temples of isolation, rigid silos within which their rules can prevail—where cults, sects, terrorist groups, and others can practice their belief systems without interference—and including silos designed to protect the turf of a given profession (e.g., obstetrics) against others with overlapping claims to parts of that turf (e.g., midwives). Fundamentalists and fanatics hold tight to their concrete silos, standing firm against the swirling, constantly changing cultural forms of our late modern technocracy. Cultural relativists would have no grounds for criticizing these cultural and professional silos, whereas global humanists would want to ensure that everyone within them chooses freely to be there and has their rights as human beings honored, even when they step outside the silo box—which is so often not the case. Thus, *Stage 1 fundamentalists and fanatics abhor global humanists, and global humanists abhor the efforts of Stage 1 thinkers to take away individual rights and freedom of choice.*

Stage 1 fundamentalists and fanatics work very hard to *reinterpret and remake* Stage 4 thinking into an "alternative" and distorted concrete system. For instance, right-wing true believers may code global humanists as "left-wing do-gooders," "socialists," and the like, while left-wing fanatics may code global humanists as bourgeois capitalists, Western puppets, and so on. Yet people of any party and any persuasion can be Stage 4 thinkers, in the sense of people who "think beyond" fundamentalism/true-believing, ethnocentrism, and even cultural relativism, who are open and willing to explore all thoughts and all possibilities, even while they identify themselves, in sociocultural terms, with one party or another, one religion or another, one culture or another. As Republican President Dwight Eisenhower famously said in his "Chance for Peace" speech (April 15, 1953[2]), "Every gun that is made, every warship launched, every rocket fired signifies, in the final sense, a theft from those who hunger and are not fed, those who are cold and are not clothed …"

The Conflicts between Stage 1 Fanatics and Global Humanists

Stage 1 fanatics tend to persecute humanists whenever they get the chance, as we have seen throughout history. One quick and apt example is provided by the Spanish Inquisition that began in 1492, in which, after 700 years of "Moors"/Muslims, Jews, and Christians all living together in peace under Moorish rule, King Ferdinand and Queen Isabella drove the Moors out of Spain and instituted a horrifying example of religious fanaticism under which all "heretics" who did not convert to Christianity were exiled, tortured, and/or killed.

The frequent conflicts between Stage 1 true believers (fundamentalists and especially fanatics) and Stage 4 fluid thinkers lie behind many of the troubles that pervade our contemporary global society. Stage 4 fluid thinking often produces social movements to create a world in which we do so much more than "just get along" and tolerate difference—a world in which higher ethical, humanistic standards guarantee basic human rights to every global citizen, regardless of their racial, ethnic, cultural, religious, political, or socio-economic background or gender/sexual orientation. Examples of these include the "Truth and Reconciliation Commissions" held in South Africa to formally apologize for apartheid, and in Canada to formally apologize for forcefully removing Inuit children from their homes and families to place them in residential schools to "stamp out the Indian in them" (see Daviss 2021: 22–25).

Table 8. 1. The 4 Stages of Cognition and Their Anthropological Equivalents. Table created by the authors.

Stages of Cognition	Anthropological Equivalents
Stage 4: Fluid, open thinking	**Global humanism:** All individuals have rights that should be honored, not violated.
Stage 3: Relative, open thinking	**Cultural relativism:** All ways have value; individual behavior should be understood within its cultural context
Stage 2: Self- and culture-centered semi-closed thinking	**Ethnocentrism:** "Other ways may be OK for others, but our way is best."
Stage 1: Rigid/concrete closed thinking, intolerance of other ways of thinking	**Naïve realism:** "Our way is the only way that matters"; **Fundamentalism:** "Our is way is the only *right* way"; **Fanaticism:** "Our way is so right that all others should be assimilated or eliminated."
+**Substage:** Non-thinking; inability to process information; lack or loss of compassion for others	**Cognitive regression:** Intense egocentrism, irritability, inability to cope, burnout, breakdown, hysteria, panic, "losing it," abusing or mistreating others

Note: +We will discuss "Substage" later on in this chapter.

Ritual and the 4 Stages of Cognition

Stage 1: Naïve Realism/Fundamentalism/Fanaticism, Stage 2: Ethnocentrism, Stage 3: Cultural Relativism, Stage 4: Global Humanism

These Stages of Cognition and their anthropological equivalents are diagrammed in Table 8.1.

Ritual can support each of these Stages of Cognition by enacting the belief and value systems generated at each level of complexity. Ritual is a primary supporter of naïve realism, continually enacting in every ritual performance the beliefs and values of a given culture or group and the myths (origin or explanatory stories) that underlie and explain those beliefs and values. Ritual performance vivifies fundamentalists' and fanatics' sense of righteousness, reinforcing the tenets of their belief system in the hearts and minds of true believers and thereby strengthening their "true belief." Rituals are also essential to ethnocentrists, helping each group to enact, intensify, and thus reinforce and transmit its belief in its own worth. Rituals can also express cultural relativism, as when Christians deliberately replace "Merry Christmas" with "Happy Holidays" to honor and respect non-Christians during the holiday season. And ritual can enact, display, and transmit globally humanistic belief systems, as it did at the Women's Conference in Beijing, and as it does in a small school in New England where people gather every year on a giant map of the world laid out on the playground to light candles for every nation on earth, and in peace-circles held around the world in which participants name every nation and call for that nation to have peace with all other nations.

Stage 4 rituals are also exemplified in social movement songs such as this one:

> *Circle round for freedom, circle round for peace*
> *For all of us in prison, circle for release*
> *Circle for the planet, circle for each soul*
> *For the children of our children, keep the circle whole!*

Freedom and peace are two core values of global humanism, as is the salvation of our planetary environment to ensure a viable life for our descendants—whose future welfare is also a core value of global humanism. The "prison" to which the song refers can mean literal prison, or the conceptual prisons of psychological issues that keep us isolated, or the rigid ideologies that keep us apart. And this song is usually sung in a ritual frame created by a circle with everyone holding hands to keep the frame intact and generate energy within it, as previously described.

Here is another globally humanistic song, often sung at the end of midwifery conferences in particular, again forming a circle and holding hands:

> *Humble yourself in the sight of your sister*
> *You need to bow down low* [everyone bows] *and*
> *Humble yourself in the sight of your sister*
> *You need to know what she knows* [all stand up straight] *and*
> *We shall lift each other up!* [all arms are raised]

This song, "Humble Yourself," is also an apt example of globally humanistic thinking, as it expresses another core value of global humanism—that every individual knows something of value and everyone's knowledge should be honored, sought, and shared. And in keeping with two of the primary characteristics of ritual—repetition and redundancy—such songs are usually sung or chanted at least four times in a row, which aids the entrainment of the participants and enables the songs' messages to more deeply penetrate into the psyches of the singers.

Other examples of Stage 4 rituals can be found in Native American-style sweat lodge ceremonies, in which all participants of every race and ethnicity call upon "all my ancestors" to be present to the ceremony—those ancestors could and often do include colonialist conquerors and many more. Likewise, for some years, Israeli and Palestinian women weekly enacted a ritual in which they all dressed in black and stood in parks and other places, simply holding hands, in a silent statement of solidarity in their desire for peace and reconciliation.

Stage 1 rituals are exclusive, honoring only the true believers who perform them, whereas Stage 4 rituals are inclusive, honoring all. Who are you and where do you want to stand along that spectrum? And how will you use ritual to enact and facilitate your particular stance?

Ritual, Cognition, and Stress: Substage and Stabilization

When humans are subjected to extremes of stress, they may, at least temporarily, retrogress into a dysfunctional cognitive and emotional condition that we call *Substage* (see Table 8.1 above), which has various ranges, from non-thinking that may cause them to suddenly lash out, driven by their out-of-control emotions, the inability to process information, intense ego-centrism/self-focus, and lack or loss of compassion for others to extreme irritability, inability to cope, burnout, breakdown, hysteria, panic, "losing it," and taking out their stress by abusing or mistreating others. Sound familiar?

Whenever the danger of such cognitive retrogression into Substage is present, ritual plays a critical role, for it stabilizes individuals under stress by giving them a conceptual handhold to keep them from "losing it." When the airplane starts to falter, even those who don't go to church are likely to pray! The simple act of rhythmically repeating, "Dear Lord, please save us," can stabilize terrified passengers enough to avoid the panic that might increase the likelihood of disastrous behaviors.

Ritual stands as a barrier between cognition and chaos (between Stage 1 and Substage) *by making reality appear to conform to accepted cognitive categories*—that is, by making the world look the way we think it ought to, even a little bit. In other words, to perform a ritual in the face of chaos is to restore conceptual order. Even a small semblance of order can enable individuals to function under the most chaotic of conditions. Hence the following section describes the "cognitive anchors" that individuals and cultures can "hold onto" in extreme situations in order to cognitively ground themselves—to keep themselves stable and functional in the face of chaos, at least at a Stage 1 level.

Cognitive Anchors and How They Can Be Employed

Ritual action in the face of disasters is not as irrational as one might think. To repeat a familiar and ritualized action may keep the person from cognitively bottoming-out and descending into Substage. Think of the earthquake victim sweeping off her front steps when the entire neighborhood lies in ruins around her. Those steps represent one ordered cognitive category, from which she can begin to assimilate (develop new neural networks for) the chaos surrounding her. In any chaotic situation where a person is in danger of "losing it," to repeat a familiar and ritualized action may keep the person from descending into Substage. For example, anger management classes may teach a person to calmly count to ten before speaking. Or you might cross yourself, clutch the tiny saint statuette in your pocket, or touch the cross or Star of David you might wear around your neck, and take a series of deep breaths to help calm yourself. Robbie recites a special prayer and carries out a certain series of gestures that have special meaning for her just before she goes onstage to give a talk, in order to ritually initiate that "cranking gear" process we described in Chapter 6.

And when Robbie's cherished home of 30 years burned down in 2009, she got a good dose of "cognitive anchoring." Just after the fire alarms went off, dressed only in her strawberry-patterned nightgown and her blue, pink, and green paisley sleep socks, she grabbed her purse (which she always kept right by the front door in case of exactly such an emergency) on the way out. Standing in the driveway in front of her burning house, she looked down at her body to take stock. "Good," she thought, "I'm not barefoot, so the driveway won't hurt my feet. Oh, and I'm wearing my nightgown, so at least I'm not naked. And I have my purse in my hand, which means I have my cellphone, my car keys, my drivers' license, my credit cards—which means that I can still function in the world—oh, WOW, I have everything I need!" Others have said she was just in shock, but for Robbie, that experience was an epiphany about how little we actually need to function in the world. And she found a great deal of grounding and calm in those cognitive anchors, few as they were compared to all that was going up in flames behind her.

Two days in the hospital for smoke inhalation gave Robbie even more calm and grounding because family and friends were constantly there to support her. Her son Jason came to say, "Mom, you need to *get this*—the house is barely there—the fire went into the attic and the ceilings collapsed, so everything is buried in gray muck." Those words gave Robbie the chance to form new neural networks—new images—that helped her to face what she would find when she returned to her house two days later to begin the salvage work. She was prepared for the horrible mess, yet totally unprepared for the new cognitive anchors that would gradually emerge from the muck—the tiny figurine that had belonged to her mother sticking its hand out of a huge pile of ashes and emerging undamaged while all its former companion figurines lay in ruin, her long-collected Mexican pottery shining fresh and clean in the dishwasher (which she had turned on before going to bed) in the midst of a shattered kitchen, and, most importantly, Peyton's altar (which was in a closed closet with an intact ceiling) impeccably preserved, along with the beautiful urn that contained Peyton's ashes and all the small mementos—her Guatemalan wallet, her passports, her journals, her dolphin sculptures, her dream catchers—that so indelibly evoked Peyton's personality and spirit. These for Robbie constituted tiny islands of cohesion in the face of the utter chaos that lay all around—cognitive anchors that Robbie clung to during the ten-day cleanup of the ashes and muck, which later became meaningful ritual artifacts that Robbie could incorporate into her new home, evoking continuity between her past and her present home lives.

Most ironically, the house burned in a very disordered way after Robbie and her Jewish partner Alan had hosted a Rosh Hashanah dinner for a group of Alan's friends from his synagogue—a lovely and well-ordered ritual, after which Robbie and Alan left the ashes cooling in the charcoal grill outside on the wooden deck. Evidently a hungry raccoon climbed up to get that last sweet potato, knocking the grill over and spreading the still-burning ashes over the deck, which caught fire, and the fire then spread up the outside walls to the attic.

In that attic, Robbie had stored all the ritual artifacts that she had hoped to give to her grandchildren when they arrived—her christening gown, the red velvet Christmas outfits her children had worn, her own favorite toys and dolls from childhood, and all of her mother's Christmas decorations, collected over 40 years. Few of these ritual artifacts had any monetary value, yet they all had ritual value to Robbie and to her son Jason. It speaks to the efficacy of ritual and its symbolic artifacts to note that the loss of these mementos caused Robbie deep emotional pain, whereas the loss of the many practical and daily useful items that vanished in the fire did not, as they carried no special, sacred significance for her. Amazingly, many of the objects that did carry such significance were saved by the firefighters, like her godmother's beautiful armoire and her mother's chests of drawers, dining table, and gorgeous colored crystal wine glasses.

Cognitive Anchors and Rituals of Stabilization

Rituals—such as prayer, or crossing oneself, carefully setting the table, lighting candles for loved ones in danger, pulling out the Christmas decorations or the Passover Seder plates, holding a feast for the devil after the mine shaft collapses (see Chapter 6), or a healing ceremony when illness strikes—provide their participants with many such cognitive anchors. Ritual thus has high evolutionary value: it is a powerful adaptive technique that our ancient ancestors over 200,000 years ago must have utilized to help them continue to function at a survival level whenever they faced conditions of environmental or social stress (like earthquakes, volcanic eruptions, grass and forest fires, and the deaths of loved ones). Archaeological discoveries show that mortuary rituals may go back as much as 300,000 years to the earliest periods of Neanderthal and ancient *Homo sapiens*. For one example, when archaeologists excavated Shanidar Cave in the Kurdistan Region of Iraq, they found evidence that Neanderthals carried out mortuary rites and ritual burials around 80,000 years ago, burying skeletons in the fetal position and showering the dead with flowers (Trinkaus 1983). And by 40,000 years ago, ritual burials, as well as cave art and ritual iconography, were common (Giacobini 2007).

For many millennia, therefore, humans have understood that *groups that believe together can act together* to meet and overcome crises and danger. When belief is not shared, joint action is much more difficult—perhaps impossible—to achieve. Even warring armies often rely on a number of shared beliefs, symbols, and rituals—the Geneva Conventions, the red cross or red crescent of medical facilities, the white flag of truce, the process of formal surrender. These are rituals of stabilization that can work even in the face of the chaos of war.

Eustress and Distress: Ritual and Stress Reduction

The endocrinologist Hans Selye (1907–1982) distinguished two types of stress. *Eustress* is "good stress" in that it challenges us to peak cognition, positive feelings, and adaptive action (Selye 1974). *Distress*, on the other hand, is "bad stress" that can drive us into Substage, and, if ongoing, can lead to physical breakdown, heart attacks, cancer, and other diseases and mental problems. The relationship between the level of complexity of cognitive functioning and performance on the one hand, and the amount of environmental challenge/stress on the other hand, may be represented by an inverted U-curve (see Schroder, Driver, and Streufert 1967; McManus 1979; and Figure 8.1).

For instance, highly stressful jobs like those of paramedics, emergency room physicians, police officers, firefighters, and soldiers may easily lead to not being able to "leave it at the office"—becoming unable to "let go" and take a rest from the environmental stressors such individuals are forced to deal with day in and day out. We know that we are under some degree of distress if it takes us a week to "come down" from the job when we are on our two-week vacation. In this sense, a "vacation" amounts to a ritualized break from the daily stress—a period of time during which we may actually have to "vacate" our homes and go somewhere else in order to de-stress and revitalize ourselves. Coffee breaks, regulated work hours, guaranteed lunch hours, and so forth are rituals that buffer to some extent the distress inherent in a job. Successful businesses take the need for these ritual buffers fully into account and increasingly offer, in addition, on-site gyms, walking trails, and daycare centers. Those businesses that do not institute such ritual buffers suffer the consequences of employee dissatisfaction and "burnout."

As we mentioned above, open-minded, fluid-thinking individuals who normally function at Stage 3 or 4 can be reduced to Stage 1 thinking, and even to Substage, by stress, or rather *dis*tress. Persistent distress can cause information overload and the development of "tunnel vision"—the need to shut out extraneous stimuli and focus on one thing only. In other words, (dis)stress can make fluid thinkers become rigid/concrete, if only for a while. Usually rest or a vacation will restore us to our normal fluid state. But if the stress continues, we can disintegrate into Substage. Under such conditions, as we have shown above in our discussion of cognitive anchors, ritual can stabilize us at Stage 1, thereby preventing us from degenerating into Substage behavior. In times of crisis, of information overload, of too much stress, the most stabilizing behaviors over time are at least a temporary return to Stage 1 rituals—often those of our childhood, like a return to the

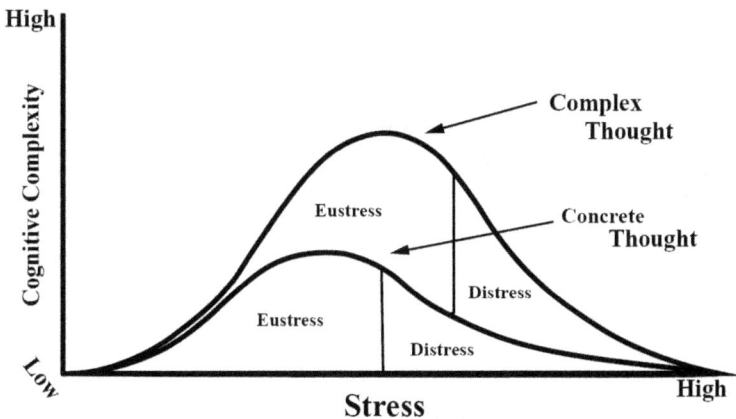

Figure 8.1. The complexity of a person's optimal level of cognition in part determines how easily they adapt to increasing stress. The more complex the mind, the more environmental stress may be encountered and processed before the cognitive system is overwhelmed (adapted from Schroder, Driver, and Streufert 1967: Figure 10.4).

religious institution in which we were raised—that generate a sense of peace and calm (and renewed hope for a brighter future) and allow us to regroup and recoup.

Individuals facing extreme loss may suddenly become extremely religious, even fanatical, when they never were before. Other individuals facing extreme stress may suddenly develop obsessive-compulsive disorder (OCD), ritualizing their every move in an enormous effort to stabilize their lifeworld. The trick is not to stay in Stage 1 too long. Once the individual is stable, change can be tried at a gentler pace. When the stress subsides, we can move back into fluid thinking, secure in the knowledge that there is order in the world (most of the time).

We suggest that contemporary humans, especially those living in modern, industrial, or post-industrial technocratic societies, must be able to move up and down the rigid-fluid continuum in order to cope both with high levels of stress and with the need to keep up with our constantly changing world—a major stressor in itself. Conscious use of ritual can make all the difference.

As we saw above, Stage 1 rituals can ground and stabilize us in times of great stress and confusion. For example, many of those in the United States can vividly remember the flags flying from almost every household after 9/11—powerful cognitive anchors that were also symbolic and ritualistic expressions of love of country when that country was attacked on its own soil, for the first time in over two centuries. Stage 2 rituals can reinforce our belief in the "okay-ness" and goodness of our own, culturally influenced lives. Jews celebrate the Passover Seder to honor and celebrate their exodus from Egypt and the 3000 or so years of cultural continuity they thereby gained. Christians celebrate Easter—a ritual enactment for them of the "risen Christ." Muslims fast during the month of Ramadan and strive to make the pilgrimage to Mecca at least once in their lives, thereby vivifying/instatiating their religion and their religious beliefs. Wiccans stage rituals to honor the Summer Solstice and the ever-repeating cycles of the Earth, Our Mother. (And on and on). Stage 3 (culturally relative) rituals like our "Happy Holidays" example above can express our awareness of cultural diversity and can honor that diversity. And Stage 4 rituals can enact the core values of global humanism—that all people have rights, that no one should suffer unjustly, that justness does or can exist, that we can strive to be fair even when life is not.

One of the things that the inverted U-curve above shows is that we do not do our best, either in thinking or in doing, unless the environment around us presents some kind of challenge. "Challenge" in this sense has to do with the amount of information coming at us. This information may be redundant—nothing new. If we are dealing with the same situations, day in and day out (making breakfast, driving to work, doing our job, bathing the baby, etc.), our brain tends to routinize—quite literally ritualize—its activities.

We feel that we have to stop a moment to note again, as we did in the Introduction, that we see routine, habit, and full-out ritual performance on a *spectrum of ritual*. It is the essence of "habit" not to think about the actions we are performing, allowing us just to perform them in routine ways. Yet how often do we talk about our morning or nighttime "rituals"— the simple self-grooming ways in which we start our days, and the simple, routinized ways in which we end them? Such tiny acts of individual habit or routine may be unconsciously or consciously performed, yet we insist in this book that all these activities are in fact rituals—*patterned, repetitive, and symbolic enactments of cultural or individual beliefs and values*—that exist on a spectrum ranging from habit and routine to full-scale ceremonies. All such acts are ritual performances of our beliefs and values, no matter how grand or how mundane.

Returning to our present topic of ritual and stress reduction, we note that the information coming at us is mostly considered redundant by our brains. But when some novelty pops up in our environment, perhaps placing an obstacle in our way (ran out of milk, the car won't start, the computers are "down" at work, we are out of diapers, etc.), our brain perks up, gets interested in what is happening, and perhaps applies some creative thinking to resolve the problem. Our brains, in other words, are designed to operate at peak efficiency when the environment is complex, novel, and challenging— in a word, "stressful" in a positive sense.

But our tolerance for novelty has its limits. If things get too complex, too novel, and information is coming at us too fast, then our brains may start to shut down and cease to operate effectively. We begin to experience information overload (Klingberg 2008; Eppler and Mengis 2004)—known in the common US vernacular as TMI—"too much information." If this information is perceived to be coming at us too fast, or in bundles that are too complex for us to deal with—we tend to react with anxiety and may even panic/regress into Substage—as happened to many during the corona-virus pandemic, which is still ongoing as we write (February 2022). Rigidly following preventive measures/rituals of containment, including self-iso-lation and quarantine, often helped—and still help—such people to cope with their pandemic-related stress (see Ali and Davis-Floyd 2022).

One of the major factors in determining information overload is the stage of cognitive complexity that we are capable of bringing to bear in pro-cessing environmental information (Schroder, Driver, and Streufert 1967). Peak efficiency for the concrete/rigid mind occurs at a level below that of a very complex mind (everything else being equal). Notice in Figure 8.1

that it requires more environmental challenge to stimulate peak complexity and efficiency in the complex mind than for the concrete mind. As the environment begins to become more complex or more information rich, the concrete mind will peak out earlier than the complex mind, but if the challenge becomes too great or goes on too long, eventually both kinds of minds will begin to decrease in efficiency and complexity of information processing until they both bottom-out and are in danger of Substage reactions.

One of the functions of ritual is to act as a buffer between environmental challenge and cognitive effectiveness—again, *ritual stands as a buffer between cognition and chaos.* Anthropologist Anthony Wallace (1956a, 1957) once researched individuals' reactions to a tornado in 1953. He found many people so stressed-out that they completely denied that something horrible had happened. To give that phenomenon a name, he coined the term "disaster syndrome." It was as though the terrible destruction had wiped people's minds of any reality grounding and effective responses. He observed peculiar behaviors, such as a woman carefully sweeping her front steps when the house behind her had been completely blown away—an example we mentioned above as a search for a "cognitive anchor."

The other really important thing he found was that *those people who had gone through disasters before were much more able to cope with the tragedy than those who had not.* In our terms, such individuals had formed new neural networks while dealing with the original tragedy or trauma that stayed in place and were thus available to help them more rapidly adapt to a new tragedy or trauma. For another example, Charlie's work among the So, who had repeatedly experienced devastating droughts throughout their history, showed that cultures confronting periodic disasters tend to be ritually structured so as to buffer the effects of the disaster on their people (Laughlin 1974; Laughlin and Brady 1978).

And in 2004, as our readers will know, a huge, magnitude 9.1 earthquake struck Sumatra in Indonesia (the "Sumatra–Andaman earthquake"). It produced horrible damage on the island, and caused a tsunami (gigantic wave) that struck coastlines all over the Pacific. It is estimated that over 400,000 people lost their lives in 14 countries. As rescue efforts unfolded, anthropologists who had lived among the peoples of the Andaman Islands feared that their hosts might have been badly harmed or wiped out. Quite to the contrary, virtually all of the people on those islands had retained folklore about past massive tsunamis and hence knew the signs immediately. Some saved themselves and their fishing boats by heading far out to sea where the giant waves just passed harmlessly under their keels; the rest immediately headed inland, away from the coasts. Few sustained casualties, with the exception of the Necobar Islanders, who had given up their traditional culture and had converted to Christianity, and hence were unprepared to recognize the signs of impending disaster and take appropriate action; many of them drowned. We cannot emphasize enough that the knowledge of their environments gained over many generations by traditional societies—always encoded in their myths and rituals and therefore always embedded in their brains' neural networks—is invaluable, and often cannot be replaced once it is lost.

Robbie's personal experience comes in handy as another example of developing *new* neural networks to deal with an original tragedy that, once in place, facilitate a family's ability to deal with subsequent tragedies. As Robbie puts it,

> Since my daughter Peyton died in 2000, our family has experienced other significant losses. We have almost become used to dealing with death, so we have developed a formula that we ritually follow. First we collectively write the dead loved one's obituary, then we plan a family viewing, and then we plan a beautiful Memorial Celebration of that loved one's life. (We are not into "funerals" but rather Life Celebrations.) We have collectively developed neural networks for dealing with death, which develop further with each new death and help us to know what to do, how to proceed. Of course, we are still massively shocked by the bad news when it comes—yet we have been through this enough times that we are perhaps more prepared than others to process the shocking information and channel our shock into rituals that we know will carry us and others through that initial shock.

Robbie has written a manual for dealing with death and grief called *The Art of Grieving Gracefully*.[3]

Rituals as "Life-Hacks"

Ritual researcher Dimitris Xygalatas (quoted in Handcock 2020) calls rituals both "mechanisms of resilience" and "life-hacks," meaning that people use them to relieve stress and anxiety and create a sense of calm. He demonstrates that rituals actively work in the human brain to achieve those goals, explaining that, as noted above:

> Stress acts as a motivation that helps us focus on our goals and rise to meet our challenges … but beyond a certain threshold, stress…can even be dangerous. Over time, its effects can add up and take a toll on your health, impairing cognitive function [and] weakening the immune system … This type of stress can be devastating to our normal functioning, health, and well-being. (Quoted in Handcock 2020: 1).

Xygalatas and his colleagues conducted an experiment on the island of Mauritius. In a stress-inducing scenario, the researchers asked participants to prepare a plan for dealing with natural disasters, which are constant threats there. Afterward, half of the group performed a familiar religious ritual at the local temple, while the other half were asked to sit and relax in a non-religious space. "The researchers found that ... those who performed the religious ritual experienced a greater reduction in both psychological and physiological stress, which was assessed by using wearable technology to measure heart rate variability." Said Xygalatas (quoted in Hancock 2020: 1), "The mechanism that we think is operating here is that ritual helps reduce anxiety by providing the brain with a sense of structure, regularity, and predictability." He recommends the performance of rituals as an effective way to cope with anxiety, noting that ritual is a powerful "mental technology" that we can use "to trick ourselves into [calming down]. That is what these rituals do—they act like life hacks ... that have been with and have served us well since the dawn of our kind." Thus, when you find yourself overwhelmed and about to regress into Substage—or need to pull yourself out of Substage—we suggest that you use the power of ritual to "life-hack" yourself back to cognitive stability.

Summary: Rigid and Fluid Thinking, the 4 Stages of Cognition, Ritual, and Stress

In this chapter, we have described two basic types of thinking—concrete/rigid and fluid—and 4 Stages of Cognition, and more or less equated those 4 Stages to the anthropological categories of naïve realism/fundamentalism/fanaticism (Stage 1); ethnocentrism (Stage 2); cultural relativism (Stage 3); and global humanism (Stage 4). For Stage 1 thinking, we have described the deep differences between naïve realism—not knowing any other way or not wishing to know any other way; fundamentalism—knowing that there are other ways of thinking and believing, yet truly believing that your way is the only right way; and fanaticism—believing so much in the rightness of your way that you also believe that all other ways should be assimilated or eliminated. We have shown that ethnocentrism's light, positive side simply results in a culture's celebration of itself and in attempts on its members' parts to preserve and perpetuate that culture, while the dark, negative side of ethnocentrism can result in one group persecuting or attempting to persecute, enslave, impoverish, exploit, or get rid of other groups—for example, by sending unwelcome immigrants "back to where they came from" or by committing genocide on entire peoples.

We have also shown the weakness of Stage 3 cultural relativism—simply acknowledging the right of every culture to exist and to have its own lifeworld and lifeways can result in accepting behaviors like wife-beating, aborting female fetuses, widow-burning, and torture as acceptable in a general sense because they are acceptable within the parameters of that culture. And we have described global humanism as Stage 4 thinking: the ongoing effort to find that elusive "higher ethical ground" that ensures universal rights to all human beings.

We have shown how ritual can be utilized to enact, display, and transmit the beliefs and values held by Stage 1, 2, 3, and 4 thinkers, as well as to, again, stand as a buffer between cognition and chaos by stabilizing every level of thinker at Stage 1 in times of crisis and distress, in order to prevent them from regressing into Substage—from "losing it." And we have noted that fluid thinking is a type of cognition that readily deals with diversity and change. In multicultural and constantly changing societies, fluid thinking is far more adaptive than rigid naïve realist, fundamentalist, or fanatical (Stage 1) or ethnocentric (Stage 2) thinking.

We have also shown that even fluid thinkers can be reduced to lower cognitive levels by daily stress overload or major disasters, and how the conscious performance of ritual as a "life-hack" can help them find "cognitive anchors" to keep them from regressing into Substage—or to pull them out of it—and to help them "get a grip" on their new reality, giving them time, space, and the energy needed to grow the new neural networks they will need to cope with the stress-full challenges they face. And we have shown how cultures and individuals that have already developed cognitive systems to cope with death and loss are generally better prepared to deal with new tragedies, as their neuronal structures for doing so are already in place—often encoded in cultural memory and enacted in ritual to keep those neural networks in place over generations.

We conclude this chapter by noting again that ritual, among other things, is a set of techniques that can be used in multiple ways to enact, justify, and perpetuate multiple ways of thinking, multiple worldviews, and all of the 4 Stages of Cognition, and with the suggestion that ritual be used consciously and wisely to achieve its desired purpose while "doing no harm."

Notes

1. See also "Obstetric Violence: Research & Policies." Retrieved 15 November 2021 from https://www.obstetricviolence-project.com/.
2. Available on https://eisenhowerlibrary.org, last accessed 15 December 2021.
3. This manual is freely available at www.davis-floyd.com.

Chapter 9

RITUAL'S PARADOXICAL ROLES
Preserving the Status Quo and Effecting Social Change

⸺∰◯

Cultural Conservatism and Cultural Change

Culture is essentially conservative, and yet the world is ever-changing. So, as previously noted, that conservatism, while it may lead to initial success and long life for a number of generations, can also lead to that society's demise when it does not adapt rapidly enough—"true itself"—to changing life and environmental circumstances. Change happens, and societies either develop new belief systems, myths, or paradigms and new rituals to enact them that can help them to adapt to that change, or they do not. And if they do not, in the end they may well disappear, as have many thousands of traditional and other societies over the past several centuries. (If you had lived in the heyday of Ancient Rome, when the Pax Romana stretched across continents, you might never have imagined that one day, Rome itself would fall.) The possibility of disappearance confronts us today: nuclear or chemical warfare, air, water, and ground pollution, the Climate Crisis, global pandemics, even an asteroid collision—any of these and more could destroy some or all of us, or profoundly change life as we know it—just as the coronavirus pandemic has done. Our ability to survive and thrive will depend in large part on our ability to tap our human flexibility and creativity and the power of ritual for its adaptive capabilities—as we have done for COVID-19 by changing our social patterns as mentioned above. These shifts in our daily patterns are examples of rapid ritual change.

Other such rapid changes may need to occur. If freshwater becomes scarce due to global warming and subsequent drought, can we find more creative ways to perform our daily rituals of dishwashing and bathing—like the four-minute shower already obligatory in some parts of Australia, where water is already scarce? Can we learn to live without non-renewable resources like oil, gas, and coal? The huge global dialogue about such issues has resulted to date in not enough concrete action, because the citizens of contemporary technocracies are accustomed to the comforts that come from consuming such non-renewable resources and to the billion-dollar businesses they sustain. Our daily rituals and large-scale ceremonies depend on those resources, not to mention our lifestyles and the technocratic worldview on which they are based.

Within our lifetimes, we may all have to acknowledge that human actions have played a major part in environmental change, to completely revamp our lifestyles in order to adapt to our changing environment, and to change our rituals to enact new values on conservation and living well with less—what Howard and Elisa Odum (2008) called "a prosperous way down." Many of us are engaged in such ritual change (see Grimes 2003a)—we religiously recycle everything we can (yet have to use the precious resource of water to rinse much of what we recycle). We turn off our taps while brushing our teeth instead of letting the water run (a major ritual/habitual change for those of us who were raised to let that water run while we took our sweet time to brush our teeth). We support organic, especially local, growers by buying their products or encouraging our local grocery stores to do so. We purchase electric cars or cars that use less gas, grow our own gardens, and note that many US grocery stores now only offer paper bags instead of those formerly ubiquitous plastic bags, and encourage us to bring our own—as has long been done in Europe, where you have to bring your own bags, as no other bags are offered. "Freegans" forage for food inside the trash bags that grocery stores throw out, finding lots of packaged food discarded simply because the package was damaged in some way.

Many of us in high resource countries are changing our daily rituals in environmentally conscious ways—yet our efforts still constitute only a tiny drop in the vast ocean of human over-consumption. We must do better. Large corporations must change their ritualized practices of generating massive amounts of waste—these practices enact their core values on showing profitability at the expense of all else (some are trying), and on and on. Whether our contemporary technocracies prove to be sustainable or not in the face of the onrushing Climate Catastrophe (see Wallace-Wells 2020) will depend in large part on profound changes in thinking and belief and on the rituals that may come to enact those changes.

Cultural Reminders, Cultural "Memories"

As we saw in the preceding chapter, information stored within sacred stories and folklore over many generations and enacted in ritual may make the difference between high casualty rates or no casualties at all among people confronting potential disaster. Some scholars have interpreted this cultural transmission of information as a kind of "cultural memory" that influences our reactions to events in the now—as with those Andaman Islanders who escaped the tsunami because of their cultural memories, encoded and transmitted to them over generations via myth and ritual.

Cultural artifacts and institutions like art, monuments, writing, storytelling, architecture, folklore, and more can operate as reminders (*mnemonics*) of information relevant to both the past and the future. For certain Indigenous societies, "cultural memory" can go back hundreds, even thousands of years. Some Australian Aboriginal myths tell of the time far back in the past when "the earth exploded." These myths (origin or explanatory stories) seem to refer to the eruptions of volcanoes in various places in Australia—for example, of Mount Wilson near modern day Sydney—that happened thousands of years ago yet are still encoded in contemporary Aboriginal myths, just as *Genesis* still encodes the historically forced transition from hunting and gathering to large-scale agriculture. (And see Cheyney and Davis-Floyd [2020a, 2020b, 2021] for a description of how the folktale of the "Three Little Pigs and the Big Bad Wolf" more elaborately encodes the transition from hunting-gathering to horticulture to agriculture—can you figure out how?) The most powerful system of cultural mnemonics/reminders among traditional and modern peoples alike is their belief system/myth/paradigm-ritual complex. Through explicit performance of a culture's cycle of meaning, ritual works both to preserve and to transmit the society's belief system, and so becomes an important force in the preservation of the status quo in any society (see Taylor 2003). Moreover, when one sub-group within a given society gains control over mnemonic performances, it can exercise a great deal of political control over its members.

In the early years of the formation of the Christian church, for example, there was a struggle for control over scriptural interpretation and the liturgy. Those who wanted people to share equally in the practice of their faith were labeled "Gnostics" and declared "heretics" (and even killed) by the patriarchal priesthood whose members wished to control access to both the scriptural canon and the liturgy—and of course the wealth accumulated by the Church. Those testaments that seemed to reinforce the "natural" power of the clergy were gathered together into what came to be called the Holy Bible, and alternative testaments were disavowed and relegated to the historical trash pile (see Pagels 1989). It was not until the

15th and 16th centuries that the German monk Martin Luther and others fomented what came to be called the Protestant Reformation, which essentially pivoted on the notion that *everyone* has the right to read and interpret the scriptures. This "Re-Formation" led to the wresting of power from the hands of Catholic priests and the formation of many of the Protestant sects that have flourished to this day, and to the creation of multiple rituals that enact, reinforce, and transmit the newer belief systems of those Protestant sects.

From Kings to Dictators: Changing and Then Preserving the Cultural Status Quo through Ritual

As we saw in the preceding chapter, the many anthropologists who have studied literally thousands of cultures around the world usually find that those in power in a given social group tend to exercise unique control over ritual performances. They utilize ritual's tremendous power and influence to reinforce both their own importance and agendas, and the importance of the belief and value system that sustains them in their positions.

Europe's feudal lords organized annual ceremonies during which their peasants/serfs presented their tributes in the great hall and received acknowledgement and recognition of their services. Europe's kings and queens received the tributes brought to them by the nobles with great ceremony and royal recognition—often knighthood and/or admission to one or another prestigious group. Their status was enhanced by any personal charisma they might have had, yet the social structure was so tightly organized around the king's "God-given right" to hold the throne and the many rituals that supported that right (e.g., coronation) that they could hold that position even if they were dull, boring, non-charismatic people.

In contrast, 20th- and 21st-century totalitarian dictators often arose from humble beginnings. Like the "big-men" of various tribal societies, they used their personal charisma, the ritualized techniques of gift-giving (and bribes), and a deep understanding of their native cultures to develop/invent rituals that could tap the core values of their respective cultures and associate themselves with those core values to rise to ultimate positions of leadership that gave them close to total control of their respective nations. Hitler of Germany, Mao Zedong of China, Pol Pot of Cambodia, Idi Amin of Uganda, Saddam Hussein of Iraq, Kim Jong-il of North Korea—all (and many, many more) are cases in point. They all heavily manipulated ritual to put themselves in positions of control and keep themselves there, as Vladimir Putin of Russia and Kim Jong-un of North Korea are doing today. And then they continued (and many still continue) to manipulate the power of ritual to keep their populations under subjugation and control.

A strong case in point comes from a very moving book by North Korean defector Hyeonseo Lee (2015: 220). She writes:

> One day early in the first semester, our teacher had an announcement to make. Training and drilling for the mass games would soon begin. Mass games, he said, were essential to our education. The training, organization, and discipline needed for them would make good communists of us. He gave us an example of what he meant, quoting the words of Kim Jong-il: since every child knew that a single slip by an individual could ruin a display involving thousands of performers, every child learned to subordinate their will to that of the collective. In other words, though we were too young to know it, mass games helped to suppress individual thought.

Ritualized Control and Ritual Change through Social Consensus

Yet we must emphasize that it does not take a totalitarian leader to keep a population under control through ritual (and the myths, belief systems, and paradigms that rituals are designed to enact). *All societies on earth work to maintain social order through ritual.* The laws intended to enforce order cannot be fully maintained solely by the judicial system of any society nor by the power of its leader. Most people in high resource countries ritually/habitually stop at stop signs and red lights and refrain from speeding, not because they are afraid of getting caught and ticketed, but because they have been socialized into doing so and recognize that this socialization is reasonable because it prevents traffic accidents. They *consensually choose* to obey the laws and to enact the rituals (patterned, repetitive, and symbolic behaviors) that obey and reinforce those laws, especially when the laws seem reasonable to them. But when laws appear to be unreasonable, many people *choose to disobey* them. And when many people in a given society choose to disobey a given set of laws, those laws in general cease to have any great effect on societal behavior.

The prohibition against alcohol in the United States during the 1920s is a case in point—although there were laws against the manufacture, selling, and drinking of alcohol, so many people defied those laws that eventually the laws were rescinded. Today, so many people in the contemporary United States defy the laws against growing, selling, and smoking marijuana that those laws are now in question and have given way to the legal sale of marijuana "for medical reasons" in 37 states as of February 2022, and to its use for recreational purposes in 18 states. These laws constitute the simple recognition on the part of lawmakers in these states that popular use and opinion trump previous official policy. Likewise, increasing numbers of women in the United States are choosing to give birth at home with midwives in attendance. Their choices have helped lead to the legalization of homebirth midwives in 37 states as of February 2022, with others on the way.[1]

In all these cases, ritual has played a significant role. People in the United States in the 1920s desiring to drink alcohol and have fun went to "speakeasies"—a window opened in the door when they knocked, they gave the proper ritualized information, and were admitted. And the dances they participated in while drinking alcohol were ritualized enactments of their values on altering their states of consciousness through alcohol in order to let go of their socialized inhibitions and to have fun as a result of that letting go. Marijuana growers and smokers hold annual conventions in the Netherlands to both celebrate and ritualize the practice of marijuana smoking. Many regard the marijuana plant as sacred, in part because of the sparkly crystalline structure of marijuana buds, which can be seen under a microscope. Friends of mothers-to-be often hold New-Age adaptations of Native American Blessingways to honor and bless those mothers and their babies. And, during the birth process, homebirthers may, along with their support people, perform many rituals, such as lighting fires or candles and "throwing their fears into the flames," drumming, chanting, dancing, ringing soft bells or chimes—all designed to help them entrain their psyches with the physiologic rhythms of labor and thereby to achieve the normal physiologic births that they desire (Cheyney 2011; Davis-Floyd 2022).

Effecting Social Change through Ritual

As we mentioned previously, although culture is conservative, it is also dynamic. Culture has to be dynamic and flexible in order to prepare each generation to confront the realities of contemporary life and to align ("true") its members to those realities. Paradoxically, ritual, with all of its insistence on continuity and order, can be an important factor not only in individual transformation (as we have shown in previous chapters) but also in social change. New belief and value systems are most effectively spread through new rituals designed to enact and transmit them—as with the COVID-19 preventive measures/rituals of containment. The new belief and value system enacted in such rituals involves an intensified respect for a microscopic virus and for the routes of viral transmission, and the need to protect oneself and others from potential contagion, as most people around the world have been doing. But many—most especially rural people, for example in Pakistan (see Akram and Alam 2022; Ali, Saddique, and Ali 2022)—have little knowledge of or respect for viruses and such deep distrust in their governments that they do not believe the coronavirus is real, but rather is a government plot to gain more foreign aid. So they do not follow preventive measures, continue to engage in marriage ceremonies and large festivals, and suffer massively increased "coronaviral" spread as a result. In other words, in this case, their lack of belief in the existence of the virus, and the multiple rumors and conspiracy theories about it that they tend to believe instead, do not "true" them to the world they are living in.

On the other hand, and as previously noted, for those who do believe the coronavirus is real and that rituals of containment/preventive measures should be followed, the world has experienced perhaps the most massive change in ritual performance ever in human history. We have had to let go of our deeply, habitually entrenched, and meaningful greeting rituals such as handshaking, hugging, and kissing each other on the cheek in favor of, for example, the "elbow bump" and/or a friendly nod, and a smile that can't be seen because of the mask we are wearing. Many of us have had to self-isolate or enter quarantine—a complete disruption of our normal rituals of daily life. The fact that so many around the world have been engaging in these Covidian rituals of containment for around two years now shows that rapid culture change is possible when spurred by a global crisis. We humans can adapt, and adaptation in this case has involved major ritual change.

Yet even if a ritual is being performed for the very first time, its stylistic similarities with other rituals make it feel tradition-like, thus giving entirely new belief systems the feel and flavor of being strongly entrenched and sanctioned by ancient tradition—a phenomenon called "invented tradition" (see Hobsbawm and Ranger 1992)—especially when the new rituals take their place within an altered cycle of meaning—including that engendered by a pandemic.

How is a cycle of meaning changed? We have provided examples of Covidian change above. We hope you remember that in Chapter 2 (on the cognitive matrix/belief system that rituals enact), we said that the cycle of meaning includes the ongoing experiences of participants. When people's experiences begin to diverge from the ways things are expected to happen, new information in the form of new interpretations begins to enter the system. Eventually the society's worldview shifts. For one instance (not involving the pandemic), apparently the only members of the US military who opposed the end of so-called "don't ask, don't tell" policies pertaining to gays in the services were older men, especially older noncoms and officers. The younger generations in the military have little or no trouble with openly gay soldiers because the values of their generations have changed over time due to increased openness about the issue as they were growing up.

And we are certain that our readers can come up with many other examples on their own of recent significant changes in their own societies' cycles of meaning, for the contemporary world is in a process of rapid technological and sociocultural change, now intensified by the coronavirus pandemic and the Climate Crisis.

Moreover, *entrenched belief and value systems are most effectively altered through changes in the rituals that enact them*—again because of the systemic relations among the various components of the cycle of meaning. Indeed, ritual represents one of society's greatest potentials for the kind of revitalization that comes from internal growth and change in response to changing circumstances. Margaret Mead (1901–1978) took the view that when we examine any culture over lengthy periods of time (say, over several generations), the culture is so constituted that at all times it both *transmits* and *transforms* knowledge (Mead 1979, [1955] 1989). Keeping in mind that a culture is a pool of information more or less available to individual members of the group, we can see that not everyone shares exactly the same information, or understands things in exactly the same way, or has the same experiences, opinions or memories, or for that matter agrees about meanings. In many societies, there are recognized specialists who are considered to know more about the cosmology (or corporate or professional culture) and its implications than everyone else, and they are often the very same people who are in charge of ritual—perhaps the shamans, chiefs, priests, preachers, political leaders, or CEOs, depending on the society in question. Below we provide examples of the power of individuals to effect social change through their manipulation or creation of myths, paradigms, and the rituals that enact them.

Revitalization Movements and Collective Rituals: Failure and Success in Effecting Social Change

No one is a passive "culture-bearer," for culture is entangled with direct experiences of contemporary social and physical life, both of which change over time. As we saw in previous chapters, ritual is used in various ways to re-enforce the group's belief system (rites of intensification), to transform people as they grow up and age (rites of passage), and to foment revolutionary change (rites of transformation). Yet each of these types of ritual uses the same drivers (see Chapter 4) and other operations to attain the intent. Moreover, it is well to keep in mind that all human beings make an effort to interpret their daily experiences as meaningful in terms of their worldview. When a society's worldview becomes out-of-date, a movement will usually arise to change things to make that worldview up-to-date with—trued to—contemporary life.

For example, the Roman Catholic Church has steadfastly outlawed the use of contraception in family planning, yet numerous polls in various countries suggest that a majority of Catholic women are in favor of the use of contraception. Insofar as the Catholic Church remains intransigent on the issue, there will continue to be a mismatch between what the Church says people ought to do and what a majority of people actually do. In time it seems likely that the Church will be forced to update its views and teachings if it is to continue to have credibility with much of its membership. If it does not, it is highly likely to lose credibility. (Yet people do not abandon their deeply held religions lightly—mostly they just choose to ignore some of their religion's tenets while continuing their religious practice in selective ways.)

Anthropologist Anthony Wallace (1956b: 265) called such a shift in a people's worldview a *revitalization movement,* which he defines as a "deliberate, organized, conscious effort by members of a society to construct a more satisfying culture" (see also Harkin 2007). As his definition implies, revitalization movements (which include prophetic, nativistic, messianic, and millenarian movements) tend to crop up in situations in which people are suffering chronic distress, as well as where groups or classes of people perceive themselves to be undergoing *relative deprivation* compared with another group or class (Walker and Smith 2001).

Revitalization Movements among Traditional Peoples

Cargo Cults as Failed Revitalization Movements

The classic and heart-rending examples in anthropology of failed attempts at cultural revitalization are the millenarian-type movements called "cargo cults" (Trompf 1990). During World War II, the Allies suddenly appeared on many islands of the Pacific and built airfields so that soldiers and war materiel could land. The natives on these islands had little choice in what was happening to them, so day after day they watched the great material wealth of the war effort magically stream in from the air in the holds of the "great birds" (cargo planes). At the end of the war, the Allies disappeared just as suddenly. Gone were the "great birds" that brought such wealth. The natives were left behind in whatever poverty conditions prevailed at the time. Feeling deprived, and wanting the "cargo" to come back, some native groups developed rituals that involved acting out perceived "white American" mannerisms and re-creating the airfields with the flashing fire-lights and other features, the intent of which was to attract the great birds to return. Some groups, led by charismatic cargo cult leaders, sold or abandoned their homes and their possessions and went to sit on an airfield at the appointed time to await the arrival of the great cargo plane. And of course the sad tragedy was that the "great birds" did not return, and the cult members who had believed that the power of their belief and the rituals they developed to enact and express that belief would bring back the cargo, just for them, were left utterly bereft and massively disillusioned. Their belief system did not "true" their imagined worldview to the world they actually lived in.

There have been many examples of revitalization movements in history and across cultures, some of which (like the Sun Dance) caught on and "worked," and some of which failed. The Protestant Reformation began with a revitalization movement against the wealth, power and privilege of the clergy (Hillerbrand 2009). Back in the 16th century, the Catholic Church was far more split than it is today, with more than one figure claiming to be Pope, and with clergy selling "indulgences" (clerically granted forgiveness of sins) to bring in wealth and clerical control of the liturgy and scriptures. As every informed Christian knows, Martin Luther and others demanded changes in the Church, and when their demands were not granted, they created their own protesting (hence "Protestant") organizations with transformed liturgy and ritual that aligned their worldview with the new one that Martin Luther and others had created.

Wovoka and the Creation of the Ghost Dance Religion: A Successful Revitalization Movement

In a similar vein, as briefly mentioned above, in the wake of draconian 19th-century US government policies pertaining to Native American societies that drove native peoples onto smaller and smaller reservations, a Paiute Indian prophet named Wovoka (aka Jack Wilson) accumulated practices and beliefs from various Native American cultures and reformulated them into what became known as the Ghost Dance religion (Kehoe 2007). During a solar eclipse, Wovoka, already a trained "weatherworker," as described above, had a vision in which the Great God gave him instructions on how the people should change their lives to make things better. Keep in mind that no Native American language has a word that means exactly what our English word "religion" does. The closest one can get in many of these languages is something like "moving around ceremonially."

Hence, the central ritual of the Ghost Dance was the ancient "circle dance"—dating back to prehistoric times, these dances symbolized the sun's cyclical movement around the sky and involved drumming, whistling, and chanting. (The Ghost Dance was originally called "Dance in a Circle" or "Spirit Dance"—the word "spirit" was translated into English as "ghost.") Wovoka's vision was that if the people carried out the right activities— living clean and honest lives, and especially if they danced properly—a new era would arrive in which the white man and the Indian (they were still called "Indians" then, and often still use that term for themselves) would come to love one another and live in peace, and prosperity would reign with the return of the buffalo and other crucial resources. As the Ghost Dance spread from its original source among the Nevada Paiute, Native American tribes synthesized selective aspects of the ritual with their own beliefs—a process that often created changes in both the society that integrated it and in the ritual itself.

The Lakota Sioux adaptation of the Ghost Dance, for example, took on a millenarian tone and ended tragically during the 1890 massacre at Wounded Knee Creek in South Dakota. Fearing that the Ghost Dance was a source of social unrest and potential uprising, the US government sent troops to Wounded Knee to stop the dancing, yet the Lakota continued to dance in the hope of salvation. (The crops they were supposed to produce on the reservations to which they had been confined failed because the soil was too poor, the buffalo were gone, and the people were starving.) A tragic series of mistakes, miscommunications, and the accidental firing of a gun led to the massacre of 153 Sioux, most of whom were women and children. As we noted above, the special "ghost shirts" the Lakota wore were supposed to magically ward off bullets, but failed to work, leading to the Lakota's rejection of the Ghost Dance religion. Nevertheless, that religion is still alive and well among some Native American groups—it remains essentially a pacifistic religion advocating love and proper behavior. (Interestingly enough, it was never picked up by the Navajo, who have an intense dislike of "ghosts.")

Charlie Yahey: A Dane-zaa Dreamer and His Invention of a Revitalizing Myth

Another way that a cycle of meaning may be changed is by changing the stories that express a people's worldview. We asked earlier, who creates myth and ritual? And answered that few in traditional societies know—"it is just the way it is." Yet here we have an actual example of the creation of a new myth/origin story among the Dane-zaa Northern Athapaskans (also known as the Beaver Indians), who are a First Nations/Indigenous people living in the Canadian Subarctic. They were seasonally nomadic hunter-gatherers until white colonizers forced them onto reservations after World War II. In an effort to explain this historical circumstance that so massively affected the lives of his people, one of their "Dreamers," a man named Charlie Yahey, came up with a story that gave agency for this change to the Dane-zaa people. According to anthropologists Robin and Jillian Ridington (2006), who have long studied the Dane-zaa:

The story relates that long ago, the creator gave the people a choice of how they would make a living. One option was to write a design for whatever they wanted on paper and have it come true without further effort. The other was to make a living using the tools of "dogs, snares and cartridge belts." The story illustrates both essential features of Dane-zaa technology and also its adaptability. Here is the story as [our Dane-zaa colleague and interpreter] Margaret Davis translated it:

God made everything on this world by drawing out the design for it on a piece of paper.
He made dogs, snares, and cartridge belts.
Then, he took these and the paper for drawing designs to the people of long ago.
He put these things before the old men.
He said, "Anything you want from this land when I have finished making it, I will write down on this piece of paper. You can choose which gifts you want:
the paper to make anything you want,
or the dogs, snares and cartridge belts."
But the Indians said to the paper,
"We won't get anything from this piece of paper,"
and they took the other gifts instead.
Dogs barking.
People can live from the dogs.
When people go to hunt they take the dogs with them
and the dogs show them where to hunt.
"From this paper we will get nothing," they said.
So they took the snares and cartridge belts
and they knew about them.
The white people took the piece of paper.
They can make everything: wagons, stores.
He wrote it down on that piece of paper for them.
Even these airplanes he made for them.
This world is not big enough for them.
He made us Indians to live in the bush,
to do hard jobs and to make our living.

The white people, Charlie Yahey said, can make everything from a piece of paper. Now, the white people with their paper-based technology that produces "wagons, stores," and "airplanes" have taken the world to a condition of ecological imbalance. It is "not big enough for them." Indians, according to Charlie Yahey, chose dogs, snares, and cartridge belts. When I heard Margaret Davis's translation of this story, I was initially surprised and disappointed to hear cartridge belts listed as part of an original Dane-zaa technology. Surely, the people of long ago used bows and arrows, not breech-loading rifles. Other stories told clearly of a time, not so long ago, when the Dane-zaa first learned about muzzle-loading muskets.

Then I asked her what word in Beaver Charlie Yahey had used. She replied that it was "atu-ze" which she told me confidently was how you say "cartridge belts" in Beaver. Both she and I knew, of course, that "atu" means "arrow" and "ze" means "real," "proper to" or "belonging to." Thus, atu-ze could be translated literally as something like "belonging to real arrows" and may have once meant either arrow holder or bow. But Margaret insisted that atu-ze is "our word for cartridge belts."

Suddenly it dawned on me that rather than being an example of cultural contamination and anachronism, this story demonstrates a continued cultural vitality and adaptability. It is about the essence of Dane-zaa adaptive strategy and how it differs from that of the white men.

Indians make their living from their knowledge of the environment. They make it through negotiating social relations with sentient non-human persons. The particular instruments of this technology are not essential to its successful operation. Once, people used bows and arrows. Now they use rifles and cartridges. The essence of their technology is situated in the mutually understood social relations of production they negotiate with human and nonhuman persons, rather than through the possession of any particular artifact. "Real Indians" are not constrained by the artifactual inventory of their ancestors. Real Indians, Dane-zaa, use whatever instrumental extensions of their intelligence that are available to them. (Ridington and Ridington, personal communication, 2015)

This creative thinker, Charlie Yahey, gave his people a story within which their present subjugation made sense—in our terms, his story served to "true" them to their present reality—not to mention empowering them through this story because *they were the original people and the original choice was theirs.*

A similar story comes to us from the Ju/'hoansi (San) people of the Kalahari (formerly known as the !Kung) that describes how the Black Herero people who showed up in the Ju/'hoansi traditional hunting-gathering grounds ended up with cows that they could milk while the Ju/'hoansi got stuck with "gathered raisins" instead of milk:

/'Oma /'Oma, a Ju/'hoan man, had the first cattle and herded them alone, but they had no kraal [corral]. A Black man came and asked whose cattle they were. The Ju/'hoan man said they were his, but agreed to herd them back to the village with the Black man to spend the night. One of the cows had given birth, so the Black man said, "Let's milk her and taste the milk." /'Oma /'Oma was afraid of the cow, so he asked the Black man to tie her up with a leather riem [thong] … Then /'Oma /'Oma gave the Black man a leather riem that was tied to a piece of string. The two of them together pulled on its opposite ends. It soon broke, and the Black man got the riem, while /'Oma /'Oma got the string. The Black man said that he would keep the cows and the Ju/'hoan man would be his servant. /'Oma /'Oma had to go off and eat little things like the three kinds of raisin berries, and the Black man began to cultivate sorghum and maize and ate them along with beef and milk. (Biesele 2009: 39)

This story, told to anthropologist Megan Biesele some years ago by its creator, a Ju/'hoan man named Di\\xao Pari \Kai, encapsulates the struggles of the Ju/'hoan people (whose skins are lighter) to adapt to the presence of Black Herero cattle herders, who took over Ju/'hoan traditional watering holes for their cattle plus a great deal of their land for planting crops, often leaving the Ju/'hoansi without sufficient water and greatly diminishing their ability to hunt and gather, as they had previously done in that area of Botswana and Nambia for many thousands of years.

Subjugated peoples like the Dane-zaa and the Ju/'hoansi can feel empowered if their creation stories tell them that they had the original choice, even if that choice eventually led to their disempowerment. At least, it was *their* choice! Here again we can detect the "truing" function of myth—such creation stories "true" people to their present environments by helping them make sense of why those environments currently exist and, thereby, to adapt to those current environments. Similarly, Wovoka's Circle/Spirit/Ghost Dance helped thousands of Native Americans adapt to their own radically changed circumstances. It did not tell them *why* they had been so subjugated, as Yahey's story did for the Dane-zaa and Di\\xao Pari \Kai's story did for the Ju/'hoansi, yet it did offer them a way to "true" themselves to their present environment by giving them something to do about it—live a good life, live in harmony and peace with others, and dance to revitalize their cultures and themselves. (In contemporary US youth parlance, "True dat!")

Current Revitalization Movements

Revitalization movements continue to arise in modern societies, especially those in which people in sufficient numbers suffer relative deprivation of resources, wealth, health care, education, and political power.

Collective rituals can always express the changing beliefs of the masses and their desires, yet they cannot always effect change. In order for them to do so, there has to be a "tipping point"—a point at which the government in power has reached the limits of its ability or its willingness to repress change—as occurred in the United States with the re-legalization of alcohol ownership and consumption after the Prohibition Era of the 1920s, and decades later, when the FDA, under pressure from the American Medical Association, tried to ban nutritional supplements back in the 1990s and failed due to tremendous popular resistance. This kind of change is currently occurring with marijuana in the United States, and also with the "green movement" and the environmental protection laws it is seeking to put in place and enforce. It is also happening with Indigenous rights, civil rights, and feminist movements, such as Black Lives Matter and #metoo; the "human rights in childbirth" movement (see Daviss and Davis-Floyd 2021); the movement to end violence; the fair trade and "occupy" movements; and other social movements working to effect radical social change, with varying degrees of success. The participants in all these contemporary social movements, just like those in the past and those among traditional societies, inevitably ritualize their actions. They hold their ritual rallies, repetitively chanting their ritual slogans and carrying their often-handmade signs signifying/symbolizing what they stand for and what changes they are trying to effect. As we will further discuss below, the environmental movement may be moving closer to its "tipping point" as more and more national governments are setting goals to reduce carbon emissions—we hope in time to prevent the worst effects of the Climate Crisis.

The Contemporary Invention of Ritual: Effecting Social Change

As previously noted, those who seek to accomplish a "paradigm shift" within a culture or company fail if their retooling does not address the rituals, visible and invisible, that keep the old paradigm in effect. *If you want to change the paradigm, you must change the rituals first.* Here we provide examples of exactly how that can be done, from one of Robbie's fieldwork projects.

The Paradigm Shift of Holistic Obstetricians: "The Good Guys and Girls" of Brazil

In Chapter 2, we described paradigms and presented as examples "the technocratic, humanistic, and holistic paradigms of medicine." Here we focus on a certain type of medical practitioner—the obstetrician—asking, why do some obstetricians choose to change? In other words, why would obstetricians (obs) fully trained and socialized into the Stage 1 technocratic model choose to switch ideologies and style of practice, from the technocratic/mechanistic to the Stage 4 holistic/integrative approach to maternity care? In so doing, they go against the cultural grain and risk persecution and ostracism from their obstetric colleagues and employers, so why would they do that? This question is most poignant in Brazil, a country with one of the highest cesarean rates in the world (56% in 2021, compared to 40% in Mexico and much of Latin America, 32% in the United States, 23% in the United Kingdom, 19% in Japan, Iceland, Finland, Sweden, and Norway, and 16% in the Netherlands (see Davis-Floyd 2022). In December 2011 and

July 2012, Robbie and her colleague Eugenia (Nia) Georges conducted 32 interviews with Brazil's humanistic and holistic obs, who call themselves "the good guys and girls" (Davis-Floyd and Georges 2018).

They introduced themselves to Robbie by that name when she first met a group of them at the I International Congress on the Humanization of Birth, held in Fortaleza, Ceara, Brazil in 2000. They used that name because it fully differentiates them from the "bad guys"—obs with extremely high cesarean rates (often 80% or higher), who practice obstetrics according to their technocratic ideology and their own convenience (cesareans take less than an hour to perform, whereas waiting at the hospital for birth to proceed normally can take many hours, and Brazilian obstetricians are paid the same for both vaginal and cesarean births). During their interviews with these "good guys and girls," Robbie and Nia found that these humanistic, and often also holistic, obs generally have extremely low cesarean rates because they dedicate themselves to helping mothers and babies achieve normal, physiologic births. They practice in varied settings—some of them will only attend home births, others attend births in both home and hospital, and some only in hospital, where they train staff to give Stage 4 humanistic evidence-based care. They were all trained—heavily socialized—in the technocratic paradigm. So how did they change their internalization of that paradigm?

Well, again, *if you want to change the paradigm, you first have to change the rituals that enact it.* For many of them, that change in ritual performance started with giving up episiotomies. An episiotomy is a cutting with scissors of the vaginal tissue that opens the perineum more widely and gets the baby out faster. Many obs still today, especially in low-resource countries, believe that "the perineum will explode" as the baby's head comes out if they don't perform an episiotomy. Thus this surgical procedure is performed on 100% of women who give birth vaginally in countries ranging from Croatia, Romania, and Bulgaria to almost every Latin American country. These beliefs are erroneous. There is a huge body of scientific evidence (see Davis-Floyd 2022 for a compilation) that shows that there is no need whatsoever in the vast majority of cases to perform that ritual procedure, which enacts the belief that the birthing woman's body-machine cannot deliver the baby without technological help.

Robbie's and Nia's interlocutors actually read some of that evidence, were intellectually convinced, and so stopped performing episiotomies. (Most of them were additionally motivated to do so by emotional appeals from their patients who wanted to avoid episiotomies.) They found that only patience was required to replace the episiotomy—if they just waited for the perineum to stretch on its own as the baby's head crowns and recedes, then crowns, recedes, and crowns again, they found (sometimes to their actual amazement) that the perineum did in fact stretch sufficiently and the baby could be easily born. Of course, they had to sit or stand in front of the birthing mother for extra minutes waiting (obstetricians are not trained to wait but rather to get in there and "do something"—perform the episiotomy, apply the forceps or the vacuum extractor—anything to get that baby out as quickly as possible and get on to the next patient). Yet, intellectually convinced by the evidence, these obs chose to start waiting, and were richly emotionally rewarded by normal births in which they did not have to do harm to women to "get the baby out." Their emotions were now engaged in their process of paradigm-shifting.

They were encouraged by the happy results of letting go of the ritual performance of episiotomy—well, they had all read Robbie's books and articles, so they already understood that episiotomy and the other "routine procedures" they had been trained to perform were rituals. And they read more of the scientific evidence and over time became intellectually convinced that birth works better in upright positions. So they began to abandon the traditional lithotomy position (flat on the back with feet up in stirrups)—a huge shift for them as it meant that they had to change their own physical position—and thus their social status—relative to the woman. They could no longer be "on top"—they had to become willing to get down on their knees, or sit or squat down in front of upright women—to actually and symbolically serve them instead of dominating them. Realizing over time (from reading the evidence) that women usually get exhausted during labor because they are hungry or thirsty, they started encouraging women to eat and drink during early labor at least.

Reading more, they started encouraging women to move around a lot during labor to assist fetal descent and pelvic/cervical expansion. A moment of further enlightenment occurred for these "good guys and girls" when they realized that women *can't* move around when they are attached to the electronic fetal monitor, so they let go of continuous monitoring unless the woman chose to have an epidural—in which case, continuous monitoring is absolutely required by hospital protocol. Reading and experientially observing (with their new awareness) that the epidural necessitates many other interventions, they started encouraging their patients to use doulas (women trained to give labor support) and get into showers or baths for pain relief instead of resorting to an epidural. And through additional reading and further experiential observation, these obstetricians came to realize that most of the time, there is no reason to artificially speed up labor with Pitocin. In fact, they realized, artificial induction or augmentation of labor causes problems down the line, because if the woman's body is not ready to go into full labor on its own, forcing it to do so through drugs often results in a dysfunctional labor that ends with the baby going into distress and a cesarean that was "needed" because the interventions they performed caused that fetal distress—the "cascade of interventions" or "ritual train" effect we mentioned previously, which Robbie calls "the vicious circle of technocratic birth."

As these obs became known in their communities as supporters of normal, physiologic birth, more and more women who wanted normal births started seeking them out. And the more these doctors saw normal births, the more they were thrilled when they could facilitate women to achieve them. Over time, these obstetricians let go, one by one, of the ritualistic interventions they had been socialized into, and learned to find delight and personal fulfillment in attending normal, physiologic, vaginal births that, most importantly, delighted and empowered the women who achieved them and their partners. Massive emotional engagement on the part of all parties!

And over time, these obs invented new rituals to enact their new holistic paradigm—spending lots of time with the mothers they attend, engaging in deep conversations with them to answer all their questions and to find out if the client had any psychological issues that might impede the birth, developing strong personal relationships with them, and enacting the values they placed on those relationships by choosing to let go of their busy schedules to spend many hours with those women when they went into labor. Some of them informally call themselves "midwives" because they are practicing what is internationally known as the "midwifery model of care" (see Davis-Floyd 2018c and 2022 for full descriptions of this model).

These obs often limit the number of clients they take on per month in order to ensure that they will have that time to spend, and many of them accept only clients who truly want the kind of normal, physiologic births these obstetricians offer—an ideological match that benefits them and their clients. (Yet some of them accept every client who seeks their services, no matter what kind of birth she wants, because they believe that every woman deserves the very best and most humanistic care, whether she wants a home birth or a scheduled cesarean.) They usually make less money than their technocratic colleagues, but according to their own reports, they are much happier in their practices—in spite of the persecution they often experience from their Stage 1, silo-oriented technocratic colleagues and "the system."

Brazil's humanistic and holistic obs, who live and work in the modern technocracy, are not subjected to torture or burning at the stake, yet they are often subjected to internal hospital reviews and/or fired by their hospitals because other obs object strongly to their countercultural and counter-hegemonic practices. They find their much-needed social support from their humanistic colleagues, who by now can be found in almost every Brazilian city and who are all members of the national network ReHuNa (Network for the Humanization of Childbirth), and, in their own communities, from local birth activists, doulas, and midwives (if they are present—professional midwives currently attend only around 12% of

Brazilian births, around the same percentage as US professional midwives), and their usually very happy clients.

One of them, a holistic obstetrician named Jorge Kuhn, expressed public support for home birth in a national media interview in Brazil in early 2012. (He had previously attended home births with midwives and doulas but had stopped because of pressure from the medical board.) The obstetric society of Rio de Janeiro immediately denounced him (even though he was no longer attending home births) and called for resignation of his license. Brazilian women responded to that challenge to Dr. Kuhn and to home birth with a country-wide march on Saturday and Sunday June 16–17, 2012 that saw more than 5000 women, husbands, partners, and children parading in the streets of 31 Brazilian cities wearing T-shirts and carrying signs and placards supporting home birth—the initial, powerful, ritual step of a social movement that is continuing to grow.

To recap and summarize, these Brazilian holistic obs accomplished their paradigm shifts by: (1) reading, learning, and accepting the scientific evidence in favor of normal birth on an intellectual level, which required the time and energy to develop new neural networks in order to assimilate/be penetrated by this new information; (2) giving up, one by one—or sometimes all at once—the rituals that enact the technocratic paradigm of birth, thereby experiencing the joy and fulfillment of attending normal, physiologic births (recall that belief follows emotion); (3) developing new rituals of personal engagement with their clients that enabled them to complete the paradigm shift from technocratic to humanistic or holistic practice; and (4) a resultant "truing" of their new ideology with their new experiences. As they lowered the number of interventions they performed, including massively lowering their cesarean birth (CB) rates (many of them have CB rates of around 15% percent, which is the rate recommended by WHO), they achieved better and better birth outcomes—healthy babies, happy and fulfilled mothers and partners, and happy and fulfilled obstetricians. Yet again we must note that this happiness was often mitigated by ostracism, bullying, and outright persecutions by their Stage 1 fundamentalist, and often fanatical, technocratic colleagues (for heart-rending descriptions, see Rosana Fontes, forthcoming, and Ricardo Jones, forthcoming).

Herb Kelleher and Southwest Airlines: The Intentional Creation of a Consciously Alternative Corporate Culture

In *Nuts! Southwest Airlines' Crazy Recipe for Business and Personal Success* (1996), authors Kevin and Jackie Frieberg begin with the original vision for the creation of Southwest Airlines (SWA), which was co-written on a cocktail napkin by founder and first CEO Herb Kelleher and one of his law clients, Texas businessman Rollin King. The authors continue with a description of a corporate culture built on the values of having fun via providing excellent and dependable service from city to city in inner-city, smaller airports that would get people closer to where they wanted to go. According to Wikipedia,

> During his tenure as CEO of Southwest, Kelleher's colorful personality created a corporate culture which made Southwest employees well-known for taking themselves lightly—often singing in-flight announcements to the tune of popular theme songs—but their jobs seriously ... Southwest is consistently named among the top five Most Admired Corporations in America in *Fortune* magazine's annual poll. Fortune has also called him "perhaps the best CEO in America."

Prospective Southwest employees were encouraged to write extraordinarily creative letters of application that fully demonstrated their sense of humor—a basic requirement for SWA flight attendants. Robbie well recalls her first flight on Southwest many years ago—attendants hidden in the overhead bins popped out announcing that "the bins are full—of us!" and the announcement during takeoff noting that smoking was available on the outside "wing lounges" where the air was cool and the wind blew free! While insisting on an intense work ethic, Kelleher also insisted on making that ethic fun to instantiate. At the annual Southwest Airlines (highly ritualized) conventions, Kelleher was famous for employing the ludic (playful) aspect of ritual by cracking hysterical jokes and stating that he trusted his employees so much that he was willing to entrust his body and his life to them—and then ritually enacting that trust by literally jumping off the stage into the waiting arms of the dozens of employees who caught him and carried him to safety. Chapters in *Nuts!* include titles and subtitles such as: "Hire for Attitude, Train for Skills," "Kill the Bureaucracy," "Be Creative, Color Outside the Lines," "Honor Those You Love," "Make Work Fun," "Customers Come Second, and Still Get Great Service," "Employees Come First: Great Service Begins at Home." These captions show us that Kelleher created his corporation in defiance of traditional corporate norms that focus on serving the customer and not on the well-being of employees, choosing instead to create and enact alternative norms focused on enhancing the wellbeing of employees in the belief that the happier the employees, the happier the customers they serve. (For a full description of the rituals that Kelleher and his colleagues created to enact their corporate values on keeping fares low, taking people where they want to go, and opening the skies to the democratic value of "availability to all," read *Nuts!*)

We must note that it now appears that Southwest Airlines has mostly abandoned this original and very successful model. Today we (and many others) find that flying SWA is like flying almost any other airline. The playfulness seems to have disappeared—perhaps it has disappeared from the corporate SWA culture as well. It is often the case that originally innovative models lose that original energy over time and turn into typical corporate models that are just about providing efficient service and making money via the sort of efficiency-based rituals that pervade business practice. Ritual spontaneity morphs into ritual bureaucracy as the cultural core values change—a very old and ongoing story that is highly reminiscent of the bureaucratic causes of the *Challenger* explosion as described in Chapter 3.

Summary: Ritual, Cultural Preservation, and Social Change

Through explicit enactment of a culture's belief system, ritual works both to preserve and to transmit that belief system, and so becomes an important force in the preservation of the status quo in any society. Thus, one usually finds that those in power in a given social group have unique control over ritual performances. They utilize ritual's tremendous efficacy and power to reinforce both their own importance and the importance of the belief and value system that sustains them in their positions.

Yet the power of ritual is even more strongly manifested in people's habitual choices to behave in the ritualized ways they have been socialized into since early childhood. Laws and explicit rules in every society may officially dictate appropriate behavior, *yet most people behave appropriately most of the time because of their ritualized socialization* to stop at stop signs and red lights, to hold the door open for the one who comes behind you, to obey the laws (most of the time), and in pandemic times, to dutifully follow the preventive measures/rituals of containment. When cultural behavior changes dramatically and official laws and rules cease to match or mirror those changes, those laws and rules usually get changed. When they do not, social resistance movements (such as labor union strikes) often manifest to work for the needed changes, unless that society is totalitarian and does not allow social resistance and change. Yet even totalitarian societies can be overthrown by massive social resistance in the form of huge public rallies and other collective rituals—as happened in Myanmar/Burma when Aung San Suu Kyi was finally released from house arrest due to public pressure and allowed to exercise political power—at least for a while. When those collective rituals don't work, all-out internal warfare can become the agent of social change. (Of course, it is better to effect such change through collective ritual than through war—if only those in power would listen to the messages those rituals are sending them!)

Again, as we have seen in this chapter, ritual, with all of its insistence on continuity and order, can paradoxically be an important factor not only in individual transformation but also in social change. New belief and value systems are most effectively spread through new rituals designed to enact and transmit them. Even if a ritual is being performed for the very first time, its stylistic similarities with other rituals make it feel tradition-like, thus giving entirely new belief systems the feel and flavor of being strongly entrenched and sanctioned by ancient tradition. Moreover, entrenched belief and value systems are most effectively altered through alterations in the rituals that enact them, just as a change in beliefs can lead to changes in ritual practice, as the "good guy and girl" obstetricians of Brazil exemplify. As they changed their ritual practices around birth, many of their students and others who worked with them also incorporated those changes, resulting by now (early 2022) in the humanization of entire labor and delivery wards in their respective hospitals. Indeed, ritual represents one of society's greatest potentials for the kind of revitalization that comes from internal growth and change in response to changing information and circumstances, such as the coronavirus pandemic and the Climate Crisis, which is likely to turn into a Climate Catastrophe if we do not develop new rituals focused on enacting the ecological values of planetary health.

Note

1. See "Midwives Alliance North America." Retrieved 23 February 2022 from http://www.mana.org/. Most homebirth midwives in the US are certified professional midwives (CPMs). As of February 2022, there are around 3000 practicing CPMs attending around 2% of US births in homes and freestanding birth centers. Of the estimated 13,000 practicing certified nurse-midwives (CNMs) in the US, only around 200 of them attend out-of hospital births (see Davis-Floyd 2022).

Chapter 10

DESIGNING RITUALS

Jerusalem

A few years ago, Robbie had the good fortune to be invited to give talks in Israel. She was simply stunned by Jerusalem. Because she was raised as a Presbyterian Christian, the name itself already had powerful symbolic connotations for her. Actually being there was far more powerful. Robbie found herself standing at the intersection of three of the world's great global religions—in historical order, Judaism, Christianity, and Islam. There she experienced both religious history and religious tolerance—and gender division. At the Wailing Wall (aka the Western Wall)—the most sacred site in Judaism—she witnessed hundreds of Jews, segregated by gender (because the Western Wall Plaza operates as an open-air Orthodox synagogue, and the Orthodox Jews insist on gender segregation), standing and praying in front of what to Robbie appeared to be just a huge stone wall, kissing its stones, and slipping paper notes containing prayers into the crevices between those stones. The Wall is a symbol and its historical context is the meaning of the symbol—that wall represents all that is left of the sacred second Jewish Temple. The first was built by Solomon in 957 BCE and destroyed by the Babylonians in 586 BCE. The second Temple was constructed in 516 BCE and destroyed by the Romans in 70 CE; the Wall is the foundation on top of which the Temple was built. The worshippers in front of the Wall were symbolically honoring the Temple—the most powerful symbol of Judaism itself—which now exists only in their historical cultural memory. (Numerous shops in the Jewish Quarter of Old Jerusalem display small wooden mockups of what the Temple might have looked like.) Above the Wall, hundreds of Muslims were at the same time worshipping in the shrine called the Dome of the Rock (which was built between 689 and 691 CE on the site where the Temple used to stand). This shrine is a holy Islamic site because the prophet Mohammed, founder of Islam, is believed to have ascended into heaven, accompanied by the Angel Gabriel, from the Rock of Moriah, which lies inside that shrine and which many Jews believe to be the ancient location of the Holy of Holies (the inner sanctum of the Temple), and also the site where Abraham prepared to sacrifice his son Isaac at God's command, then stopped because God changed that command. Needless to say, some Jews would love to tear down the Dome of the Rock and rebuild their Temple—which of course is never going to happen.

And within a ten-minute walk, Robbie was in the Church of the Holy Sepulcher, where Jesus Christ is believed to have been crucified and buried in the sepulcher that is now inside the church. She had expected it to be as beautiful as the huge cathedrals of Europe, yet it is not—it is a rough-hewn hodgepodge of large spaces and pigeonholes, first constructed by Crusaders, then damaged and reconstructed many times by various groups across the centuries. The Roman Catholic, Greek Orthodox, Eastern Orthodox, Armenian Apostolic, Coptic Orthodox, Ethiopian Orthodox, and Syrian Orthodox have their own shrines inside the Church, carefully delineated from each other (down to who cleans which part of the continuous floors), containing their own altars where priests robed in differing raiments prayed. And yet, as Robbie was told by her guide, two Muslim families have for around 700 years held the keys to this sacred Christian church, because the vying Christian sects could not agree on which one should hold those keys.

These three major religions hold Jerusalem sacred, and each religion claims to be the only valid and true one, as does each sect within each religion. From a logical, rational perspective, they can't all be right! Yet each claims to be right and true—in our terms, their cycle of meaning "trues" them to the world they live in sufficiently. If a myth—a creation, origin, or explanatory story—sticks close enough to lived reality, it can shape that reality into a viable belief system to which its followers can adhere, each believing that their way is the right and true way, each living within the reality that their belief system expresses and performing the rituals that enact and vivify/instantiate that belief system. In our terms in the preceding chapter, the members of these sects would be Stage 1 fundamentalists: "Our way is the only right way"—and yet, as we showed in that chapter, there are many depths and layers of meaning in each of these religious systems that can take a lifetime to fully study and understand.

All these varied religious groups have managed for many years to peace-fully co-exist within the same square mile. This peaceful coexistence is enabled by the continuous presence of police and the strict regulations of the Israeli government and the Jordanian Waqf; the latter is responsible for everything that happens on the platform above the Wall where the two mosques stand, and Israel is responsible for the security around the perimeter. This status quo protects the Dome of the Rock. The Temple Mount area is a highly charged site that has long been the focus of political struggles not only between Jews and Muslims but also among various Jewish sects. Yet for now, a fragile ethnocentric tolerance prevails there.

Religious Syncretism as Adaptive Ritual Strategy

We now turn away from the marvels of Jerusalem to a brief descrip-tion of the religious *syncretism* that characterizes the Christianity of many Indigenous peoples. (Religious "syncretism" exhibits the blending of two or more religious belief systems into a new system, or the incorpora-tion of beliefs from unrelated traditions into a religious tradition.) Don Lucio's huge altar, like that of his friend Don Julio (see Chapter 6 on ritual frames), contained both Catholic icons and pagan artifacts. Don Lucio could tell you one moment that the sudden weather change was due to the displeasure of the mountain spirits, and in the next moment instruct you to pray to a particular Catholic saint! When anthropologist Evon Vogt lived with the Chamula of Highland Chiapas, he often saw their shamans kneeling on the mountainside in front of large wooden crosses festooned with evergreen boughs. Most observers would assume that they were pray-ing to the risen Christ, when in fact those crosses were believed by the shamans to constitute portals (at the intersection of the bars) through which the mountain spirits could manifest themselves and become avail-able to hear the prayers and petitions of the shamans, assisted in doing so by the living evergreen boughs (which "vivified" the crosses—brought them to life), and *at the same time*, to represent the risen Christ (Vogt 1976). This sort of religious syncretism has enabled Indigenous peoples around the globe to appear to be good practicing Christians while at the same time maintaining (vivifying, revitalizing, and transmitting) some of their ancient traditions, values, and beliefs. Once again, the human brain can be plastic, fluid. It can encompass various explanations of reality and meld them together through the performance of ritual. Or the brain can become concrete, rigid, its neural networks entrained to one and only one view of reality by the consistent performance of inflexible rituals that enact that one view.

Implicit versus Explicit Ideologies and Their Enactments in Ritual

We find it striking that *clearly articulated belief systems can make do with soft and fuzzy rituals, while belief systems that are not clearly articulated often require very clear rituals.* For example, the technocratic model of medicine that we described in Chapter 2 is *not* clearly articulated. Professors of obstetrics do not say to their students that "the body is a machine, the female body is a defective machine, and therefore we need to correct its defects through massive technological interventions in birth." The ideology is not verbally expressed; rather, it is actively performed and transmitted through the rituals of hospital birth and implicitly encoded in the official textbooks. Take for example the following quotation from *Williams Obstetrics* (1989), the most widely used US textbook for obstetricians:

> The uterus is a muscular organ that is covered, partially, by peritoneum, or serosa. The cavity is lined by the endometrium. During pregnancy, the uterus serves for reception, implantation, and nutrition of the conceptus, which it then expels during labor … Birth is the complete expulsion or extraction from the mother of a fetus irrespective of whether the umbilical cord has been cut or the umbilical cord is still attached. (Cunningham et al. 1989: 877)

Then contrast that quotation with the following one:

> We value pregnancy and birth as personal, intimate, internal, sexual, and social events to be shared in the environment and with the attendants a woman chooses. We value the oneness of mother and child, an inseparable and interdependent whole. (Midwives Alliance of North America (MANA) Statement of Core Values and Ethics 1994: 1–2)

The quotation from *Williams Obstetrics* seems to be simply "scientific"—yet without saying so, it implicitly expresses the technocratic ideology of the body as machine, whereas the MANA statement explicitly expresses a holistic ideology of birth.

While the technocratic model of birth is taught implicitly through its texts and through the rituals of hospital birth, the home birth/midwifery model is explicitly written down in many articles and books, explicitly taught in childbirth education classes, and explicitly articulated by homebirth midwives, doulas, birth activists, and mothers. They have to be explicit about their model and their belief system around birth because it is alternative, counter-hegemonic, not recognized by society-at-large. (To recap, the midwifery model holds that the female body is a healthy organism; birth is a normal physiological, psychological, social, and spiritual experience that should be facilitated by midwives and accomplished by mothers; and that women can give birth under their own power without any need for interventions in the vast majority of cases.) The more counter-hegemonic a given culture or subculture, the more explicitly its members will tend to develop and articulate their own countercultural belief system. This explicit model is enacted in rituals, yet those rituals, at least for home birth, can be soft and fuzzy—as we mentioned previously, lighting candles or a fire and "throwing your fears into it," chanting and singing, and so on. In contrast, implicit models like the technocratic paradigm of birth have to be massively enacted in ritual so that the students being imbued in that model will "get it" without being explicitly told what "it" is—in what is called technomedicine's "hidden curriculum."

Quesalid and Implicit versus Explicit Rituals

Quesalid was a Kwakiutl shaman who became a shaman because he did not believe in shamanism and wanted to learn more about it so that he could confirm his skepticism (H. Whitehead 2000). He studied under senior Kwakiutl shamans, learning techniques like "sucking the illness out" of a person and then manifesting what he had "sucked out" by showing a bloody piece of blob (which he had previously tucked into his pocket). To his surprise, most of the ill people for whom he performed this "healing" ritual actually got well! He ultimately came to recognize the psychological effects of this sort of ritual performance and continued his shamanic work to great cultural acclaim. He never believed he was actually sucking anything out of anyone, but he did come to believe, through lived experience, that if his patient *believed* that their illness had been sucked out, that belief could help them to heal—what we in contemporary times would call "the power of visualization" (which we described in Chapter 7 on ritual as performance). The belief system Quesalid was taught by other shamans was explicit, and the people he treated believed in that explicit belief system. Thus it was implied through his healing performances that the ritual would work. And since it usually did, he eventually came to value implicit ritual performance that utilized, to great effect, the core beliefs of the explicit belief system. Ritual can work both ways! You can first believe in the "belief system" and so experience the "truth" of ritual through performing the rituals that enact that belief system. Or you can believe in nothing, as Quesalid initially did, then perhaps gain a different sort of belief through the performance of rituals when you perceive that those rituals do in fact produce results. As we have previously stated, ritual is inherently paradoxical.

The Intentional Creation of Personal Rituals: Two Memorial Services, Two Weddings, and One Birthday Party

Thus far in this book we have mostly spoken about ritual as a social and cultural enactment of values and beliefs. But ritual also has the ability to enact extremely individual and personal beliefs, and here we home in on that ability, using as examples the Memorial Service that Robbie and her family members created to honor Peyton shortly after she died (an extremely successful ritual), a second Memorial Service that Robbie planned on her own one year later that went all wrong in the end (a failed ritual), and the extremely successful ritual weddings of Chris and Lisa.

Peyton's Memorial Service/Birthday Party: A Conscious Ritual Enactment of Personal Beliefs and Values That Worked

Written by Robbie

We called it a Memorial Service because we hated the word "funeral." More than mourning her death, we wanted to celebrate her life. Within a day of her death (September 12, 2000), it had become apparent to us all that the event *had* to happen on her 21st birthday, September 16. It would be the birthday party she never got to have, plus some! Our friends—our massive support system—flew into action. Our dear friend Robert Smith found Umlauf Sculpture Garden, a gorgeous outdoor site that would both honor Peyton's love of nature and accommodate the 400+ people who were expected to attend.

Now to constructing the program—how should this Memorial Service proceed? What should be its ritual order? Peyton was highly spiritual yet belonged to no organized religion, so obviously, if we really wanted to honor her and who she was, no minister or preacher could preside. Clearly, we needed a Master of Ceremonies, and our 16-year-old son Jason took on that ritual role.

We also agreed that into this Memorial Service we would put all the money we had been saving for Peyton's ongoing university tuition, her college graduation party, her eventual (we had hoped) wedding, the baby showers—now none of those events would ever happen. So we decided to throw all our "Peyton savings" into this one event—this massive celebration of Peyton's life. It would be a party beyond all parties! Since Peyton had just graduated from the Natural Gourmet Cookery School in New York, obviously the catered dinner we were planning would use the vegan menu she had cooked for her graduation. (She had sent it to us as a booklet, complete with recipes for each dish and photos. Our caterer found it a huge challenge, yet he succeeded—the food was beyond delicious!) Since Peyton loved Texas wild-flowers, obviously our florist should decorate Umlauf Garden with the most beautiful Texas wildflowers he could find. And because carrot cake was her favorite dessert, obviously we should celebrate her 21st birthday with a huge carrot cake.

Two days before the Memorial Service (that is, two days after she died—this had to happen fast!), all of Peyton's closest girlfriends came to my home to help me unpack her luggage (which I had fetched from the wrecked car in Roanoke, Virginia) in order to select the clothes her body should be dressed in for the viewing. (Viewing the dead corpse is a tradition for many in the United States, a way to really comprehend that the person is dead, a chance to say goodbye. That tradition makes millions of dollars per year for the funeral industry [see Mitford (1963) 1998], yet we tend to cling to it because we really want to see them just that one more time.) Together, we unpacked the bags and selected just the right clothes. And then, what else should go into the casket to be cremated with her? These objects needed to powerfully symbolize her values and her life. So, her toe shoes, of course—she was such an amazing dancer. Her Natural Gourmet chef's hat. A T-shirt from Broadway Dance, where she was training in New York City to dance on Broadway. A dolphin figurine, to symbolize the seven summers she spent dancing in the ocean with wild dolphins off of Key West with Captain Victoria Impallomini, Peyton's love of the oceans, and her deep respect for their ecologies and of the need to protect our earthly environment.

At Umlauf Garden, we had Peyton's body in its wooden casket filled with those ritual artifacts placed in a beautiful, wildflower-decorated grove some distance away from the large patio where the actual service took place—so that those who did not wish to see her body did not have to—and provided cards and colorful pens for people who did wish to see her to write farewell wishes to Peyton to place in her casket and be cremated along with her.

Jason did a great job as Master of Ceremonies, dressed in a Hawaiian shirt and beach trunks in symbolic honor of his sister's love of the ocean. The order of events—of the smaller rituals that constituted this large celebration of Peyton's life—was formal and pre-planned. To open the formal part of the ceremony, Peyton's close friend Brian Hudson played and sang "Sweet Dreams"—a lullaby he had written for Peyton before she died. As the perfect follow-up, my cousin Rocky sang "The Impossible Dream" in his operatic voice. People came forward one-by-one to tell Peyton Stories that had everyone either crying or laughing—remember the importance of the ludic element of ritual? It truly felt like there was a magical frame of energy surrounding the entire event, and the laughter did not break, but rather strengthened, that ritual frame.

After the formal, framed, and heavily ritualized part of the Memorial Service ended, dinner and refreshments were served. The ritual frame that had been the roofed patio felt "open but unbroken"—despite the informality of the dinner. We allowed plenty of time, so that no one felt rushed to finish eating. When the caterers called me to attend the lighting of the candles on the birthday cake, I told them to "STOP and hold it" for a little while, and then I took my sweet time to walk around the beautiful gardens to note how friends and relatives had clustered to eat and to talk about Peyton—forever engraved in my memory are the shining candles and my equally shining relatives and friends. I had learned not to simply ride the ritual train, but to *stop it* for a little while, so that I could simply bask in the moment to drink in from the ritual every single thing it could give me—to let it all penetrate deeply into my being. Peyton's death was far too sudden; I did not want this precious and powerful celebration to stop suddenly in any way, and I succeeded in achieving that very important goal.

When and only when I felt ready, we lit the candles on the cake and sang "Happy Birthday" and "Las Mañanitas" (because she had spent time in Mexico to learn Spanish) to Peyton for her 21st birthday. (Only a few of us knew the words, so we sang them at the top of our lungs!) Then Robert and I closed the casket and the pallbearers—Peyton's dad, brother, and closest male friends—gathered to carry it out. We made a spontaneous ritual of that—my godson Hank gathered the pallbearers and me in a circle and asked us to call in every ancestor and historical figure whom we thought should grace this occasion with their presence—he started with Susan B. Anthony and we went on from there! Then I brought up the rear of the casket procession carrying the gorgeous wildflowers that had graced the closed portion of the casket, and ritually placed them in front of that casket after the pallbearers loaded it into the hearse. Endorphin-producing beauty all around!

After the hearse drove away, many of the attendees didn't feel like leaving and so hung out for a very long time. I vividly remember my son Jason standing in the middle of a huge group hug given to him by his many friends who were there. There was never any rush—we took our needed time—I had learned that lesson in the hospital where I spent almost all day with P's body—bathing her, loving on her—it was so incredibly valuable and important to me that nobody rushed me, so I worked hard to make absolutely sure that nobody would rush this Birthday Party. And nobody did. Oh, you know, we *can* control *some* things in life!

It was the best party ever!—as any and all of the 400+ people who attended will attest to this day. The success of this ritual event—meaning that it succeeded in celebrating Peyton's life, honoring her multiple contributions to the world and the people she touched, completely acknowledging who she was, and leaving all participants on a "high"—carried us for a good while, and helped us in the long term to survive the pain of her death. In terms of this book, this ritual celebration worked at a Stage 4 level: it did not enact any specific religious or cultural beliefs, as most "funerals" do—it simply enacted our personal valuations of Peyton and the globally humanistic life that she lived. She was always and ever the defender of the abused—she was both renowned and respected from kindergarten through high school for openly "jumping the case" of anyone who abused or belittled anyone else. Always fearless in the cause of justice and the right, she called the bullies on their bullying and made them stop! She believed, in a Stage 4, globally humanistic way, that everyone has rights to personal dignity and respectful treatment, and she enacted those beliefs on a daily basis—that's a small part of why she was so loved by so many.

Peyton's Second Memorial Service: A Ritual That Failed

One year later, I planned a second Memorial Service for Peyton on what would have been her 22nd birthday, in the hope that it would carry me through my ongoing grief for some months as the first one had so success-fully done, and be cathartic for others as well. And it should have worked—it almost worked—yet for me this very carefully planned ritual utterly failed in the end. I had rented a school auditorium for the event. I recruited some of Peyton's best friends to sing songs and tell stories about her. Some of her dance teachers even came out of retirement to perform a dance they had created in her honor to the song "Sweet Dreams" that her friend Brian had written as a lullaby for Peyton—such a beautiful dance. We showed some of her dance videos—she was a dream on screen!

This second Memorial Service for Peyton was a major performance, yet there was no dress rehearsal, so we got the timing all wrong. Some of the people who came on stage to speak about Peyton talked for way too long. There were problems with the visual and sound effects, causing further delays. It dragged and lots of people left far before the end. And at that end, which I had planned to be cathartic, absolutely everything went wrong. By then, those remaining had gathered, according to my plan, into a circle around the auditorium, holding hands. I had printed a program that included words to circle songs that we all were to sing together, but the sound system went crazy and the music was too loud for anyone to hear anyone else. I regret to this day that I didn't STOP everything at that point and get the sound manager to fix the system before we continued. And I understand that I was carried, at that point, by the ritual train—even I, who had designed the ritual, could not bring myself to stop it in order to make it better, despite the lesson I had learned at her first Memorial Service. So we sang the songs in our circle, yet nobody could hear anybody else singing, and instead of the closure I was hoping for and expecting, everyone just kind of drifted off in disarray.

I was devastated, and all the more so because this long-planned ritual happened just a few days after 9/11, when the Twin Towers fell and so many people died. Its failure, in combination with that terrible attack, and other very bad things that happened to me in the preceding and ensuing days (on top, of course, of Peyton's death one year before), led to my having a massive nervous breakdown that led into a deep depression, which took me many, many months to recover from. Ritual can carry you, but if it fails, it can also majorly screw you up! All I can say is remember ice-skater Debi Thomas, whom we mentioned earlier, and be very, very careful in how you choose to employ ritual, and work hard to get it right. And if you see it going wrong, *stop everything and fix the problem*! If you don't, given that your emotions and those of everyone participating will probably already be massively engaged, the ritual will *not* carry you through and you will suffer more as a result. (For a fascinating analysis of the multiple ways in which ritual can go wrong, see Grimes 1996b.)

Two Weddings That Worked: Chris and Lisa

Chris and Lisa got married twice, because their respective grandparents lived in different states (California and Pennsylvania) and were unable to travel. Yet we will describe these two weddings as if they were one because of their structural similarities (and to save space). The guests are gathered in a beautiful outdoor setting that enacts and displays the couple's love of nature. White chairs are set up in formation in front of a huge table—the wedding altar. Instead of bridesmaids and groomsmen, each family member proceeds down the aisle holding a flower, which he or she places in a large, water-filled vase on the table/altar, ultimately creating a huge bouquet that symbolized, as Chris and Lisa later explained (ritual interpretation/thick description, this time by its designers), the creation of the extended family to which they both were about to belong. The family members take their seats on rows in front of the altar, facing the wedding audience—a further manifestation of family solidarity. In overt rejection of traditional norms, nobody is to give anybody "away." Lisa and Chris walk the aisle individually, put their own flowers into the now-almost-overflowing vase (it was a large Irish family!), and turn to face each other with deep smiles. And then, they each turn to face the "audience" and tell their individual stories of how they had met and how, when, and why they fell in love. And they tell moving stories about how their present family members and friends had affected their lives and how they were enriched by those relationships. And then they turn toward their minister—a family friend in both cases—and recite vows to each other that they had written themselves. The following receptions, which included full dinners, were enlivened by singing, guitar playing, and

Irish dancing—all performed by friends and family and by Chris and Lisa themselves.

In terms of our book, these wedding rituals enacted and vivified Chris and Lisa's personal values on their relationship, their families, and their friends. Both weddings "worked" as rituals, meaning that all participants, including Chris and Lisa, left with feelings of satisfaction and transformation—family and friendship ties were expressed and thus deepened by the rituals, as was their love for each other, which continues in their happy marriage to this day. The rituals they personally created and carried out worked for them and for their participants. And of course, as we have seen, rituals don't always work, but that doesn't mean that we shouldn't try! Because when they do work, they can be positively transforming in very good ways.

Weddings and Funerals: Lessons from Personal Rituals

Our friend and colleague Betty Sue Flowers, author of the Foreword to this book, notes here (personal communication 2012):

> I've never been to a wedding that didn't work, because the spirit is usually one of shared happiness for the couple. But I've been to many funerals that didn't work, usually because the master of ceremonies (the minister) didn't know the deceased and "went through the motions" of the ritual—thus not matching the feelings of those present. I think there's a key point here that hasn't been mentioned yet—that a public ritual must embody the feelings of those present. A wedding almost always is a happy occasion; but a funeral/memorial service is far more variegated depending on the different extents to which people are mourning for the deceased and how they remember him/her. What made Robbie's Memorial Celebration for Peyton so powerful (I was there, so I know!) is that it was so beautifully done that people joined in a similar feeling in the end (here "not rushing" was important so that people took the time to reach the same shared feeling).

We follow Betty-Sue's astute observation with an example of another ritual that joined people in a similar shared feeling by the end.

Rima's "Sensational at Sixty" Surprise Birthday Ritual

When Robbie's best friend Rima Star was about to turn 60, Robbie decided not only to throw Rima a huge party but also to design a ritual that would hold psychological and spiritual significance for her. Robbie knew Rima quite well enough to understand her core values on breath, spirit, healing, natural childbirth in water, dolphins and consciousness, and ballroom dance as a form of art, self-expression, and exercise. So Robbie did her best to create a ritual that would display and enact those core values. She enrolled the assistance of a women's support group that she and Rima had both been participating in since 1993 called The Wild Women Tea Party and of Rima's three grown children Mela, Orien, and Hank. All of this planning and the number of people invited were kept a secret from Rima.

Robbie took advantage of her big circular driveway deep in the woods to place signposts at measured intervals around the circle marking each decade of Rima's life (ages birth to 10, 10–20, 20–30, 40–50, and 50–60). At each signpost stood one of Rima's children or Wild Women friends, who facilitated the ritual by asking these questions: *What was most memorable during this decade? What did you learn? What are you grateful for?* If someone felt that Rima was leaving out significant experiences, they would shout them out and she would respond. When she received an ovation for that decade, she could move on to the next decade station. Often she would blush, take a deep breath and share experiences of profound pain, meaning, or exhilaration. Her former husband Jerry Cunningham was another surprise—a guest Rima had not expected to see. When she got to the decade of their marriage, she suddenly experienced and expressed a deep sense of loving forgiveness toward him. Everyone, including Jerry, was moved. After their reconnection at the party, they began to spend time together every now and then and remained close friends until his death (Star 2016). Rima later noted that the ritual helped to open her heart and make that forgiveness and their ensuing friendship possible. (Robbie of course was delighted at this unexpected outcome of her ritual design.)

At the end of the circle, Robbie asked the entire group of more than 60 people to form two lines with their arms raised to touch the hands of the person on the other side, symbolically creating a birth canal (a gentle gauntlet[1]) through which Rima was to move slowly, receiving kisses and embraces from the friends on each side to help "birth" her into her new, *sensational* (her choice of term), sixties. Emerging from the "birth canal," Rima was carried by two male friends into a throne-like chair in Robbie's living room that had been decorated especially for her and placed in the center of the room. As Robbie settled a sparkling rhinestone tiara upon Rima's head, she dramatically intoned, "By the power invested in me as your best friend, I hereby crown you Rima, Sensational at Sixty, Queen of Breathwork, Waterbirth, Dolphins, and the Dance!" to much applause and acclaim.

Next, Rima's friends were invited to step forward and say anything loving and affirmative they wanted to say to Rima—this was a very beautiful part of the ritual, as some had written lovely poems, had chosen special readings, or simply spoke from their hearts about what Rima meant to them and all they had learned from her. The formal, orchestrated part of the ritual ended, of course, with a huge birthday cake and 61 candles ("one to grow on") and everyone singing "Happy Birthday" as a slow chant in three-part harmony! With impeccable timing, precisely as the song ended, our chef Alan gleefully announced that dinner was served, and the formality of the ritual gave way to the casual, fun and meaningful (ritualized) feasting and toasting that characterize any good birthday party anywhere.

For Rima, this ritual was a huge success in that it helped her achieve her personal goal of having a positive attitude about entering her seventh decade of life. When Robbie first proposed the idea of this birthday party, Rima had responded, with a puzzled look, "But who will come?" Thus this ritual and its surrounding party was also for Rima a strong manifestation of how very many dear friends and relations she has and the many ways in which they value their relationship to her. For Robbie and all others present, this ritual succeeded in clearly demonstrating their love to Rima and their understanding of her individual values on healing, presence, consciousness, and life as an ongoing lesson. It made each of us feel good to help her feel good; we were very happy to turn the power of ritual to that worthwhile end, and to internalize the message that one can indeed be "sensational at sixty"—an empowering notion for us all.

Ray Robertson Designs a Puberty Rite

As we saw back in Chapter 7, many rites of passage around the globe involve a recognition of puberty and sexual maturity and are designed to help young people accomplish that transition in socially appropriate ways. How youths are prepared for adulthood varies from society to society. Many traditional societies do not recognize the extended childhood phase that we call "adolescence," which may last from around 13 years of age to around 20 years of age (Benedict 1950)—in such societies, you simply go from being a boy or girl to being a man or woman via an initiatory rite of passage. But in modern technocratic society, there is usually nothing like a transformative ritual marking puberty or the beginning or end of "adolescence" or adulthood.

Raymond Robertson is an anthropologically trained social worker in Canada who recognized a great need for a consciously designed rite of passage for students 12–14 years of age who were participating in a Unitarian Universalist church school program in which Ray was involved. (We first met Ray when he and Charlie confronted Darth Vader back in Chapter 1.) So Ray decided to experiment with consciously designing a rite of passage for these students, basing his design on his studies in anthropology, especially the writings of Victor Turner. He began by preparing them for this ritual during the several months prior to the event—thus mimicking the periods of "bush school" type preparation that many children in Indigenous societies undergo before their coming-of-age ceremonies. Ray writes:

> The students learned about symbology. They were asked to submit a written statement of what their childhood had meant to them. We kept our requirements for this statement deliberately vague and open-ended to encourage personalization. The students were asked to choose a private, secret name for themselves, different from their birth name. These new names were then printed on name tags. The students also used plaster gauze wrap to make a mask—a cast of their own faces—which they then decorated as they wished. Finally, the students were asked to write their own personal summary of their religious views.
>
> On the night of the ritual, the students were dropped off by their parents. They were greeted by two of the adult leaders who told the parents, "Say goodbye to your child, you will never see her/him again" because their expected ritual transformation was planned and designed to transform them from children to adolescents. When all the students were gathered, the leaders then donned robes and masks, entered the room where the students were waiting, and placed a robe over each student, all of whom had a name tag with their birth name on it. They were blindfolded and led as a group through the building by a circuitous route, to a room where they were to wait in silence, keeping vigil.
>
> One by one they were taken to another room where they were asked, "What do you seek?" They responded as previously coached, "Light!" Their blindfold was removed and they found they were in a candle-lit room facing a table which held the four symbols of the Tarot's minor arcana: pentacle, sword, cup, and wand. They were asked for their statement of childhood, and told, "I now take your childhood from you," and the statement was placed in a box.
>
> Students were asked for their birth name. When they responded, the leader replied, "That was your name as a child, I take it from you now." Their name tag was removed and burned. They were then instructed, "Look into the mirror." A curtain above the table was drawn briefly aside, and the student saw an empty frame through which they could see a table, arranged identically to the table on their side of the curtain. This created the illusion that they were looking into a mirror that had no reflection. (Several of the students gave a visible start in reaction.) The curtain was then replaced.
>
> The leader said to the student, "You have no image, you have no name, you are no longer a child, but not yet an adolescent. What remains? Think on this when you have left this place. For now, we need a name by which to call you. I give you the name you have chosen for yourself." A name tag with that name was placed on the student's robe. "We need a way to recognize you, therefore wear this." Their mask was placed on their face. "Go now, and think on what has happened here, and speak to no one." Their blindfold was then replaced and they were led back to keep vigil.

When all the students had gone through this part of the ceremony, they were gathered together and their blindfolds were removed. They were told that they had a test to pass before they could be recognized as adolescents. They were then asked to state their personal beliefs regarding the existence of a deity, life after death, and what constitutes a moral life. (It is interesting that several adults had questioned whether this was too difficult a task to expect of people this age, yet every student rose admirably to the task.)

When all had done so, they were told that they had passed the test and were accepted into our community as adolescents. They were instructed not to reveal what had taken place to any younger person (but could share as much as they liked with their parents). All were gathered outside where they fed their statements of childhood into a small fire. They then removed their robes and masks and shared a communal meal.

After a sleepover, all [of these] students attended the church service the next morning. The students had chosen the music for the service, mostly by contemporary artists whose music spoke to them. They were presented to the congregation as our newest adolescents, came masked to the dais, removed their masks, and placed them at the front of the dais. The students were welcomed by the community with applause, ending the ceremony on a note of celebration. (Raymond Robertson, personal communication, 2012)

That was the "thin" description of this purposively designed ritual. Now we layer in the "thick description" (Geertz 1973) of Ray's reasoning behind the symbolism:

This ceremony is a way of externalizing and concretizing the transition from one stage of life, childhood, to another, adolescence. This transition is known to be problematic for many young people, because their culture does not normally prepare them for what is expected of them. A common parental lament is that teens often seem stuck in childhood, and "don't act their age." The process of removing and destroying markers of childhood symbolizes that this stage of their life is over, and the time has come to let go and adopt a new self-concept. The process of replacing these markers with self-chosen aspects of identity symbolizes the process of individuation. The message is to make one's own choices, and take responsibility for one's self-concept, identity, and beliefs. As such, this ritual performs a function similar to psychodrama. In making this transition from childhood to adolescence ceremonial, the transition, rather than being open-ended and indefinite, is compressed into a single night. (Raymond Robertson, personal communication 2012)

When Robbie wrote Ray in June 2021 to ask about the aftereffects of this puberty rite, he responded:

This puberty rite was conducted several times, according to the inclinations of the teachers. Teachers are volunteers, and the rite and preparation leading up to it represent a considerable investment of time and energy. The first time this rite was performed, it was myself and 3 like-minded teachers who felt this was worthwhile. My memory is that the kids fairly glowed when we were done. One of the younger students, a girl who had only turned 12 during the 2nd term (the rite was held in May) spotted the minister entering the building, made a bee-line to him and announced, "I'm an adolescent now!" He sincerely congratulated her and they hugged. The next morning during worship services people remarked on how these now-official adolescents seemed. Heads up, smiles, no slouching as they were presented to the congregation. These rites were conducted until I moved away, and I don't know if they were continued after that … But years later, when I ran into the mother of one of the participants, she told me that she was forever grateful for what I had done for her son [as the rite of passage had generated in him a maturity and self-acceptance that most of his friends who had not gone through the rite did not share].

It has been argued (Muuss 1975) that the failure of modern societies to ritually underscore and symbolically manipulate the puberty crisis in young people is responsible, in part at least, for the uncertainty and chaos so many young people experience during their teen years. Such societies leave their young people in a kind of identity limbo where they are vulnerable to peer pressure, role uncertainty, and dependence upon family even as they reject/rebel against many of their family-assigned roles and ties. Consciously designed rituals like the one Robertson created can empower young people to make the transition from childhood to adolescence in full awareness of the meaning of this transition, thereby enabling them to reconcile its inherent paradoxes and to move into their new social status in conscious and healthy ways—as opposed to, for example, going through a gang initiation.

Such consciously designed rituals can be especially important to young girls experiencing their menarche—a much more dramatic transition to adolescence and later adulthood than boys experience. Boys entering adolescence grow facial hair and experience the lowering of their voices, all major biological transitions. Girls entering adolescence experience breast development and bleeding when they first get their "periods." When girls receive little or no information from their parents about the biological processes they are undergoing, they can become massively confused and can experience a major sense of shame for the "messiness" of bleeding and sometimes unwelcome sexualized comments about their budding breasts (or their odor) from their male or female peers. Rituals that honor and appropriately channel these biological transitions can be of enormous help to adolescents by endowing their physical changes with deep cultural meaning, as the following section will describe.

Our Pink and Ruby Tents for Adolescent Girls

Written by Jeanna Lurie

Several years ago, my dear friend Jennifer Penick started leading Red Tent evenings in our community in Silicon Valley, California. These monthly circles offer women the opportunity to connect with one another and reflect on their lives in an intimate, supportive, and celebrative setting. It was important to Jennifer to create a space for women, not just to connect socially, but to gather on an emotional and spiritual level as well. She felt that was the environment described in Anita Diamant's famous book *The Red Tent* (1997). Like the environment in the book, Red Tents include women of all generations, from menarche on. The age range so far has included young girls of 11 years to women in their 70s.

During a Red Tent some years ago, in which we reflected on our experiences of our first menstruations, it occurred to me how valuable it would be to have this same discussion in the company of my daughter, who was ten at the time. With Jennifer's support, just a few months later "Pink Tents" for girls ages nine to 13 with their mothers and "Ruby Tents" for teen girls were born. The colors—variations of the red color palette (evoking menstrual blood)—came to mind automatically and stuck. Pink had a soft connotation that seemed to match the younger set and ruby gave a feeling of sparkle, flashiness, and sass that fit teens. The groups have been open to the public and Pink Tents in particular are always full, with about 12 mother/daughter pairs. Because teens are at a stage in which they are finding themselves and appropriately seeking autonomy from their families of origin, it felt natural to not include their mothers in the Ruby Tents, which average about six girls. While there is great interest, teens have very busy schedules and we are finally just settling into a time that seems to work. Each circle is a separate event, so while many of the girls have attended regularly, each month the mixture of attendees has been slightly different. Everyone is invited to wear pink or red and bring food to share.

Similar to Mother Blessing circles used to honor new mothers in our community (which I'm sure may have been part of what inspired Jennifer), all Red Tents, Ruby Tents, and Pink Tents include the string ritual in which each woman shares her name and the names of her female relatives while wrapping a string around her wrist, then passing it to her neighbor to do the same. This ritual literally connects the women in the circle. After the string makes it around the entire circle, it is cut and tied around the wrist as a reminder of our connection to and support of each other. Pink string is used at Pink Tents and at Ruby Tents we use a sparkly red.

Although I researched before we started to see what similar rituals others had created and to get ideas for our new group, our ritual was developed for the most part through my own experience participating in Mother Blessings and Jennifer's Red Tents, a bit of creativity, and trial and error. Our first Pink Tent combined both education and storytelling. We started with an activity to diagram the female anatomy, and then discussed the mechanics of the menstrual cycle. The mothers in the group shared their stories of their first periods—what it was like, what they wished they had known. I also brought in examples of menstrual products, from reusable cloth products and menstrual cups to the typical disposable pads and tampons, and each girl received samples from a couple of different menstrual product companies. And throughout the circle we indulged in "goodies"—strawberries, chocolate, brownies, tea. Our first circle was quite long, but all of the girls who participated had a great time and couldn't wait to return.

In the following months, our topics came to include other "girl stuff" (bras, armpit and leg shaving, make-up ...), relationships, and finally reproduction. Every circle opened with a simple meditation using the breath to fully "arrive," and included time at the end for anonymous questions written on scraps of paper, then read aloud and discussed within the group. While the mothers and I all wanted to make sure our daughters received factual information, we put just as much emphasis on their feelings, curiosities, and the need to simply be witnessed in this stage of their lives. Depending on the topic, we used a number of creative activities to explore thoughts and ideas. For example, in our second circle, the girls used magazines to create collages representing what it meant to them to be female. Most circles included poems or readings, and sometimes Jennifer, who has a beautiful voice, led us in song or played her harmonium.

The first few Ruby Tents followed the same topics as the Pink Tents: menstruation, relationships, reproduction, but since the participants were older and more experienced, and I was the only adult in the circle, I left the activities a bit more open-ended. We always started with a simple opening meditation, and passed the string around while acknowledging the women in our lineage, but mostly our time together consisted of a juicy discussion on the evening's topic. Often we strayed from the subject—I felt it was important for the girls to "own" their circle and have the time to talk about what was most important to them. Sometimes they brought poems or readings to share—once, one of the girls performed a long poem she had written and memorized.

After our first four months, we had a party and invited any girl who had attended a Pink or Ruby Tent and her mother to join us. At this party we shared food and an amazing storyteller, who entertained us with stories starring empowered women. It was a special celebration just before the winter holidays to wrap up the first installment of these unique circles.

In the New Year, we took a slightly different approach to the Pink Tent based on the most successful elements of the previous circles. It was clear that the girls attending had mothers who were giving them a fair amount of factual information. What the girls needed more than a clinical sort of education was the opportunity for self-expression, to share their stories and hear others, and to ask questions in a safe space. Our topics changed from concrete subjects like menarche and reproduction, softening into topics like boundaries, authenticity, and finding one's passion. Interestingly, the concrete clinical issues often come up within the context of open-ended topics, and when they do, everyone is able to relate to the clinical information more deeply. No longer abstract, it can be applied to real-life situations they are likely to encounter or perhaps have already encountered on some level. The girls love the opportunity to ask anonymous questions (written down on paper). These mostly request advice regarding situations with other kids at school. The irony is that these questions never stay anonymous: "Um ... that question was mine ... and ... what happened was ..." This speaks to the comfort the girls feel within the intimacy of the group.

The Ruby Tents continued with the support of Zoe Beaman, a faithful member of the circle who decided to form a school-sponsored club. Like any school club, they meet on a regular basis during lunchtime. This has helped teens new to the ritual to understand what to expect and get them committed to attending the actual Ruby Tent circles off-campus. At our most recent gathering, I gave them a short, simple writing exercise to reflect on a topic and all were very willing to share what had come up for them. The topic was "Yes, no, maybe so," exploring how and why we set boundaries. I asked, "Can you think of a time when you agreed to do something that you didn't really want to do? Or you had an opportunity that you turned down and later regretted? How did it make you feel?" The girls took a few minutes to jot down thoughts, words, or pictures, which quickly turned into a discussion. The energy of the younger Pink Tent girls has demanded that I take a more active role as facilitator. With the Ruby Tent teens, I merely need to give them a topic and hold the space.

Pink Tents can be personalized to honor a girl experiencing her first menarche, as we did with my daughter Jeannessa last fall. For Jeannessa's special circle, it was up to her to decide whom to invite. It was important that everyone in the circle was someone with whom she felt a special connection. My extrovert daughter had quite the guest list, including her grandmothers, aunts and cousin, friends of all ages, and a number of girls and their mothers from our monthly Pink Tent. All were asked to wear red or pink.

With my guidance, Jeannessa chose the activities for her celebration with inspiration from each of the menarche circles that were held in honor of Zoe and her sister Isobel a few years prior. Jeannessa's circle was held in our backyard on a September evening. A special chair draped with pretty tapestries was reserved at the head of the circle for her. In the center of the circle was a small altar with trinkets symbolizing fertility or the feminine and three candles: pink for the girls who had not yet started to bleed, red for those that have a monthly cycle, and plum for the elders who had experienced menopause. As each guest came into the backyard, they were smudged with a stick of burning sage [an ancient cleansing ritual]. After everyone was settled in the circle, the candles were lit and we opened with a short guided meditation focused on the breath. A dark pink string that matched the dress Jeannessa chose especially for this occasion was passed around as everyone acknowledged their children, mothers, and grand-mothers. About two-thirds of the way around the circle, we ran out of string! Luckily, I had the Ruby Tent string on hand and we were able to tie it on and continue the string ritual. Nothing happens by accident! It was a perfect symbol of Jeannessa growing out of the "pink" stage and into "ruby."

Next, everyone in the circle had the opportunity to say how they knew Jeannessa, and to share any poems, readings, or special gifts they had brought for her. It was touching how much thought everyone put into the mementos they brought! I too had gifts for her: a box I made with a red fabric lid for her to store any strings or tokens from Red Tents (which she was now able to attend since she had gotten her period), Ruby Tents, or Pink Tents, and a matching journal that we can use to communicate on issues that may be a little awkward face to face.

Then it was Jeannessa's turn to acknowledge each person in the circle. She walked around, stopping to tell each person what she meant to her. She carried a basket filled with pink, red, and plum tea light candles, every person taking one that corresponded to her own stage of life—pink for not yet bleeding, red for bleeding, plum for post-menopausal. I then brushed Jeannessa's hair and massaged her feet and hands with lotion as a reminder that she is nurtured by the women in her circle and to continue to nurture herself. We then closed the circle by acknowledging the four directions, and Jennifer led us in song.

Afterward we celebrated with a wonderful spread of food—Jeannessa's favorites that were red or pink: pomegranate juice, strawberries, shrimp cocktail, ravioli with meat sauce, and an antipasto platter my mother prepared as she always does for special family gatherings.

For years Jeannessa knew that there would be a celebration in honor of her first menarche, and so she looked forward to menstruation. At the Pink

Tent, most of the girls have expressed enthusiasm and positivity as they look forward to getting their first periods. Mothers are certain their daughters are gaining insight that they probably would not have found without the circles. Providing pre-teen and teenage girls the space to celebrate being female and seeing how much it has positively impacted their lives thrills me! I feel blessed and honored to connect with girls and their mothers through our Pink and Ruby Tents.

Robbie adds here that she would have been thrilled to participate in Pink and Ruby Tents as a young girl and then teenager. Like so many middle-class parents in many countries whose children were born in the 1950s and 1960s, Robbie's parents found themselves simply unable to talk to her about her biological transitions. Her first period found her alarmed and scared—she ran to her mother, who simply handed her a book explaining the biology of menstruation, and a box of Kotex. The book was instructive and helpful—it did answer her concrete questions with specific information, yet gave her no context for the *knowledge and spiritual understanding* that she would have delighted in at the time. She would have loved to be imbued with the power of the Pink and Ruby Tent rituals, and she was deeply grateful that her daughter Peyton did receive this kind of ritual initiation into young womanhood via her then-mentor Captain Victoria Impallomeni in Key West, Florida, on the beach with a fire and the wild dolphins nearby.

Charlie's Personal Tantric Rituals

As we mentioned earlier, Charlie spent years as a Buddhist monk studying Tibetan Tantric-style meditation. What "Tantric" means is way too complicated, abstruse, and confusing to get into here. What is important here is that Tantrism in all of its forms engendered ritual practices that offer some of the richest examples of symbolism found in the world today. Meditation upon symbols is older than Buddhism. Most of the meditation techniques the Buddha reputedly taught were borrowed from earlier traditions. In those traditions, simple objects like bowls of water, clay circles, fire, mandalas, etc. were used as foci for intense concentration. These meditations were frequently embedded within more complex rituals such as *pujas*—rituals of worship within the Hindu and Buddhist traditions. Tantric practices continue in that vein, but often use more complex and elaborate symbols and rituals, performed repetitively until their intended meanings arise in an ASC (altered state of consciousness). Tantric practitioners have developed complex meditations embedded within *pujas* (or *sadhanas*) involving the visualization (often with the aid of a precise description, a picture or a painting) of a "deity" or spiritual being, often shown in sexual union and dancing in flames. Access to the instructions for each type of meditation practice is via what is called by Tibetans a *wangkur* (or simply a *wang*; an initiation or "empowerment") during which the teacher (lama) will enact the ritual practices and meditations, presumably transforming him or herself into the appropriate deity and bestowing sublime blessings on the initiate. The *wang* stands as official permission for the initiate to perform the meditation practices associated with that particular deity (e.g., *Mahakala, Demchog, Dorje Palmo,* and so forth).

By practicing these rituals in a group or individually—especially practicing the appropriate visualizations—the practitioner is in essence creating the possibility of evoking profound experiences and insights that are in fact the intent of the rituals. These visualizations—indeed any visualization carried out with persistence and concentration—can result in symbolic penetration into the unconscious mind and may result in the arising of certain feelings, sensory experiences and insights; thus such practices are called *arising yogas*. Charlie attended scores of *wangs* over many years, but only practiced a few of them diligently (Laughlin, McManus, and Webber 1984; Laughlin 1994). Each deity is associated with a series of visualizations and reciting of mantras literally hundreds of thousands of times—a process that can take months to complete. Once a practitioner has learned the essential methodology of Tantric meditation, he or she can easily adapt those methods and form new configurations.

An Aside: "Tantra" in the West

If you are like most Westerners, you will likely associate "Tantra" or "Tantric" with exotic ways for making love/having sex. When Western explorers first discovered temples full of art exhibiting the Tantric symbolism of male and female forms in various sexual postures, they were shocked and made the natural but erroneous assumption that Tantric practitioners must be profligate hedonists who only had sex on their minds. Only later did more careful explorers discover that Tantric sexual iconography was intended as an aid to visualization meditations—manipulating archetypal symbols that had more to do with unifying consciousness than having coitus. Very few Tantric practitioners used actual sexual liaisons in their meditation work, and only those who had reached a very advanced state of proficiency were allowed to practice Tantric sex. But by the time the true meaning of the iconography was understood, the previous interpretation had become widespread in the West, leading of course to a systematic misunderstanding of Eastern Tantric practices, and to all kinds of "Tantric" sex programs propagated through books, tapes, and workshops. Totally lost have been both the meditational importance of true Tantric practice and the accompanying sexual abstinence required of all but the most advanced practitioners.

Nevertheless, thousands of people practice "Tantric sex" in the West and ritualize their encounters so as to evoke special, even extraordinary, experiences. So here we provide an example of ritualized "Tantric" sexuality as practiced in the contemporary United States:

> Deeply and passionately in love, a woman and a man (the man had been trained in Tantra, the woman had not, yet she was receptive), spent time in a hot tub together somewhere in Northern California. And when they began to make love, the experience for both of them melted into not only ongoing ecstasy but also a profound sense of timelessness. With their bodies fused together through total symbolic and physical penetration, they sat on the edge of the hot tub without moving, for what could have been hours for all they knew or cared, experiencing an ongoing orgasm so intense that it seemed to grow from deep inside their fusion and eventually expanded until they experienced oneness not only with each other, but also with all that was around them, and then, as the mighty orgasm continued, with the heavens and stars above.

The couple who told us this story experienced this fusion as life-transforming and as an affirmation of the Tantric declaration that during sex, the participants' energy fields are united and they can then experience a sense of "cosmic consciousness." According to Wikipedia:

> Tantric texts specify that sex has three distinct and separate purposes—procreation, pleasure, and liberation. Those seeking liberation eschew frictional orgasm for a higher form of ecstasy, as the couple participating in the ritual lock in a static embrace. The sexual act itself balances energies coursing within the *pranic ida* and *pingala* channels in the subtle bodies of both participants. The *sushumna nadi* is awakened and *kundalini* rises upwards within it. This eventually culminates in *samadhi*, wherein the respective individual personalities and identities of each of the participants are completely dissolved in a unity of "cosmic consciousness." Tantrics understand these acts on multiple levels. The male and female participants are conjoined physically, and represent *Shiva* and *Shakti*, the male and female principles. Beyond the physical, a subtle fusion of *Shiva* and *Shakti* energies takes place, resulting in a united energy field. On an individual level, each participant experiences a fusion of one's own *Shiva* and *Shakti* energies.

Tantric Dreamwork

Returning to the non-sexual yet equally fascinating realm of dreams, we note here that Charlie was early-on drawn to the Tibetan Buddhist practice of *dream yoga* (*mi-lam*; see Laughlin 2011 for a detailed description). Dream yoga amounts to the application of Tantric meditation methods to retain and enhance awareness during dreaming. The specific intention of Buddhist dream yoga is to retain awareness across warps and throughout all SOCs and to come to realize that each and every one of them is an illusion produced by the mind for its own consumption. Furthermore, once one has learned the simple properties underlying the various yogas (regardless of tradition, by the way), one can begin to manufacture yogic rituals for oneself. When Charlie began working on "incubating" (ritualizing the process of falling asleep) his dreams, he learned that the only things necessary to increase dream recall were to develop an intense interest in his dreams and to put a tablet of paper and a pen next to his bed and write down every scrap of dream that he could recall immediately after waking. It was as though his unconscious "got it" that ego-Charlie had become interested in dreams, and the unconscious obliged by upping his nightly dose of conscious dreams. He also drank half a glass of water before falling asleep and finished the glass of water upon waking—a common practice among dream enthusiasts to help ritualize the process of going to sleep and waking up. He would fall asleep focusing upon an intention to become more aware of his dreams, or upon a problem he wished to solve with the help of the "depths." Charlie found that all of these ritualized pre-sleep practices had a positive effect and deepened his conscious involvement in his dream life.

Then, at age 40 or thereabouts, Charlie was introduced to Tibetan dream yoga. The Tibetan methods essentially changed Charlie's ritual practice to a more active concentration during the process of falling asleep. He began his nightly practice by going to bed before he was actually tired. He then focused his attention inward, first visualizing a neon red English letter 'A' at the base of his throat (Tibetans use their letter corresponding to the "ah" sound in the "throat chakra"), and later simplified this image to a pea-sized red bubble (Tibetan: *Tig Le*). At the same time, he chanted "ahhhhhh" softly in his throat. Ritualizing his going-to-bed practices and using these simple techniques, Charlie found that he could enter sleep onset—what psychologists call the "hypnagogic" state—in an alert, energized, and focused state of awareness, and eventually found that the hypnagogic state (usually lasting only a few seconds in normal sleep onset) began to stretch out into minutes of intense kaleidoscopic imagery, which began as a kind of gorgeous two-dimensional slide show, but then deepened into dynamic, four-dimensional experiences (time being the fourth dimension). In addition, his dreaming became more vivid and even lucid—that is, he could remain aware that he was dreaming while still in the dream.

But Charlie remained frustrated because he would eventually become tired and lose consciousness. Heretofore he had carried out these ritual practices while lying flat on his back in bed. He realized that he was struggling against a lifetime's conditioning to lose consciousness when he laid down, so he decided to remain sitting up in half-lotus posture, meditating his way into sleep onset. This worked to some extent in prolonging the hypnagogic state and even entering deep lucid dreaming, but again, the conditioning was too strong and he would wake up after a while lying flat-out on the rug. He even tried the Tibetan trick of using a wide strap around his legs and torso to maintain proper posture, to no avail. He would still wake up lying on his side.

Charlie finally decided to make it impossible to lie down during the night. He built a box out of plywood approximately four feet square and higher than his shoulders when sitting in half-lotus posture. He lined the bottom and sides of the box with foam pads thick enough that it made the inside comfortable. He left the corner of the box in front of him open, as the two sides that would have met to form the corner extended only half the length of the side of the bottom. This configuration left a corner for his back and two angles on each side for his knees, and an opening in front to enter the box and to place objects (water, tablet and pen, rosary, etc.) within easy reach on the floor. He slept sitting up in this box for many months, and although he never succeeded in remaining conscious throughout the night, he spent much of his sleep in lucid dreaming, wafting in and out of the waking and dream states and recording experiences on the note pad as he could.

Charlie's dreams during the sleeping box phase of his practice were a mixture of the chthonic (earthly) and the sublime. Many were dark and disturbing, and some downright frightening. Charlie's Buddhist studies came in handy once again, and he built into his sleep-ritual practice another Tibetan method. He visualized his dream-ego as a particular fierce "deity" he had been assigned by one of his teachers. The figure was that of his *yidam*, or personal protector, and was called Mahamaya, the Great Sorcerer, who is depicted in Tibetan paintings (*thangka*) as a huge light blue figure dancing in flames with four multicolored heads, each with a mouth with fangs and two red eyes and a "third eye" just for good measure, two sets of arms with hands holding various implements for dealing with scary apparitions, clothed in a tiger skin and wearing a necklace of human skulls. After some practice, Charlie was able to assume this dream body at will, and this practice alone transformed encounters with the unconscious to a less terrifying tone. His dream experiences often informed Charlie of the real meaning behind some of the meditative rituals he had been taught to do while awake—hence, these practices took on a quality in which one SOC influences or shapes another via continuity through the warp (see Chapter 4).

One of the "foundation" rituals in Tibetan Buddhism is to complete 100,000 repetitions of deep prostrations to the guru—for the more sophisticated student, the "guru" represents the goal of perfect enlightenment (see Pabongka Rinpoche 2006). This practice is accomplished while standing before an altar, or while visualizing the guru, and then moving from a standing posture to a position of total prostration, repeated over and over, hour after hour. Charlie was well into this practice when he had a lucid dream while in his sleeping box, in which he was starting a prostration before a colorful altar at the end of his in-breath, and by the time he had reached the end of the out-breath and completed the prostration, his dream body had exploded and his consciousness expanded into a vast, infinite void, accompanied by intense ecstasy. When he awoke, it was with the certain understanding that if one were to do a prostration properly, only one repetition would do the trick to evoke the transcendental mind state toward which the ritual is pointing. This experience highlights the ability to shift one's state of consciousness from egoistic to universalistic with an act of will, an ability greatly prized in Buddhist psychology.

The practice of arising yoga (meditation on an object such as a mandala, flower, bowl of water, etc., which may produce a spiritually significant experience) is thousands of years old within Eastern meditation traditions. We have seen how Charlie (like countless other yoga practitioners) manipulated the principles of repetitive rituals and concentration to evoke experiences that then became the meaning, for him, of the symbols used in the rituals. This process completed a spiritual cycle of meaning for Charlie—a process that continues to unfold in his dreams and other SOCs (states of consciousness) up to the present day.

Prayer Practice among Evangelical Christians

Some practitioners in Western Christian spiritual traditions have discovered more or less the same principles in order to ground their spiritual lives in the direct experience of the sublime. Anthropologist Tanya Luhrmann (2012) has done ethnographic fieldwork on US evangelical Christians, specifically members of a sect known as The Vineyard. It is very important to members of The Vineyard, and of course to many other evangelical Christians (Rose 1988), that a personal relationship be established with God. But just how is this personal relationship to be established? The answer is "through prayer." As Luhrmann (2012: 133) says: "Prayer is understood as the only way to create a relationship with God and indeed the only way to reach God at all."

As her hosts told Luhrmann, most people require training in order to pray properly and effectively. Some people are better at it than others, and some enjoy praying while others do not. Moreover, there is an awareness that part of the training is to interpret signs, images, and insights in the "right" way. As people become more proficient at prayer, the clearer and more detailed their imagery becomes. As one of her interlocutors noted, "Depending on the prayers and depending on what's going on, the images that I see [in prayer] are very real and lucid" Luhrmann 2012: 135). Luhrmann's interlocutors made it clear to her that praying is a technique (see Chapter 5 on ritual techniques and technologies)—a set of ritual procedures that must be learned and that operate to invite or evoke the presence of the divine within the individual consciousness.

Prayer practice involves working with (concentrating upon) images— indeed, it is essentially a meditation upon imagery. One of Luhrmann's interlocutors worked with the images of flowers, and the more adept she became, the less control she (her waking ego) had over the images, and the more lucid and revealing they became. In other words, images "came alive," as well as ideas, and were interpreted by her as communication with God (Luhrmann 2012: 134). The more she meditated/prayed, the clearer and more complex her imagery became, and the more she experienced "flow" and openness to the depths. Moreover, over time these practices changed "how her mind worked." She spoke of her prayer practices as the "technical" aspect [read: ritual] of praying—setting things up so that the voice of God could get through to her. In addition, she believed that when she was praying for someone else, her technical practice of prayer opened a conduit for the Holy Spirit to reach her prayer target.

Another of Luhrmann's interlocutors carried out a number of other ritualized practices, some of them drivers (Chapter 4). When he began his practice, he would first read scripture and then pray for an hour in a closet on his knees (Luhrmann 2012: 141). He later used fasting and praying in a rural field. Eventually he was able to enter into a profound state of rest and openness. Later still, he found that imagery popped up spontaneously, sometimes of people he knew, for whom he would then pray. His experience was that God eventually talked to him a few times. Still other interlocutors told Luhrmann they had gone on retreats or "Holy Weekends" that resulted in out-of-body and transpersonal experiences, profound bliss states ("electricity in the body"), speaking in tongues, and the physical presence of God. Once again, the results of ritual practices may have a profound and transformative impact upon practitioners.

Designing Personal Rituals: Healing and Danger

It is very unlikely that people who are designing a ritual for themselves or a group will, with the exception of high-tech artifacts, discover a ritual element that has not been found in rituals already extant in other cultures and used for thousands of years. As in the case of prayer practice among evangelical Christians, the age-old principle of "arising yoga" may be re-discovered over and over again when people find ritual methods for evoking spiritually poignant experiences. Many of the characteristics of the anatomy of ritual may be used, such as designating a special (holy, sacred) ritual frame, and making the occasion even more special/ritualistic through clothing and iconography, etc. Various nervous system drivers may be used, including singing, dancing, fasting, chanting, blindfolding, and more.

The really important thing to realize here (as we have already emphasized) is that *there is no such thing as an experience that is interpretable in one and only one way.* For example, one of Luhrmann's evangelical Christian interlocutors heard an internal voice in her dream that "… startled her awake. *Read James,* the voice said, and she knew it was God" (Luhrmann 2012: 138). Charlie had a similar experience (Laughlin 2011: 191). He wrote:

> After what was perhaps the most intense and transformative meditation retreat of my life, which lasted for months, I had a uniquely profound dream. I dreamed that I was standing hand in hand with my child self under a fiery arch that had morphed from two enormous serpents that had arisen on each side of us and touched their heads above us. I was lucid and watching the scene from a position behind the fiery portal and my dream selves, so I could see they were located on a vast plain upon which stood the ruins of a city. I knew in the dream that I was looking at the transformation of myself after the realizations of the past retreat. I was beginning to awaken from the dream … when a fiery golden chariot being drawn by huge golden horses appeared out of an intense, almost blinding golden light, and a deep, booming voice called out, "Read Ezekiel!"

Charlie quickly acquired a Bible, read Ezekiel, and was astounded to find that the section in question began with a visitation by a fiery chariot and outlined instructions from God about building a new city over the ashes of the old city. But the difference between Charlie's interpretation of the experience and that of Luhrmann's interlocutor is that Charlie is a Buddhist, not a Christian. So what for Luhrmann's interlocutor was God talking to her was for Charlie a message from his unconscious depicting transformations happening at the time in his psyche. He further understood how any theist could well interpret his dream as a message from God.

From our earlier discussions, you will (hopefully) appreciate that in order for ritual to do its work appropriately, *it must be lodged within a cycle of meaning.* The Buddhist and Christian contexts of Charlie's and Luhrmann's interlocutors' respective experiences are quite different. Each has an explanatory framework that allows the integration of the experience within a distinct worldview. If no such cycle of meaning is available to a practitioner, they must either find one or build one themselves. It is quite possible to construct a *personal mythology,* a process that integrates one's own experiences into a coherent story line (see Feinstein 1990; Feinstein and Krippner [1988] 2009). After all, somebody, or somebodies, had to originally invent all cycles of meaning. Why not invent one's own? Many people do, with varying degrees of success.

Robbie, for example, built her own cycle of meaning out of Peyton's death. Forced by her desperate need to find meaning in her daughter's apparently random death in a random car wreck, and led by the rituals she, her family, and Peyton's friends constructed to memorialize Peyton's life and her many contributions to the lives of others, Robbie formulated the only meaning/ interpretation she could—namely, that Peyton's death had something to do with her multiple contributions to life while she lived. Perhaps, Robbie thought then and believes now, Peyton had already accomplished her purpose in life and God was calling her home to rest, and then to send her spirit to help others in spirit form or maybe in another incarnation? Questions with no answers—yet we have to ask, we always ask, "Why did this horrible thing happen? Where is the meaning, the sense of it—does it, can it, make any kind of sense?" The rituals that Robbie and her family and friends performed around and about Peyton's death and life, the successful ones and even the failed one, gave Robbie a very clear sense of her daughter's many accomplishments at such a young age—she did so much for so many—maybe she was simply done with her work on this planet.

When Peyton appeared to Robbie in a dream three weeks after her death, Robbie was full of questions: "Why did you die? Why did you have to die?" And Peyton said, "Mom, it was my time, it was just my time!" And Robbie asked, "Where are you now, what are you doing now?" And with a huge smile, and spreading her arms out wide, Peyton answered, "Mom, I am everywhere, I live everywhere!" Robbie then asked, "But how am I to live without you—and your dad and your brother? How can we live without you?" She grinned, and said "Mom, I will take care of you all," and, touching Robbie's heart with a glowing finger, she said, "Mom, it's just like ET—I live right here, inside your heart!" And many years later, Robbie, lying awake in bed, experienced Peyton's presence and heard her say very clearly, "Mom, I have the best job in the universe now—finding and healing lost souls. You cannot imagine the incredible joy I am constantly feeling—and that's why I had to die so young, Mom—because this job is what I have always been meant to do." And Robbie even asked Peyton, "Is this really you? Or just my higher self talking to me?" And Peyton laughed, and responded, "Mom, (1) it really *is* me; and (2) it doesn't matter, because our souls are always interlinked."

At the same time as we note that Robbie's EMDR experience at Sierra Tucson led her younger, formerly frozen self to find Peyton in Robbie's heart (see chapter 7), we have to ask, as Robbie asked, did Peyton's spirit really come to Robbie, or did Robbie dream and later conjure Peyton up to get the answers Robbie needed from her own psyche, her own unconscious mind? And we collectively answer now that it doesn't matter, because the effect is the same. Robbie got the answers she needed to help her make sense of and thus reconcile, over time, to her daughter's death. Whether those answers came from Peyton's spirit or from Robbie's deep unconscious or "higher self," they helped Robbie to find the meaning she sought. And that is precisely what rituals and the myths, belief systems, and paradigms they enact do for their participants—when they work.

Yet we must be cautious here, for people suffering from various psychopathologies quite commonly invent a cycle of meaning for themselves that is far from wholesome, far from integrative, and far from peaceful. The rituals that individuals create for themselves, along with the stories those rituals enact, can help to true them to their sociocultural reality or can lead them into an individually constructed reality that may or may not help to true them to the world they live in. A powerful example is detailed by Joanne Greenberg (1964, a book written under the pen name Hannah Green), in which she describes the schizophrenia that led her to invent for herself the imagined world of Yr, whose gods over time became tyrannical dictators who controlled her each and every word and action and made her enact rituals that were harmful to her.

And a powerful counter-example is Robbie's construction of that cycle of meaning around Peyton's death, and the rituals she has constructed to enact that cycle of meaning over time, such as the annual Birthday Parties that Robbie still holds for Peyton on her birthday both to honor her life and to stay connected with Peyton's closest friends, who often drive from other cities to attend these parties. They come to ritually remember Peyton—Robbie always serves Peyton's favorite carrot cake and all sing "Happy Birthday" to Peyton—but now mostly to re-connect with Robbie and with each other.

Summary: Designing Personal Rituals—Failure and Success

We began this chapter on designing rituals with a discussion of Jerusalem and its multiple symbolic implications for the followers of three major world religions—Judaism, Christianity, and Islam. We recognized that every enduring belief system manages successfully to true its adherents to their conceptual world through their lived reality as expressed in ritual. And then we explained religious syncretism as adaptive ritual strategy, showing how peoples whose reality changes dramatically can combine traditional rituals with new ones that blend old and new beliefs in successful, synthetic, and syncretic forms. In our discussion of explicit versus implicit ideologies, we explained that implicit ideologies (like the technocratic model) need explicit enactment in ritual to enact and transmit those ideologies and their underlying values and beliefs, while explicit ideologies (like the humanistic/holistic midwifery model of care) can make do with soft and fuzzy rituals because their countercultural belief and value systems are so explicitly detailed in their writings and communications.

We used the example of the Kwakiutl shaman Quesalid to show how a practitioner who did not initially believe in his ritual practice came to understand that it worked psychologically if not physically—his physical presentation to his clients of the bloody glob he supposedly sucked out of their bodies enabled them symbolically to believe that they were healed. Thus we noted that ritual is inherently paradoxical: you can first believe in the belief system and so experience the "truth" of ritual through performing the rituals that enact that belief system—or you can believe in nothing, as Quesalid initially did, then gain a different sort of belief when you perceive that the rituals you perform do in fact produce results.

We described the intentional creation of personal rituals through the examples of two memorial services (one worked, the other failed) and one wedding (held twice), illustrating the happy consequences of successful rituals as well as the potentially dire consequences when ritual fails. We followed up with detailed descriptions of an intentionally designed puberty rite that worked for the adolescents who participated in it, of the Pink and Ruby Tents designed to help adolescent girls and teens find meaning in their biological and cultural transitions, and of the prayer rituals that some evangelical Christians design for themselves or within their prayer groups, which affirm and reaffirm their close relationship to God as they perceive and experience "Him."

We noted, quite emphatically, that in order for ritual to do its work appropriately, *it must be lodged within a cycle of meaning*—which can be created by a society or group, or by an individual. We also noted that people suffering from various psychopathologies quite commonly invent a dysfunctional cycle of meaning for themselves. We conclude by once again stating that ritual, even when individually designed, can be powerful and should be employed with consciousness and caution. (And see the Appendix to this book, "How to Create and Perform an Effective Stage 4 Ritual.")

Note

1. We interpret the gauntlets created by numbers of Indigenous tribes for male initiation rites as symbolic recreations of the birth canal—yet another example of male appropriations of female physiologic processes.

Conclusion

RITUAL
What It Is, How It Works, and Why

⁓⚬⚬

Ritual is a form of repetitive and communicative behavior that humans and animals share. As such, ritual is deeply embedded in our evolutionary past. In this book, we have defined a ritual as a patterned, repetitive, and symbolic enactment of enactment of cultural (or individual) beliefs and values. More simply put, ritual enacts cultural (or individual) beliefs and values. Although seemingly easy to define, and even recognize when we see or perform one, ritual is far from simple in its structure, psychological, and cultural contexts and in its emotional and cognitive elements. The previous chapters of this book explored the many facets of ritual—its characteristics/anatomy—and isolated the anatomical aspects of ritual that account for its power, efficacy, and endurance through time.

Chapter Summaries

In our Introduction, we detailed the "anatomy of ritual"—the core characteristics that enable ritual it to do its work in the world, primarily in the human brain. To repeat, with a bit of elaboration, the core characteristics that constitute the anatomy of ritual include:
1. the use of symbols to convey a ritual's messages;
2. a cognitive matrix (belief system) from which rituals emerge, and which rituals are designed to enact, express, and transmit;

3. rhythm, repetition and redundancy: ritual drivers;
4. the use of techniques and technologies to accomplish ritual's multiple goals;
5. the framing of ritual performances;
6. the order and formality that separate the rituals on the more formal end of our spectrum from everyday life, identifying them *as rituals*;
7. the sense of inviolability and inevitability that rituals can generate;
8. the acting, stylization, and staging that often give collective rituals their elements of high drama, as they are *performed* and often intensify toward a climax.

We reiterate here that ritual operates on a spectrum, from the small, informal, thinly symbolic habitual rituals we perform as part of our daily lives to the more formal, ordered, and densely symbolic rituals (like a parade, a church service, or a presidential inauguration) at the other.

In Chapter 1, we saw that rituals use symbols to convey the messages that the group seeks to send into the individual human brain—a process we called "symbolic penetration." We described the three (core, emotional, and cortical) levels of neural processing and how ritual engages all three levels. We discussed "core symbols" and described their primary characteristics. We then described how hard anthropologists often have to work to understand a culture's core symbols, their meanings and interpretations, and their very palpable effects on cultures and individuals, providing examples from: (1) Charlie's fieldwork with the So and the "gray goop" they ritually painted on their bodies to, as Charlie eventually figured out, protect themselves from evil spirits; (2) the warnings Michael Winkelman received from the messenger mice, which he was able to interpret from his long years of experience with studying shamanic practice; (3) the experiences of Charlie and his friend upon meeting a facsimile of Darth Vader in a hotel hallway during a science fiction convention; (4) the successful efforts of Old Naro's lineage members to appease her disturbed spirit through the performance of appropriate rituals; and (5) a debate among midwives over what was the most appropriate gift to give to their honoree—a kettle or a pressure cooker?—both of which were powerfully symbolic of the midwives' varying worldviews. We concluded Chapter 1 by re-noting that symbols can penetrate individual consciousness and evoke strong emotional reactions in accordance with the system of beliefs they express.

In Chapter 2, "The Cognitive Matrix of Ritual," we explained that rituals are not arbitrary—they always emerge from a "cognitive matrix"—a system of meaning and belief that rituals are designed to express, enact, and transmit. We described myths and paradigms, what they are, and how they differ: a myth tells an origin/creation story or is explanatory of a cultural phenomenon; a paradigm consists of a set of tenets that encode a specific belief system without making it into an actual story. We also explained how belief systems constitute a broader category than myths and paradigms and can thus encapsulate them, and that a "belief system" can be defined as a set of principles or tenets that together form the basis of a religion, philosophy, or moral code.

We showed how rituals enact and thus transmit myths, paradigms, and belief systems and the group or individual values they encompass. We used the Navajo creation myth of Changing Woman and "dream incubation" as examples of the "cycle of meaning" that every culture develops to explain the origins of and give meaning to its lifeworld. For paradigms and the cycles of meaning they create, we described as examples the old and new paradigms of business and the technocratic, humanistic, and holistic paradigms of medicine.

We noted, very importantly, the partial relationship between myth and historical reality, stating that from an anthropological viewpoint, the story of Adam and Eve being cast out of the Garden is a metaphorical way of addressing, explaining, and encapsulating the long, slow transition from hunting and gathering to agriculture, and illustrated how the Tree of Life (the placenta) with the snake wrapped around it (the umbilical cord) is an archetypal symbol encoded in all human experience. We asked how readers might, in light of our anthropological interpretation of the story of Adam and Eve, interpret the long-told folktale of "The Three Little Pigs," and respond here with a brief description of Cheyney and Davis-Floyd's (2020a, 2020b, 2021) interpretation of the "three little pigs" as each representing one the subsistence strategies that evolved over the course of human *biocultural* evolution. In this interpretation, the first little pig, who built his house of straw, represents hunter-gathers/foragers, who did indeed often build small huts of straw as they went on their nomadic ways and lived within and as a part of nature. The second little pig, who built his house of sticks, represents horticulturalists, who generally moved—and still move, in the regions where they still exist—every four or five years to replant in more fertile fields and to allow the forests they had cleared to regenerate, and thus often did—and still do—build their temporary houses out of sticks, clearing the land for their gardens and around their new settlements, yet living in the midst of the forests surrounding them. And the third little pig, who built his more permanent house out of bricks, represents agriculturalists, who often did build their houses out of (mud) bricks or stones to keep nature—represented by the Big Bad Wolf—at bay.

As with the story of Adam and Eve, here again we can see how stories can encapsulate millennia of human history. Cheyney and Davis-Floyd postulate that the early agriculturalists who (likely) came up with that story (which had been passed on orally for generations before being written down), needed a way of explaining why they had to work so hard to grow their crops "by the sweat of their brows" when around them still lived multiple tribes of hunter-gathers and horticulturalists who only had to work a few hours a day for their subsistence. The answer these agriculturalists likely generated was that, in their houses of bricks, they were far safer from "nature," which they had come to separate themselves from and to control, rather than living as part of it. (There is much more to this interpretation; see Cheyney and Davis-Floyd 2020a, 2020b, 2021.)

We provided another example of how myth incorporates historical transitions from the Huichol of Northern Mexico, who were originally hunter-gatherers yet fled northwest into the mountains to escape the Spanish invasion (which came from the east) and settled down to become agriculturalists. We described the new worldview they developed—one that incorporated their ancient hunting and gathering traditions with their contemporary reality, combining the deer they formerly hunted, the peyote they use to stay in touch with alternative realities, and the maize they currently grow into one unified worldview that both informs and illuminates their contemporary lifeworld, which they encapsulate in the words "To be Huichol is to be sacred."

We noted the "cognitive imperative" to understand our lifeworlds, and described *expressive culture* and *collective consciousness*, noting through examples from Australian Aborigines that the reality expressed in myth is not merely the figment of someone's imagination, *but is reality itself imagined*. In other words, *through their myths, people collectively imagine reality, and then they live in the collective reality they have imagined*. There are no human cultures without myths and the rituals that enact them—these are cultural universals. So we went on to provide examples from contemporary technocratic societies, including the "myth of technological transcendence"—the (often unconsciously held) belief that through technology, we will ultimately transcend the limitations of nature—which enables us to sleep at night because this myth insists that the problems we have generated with technology will not lead to doom for humanity, but *will be solved with more technology*.

In Chapter 3, we looked at the nature of belief systems, showing that such systems, which vary enormously across cultures, are only partial pictures of larger realities, yet serve to "true" those pictures—to make them reflect enough of reality to ensure that the cultures that create and live through them will be able to function effectively in the world. We examined the roles of these belief systems among "sensate," "idealistic," and "ideational" cultures and how the members of these different cultural types enact their beliefs and values through ritual, as well as how they manipulate myths and paradigms and the rituals that enact them to accommodate themselves to cultural and environmental change.

The need to know about and to understand the world—the "cognitive imperative"—along with myths and rituals, are human universals. As we have explained, the worldview of a group must be kept more or less current—more or less trued—with the daily experiences of people on the ground. Otherwise, ritual fails in its primordial function, imposing the enactment of a world-as-we-want-to-force-it-to-be instead of an enactment of the world-as-is—which is exactly what we are doing today in our sensate, technocratic cultures (see Parting Remarks below). In such cases, either the culture or group must re-design its entire belief system and the rituals that enact it to "true" itself to a new reality—as in the changes in the Sun Dance and the Ghost Dance, which served to true many First Nations groups to their changed realities, and as in the massive social transformations required to avoid coronavirus transmission via changes in our ritualized habits and behaviors.

Continuing our analysis of the characteristics of ritual, in Chapter 4 we described ritual "drivers"—sensory stimuli such as drumming, chanting, singing, dancing, and even electronic fetal monitoring—that work to entrain the human central nervous system with the structure of the ritual and the sense of "flow" that ritual drivers can produce. We described states of consciousness (SOCs) and warps of consciousness (WOCs) and how ritual can generate altered states of consciousness (ASCs) by manipulating the warps between them through creating "portals" to ASCs. We also described the differences between sensate monophasic and idealistic or ideational polyphasic cultures and the roles of ritual in each. We have seen that the range of rhythmic and repetitive stimuli through which rituals act on the human body and consciousness are many and varied—yet they all in one way or another operate upon the human central nervous system. The enactment of rituals can "drive," or control, states of consciousness among its participants. By taking this approach to the anatomy of ritual, we have been able to uncover the sources of much of ritual's power, and to answer the question, "Why are ritual drivers so compelling?" by showing their profound effects on the human brain—which, again, extends throughout our central nervous systems.

In Chapter 5, we investigated the ritual techniques and technologies that make ritual so efficacious. We have seen that ritual is technique, and that most rituals are also technologized—we experience rituals not just through activity and symbols but also through physical objects and the manipulation of the causation lying behind events. We showed how many technologies—from low- to high-tech—can serve as implements of ritual practice, and asked, how on earth did the manipulation of a pair of sandals lead the African diviner to find the purloined pots? Of course no discussion of ritual technologies would be complete without examining magic. Thus we described "spooky causation," and asked, how can ritual serve as a vehicle for "divine inspiration" and "psychic power"? We also illustrated how it is possible for ancient techniques embedded in ritual to manifest and operate effectively in the contemporary high-tech and virtual worlds.

We proceeded in Chapter 6 to explore how rituals are often "framed"—set apart from ordinary reality. Framing, order, and a sense of formality, inviolability, and inevitability are primary characteristics of ritual that are essential to its efficacy and its courage-enhancing effects, and gave examples from the Trobriand Islands, Bolivian tin miners, and contemporary obstetricians. And we described how a young woman who really did not wish to get married did so anyway because she couldn't get off of the "ritual train." We described what we consider to be "invisible lines of energy" that run around the edges of ritual frames, the power that can be released when someone chooses to break the ritual frame, and how the ludic (playful) aspects of some rituals can work not to break the ritual frame but rather to intensify the energy built up inside that frame. We described the meanings, purposes, and power of shrines and altars, and the ASC called "flow," making it clear that flow most often happens inside of a clearly delineated ritual frame—*the stronger the ritual, the deeper the sense of flow.* We also illustrated and discussed what can happen when rituals fail, and how most people respond to ritual failure not by abandoning the belief system being enacted in the ritual(s), but by intensifying ritual performance.

In Chapter 7, we turned to the performative aspects of ritual—the acting, stylization, and staging that characterize ritual performances, their climactic nature, and the roles that charismatic ritual leaders, from cult leaders to priests to politicians, play in making these performances effective by generating emotional buildup and catharsis and achieving psychological transformation in their participants. And we showed that no matter what the end goal is—whether it is conversion to a cult, a religion, a military service such as the Marines or the army, a political party, or a point of view, very similar rituals are used to achieve that goal.

We examined how ritual healing can work through the sensory manipulation of repetitive and symbolic stimuli—the drivers—embedded in the ritual. We explained the excitation and relaxation nervous systems, and described how ritual can cause them both to discharge simultaneously, producing a strong sense of flow and sometimes even ecstasy—which underscores for the participant the efficacy of the ritual process, which in turn advances a belief in the healing system. We pointed out ritual performance mechanisms for generating emotion and belief—including extrinsic and intrinsic drivers, beauty, mandalas of perception, collective effervescence, and ritual drama. We looked at rites of passage and religious conversions, and showed how "raw" individual spiritual experiences can be (and almost always are) interpreted in cultural and religious terms to give them socially shared meaning. These ritual aspects—the rhythmic repetition, evocative style, and precise manipulation of symbols and sensory stimuli—enable collective rituals to focus the emotions of participants on intensifying the ritual's underlying message(s). We repeat yet again that *belief tends to follow emotion*. Ritual can generate intense emotions, even ecstasy, and intense emotion, in turn, generates belief.

In Chapter 8, we turned to ritual and cognition. We defined two basic types of thinking—closed/rigid and open/fluid—4 Stages of Cognition, and a non-cognitive state we called "Substage." We correlated the 4 Stages with the anthropological categories of naïve realism/fundamentalism/fanaticism (Stage 1); ethnocentrism (Stage 2); cultural relativism (Stage 3); and global humanism (Stage 4). Within Stage 1 thinking, we analyzed the differences between naïve realism (no interest in any other way), fundamentalism (knowing that there are other ways of thinking and believing, yet truly believing that your way is the only right way and wishing to convert others to that way), and fanaticism (believing so much in the rightness of your way that you also believe that all other ways, most especially those most opposed to yours, should be either assimilated or eliminated). We have shown that positive ethnocentrism simply results in a culture's celebration of itself and in attempts on its members' parts to preserve and perpetuate that culture, while negative ethnocentrism can result in one group trying to exploit, persecute, enslave, impoverish, or eliminate other groups.

We emphasized the weakness of cultural relativism (Stage 3)—simply acknowledging the right of every culture to exist and to have its own lifeworld and lifeways can result in tolerating behaviors like stoning, wife-beating, and torture as morally acceptable because they are accepted within the parameters of that culture. We also examined how global humanism evinces Stage 4 thinking: the ongoing effort to find that elusive "higher ethical ground" that ensures universal rights to all human beings, and how these rights play out within a global system. We showed that ritual is utilized to enact, display, and transmit the beliefs and values held by thinkers at all 4 Stages, as well as to *stand between cognition and chaos* by stabilizing every level of thinking at Stage 1 in times of crisis and distress, in order to keep individuals from regressing into Substage—"losing it." In that light, we described rituals as "life-hacks" that people can use to stabilize themselves. We noted that fluid, open thinking is a type of cognition that readily deals with diversity and change. In multi-cultural and constantly changing societies, open, fluid thinking is far more adaptive than closed or rigid thinking. We showed that even fluid thinkers can be reduced to lower cognitive levels by daily stress overload or major disasters, and how the conscious performance of ritual can help them find "cognitive anchors" to keep them from regressing into Substage and "get a grip" on their new reality, giving them time, space, and the energy needed to grow the new neural networks they will need to cope with the distressing challenges they face. And we showed that cultures (or individuals) who have already inherited or developed those neural networks are better prepared to deal with new disasters.

As we saw in Chapter 9, most rituals have a built-in conservative effect. Ritual works both to preserve and to transmit the cognitive matrix/belief system from which it stems, and so becomes an important force in the preservation of the status quo in any society. Thus one usually finds that those in power in a given social group have unique control over ritual performances. They utilize ritual's tremendous power to reinforce both their own importance and the importance of the belief and value system that sustains them in their positions. Laws and explicit rules in every society may officially dictate appropriate behavior, yet most people behave appropriately most of the time because of their ritualized socialization—including following coronaviral "rituals of containment." We showed that when official laws and rules cease to match or mirror people's actual practices—such as selling or drinking alcohol during Prohibition or using marijuana—those laws and rules usually get changed over time. When they do not, social resistance and revitalization movements often arise to effect needed changes, unless that society is totalitarian and does not allow social resistance and change. We also examined the contemporary invention of ritual by holistic obstetricians in Brazil and by Herb Kelleher, the founder of Southwest Airlines.

We have shown how ritual, with all of its insistence on continuity and order, can paradoxically be an important factor not only in individual transformation but also in social change. New belief and value systems are most effectively spread through new rituals designed to enact and transmit them. Even if a ritual is being performed for the very first time, its stylistic similarities with other rituals make it feel tradition-like, thus giving entirely new belief systems the feel and flavor of being strongly entrenched and sanctioned by ancient tradition. Moreover, entrenched belief, value, and behavioral systems are most effectively altered through alterations in the rituals that enact them—such as the massive worldwide transformations in our greeting rituals as the result of COVID-19. Indeed, ritual represents one of society's greatest potentials for the kind of revitalization that comes from internal growth and change in response to changing circumstances.

In Chapter 10 on "Designing Rituals," we provided examples of how some people have designed and carried their own ceremonial rituals, and how such contrived affairs either work well, or don't—from two Memorial Services to two weddings (described as one) to puberty rites and "dream incubation." We explored religious syncretism as an adaptive ritual strategy, explaining how peoples whose reality changes dramatically can combine traditional rituals with new ones in successful, synthetic, and syncretic forms. In our discussion of explicit versus implicit ideologies, we explained that implicit ideologies (like the technocratic model of medicine) need explicit enactment in ritual to reflect and transmit those ideologies and their underlying values and beliefs, while explicit ideologies (like those of homebirthers) can make do with soft and fuzzy rituals because their countercultural belief and value systems are so explicitly detailed in their writings and communications. We explained that ritual is inherently paradoxical: you can first believe in the belief system and so experience its "truth" through performing the rituals that enact that belief system—or you can be quite skeptical, then gain a different sort of belief when you perceive that the rituals you perform do in fact produce results, as the Kwakiutl shaman Quesalid discovered.

We showed that intentional creation of a personal or social ritual may or may not be successful. We noted that in order for ritual to do its work appropriately, it must be lodged within a cycle of meaning—which can be created by a society, an individual, or a group. We also noted that people suffering from various psychopathologies quite commonly invent a cycle of meaning for themselves that is dysfunctional. We conclude by once again stating that ritual, even when individually designed, can be powerful and should be employed with consciousness and caution.

Parting Remarks

Now that you have traveled with us through this long and hopefully edifying journey through the anthropology and anatomy of ritual, you will find that you are much more able to isolate and identify the various elements of rituals that produce whatever effects they have on you and your fellow participants. This journey may also have placed you in the position of questioning whether or not you really want to participate in this or that ritual. You will certainly be aware of how rituals can be used to manipulate your feelings, perceptions, thoughts, decisions, and behaviors. You have likely become a more enlightened participant in your society, able to decide whether to "get into it" with this ritual, and "back off" from that ritual. Furthermore, when need be, you have at hand the knowledge to design and carry out your own ritual(s) (see Appendix), and then step back and evaluate the ritual's efficacy—understanding why it worked—or didn't—and perhaps what should be changed, added, or eliminated in order to make it more effective. You may even find yourself in the position of teaching about ritual to others (Bell 2007; Grimes 2013). You will not only be able to describe rituals in different contexts, but also to isolate the various elements that go into building a ritual—its anatomy, its constituent actions, its relations to ideology and to direct experience.

You can now appreciate the extent to which rituals facilitate daily living—again, by engendering belief, concretizing that belief, maintaining religious vitality, enhancing courage, effecting healing, initiating individuals into new social groups or new ways of being, preserving the status quo in a given society, and, paradoxically, effecting social change. You can also see how rituals may be used for your own self-discovery and transformation. This may be as simple as building in a morning run, an hour of yoga, or some form of progressive relaxation. Or, the transformative ritual you find or create for yourself may entail working with the depths of your psychic being—perhaps discovering your inner spiritual nature through phenomenological exercises like dream work, prayer, insight meditation, or guided visualization.

We repeat once again that ritual is a powerful didactic and socializing tool. To grasp its inner workings is to have a choice as to whether to accept the beliefs and values transmitted through the rituals that permeate our daily lives—as well as to be able to harness the power of ritual to enact beliefs and reinforce behaviors that we consciously choose. And we add here that such a choice is becoming increasingly important in our contemporary globalized world, where all of us confront conditions of rapid social, technological, and environmental change.

When their cultures have not been adaptively accurate enough for them to survive—sufficiently "trued" to the changing circumstances of the world they live in, thousands of traditional societies have simply died off. *Just so could Homo sapiens die off as a species*—as a result of our own behaviors—if the onrushing Climate Crisis reaches a tipping point at which our planetary environment can no longer sustain us. Thus, if we are to save life on earth as we now know it, our technocratic systems *must* change into globally humanistic systems "trued" to the realities of the Climate Crisis and to the actions we must take to thereby stop it from turning into a Climate Catastrophe. If we make the right choices now for our collective and individual human future, we can consciously use rituals to reflect, express, and enact those choices and the new belief and value systems such choices will inevitably entail, and thereby transmit those new, planet-wide worldviews to future generations.

How to Create and Perform an Effective Stage 4 Ritual

Things to Remember and Include

—⁂◯

This Appendix is a checklist based on all that we say about ritual in this book. It won't make full sense to you unless you actually read the book! And please note that these recommendations for carrying out a ritual do not reflect the myriad of ways in which rituals can be performed.

- Be clear about the beliefs and values you want to enact. Make sure that those who will be performing the ritual with you either share these beliefs and values, or wish to share them.

- Choose meaningful symbols. If the ritual is new, explain the symbols before you begin the ritual—by engaging the intellect in advance, you increase the chances of an emotional response. You might want to create an altar with candles for the center of the circle that holds meaningful artifacts, and to explain their meaning. The power of the altar can be magnified if it is in mandalic form.

- If the ritual is for healing purposes, if possible, place the person or people to be healed in the center of the circle and construct an altar, or mandala, around them, or place a rug containing a mandala underneath them. If the one(s) in need of healing can't be present, place a large photo or photos of them on the altar, or perhaps four such photos, so they can be seen from all directions. Clearly state the person's name(s), state the reasons for their need to be healed, and the intention to heal them. Ask everyone present to focus on sending healing energy to that person or those people.

- *Hold the center.* People often feel silly performing rituals, especially new ones. Several people, or only one, who can hold the center for the group can create a sense of specialness (even sacredness) and acceptance that everyone can eventually feel if the ritual works.

- Tell the participants in advance, especially if they are new to such rituals, "If you feel ridiculous, let the feeling wash over you and pass away."

- Once it is established, don't break the ritual frame. If it gets broken, reestablish it as quickly as possible. (Remember that what generates "flow" is a narrowed, focused cognitive field.) If your ritual is being performed in a circle of people holding hands, make sure that everyone understands that if they need to leave the circle, they should depart silently and engage the hands they were holding with those next to them in the circle.

- Evoke mystery when appropriate—use semi-darkness, flickering candles, and so on—for their neurological opening effects.

- Allow for spontaneity and playfulness. There is a certain quality of playfulness in ritual that does not break, but strengthens, the frame. Laughter and lightness alternating with seriousness can make the ritual more powerful by making the energy come in waves that can build in intensity.

- Ritual drivers include: drumming, chanting, singing, dancing, mantric meditation, privations, ordeals, hazing/physical challenges, isolation, sensory deprivation, and others. *Treat them with respect!*

- Utilize the power of repetition. To generate a lot of energy and a strongly special or sacred atmosphere, the drumming and/or chanting/singing should go on for a long time. The more repetitive the rhythm, the more powerful the neural entrainment.

- If you are including songs in your ritual, make sure there is someone with a strong voice who knows the songs to be sung or chanted. That person can "hold the center" for the songs.

- Keep the songs short, so they can be easily learned without need of paper (or put them up on Powerpoint), and sing them at least four times. That's really important—it takes at least four repetitions of the songs for everyone to learn them, sing them properly, and figure out appropriate harmony, and for their messages to fully penetrate the psyches of the participants. But don't sing them more than four times—that can get boring! (Chants are a different matter—they can go on for hours.)

• Provide a strong opening that clearly establishes the ritual frame, and a definite closure at the end—a cementing song, or prayer, or "so be it," "Amen!" "We love you all!" or the Wiccan "Blessed be!" or "Let the circle be open yet unbroken!" Clear closure holds the integrity of the frame until it is intentionally dropped, and allows participants to leave with a feeling of completeness.

• *Be aware of ritual's power for transformation, and be responsible in its use!*

Appendix 2

LIST OF DOCUMENTARY FILMS ABOUT RITUAL

‑∰☉

March of the Penguins
(best suited to Chapter 1)

In the Antarctic, every March, the ritual quest begins to find the perfect mate and start a family. This courtship will begin with a long journey—a journey that will take these penguins hundreds of miles across the continent by foot, in freezing cold temperatures, in brittle, icy winds and through deep, treacherous waters. They will risk starvation and attack by dangerous predators, under the harshest conditions on earth, all to find true love.

Found at: March of the Penguins—YouTube

African Tribes, Traditions & Rituals
(best suited to Chapters 1 and 5)

In this region in the west of the Ivory Coast, there are still ancient jungles, such as the Tai jungle, and leafy forests that are home to different ethnic branches of the Mande group. The most characteristic of these are the Dan, who are related to the Guéré. Their villages are very distant from each other—they do not form a large community, but rather isolated groups, which only come together in exceptional circumstances to defend themselves against some common threat. Masks are institutions of the Guéré that order, legislate, and codify the social life of the different ethnic groups that live in this region. A great part of the mythology of the Dan is born in the heart of the jungle where their deities live, and where nature and magic melt into one. In the interior of this green world, we find bridges of the spirits built by the supernatural beings of the forest to make it easier for the people who live here to move through the forest. Hundreds of lianas, the resistant living limbs of the jungle, are woven together in the dead of night by the spirits. At dawn, a new bridge connects the opposing banks of a river, or crosses a deep ravine. No one knows how or when they are built. But for them they are sacred, because they are made with lianas, and everything that comes from the jungle is revered. That is why they take their shoes off before crossing, as a mark of respect.

Apart from the daily chores, the women occupy a very important position in the social structure of the Ubi. As in the majority of the 60 or so different ethnic groups that live in the Ivory Coast, the women form secret societies, which have a decisive influence in the village about sex rituals. In their meetings, which no man may attend, they deal with matters exclusive to the women, though their attention has been centered on just one subject for some time now. In the main cities of the Ivory Coast, associations have been formed to fight to eradicate the traditional mutilation of female sex organs. Periodically, women from these associations travel to the most remote villages to speak with the leaders of the secret societies and try to convince them to abandon this custom. Every village in the Ivory Coast has an area of the nearby forest where the spirits of their ancestors live. Here, the young men are brought to be initiated, circumcisions are carried out, they speak to the masks of wisdom, and justice is imparted.

Found at: African Tribes Traditions & Rituals | Full Documentary—YouTube

Mayordomia: Ritual, Gender and Cultural Identity in a Zapotec Community
(best suited to Chapter 2)

No description available.

Found at: https://doi.org/10.1525/jlca.1991.3.1.41

In Her Own Time
(best suited to Chapter 2)

Based on the fieldwork of Dr. Barbara Myerhoff, this is a documentary exploring the diverse Fairfax district Jewish Community in Los Angeles, California.

Found at: https://www.imdb.com/title/tt0158672

Islam in Africa: History of Africa [Episode 9]
(best suited to Chapter 2)

Zeinab Badawi travels to several countries and looks at the early spread of Islam in Africa and how many Africans practice to this day a mystic, Sufi form of the religion. She shows how not only Islam but also Arab culture came to influence a large part of the continent, particularly in the north. And she charts the rise of the powerful Islamic dynasties of North Africa that built magnificent monuments, mosques, and empires, including a part of southern Europe, and who helped determine the path of this part of the continent.

Found at: Islam in Africa—History of Africa with Zeinab Badawi [Episode 9]—YouTube

Sansari: The Goddess and the Corona in the Himalayas
(best suited to Chapter 3)

At the end of March 2020, in a village in Nepal, affected like the rest of the country—and the world—by lockdown, news of the virus spreads. Some villagers decide to perform the Sansari (Goddess of Epidemics) ritual, adapting it to the current circumstances. This film shows their relationship to politics and to nature, the place of the stranger in their society, respect for tradition and adaptation to change, human and divine responsibility, rumors and learned discourse. We watch these villagers search for what to think and what to do and cobble together uncertain answers. The primary language is Nepali but you can choose either English or French subtitles. 19 minutes.

Found at: https://www.canal-u.tv/video/universite_de_nice_sophia_antipolis/sansari_the_goddess_and_the_corona_in_the_himalayas.56277?fbclid=IwAR1AAFr6LA24v5MbMpcyDZXE7ZnfBAhuQKIqwaEhe1lJ7OuJXnDfNLr_DBc

Twist of Faith
(best suited to Chapter 3)

This series of films follows documentary filmmaker Martin Himel on a global journey to discover how religions and spiritual traditions influence societies and individuals around the world. While not everyone may practice a spiritual discipline or subscribe to a conventional faith, we are all affected in one way or another by the rich diversity of the world's faiths. 13-part series, 22 minutes each.

The series includes : Jesus of Siberia: Twist of Faith | Faith Healing: Twist of Faith | Women in Islam: Twist of Faith | Religion and Conflict: Twist of Faith | Ethiopia's Christianity: War on Terror—Twist of Faith | Future of Judaism: Twist of Faith | Catholic Priests: Controversy—Twist of Faith | India's Dalits: Twist of Faith | Marriage and Divorce: Twist of Faith | Islam in China: Twist of Faith | Spirit Women: Thailand—Twist of Faith | South Africa: A Pastor Fights HIV—Twist of Faith | Temple Mount Controversy: Twist of Faith

Found at: https://www.films.com/ecTitleDetail.aspx?TitleID=28246. Please note: These films are extremely expensive if you seek to purchase them, but leasing arrangements can be made and perhaps you can get them for free from your library.

Hajj: The Sacred Journey
(best suited to Chapters 3 or 7)

Millions head toward the greatest pilgrimage to Mecca every year, performing their Islamic rituals. Hajj group leaders describe their experiences in preparation for this lifetime journey.

Found at: Hajj: The Sacred Journey—Documentary—YouTube

Essentials of Faith: Paganism
(best suited to Chapter 3)

Drawing on ancient spirituality, most pagans sum up their chosen form of worship within a modern "green" context. Some follow Druidry, others Wicca, while a third brand depicts the shamanism of hunter-gatherer cultures. This program sheds light on various examples of pagan devotion put forward by four observers of ancient religious rites and customs. Through straightforward explanations and heartfelt expression, the sundry shapes and species of paganism are explained by Druid priestess Emma Restall Orr, Professor Ronald Hutton of the University of Bristol, British coven organizer Jeanette Ellis, and shamanic practitioner Leo Rutherford. 24 minutes.

Found at: ffh.films.com/id/13171/Essentials_of_Faith_Paganism.htm

Witchcraft: The Magick Rituals of the Coven
(best suited to Chapter 3)

The history and craft of modern-day witches. Karen Frandsen from Eerie Investigations interviews Jeanette Ellis, lecturer on traditional British Witchcraft, and author of *Forbidden Rites*. Jeanette reveals the truth behind many aspects of witchcraft, includes the history of traditional witchcraft in the United Kingdom, and depicts how witches practice their craft.

Found at: Witchcraft: The Magick Rituals of the Coven (2011) – (Documentary) – Bing video

Macumba, Candomble, and Umbanda: Brazilian Spirituality
(best suited to Chapter 4)

No description available.

Found at: Macumba, Candomble, and Umbanda: Brazilian Spirituality— Bing video

Ritual Magic: Candomble & Obeah
(best suited to Chapters 4 or 5)

No description available.

Found at: RITUAL MAGIC: CANDOMBLE & OBEAH—YouTube

One of Us
(best suited to Chapter 8)

This documentary profiles three different Hasidic Jews as they attempt to leave their ultra-orthodox communities. While you get a glimpse into some of the unique routines and practices of the Hasidic lifestyle, what this religion documentary really focuses on are the extreme hardships tied to trying to leave the community, as well as the hardships that exist years later.

Found at: Netflix

Going Clear: Scientology and the Prison of Belief
(best suited to Chapter 8)

As one of the most recently established (and controversial) religions of our era, Scientology has drawn a lot of attention. This documentary sheds light on some of the darker sides of this relatively new faith and will certainly stay with you long after you've finished the documentary. Scientology's celebrity status, their "auditing" techniques, and the immense difficulty faced by those trying to leave the church are all covered in this captivating film.

Found at: Watch Going Clear: Scientology and the Prison of Belief | Prime Video (amazon.com)

David's Story: The Childhood Ritual Abuse of David Shurter
(best suited to Chapter 8)

No description available.

Found at: https://www.youtube.com/watch?v=d9__tMLGZUc

Believer
(best suited to Chapter 9)

A documentary that focuses on a very specific area of the Mormon religion: their lack of acceptance of the LGTBQ community. The Mormon faith has notoriously taken a very harsh stance against its LGTBQ members and the effects are startling, including the highest teen suicide rate in the country. *Believer* is an extremely inspirational documentary that provides hope for much-needed change in a strong religion.

Found at: Watch Believer | Prime Video (amazon.com)

Documentary on Arranged Marriage | *The Only Son*
(best suited to Chapter 9)

The Only Son is a Dutch documentary directed by Simonka de Jong. It is a story about the challenge of keeping Dolpo's ancient culture alive as the area becomes less isolated. The film centers on Pema's parents' expectation that Pema will return to Dolpo, Nepal when he completes his education, marry a Dolpapa woman, and manage the family's land. As the only son, this is his role in Dolpo's traditional culture. Pema is torn between his duty to the family and his desire to live the modern life that he now prefers. The film is primarily shot in Karang, a village at 13,000 feet in Upper Dolpo, one of the most remote areas of Nepal. It has been shown at a number of International Film Festivals.

Found at: Documentary on Arranged Marriage | *The Only Son*—by Simonka de Jong—YouTube

Chicks in White Satin
(best suited to Chapter 10)

A lesbian couple gets married.

Found at: https://www.imdb.com/title/tt0106555/

In Pursuit of the Siberian Shaman
(best suited to Chapter 10)

Long suppressed by missionaries and then by Soviet anti-religious campaigns, Siberian shamanism has experienced an unprecedented revival following the collapse of the Soviet Union, and the number of shamans continues to rise. But who are these new shamans? Are they tricksters, magicians, businessmen, or cultural activists? This film takes a behind-the-scenes look at a Buyrat shaman living on an island in the Lake Baikal as he moves between intimate shamanic rituals performed for local clientele and shows performed at various resorts for Western tourists in search of "primitive" cultures. The film captures cross-cultural miscommunication as the shaman and tourists misunderstand each other, usually comically, sometimes disturbingly, made all the more poignant by the conflict between the dominant Russian Orthodox Church and the local shamanic tradition. Juxtaposing 1920s archival footage of a shamanic performance with its contemporary counterparts, the film grapples with the long-standing tension between the "Indigenous" and the "cosmopolitan" in a transnational world. 75 minutes, color, in Russian and Buryat with English subtitles.

Found at: In Pursuit of the Siberian Shaman | Kanopy

Split Horn: The Life of a Hmong Shaman in America
(best suited to Chapter 10)

The sweeping story of a Hmong shaman and his family living in Appleton, Wisconsin. Documenting the journey of Paja Thao and his family from the mountains of Laos to the heartland of America, this film shows a shaman's struggle to maintain his ancient traditions as his children embrace American culture.

Found at: https://www.imdb.com/title/tt0324048

Coming of Age: Ethnographic Profiles from a Global Perspective
(best suited to Chapter 10)

Weaving a worldwide narrative of rites of passage, this program takes viewers into the lives of six children and adolescents, all of whom are undergoing critical stages in their transition to adulthood. Widely varying experiences from Russia, China, Malaysia, Uganda, the Dominican Republic, and Canada's Baffin Island produce a startling picture of the political, social, and economic issues that surround growing up. An Inuit boy's first hunt, a young Russian's involvement in a right-wing hate group, and an obligatory weeklong military boot camp for a 15-year-old Chinese girl—these and other stories show the differences and the unity of human development around the world.

Contents: Young People in China and Russia (3:55)—Coming of Age in the Dominican Republic (2:43)—Inuit Coming of Age (2:02)—Chen Lu's Regimented Life in Beijing (2:57)—Young People in Malaysia and Russia (3:43)—Circumcision Ritual (1:55)—Inuit Hunting Trip and Dominican Cruise (4:01)—Beijuing: Military Camp for Chen Lu (2:00)—Andre the Skin Head (2:05)—Coming of Age: Caribbean and Arctic Circle (2:00)—Circumcision, Sex, and AIDS in Uganda (2:19)—Islamic Fundamentalist Party (2:51)—Beijing: Military Boot Camp (2:44)—Pressures on Young People (3:40)—Preparation for Initiation (4:14)—Monica's Coming Out Party (2:39)—Initiation into the People's National Party (2:38)—Nur's Graduation Ceremony (2:27)—Kumoti's Circumcision (2:21)—New Beginnings for Chen Lu and Apak (4:08)

Found at: Item details: Coming of Age: Ethnographic profiles from a Global Perspective—46699959 (tadl.org)

Ancestors, Spirits and God: History of Africa
(best suited to Chapter 10)

In this episode Zeinab Badawi examines religion in Africa—first, the enduring presence of Africa's Indigenous religions, to which millions of people on
the continent still adhere. She travels to Zimbabwe to find out more about
a remote community that follows traditional African religion. In Senegal
she meets a Muslim man who, like so many others in the continent, blends
Islamic beliefs with his ancestral ones and enjoys talking to trees. She also
charts the impact of Judaism and early Christianity in Africa and how
Africans in particular made significant contributions to Christian thinking
and practice through influential figures such as St. Augustine, who lived in
what is today Algeria. This film demonstrates that religious syncretism can
go both ways.

Found at: Ancestors, Spirits and God—History of Africa with Zeinab
Badawi [Episode 8]—YouTube

REFERENCES

Abrahams, Roger D. 1973. "Ritual for Fun and Profit (or the Ends and Outs of Celebration)." Paper delivered at the Burg Wartenstein Symposium No. 59, "Ritual: Reconciliation in Change. Wenner-Gren Foundation for Anthropological Research." Unpublished manuscript.Adler, Margot. 1988. *Drawing Down the Moon: Witches, Druids, Goddess-Worshippers, and other Pagans in America Today,* 2nd edn. Boston: Beacon Press.

Akram, Sara, and Rao Nadeem Alam. 2022. "Social Constructions of the Concept of COVID-19 in Pakistan: An Anthropological Investigation." In *Negotiating the Pandemic: Individual, Cultural, and National Constructions of COVID-19,* ed. Inayat Ali and Robbie Davis-Floyd, Chap. 16. Abingdon, Oxon, UK: Routledge.

Ali, Inayat. 2021. "Rituals of Containment: Many Pandemics, Body Politics, and Social Dramas during COVID-19 in Pakistan." *Frontiers in Sociology* 6(83): 648149. https://doi.org/10.3389/fsoc.2021.648149.

————. 2022. "My Great-Grandmother, Malinowski, and My 'Self': An Autoethnographic Account of Negotiating the COVID-19 Pandemic." In *Negotiating the Pandemic: Individual, Cultural, and National Constructions of COVID-19,* eds. Inayat Ali and Robbie Davis-Floyd, Chap 1. Abingdon, Oxon, UK: Routledge.

Ali, Inayat, and Robbie Davis-Floyd, eds. 2022. *Negotiating the Pandemic: Individual, Cultural, and National Constructions of COVID-19.* Abingdon, Oxon, UK: Routledge.

Ali Inayat, Salma Saddique, and Shabaz Ali. 2022. "Local Perceptions of COVID-19 in Pakistan's Sindh Province: Political Game, Supernatural Test, or Western Conspiracy?" In *Negotiating the Pandemic: Individual, Cultural, and National Constructions of COVID-19,* ed. Inayat Ali and Robbie Davis-Floyd, Chap. 17. Abingdon, Oxon, UK: Routledge.

Atran, Scott. 2002. *In Gods We Trust: The Evolutionary Landscape of Religion.* Oxford: Oxford University Press.

Atran, Scott, and Joseph Henrich. 2010. "The Evolution of Religion: How Cognitive By-Products, Adaptive Learning Heuristics, Ritual Displays, and Group Competition Generate Deep Commitments to Prosocial Religions." *Biological Theory* 5: 18–30.

Babcock, Barbara. 1978. *The Reversible World: Symbolic Inversion in Art and Society.* Ithaca NY: Cornell University Press.

Cunningham F. Gary, Paul C. MacDonald, and Norman F. Gant. 1989. *Williams Obstetrics,* 18th ed. Norwalk, CT: Appleton & Lange.

Baggott, Jim. 2020. *Quantum Reality: The Quest for the Real Meaning of Quantum Mechanics—A Game of Theories.* Oxford: Oxford University Press.

Beidelman, T. O. 1973. Review of Colin M. Turnbull, *The Mountain People. Africa* 43(2): 170–71.

Bell, Catherine. 1992. *Ritual Theory, Ritual Practice.* Oxford: Oxford University Press.

———. 1997. *Ritual: Perspectives and Dimensions.* Oxford: Oxford University Press.

———. 2008. "Embodiment." In *Theorizing Rituals: Issues, Topics, Approaches, Concepts,* ed. Jens Kreinath, Jan Snoek, and Michael Stausberg, 533–543. Leiden: Brill.

Benedetti, Fabrizio. 2008. *Placebo Effects: Understanding the Mechanisms in Health and Disease.* Oxford: Oxford University Press.

Benedict, Ruth. 1950. "Continuities and Discontinuities in Cultural Conditioning." In *Readings in Child Development,* ed. W. E. Martin and C. B. Stendler. New York: Harcourt Brace.

Biesele, Megan, ed. 2009. *Ju/hoan Folktales: Transcriptions and English Translations: A Literacy Primer by and for Youth and Adults of the Ju/hoan Community.* Victoria, BC: Trafford Publishers.

Bohm, David. 1980. *Wholeness and the Implicate Order.* Boston, MA: Routledge and Egan Paul.

Bongaarts, John, and Christope Z. Guilmoto, 2015. "How Many More Missing Women? Excess Female Mortality and Prenatal Sex Selection, 1970–2050. *Population and Development Review* 41(2): 241–69.

Campbell, Joseph. 1986. *The Inner Reaches of Outer Space: Metaphor as Myth and as Religion.* New York: Harper.

Campbell, Joseph, with Bill Moyers. 1988. *The Power of Myth,* ed. Betty Sue Flowers. New York: Doubleday.

Chagnon, Napoleon. 1982. *Yanamamo: The Fierce People,* 2nd edn. New York: Holt, Rinehart, and Winston.

Chapple, Eliot D. 1970. *Culture and Biological Man: Explorations in Behavioral Anthropology.* New York: Holt, Rinehart, and Winston.

Chapple, Eliot D., and Carleton S. Coon. 1942. *Principles of Anthropology.* New York: Holt, Rinehart, and Winston.

Cheyney, Melissa. 2011. "Reinscribing the Birthing Body: Homebirth as Ritual Performance." *Medical Anthropology Quarterly* 25(4): 519–42.

Cheyney, Melissa, Marit Bovbjerg, Courtney Everson, Wendy Gordon, Darcy Hannibal, and Saraswathi Vedam. 2014. "Outcomes of Care for 16,924 Planned Homebirths in the United States: The Midwives Alliance of North America Statistics Project, 2004 to 2009." *Journal of Midwifery & Women's Health* 59(1): 17–27.

Cheyney, Melissa, and Robbie Davis-Floyd. 2020a. "Birth and the Big Bad Wolf: A Biocultural, Co-Evolutionary Perspective, Part 1." *International Journal of Childbirth* 9(4): 177–92.

———. 2020b. "Birth and the Big Bad Wolf: A Biocultural, Co-Evolutionary Perspective, Part 2." *International Journal of Childbirth* 10(2): 66–78. http://dx.doi.org/10.1891/ IJCBIRTH-D-19-00029.

———. 2021. "Birth and the Big Bad Wolf: Biocultural Evolution and Human Childbirth." In *Birthing Techno-Sapiens: Human-Technology Co-Evolution and the Future of Reproduction,* ed. Robbie Davis-Floyd, 15–46. Abingdon, Oxon: Routledge.

Chick, Garry. 2008. "Altruism in Animal Play and Human Ritual." UC Irvine *World Cultures eJournal* 16(2). Retrieved 24 January 2022 from https://escholarship.org/content/qt4mv8f9px/qt4mv8f9px.pdf.

Cove, John J. 1987. *Shattered Images: Dialogues and Meditations on Tsimshian Narratives.* Ottawa: Carleton University Press.

Csikszentmihalyi, Mihaly. 1975. *Beyond Boredom and Anxiety: Experiencing Flow in Work and Play.* San Francisco: Jossey-Bass.

D'Aquili, Eugene G., Charles D. Laughlin, and John McManus, eds. 1979. *The Spectrum of Ritual.* New York: Columbia University Press.

Davis-Floyd, Robbie. 1987. "Obstetric Training as a Rite of Passage." *Medical Anthropology Quarterly* 1(3): 288–318.

———. 1994. "The Technocratic Body: American Childbirth as Cultural Expression." *Social Science and Medicine* 38(8): 1125–40.

———. 2001. "The Technocratic, Humanistic, and Holistic Models of Birth." *International Journal of Gynecology & Obstetrics* 75, Supplement No. 1: S5–S23.

———. 2002. "*Knowing*: A Story of Two Births." Unpublished article.

———. [1992] 2003a. *Birth as an American Rite of Passage,* 2nd edn. Berkeley: University of California Press.

———. 2003b. "Windows in Space/Time: A Personal Perspective on Birth and Death." *Birth: Issues in Perinatal Care* 30(4): 272–77.

———. 2018a. "The Technocratic, Humanistic, and Holistic Paradigms of Birth and Health Care." In *Ways of Knowing about Birth: Mothers, Midwives, Medicine, and Birth Activism,* 3–44. Long Grove, IL: Waveland Press.

———. 2018b. "Medical Training as Technocratic Initiation." In *Ways of Knowing about Birth: Mothers, Midwives, Medicine, and Birth Activism,* 107–40. Long Grove, IL: Waveland Press.

———. 2018c. "The Midwifery Model of Care: Anthropological Perspectives." In *Ways of Knowing about Birth: Mothers, Midwives, Medicine, and Birth Activism,* 323–38. Long Grove, IL: Waveland Press.

———. 2018d. "The Rituals of Hospital Birth: Enacting and Transmitting the Technocratic Model." In *Ways of Knowing about Birth: Mothers, Midwives, Medicine, and Birth Activism,* 45–70. Long Grove, IL: Waveland Press.

———, ed. 2021. *Birthing Techno-Sapiens: Human-Technology Co-Evolution and the Future of Reproduction.* Abingdon, Oxon, UK: Routledge.

———. 2022. *Birth as an American Rite of Passage,* 3rd ed. Abingdon, Oxon: Routledge.

Davis-Floyd, Robbie, Kenneth J. Cox, and Frank White. 2012. *Space Stories: Oral Histories from the Pioneers of the American Space Program.* Kindle E-Book.

———. 2022. *Space Stories: Oral Histories from the Pioneers of America's Space Program.* Denver, CO: Multiverse Publishing.

Davis-Floyd, Robbie, and Gloria St. John. 1998. *From Doctor to Healer: The Transformative Journey.* New Brunswick, NJ: Rutgers University Press.

Davis-Floyd, Robbie, and Eugenia Georges. 2018. "The Paradigm Shift of Humanistic and Holistic Obstetricians: The 'Good Guys and Girls' of Brazil." In *Ways of Knowing about Birth: Mothers, Midwives, Medicine, and Birth Activism,* 141–64. Long Grove, IL: Waveland Press.

Daviss, Betty-Anne. 2021. "Introduction: Speaking Truth to Power for Social Justice in Pregnancy and Childbirth." In *Birthing Models on the Human Rights Frontier: Speaking Truth to Power,* ed. Betty-Anne Daviss and Robbie Davis Floyd, 1–52. Abingdon, Oxon: Routledge.

Daviss, Betty-Anne, and Robbie Davis Floyd, eds. 2021. *Birthing Models on the Human Rights Frontier: Speaking Truth to Power.* Abingdon, Oxon: Routledge.

Deacon, Terrence W. 1997. *The Symbolic Species: The Co-Evolution of Language and the Brain.* New York: W.W. Norton.

Deliège, Robert. 2004. *Lévi-Strauss Today: An Introduction to Structural Anthropology.* Oxford: Berg.

de Waal, Frans, and Frans Lantings. 1997. *Bonobo: The Forgotten Ape.* Berkeley: University of California Press.

Devereux, Paul. 1992. *Symbolic Landscapes.* Somerset, England: Gothic Image Publications.

———. 1996. *Re-Visioning the Earth.* New York: Simon and Schuster.

———. 2008. *The Long Trip: A Prehistory of Psychedelia.* Brisbane: Daily Grail Press.

———. 2010. *Sacred Geography: Deciphering Hidden Codes in the Landscape.* London: Octopus.

Dissanayake, Ellen. 1992. *Homo Aestheticus: Where Art Comes from and Why.* Seattle: University of Washington Press.

Donald, Merlin. 2001. *A Mind So Rare: The Evolution of Human Consciousness.* New York: W.W. Norton & Company.

Dossey, Larry. 1985. *Space, Time, and Medicine.* Boston: Shambala.

Driver, Thomas F. 1991. *The Magic of Ritual: Our Need for Liberating Rites that Transform Our Lives and Our Communities.* San Francisco: Harper.

———. 2006. *Liberating Rites: Understanding the Transformative Power of Ritual.* North Charleston, SC: Booksurge.

Douglas, M. 1966. *Purity and Danger: An Analysis of Concepts of Pollution and Taboo.* London: Routledge.

Durkheim, Émile. [1912] 1995. *The Elementary Forms of Religious Life*, trans. Karen E. Fields. New York: The Free Press.

Ehrenreich, Barbara, and Deirdre English. 1973. *Witches, Midwives, and Nurses: A History of Women Healers.* Old Westbury, NY: The Feminist Press.

Eisenberg, David M., Ronald C. Kessler, Cindy Foster, Francis E. Norlock, David R. Calkins, and Thomas L. Del Banco. 1993. "Unconventional Medicine in the United States: Prevalence, Costs, and Patterns of Use." *New England Journal of Medicine* 328: 246–52.

Epoo, Brenda, Kim Moorehouse, Maggie Tayara, Jennifer Stonier, and Betty-Anne Daviss. 2021. "'To Bring Back Birth Is to Bring Back Life': The Nunavik Story." In *Birthing Models on the Human Rights Frontier: Speaking Truth to Power*, ed. Betty-Anne Davis and Robbie Davis-Floyd, 75–109. Abingdon, Oxon: Routledge.

Eppler, Martin J., and Jeanne Mengis. 2004. "Side-Effects of the E-Society: The Causes of Information Overload and Possible Countermeasures." *IADIS International Conference e-Society*, 1119–24. Avila, Spain.

Faiola, Thomas John. 2002. "The Relationships among Religious Orientation, Conceptual Systems, and Values." ETD Collection for Fordham University. Paper AAI3040394. http://fordham.bepress.com/dissertations/AAI3040394.

Farella, J. R. 1984. *The Main Stalk: A Synthesis of Navajo Philosophy.* Tucson, AZ: University of Arizona Press.

Farrer, Claire. 1991. *Living Life's Circle: Mescalero Apache Cosmovision.* Long Grove, IL: Waveland Press.

———. 2010. *Thunder Rides a Black Horse: Mescalero Apaches and the Mythic Present*, 3rd edn. Long Grove, IL: Waveland Press.

Feinstein, David. 1990. "The Dream as a Window on Your Evolving Mythology." In *Dreamtime and Dreamwork,* ed. Stanley Krippner, 21–33. Los Angeles, CA: Tarcher.

Feinstein, David, and Stanley Krippner. [1988] 2009. *Personal Mythology: Using Ritual, Dreams, and Imagination to Discover Your Inner Story,* 2nd edn. Fulton, CA: Energy Psychology Press.

Fontes, Justine and Ron Fontes. 2001. *How the Turtle Got Its Shell.* New York: Random House.

Fontes, Rosana. In press. "Repercussions of a Paradigm Shift in the Professional and Personal Life of a Brazilian Obstetrician." In *Obstetricians Speak: On Training, Practice, Fear, and Transformation,* ed. Robbie Davis-Floyd and Ashish Premkumar. Chapt. 7. New York: Berghahn Books.

Frieberg, Kevin, and Jackie Freiburg. 1996. *Nuts! Southwest Airlines' Crazy Recipe for Business and Personal Success.* New York: Bard Press.

Galanter, Mark. 1989. *Cults: Faith, Healing, and Conversion.* Oxford: Oxford University Press.

Garfield, Patricia. 1974. *Creative Dreaming.* New York: Simon and Schuster.

Geertz, Clifford. 1973. *The Interpretation of Cultures: Selected Essays by Clifford Geertz.* New York: Basic Books.

Gell, Alfred. 1992. "The Technology of Enchantment and the Enchantment of Technology." In *Anthropology, Art and Aesthetics,* ed. J. Coote and A. Sheldon, 40–66. Oxford: Clarendon.

———. 1998. *Art and Agency: An Anthropological Theory.* Oxford: Clarendon.

Gellhorn, Ernst. 1967. *Principles of Autonomic-Somatic Integration.* Minneapolis: University of Minnesota Press.

Giacobini, Giacomo. 2007. "Richness and Diversity of Burial Rituals in the Upper Paleolithic." *Diogenes* 54(2): 19–39.

Goethals, Gregor. 2003. "Myth and Ritual in Cyberspace" In *Mediating Religion: Conversations in Media, Religion and Culture,* ed. Jolyon Mitchell and Sophia Marriage, 257–69. New York: T&T Clark.

Goffman, Erving. 1961. *Asylums: Essays on the Social Situation of Mental Patients and Other Inmates.* New York: Anchor Books.

Goffman, Erving, and Joel Best. 2005. *Interaction Ritual: Essays in Face to Face Behavior.* Chicago: Aldine Transaction.

Greenberg, Joanne (pen name Hannah Green). 1964. *I Never Promised You a Rose Garden.* New York: St. Martin's Paperback.

Greene, Brian. 2003. *The Elegant Universe: Superstrings, Hidden Dimensions, and the Quest for the Ultimate Theory,* 2nd edn. New York: W. W. Norton.

———. 2004. *The Fabric of the Cosmos: Space, Time, and the Texture of Reality.* New York: Vintage Books.

———. 2011. *The Hidden Reality: Parallel Universes and the Deep Laws of the Cosmos.* New York: Vintage Books.

———. 2005. *The Fabric of the Cosmos: Space, Time, and the Texture of Reality.* New York: Vintage Books.

———. 2021. *Until the End of Time: Mind, Matter, and Our Search for Meaning in an Evolving Universe.* New York: Alfred A. Knopf.

Griaule, Marcel. 1965. *Conversations with Ogotemmeli.* London: Oxford University Press.

Grimes, Ronald L. 1990. *Ritual Criticism: Case Studies in Its Practice, Essays on Its Theory.* Columbia, SC: University of South Carolina Press.

———. 1996a. "Introduction." In *Readings in Ritual Studies,* ed. Ronald L. Grimes, xiii–xvi. Upper Saddle River, NJ: Prentice Hall.

———. 1996b. "Ritual Criticism and Infelicitous Performances." In *Readings in Ritual Studies,* ed. Ronald L. Grimes, 279–92. Upper Saddle River, NJ: Prentice Hall.

———. 2002. *Deeply into the Bone: Re-Inventing Rites of Passage.* Berkeley: University of California Press.

———. 2003a. "Ritual Theory and the Environment." *The Sociological Review* 51(s2): 31–45.

———. 2007. "Ritual, Performance, and the Sequestering of Sacred Space." *Discourse in Ritual Studies* 14: 149.

———. 2008. "Performance." In *Theorizing Rituals: Issues, Topics, Approaches, Concepts,* ed. Jens Kreinath, Jan Snoek, and Michael Stausberg, 379–94. Leiden: Brill.

———. 2014. *The Craft of Ritual Studies.* Oxford: Oxford University Press.

Grimes, Ronald L., Ute Hüsken, Udo Simon, and Eric Venbrux, eds. 2011. *Ritual, Media, and Conflict.* Oxford: Oxford University Press.

Hallowell, A. Irving. 2002. "Ojibwa Ontology, Behavior, and World View." In *Readings in Indigenous Religions,* ed. Graham Harvey, 17–49. New York: Continuum.

Handcock, Eliana. 2020. "Life-Hack: Rituals Spell Anxiety Relief." *UConn Communications.* Retrieved 15 December 2021 from https://today.uconn.edu/2020/06/life-hack-rituals-spell-anxiety-relief/.

Handelman, Don. 1998. *Models and Mirrors: Towards an Anthropology of Public Events.* New York: Berghahn.

Handelman, Don, and David Shulman. 1997. *God Inside Out: Śiva's Game of Dice.* Oxford: Oxford University Press.

Harkin, Michael E., ed. 2007. *Reassessing Revitalization Movements: Perspectives from North America and the Pacific Islands.* Lincoln: University of Nebraska Press.

Harley, George W. 1950. *Masks as Agents of Social Control in Northeast Liberia* (Papers of the Peabody Museum of Archaeology and Ethnography, Harvard University 32(2)). Cambridge, MA: Peabody Museum.

Harner, Michael J. [1980] 1990. *The Way of the Shaman,* 2nd edn. New York: HarperOne.

Hart, Mickey. 1990. *Drumming at the Edge of Magic.* New York: Harper Collins.

Harvey, Oscar Jewell, David E. Hunt, and Harold M. Schroder. 1961. *Conceptual Systems and Personality Organization.* New York: Wiley.

Heilpern, John. 1999. *Conference of the Birds: The Story of Peter Brook in Africa.* London: Routledge.

Heine, Bernd. 1985. "The Mountain People: Some Notes on the Ik of North-Eastern Uganda." *Africa: Journal of the International African Institute* 55(1): 3–16.

Hill, Anne. 1998. "Children of Metis—Beyond Zeus the Creator: Paganism and the Possibilities for Embodied Cyborg Childraising." In *Cyborg Babies: From Techno-Sex to Techno-Tots,* ed. Robbie Davis-Floyd and Joseph Dumit, 330–44. New York: Routledge.

Hillerbrand, Hans J. 2009. *The Protestant Reformation: Revised Edition.* New York: Harper Perennial.

Hobsbawm, Eric, and Terence Ranger. 1992. *The Invention of Tradition.* Cambridge: Cambridge University Press.

Hocart, A. M. 1915. "Psychology and Ethnology." *Folklore* 26: 115–37; reprinted in *Imagination and Proof: Selected Essays of A.M. Hocart,* ed. Rodney Needham. 1987, 35–50. Tucson: University of Arizona Press.

Hoffer, Eric. 1951. *The True Believer: Thoughts on the Nature of Mass Movements.* New York: Harper and Row, Perennial Classics.

Huizinga, Johan. [1919] 1996. *The Autumn of the Middle Ages,* 2nd ed. Chicago: University of Chicago Press.

Hüsken, Ute, ed. 2007. *When Rituals Go Wrong: Mistakes, Failure, and the Dynamics of Ritual.* Leiden: Brill.

Ievers-Landis, Carolyn E., et al. 2006. "Cognitive Social Maturity, Life Change Events, and Health Risk Behaviors among Adolescents: Development of a Structural Equation Model." *Journal of Clinical Psychology in Medical Settings* 13(2): 107–16.

Jones, Ricardo Herbert. 2005. *Memórias de um Homem de Vidro: Reminiscências de um Obstetra Humanista*. Encadernação: Brochura, Brazil.

———. 2009. "Teamwork: An Obstetrician, a Midwife, and a Doula in Brazil." In *Birth Models that Work*, ed. Robbie Davis-Floyd, Lesley Barclay, Betty-Anne Daviss, and Jan Tritten, 271–304. Berkeley: University of California Press.

———. 2012. *Entre as Orelhas: Histórias de Parto*. Porto Alegre, Brazil: Ricardo Herbert Jones.

———. In press. "The Bullying and Persecution of a Humanistic/Holistic Obstetrician in Brazil: The Benefits and Costs of My Paradigm Shift." In *Obstetricians Speak: On Training, Practice, Fear, and Transformation*, ed. Robbie Davis-Floyd and Ashish Premkumar, Chapt. 8. New York: Berghahn Books.

Jorgensen, Dan. 1980. "What's in a Name: The Meaning of Nothingness in Telefolmin." *Ethos* 8(4): 349–66.

Jorgensen, Joseph G. 1972. *The Sun Dance Religion*. Chicago: University of Chicago Press.

Jung, Carl G. 1964. *Man and His Symbols*. New York: Doubleday.

Kapferer, Bruce. 2004. "Ritual Dynamics and Virtual Practice: Beyond Representation and Meaning." *Social Analysis* 48(1): 35–54.

Katz, Richard. 1982. *Boiling Energy: Community Healing among the Kalahari Kung*. Cambridge, MA: Harvard University Press.

Katz, Richard, Megan Biesele, and Verna St. Denis. 1997. *Healing Makes Our Hearts Happy: Spirituality and Cultural Transformation among the Kalahari Ju|'hoansi*. Rochester VT: Inner Traditions.

Kaufman, Rafael. 2019. "Business, Management and Strategy in the New Paradigm." *Start It Up*. Retrieved 15 November 2021 from https://medium.com/swlh/business-management-and-strategy-in-the-new-paradigm-9750b28f780e.

Kehoe, Alice Beck. 2007. *The Ghost Dance: Ethnohistory and Revitalization,* 2nd edn. Long Grove, IL: Waveland Press.

Kingwatsiaq, Novaliinga, and Kumaarjuk Pii. 2003. "Healing the Body and the Soul through Visualization: A Technique Used by the Community Healing Team of Cape Dorset, Nunavut." *Arctic Anthropology* 40(2): 90–92.

Kipling, Rudyard. 2009. *Just So Stories*. Oxford: Oxford University Press.

Klingberg, Torkel. 2008. *The Overflowing Brain: Information Overload and the Limits of Working Memory*. Oxford: Oxford University Press.

Kuhn, Thomas S. 2012. *The Structure of Scientific Revolutions,* 4th edn. Chicago: University of Chicago Press.

Laderman, Carol. 1991. *Taming the Wind of Desire: Psychology, Medicine and Aesthetics in Malay Shamanistic Performance*. Berkeley: University of California Press.

Lakoff, George, and Mark Johnson. 1980. *Metaphors We Live By*. Chicago: University of Chicago Press.

Lalich, Janja. 2004. *Bounded Choice: True Believers and Charismatic Cults*. Berkeley: University of California Press.

Laughlin, Charles D. 1974. "Deprivation and Reciprocity." *Man* 9: 360–96.

———. 1994. "Psychic Energy and Transpersonal Experience: A Biogenetic Structural Account of the Tibetan Dumo Practice." In *Being Changed by Cross-Cultural Encounters*, ed. David E. Young and Jean-Guy Goulet, 99–134. Peterborough, Ontario: Broadview Press.

————. 2004a. "Art and Spirit: Brain, the Navajo Concept of *Hozho*, and Kandinsky's 'Inner Necessity.'" *International Journal of Transpersonal Studies* 23: 1–20.

————. 2004b. "Navajo Shamanism." In *Shamanism: An Encyclopedia of World Beliefs, Practices, and Culture*, vol. 1, ed. Mariko Namba Walker and Eva Jane Neumann Fridman, 318–23. Santa Barbara, CA: ABCCLIO.

————. 2011. *Communing with the Gods: Consciousness, Culture and the Dreaming Brain.* Brisbane: Daily Grail Press.

Laughlin, Charles D., and Ivan A. Brady. 1978. *Extinction and Survival in Human Populations.* New York: Columbia University Press.

Laughlin, Charles D., and Eugene G. d'Aquili. 1974. *Biogenetic Structuralism.* New York: Columbia University Press.

Laughlin, Charles D., and Sheila Richardson. 1986. "The Future of Human Consciousness." *Futures* 18(3): 401–19.

Laughlin, Charles D., John McManus, and Eugene G. d'Aquili. 1990. *Brain, Symbol and Experience: Toward a Neurophenomenology of Consciousness.* New York: Columbia University Press.

Laughlin, Charles D., John McManus, Robert A. Rubinstein, and Jon Shearer. 1986. "The Ritual Control of Experience." In *Studies in Symbolic Interaction* (Part A), ed. Norman K. Denzin. Greenwich, CT: JAI Press.

Laughlin, Charles D., John McManus, and Mark Webber. 1984. "Neurognosis, Individuation, and Tibetan Arising Yoga Practice." *Phoenix: The Journal of Transpersonal Anthropology* 8(1/2): 91–106.

Laughlin, Charles D., and C. Jason Throop. 1999. "Emotion: A View from Biogenetic Structuralism." In *Biocultural Approaches to the Emotions*, ed. A. L. Hinton, 329–63. Cambridge: Cambridge University Press.

Lee, Hyeonseo, with David John. 2015. *The Girl with Seven Names: A North Korean Defector's Story.* London: William Collins.

Léveillé, Jean. 2007. *Birds in Love.* New York: MBI Publishing Company.

Lévi-Strauss, Claude. 1963. *Structural Anthropology.* New York: Basic Books.

————. 1995. *Myth and Meaning: Cracking the Code of Culture.* New York: Basic Books.

————. 2012. *Triste Tropiques.* New York: Penguin Books.

————. 2021. *Wild Thought: A New Translation of "La Pensée Sauvage."* Chicago: University of Chicago Press.

Liese, K., Robbie Davis-Floyd, Karie Stewart, and Melissa Cheyney. 2021. "Obstetric Iatrogenesis in the United States: The Spectrum of Unintentional Harm, Disrespect, Violence, and Abuse." *Anthropology & Medicine* 28(2): 1–17.

Lewis-Williams, David J., and David G. Pearce. 2004. *San Spirituality: Roots, Expression, and Social Consequences.* New York: Rowman Altamira.

Luhrmann, Tanya M. 2012. *When God Talks Back: Understanding the American Evangelical Relationship with God.* New York: Knopf.

Malinowski, Bronislaw. 1925. *The Sexual Life of Savages in North-western Melanesia: An Ethnographic Account of Courtship, Marriage, and Family.* London: Routledge and Kegan Paul.

McCauley, Robert N., and E. Thomas Lawson. 2002. *Bringing Ritual to Mind: Psychological Foundations of Cultural Forms.* Cambridge: Cambridge University Press.

McManus, John. 1979. "Ritual and Human Social Cognition." In *The Spectrum of Ritual*, ed. Eugene G. d'Aquili, Charles D. Laughlin, and John McManus, 216–48. New York: Columbia University Press.

McNeley, James K. 1981. *Holy Wind in Navajo Philosophy.* Tucson: University of Arizona Press.

Mead, Margaret. 1979. *Culture and Commitment.* New York: Natural History Press.

———. [1955] 1989. *Cultural Patterns and Technical Change.* New York: Mentor.

Meadows, Donella H., and Diana Wright. 1980. *Thinking in Systems: A Primer.* White River Junction VT: Chelsea Green Publishing Company.Metcalf, Peter, and Richard Huntington. 1991. *Celebrations of Death: The Anthropology of Mortuary Ritual,* 2nd edn. Cambridge: Cambridge University Press.

Myerhoff, Barbara. 1974. *Peyote Hunt: The Sacred Journey of the Huichol Indians.* Ithaca, NY: Cornell University Press.

Midwives Alliance of North America (MANA). 1994. "Statement of Core Values and Ethics." Draft, unpublished. Updated Statement retrieved 24 January 2022 from https://mana.org/about-us/statement-of-values-and-ethics.

Mitford, Jessica. [1963] 1998. *The American Way of Death.* New York: Simon and Schuster.

Moerman, Daniel E. 2002a. "Deconstructing the Placebo Effect and Finding the Meaning Response." *Annals of Internal Medicine* 136(6): 471–76.

———. 2002b. *Meaning, Medicine, and the "Placebo Effect."* Cambridge: Cambridge University Press.

Molino, Jean. 2000. "Toward an Evolutionary Theory of Music." In *The Origins of Music,* ed. N. Wallin, B. Merker, and S. Brown, 165–76. Cambridge, MA: MIT Press.

Moore, Sally F., and Barbara Myerhoff, eds. 1977. *Secular Ritual.* Assen, The Netherlands: Van Gorcum.

Murphy, G. Ronald. 1979. "A Ceremonial Ritual: The Mass." In *The Spectrum of Ritual,* ed. Eugene G. D'Aquili, Charles D. Laughlin, and John McManus, 318–41. New York: Columbia University Press.

Muuss, Rolf E. 1975. *Theories of Adolescence,* 3rd edn. New York: Random House.

Nash, June. 1979. *We Eat the Mines and the Mines Eat Us: Dependency and Exploitation in Bolivian Tin Mines.* New York: Columbia University Press.

———. 1992. *"I Spent My Life in the Mines": The Story of Juan Rojas, Bolivian Tin Miner.* New York: Columbia University Press.

Nautiyal, Chandra Shekhar, Puneet Singh Chauhan, Yeshwant Laxman Nene. 2007. "Medicinal Smoke Can Completely Eliminate Diverse Plant and Human Pathogenic Bacteria of the Air within Confined Space." *Journal of Ethnopharmacology* 114(3): 446–51.

Neddermeyer, Dorothy M. 2020. "Holistic Health Care Facts and Statistics." *Disabled World.* Retrieved 1 April 2021 from https://www.disabled-world.com/medical/alternative/holistic/care-statistics.php.

Odum, Howard T., and Elizabeth C. Odum. 2001. *A Prosperous Way Down: Principles and Policies.* New York: Random House.

Pabongka Rinpoche. 2006. *Liberation in the Palm of Your Hand: A Concise Discourse on the Path to Enlightenment,* 2nd ed. Essex: Wisdom Books.

Pagels, Elaine. 1989. *The Gnostic Gospels.* New York: Vintage.

Paul, Russill. 2004. *The Yoga of Sound: Healing & Enlightenment through the Sacred Practice of Mantra.* New York: New World Library.

Prigogine, Ilya. 1980. *The Future of Life. Quest Magazine.*

Pozas, Ricardo. 1962. *Juan the Chamula: An Ethnological Recreation of the Life of a Mexican Indian,* trans. by Lysander Kemp. Berkeley: University of California Press.

Quayle, Ethel, and Max Taylor. 2003. *Child Pornography: An Internet Crime.* New York: Routledge.

Rappaport, Roy A. 1999. *Ritual and Religion in the Making of Humanity.* Cambridge: Cambridge University Press.

Ray, Sondra. 1983. *Celebration of Breath: How to Survive Anything and Heal Your Body.* Berkeley, CA: Celestial Arts.

Reagan, Albert B. 1904. "The Moccasin Game." *Proceedings of the Indiana Academy of Science* 14: 289–92.

Redfield R. 1962. *Chan Kom: A Maya Village.* Chicago: University of Chicago Press.

Reichel-Dolmatoff, G. 1971. *Amazonian Cosmos.* Chicago: University of Chicago Press.

Rest, James, D. Narvaez, M. Bebeau, and S. Thoma. 1999. *Postconventional Moral Thinking: A Neo-Kohlbergian Approach.* Mahwah, NJ: Lawrence Erlbaum Associates.

Ridington, Robin, and Jillian Ridington. 2006. *When You Sing It Now, Just Like New: First Nations Poetics, Voices and Representations.* Lincoln: University of Nebraska Press.

Rock, Adam J., Einar B. Thorsteinsson, and Patrizio E. Tressoldi. 2014. "A Meta-Analysis of Anomalous Information Reception by Mediums: Assessing the Forced-Choice Design in Mediumship Research, 2000–2014." In *Advances in Parapsychological Research* 10, ed. Stanley Krippner, Adam J. Rock, H. L. Friedman, and Nancy L. Zingrone, 123–44. Jefferson, NC: McFarland.

Rose, Susan D. 1988. *Keeping Them Out of the Hands of Satan: Evangelical Schooling in America.* New York: Routledge.

Rothenbuhler, Eric W. 2006. *Ritual Communication: From Everyday Conversation to Mediated Ceremony.* New York: Sage.

Rowlands, Mark. 2006. *Body Language: Representing in Action.* Cambridge, MA: MIT Press.

Sadler Michelle, Mário J. D. S. Santos, Dolores Ruiz-Berdún, Gonzalo Leiva Rojas, Elena Skoko, Patricia Gillen, Jette A. Clausen. 2016. "Moving Beyond Disrespect and Abuse: Addressing the Structural Dimensions of Obstetric Violence." *Reproductive Health Matters* 24(47): 47–55.Salzen, E. 2010. "Whatever Happened to Ethology? The Case for the Fixed Action Pattern in Psychology." *History and Philosophy of Psychology* 12(2): 63–78

Sax, William S. 2010. "Ritual and the Problem of Efficacy." In *The Problem of Ritual Efficacy*, ed. William S. Sax, Johannes Quack and Jan Weinhold, 3–16. Oxford: Oxford University Press.

Schechner, Richard. 1993. *The Future of Ritual: Writings on Culture and Performance.* Washington, DC: Psychology Press.

Schroder, Harold M. 1971. "Conceptual Complexity and Personality Organization." In *Personality Theory and Information Processing,* ed. H.M. Schroder and P. Suefeld, 124–135. New York: Ronald Press.

Schroder, Haround M., Michael J. Driver, and Siegfried Streufert. 1967. *Human Information Processing.* New York: Holt, Rinehart, and Winston.

Schultes, R. E., and A. Hofmann. 1980. *Plants of the Gods: Origins of Hallucinogenic Use.* London: Hutchinson.

Selleri, Franco. 1988. *Quantum Mechanics Versus Local Realism: The Einstein-Podolsky-Rosen Paradox.* New York: Plenum Press.

Selye, Hans. 1974. *Stress without Distress.* Toronto: McClelland and Stewart.

Senft, Gunter, and Ellen B. Basso, eds. 2009. *Ritual Communication.* Oxford: Berg.

Sherman, D. George, and Hedy B. Sherman. 1990. *Rice, Rupees and Ritual: Economy and Society among the Samosian Batak of Sumatra.* Stanford, CA: Stanford University Press.

Sias, Shari M., Glenn W. Lambie, and Victoria A. Foster. 2006. "Conceptual and Moral Development of Substance Abuse Counselors: Implications for Training." *Journal of Addictions & Offender Counseling* 26(2): 99–110.

Simonton, O. C., S. Simonton, and J. Creighton. 1978. *Getting Well Again.* Los Angeles: Tarcher.

Smith, Margaret. 1993. *Ritual Abuse: What It Is, Why It Happens, and How to Help.* San Francisco: Harper.

Smith, W. John. 1979. "Ritual and the Ethology of Communicating." In *The Spectrum of Ritual,* ed. Eugene G. D'Aquili, Charles D. Laughlin, and John McManus, 51–79. New York: Columbia University Press.

———. 1990. "Animal Communication and the Study of Cognition." In *Cognitive Ethology: Essays in Honor of Donald R. Griffin,* ed. Peter Marler and Carolyn A. Ristau, 209. Washington, DC: Psychology Press.

Snoek, Jan. 2006. "Defining 'Rituals.'" In *Theorizing Rituals: Issues, Topics, Approaches, Concepts,* ed. Jens Kreinath, Jan Snoek, and Michael Strausberg, 3–14. Leiden: Brill.

———. 2014. "Masonic Rituals of Initiation." In *Handbook of Freemasonry,* Henrik Bogdan, and Jan Snoek, 321. New York: Brill.

Sorokin, Peter A. 1957. *Social and Cultural Dynamics.* Boston: Porter Sargent.

———. 1962. *Society, Culture, and Personality.* New York: Cooper Square Publishers.

Southard, D., and Andrew Miracle. 1993. "Rhythmicity, Ritual, and Motor Performance: A Study of Free Throw Shooting in Basketball." *Research Quarterly for Exercise and Sport* 64(3): 284–90.

Spomer, Ron. 1996. *The Rut: The Spectacular Fall Ritual of North American Horned and Antlered Animals.* Minocqua, WI: Willow Creek Press.

Star, Rima. 1986. *The Healing Power of Birth.* Austin, TX: Star Publishing.

———. 2016. "Love Lives On." In *Surviving the Death of Your Ex: Managing the Grief No One Talks About,* ed. Robyn Hass and Robbie Davis-Floyd, 134–45. Amarillo, TX: Praeclarus Press.

Stewart, Pamela, and Andrew Strathern. 2014. *Ritual: Key Concepts in Religion.* London: Bloomsbury.

Tainter, Joseph A. 2006. *The Collapse of Complex Societies,* 15th ed. Cambridge: Cambridge University Press.

Tannen, Deborah. 2005. *Conversational Style: Analyzing Talk among Friends.* Oxford: Oxford University Press.

Taylor, Diana. 2003. *The Archive and the Repertoire: Performing Cultural Memory in the Americas.* Durham, NC: Duke University Press.

Tedlock, Barbara. 2005. *The Woman in the Shaman's Body: Reclaiming the Feminine in Religion and Medicine.* New York: Bantam Books.

Thurner, Stefan, Rudolf Hanel, and Peter Klimek. 2018. *Introduction to the Theory of Complex Systems.* Oxford: Oxford University Press.

Trakhtenberg, Ephraim C. 2008. "The Effects of Guided Imagery on the Immune System: A Critical Review." *International Journal of Neuroscience* 118(6): 839–55.

Trinkaus, Erik. 1983. *The Shanidar Neanderthals.* New York: Academic Press.

Trompf, C. W., ed. 1990. *Cargo Cults and Millenarian Movements: Transoceanic Comparisons of New Religious Movements.* Berlin: Mouton De Gruyter.

Turnbull, Colin M. 1962. *The Forest People: A Study of the Pygmies of the Congo.* New York: Simon and Schuster.

———. 1972. *The Mountain People.* New York: Simon & Schuster.

———. 1978. "Rethinking the Ik: A Functional Non-Social System." In *Extinction and Survival in Human Populations,* ed. Charles D. Laughlin and Ivan A. Brady, 49–75. New York: Columbia University Press.

Turner, Edith. 1996. *The Hands Feel It: Healing and Spirit Presence among a Northern Alaskan People*. DeKalb: Northern Illinois University Press.

Turner, V. 1967. *The Forest of Symbols*. New York: Cornell University Press.

———. 1969. *The Ritual Process: Structure and Anti-Structure*. Chicago: Aldine.

Van Gennep, Arnold. 1960. *The Rites of Passage*. Chicago IL: University of Chicago Press.

Vogt, Evon Z. 1976. *Tortillas for the Gods: A Symbolic Analysis of Zinacateco Rituals*. Cambridge, MA: Harvard University Press.

von Bertalanffy, Ludwig. 2015. *General System Theory: Foundations, Development, and Applications*. New York: George Braziller.

Wagner, Rachel. 2012. *Godwired: Religion, Ritual, and Virtual Reality*. New York: Routledge.

Walker, Iain, and Heather J. Smith. 2001. *Relative Deprivation: Specification, Development, and Integration*. Cambridge: Cambridge University Press.

Wallace, Anthony F. C. 1956a. "Tornado in Worcester: An Exploratory Study of Individual and Community Behavior in an Extreme Situation." Publication 392. Washington, DC: National Academy of Sciences-National Research Council.

———. 1956b. "Revitalization Movements." *American Anthropologist* 58: 264–81.

———. 1957. "Mazeway Disintegration: The Individual's Perception of Socio-Cultural Disorganization." *Human Organization* 16: 23–27.

———. 1966. *Religion: An Anthropological View*. New York: Random House.

———. 1969. *The Death and Rebirth of the Seneca*. New York: Random House.

Wallace-Wells, D. 2020. *The Uninhabitable Earth: Life after Warming*. New York: Tim Duggan Books.

Warner, W. Lloyd. 1959. *The Living and the Dead: A Study of the Symbolic Life of Americans*. New Haven, CT: Yale University Press.

Weil, Andrew, and Martin Rossman. 2006. *Self-Healing with Guided Imagery*. New York: Sounds True.

Whitehead, Alfred North. 1978. *Process and Reality: An Essay in Cosmology*, the corrected edition edited by D. R. Griffin and D. W. Sherburne. New York: The Free Press.

Whitehead, Harry. 2000. "The Hunt for Quesalid: Tracking Levi-Strauss' Shaman." *Anthropology and Medicine* 7(2): 149–68.

Whitehouse, Harvey. 2005. "Emotion, Memory and Religious Rituals: An Assessment of Two Theories." In *Mixed Emotions: Anthropological Studies of Feeling*, ed. Kay Milton and Maruška Svašek, 232–55. Oxford: Berg.

Wilcken, Patrick. 2010. *Claude Lévi-Strauss: The Poet in the Laboratory*. New York: Penguin.

Zakar, Rubeena, Muhammad Z. Zakar, Safdar Abbas. 2016. "Domestic Violence against Rural Women in Pakistan: An Issue of Health and Human Rights. *Journal of Family Violence* 31(1): 15–25.

Zuckerman, Phil. 2019. "Does Prayer Work? Yes and No." *Psychology Today*. Retrieved 29 November 2021 from https://www.psychologytoday.com/us/blog/the-secular-life/201909/does-prayer-work.

INDEX

www.ingramcontent.com/pod-product-compliance
Lightning Source LLC
Chambersburg PA
CBHW070909030426
42336CB00014BA/2341